# DAVID BOWIE

# DAVID BOWIE

## LIVING ON THE BRINK

## GEORGE TREMLETT

CARROLL & GRAF PUBLISHERS, INC.
NEW YORK

Copyright © 1996 by George Tremlett

First Carroll & Graf edition 1997

Carroll & Graf Publishers, Inc.
19 West 21st St., Suite 610
New York, NY  10010-6805

Library of Congress Cataloging-in-Publication Data
    Tremlett, George.
          David Bowie, living on the brink / George Tremlett.
                p.    cm.
          Includes bibliographical references.
          ISBN 0-7867-0465-9 (trade paper)
          1. Bowie, David.   2. Rock musicians—England—Biography.
    I. Title.
    ML420B754T68     1997
    782.42166'092—dc21
    [B]                                                          97-19900
                                                                   CIP
                                                                   MN

Manufactured in the United States of America

For
Tony Secunda
The Original Telegram Sam

# Contents

# Introduction

We talked of many things: from rock 'n' roll to music hall; French chansons to the Modern Jazz Quartet; Jack Kerouac to Little Richard; Buddhism to politics; John Lennon to André Gide; Dylan Thomas to The Rolling Stones; Marc Bolan to Franz Kafka; and drugs, sex, marriage, our fathers and Unidentified Flying Objects – and at some point, David Bowie said, 'You don't have to go just yet, do you?' and then we started discussing his future.

He surprised me by saying he had no intention of spending the rest of his life in pop music. 'I'm not even sure I like the music and a career like this would never satisfy me,' said Bowie, then 22. 'I shall be a millionaire by the time I'm 30 and I'll spend the rest of my life doing other things.'

It was Monday 17 November 1969. This, our fourth interview, was supposed to last just an hour. We were alone at his manager Kenneth Pitt's apartment at 39 Manchester Street, London, where Bowie had his own room. Bowie was fashionably but individually dressed, wearing light beige flowing flares and a silky shirt hanging loose at the elbows, with long blond hair falling over his shoulders.

I think it was the UFOs that took our conversation to another plane. Bowie tried to convince me he saw flying saucers every night, passing over the house soon after 6 p.m. 'You could set your clock by it,' he said with a straight face. This was not the first time a musician tried one like that on me, so I asked if he lived beneath the flight path to Heathrow Airport and, knowing his taste in drugs, said I preferred a good bottle of malt. There was a pause. Our eyes met, and his face creased with laughter.

In our earlier meetings, Bowie had been always forthcoming, answering questions on his family background, childhood, school-days, friends and girlfriends, sexuality, religious beliefs, personal philosophy and early interests in jazz and other branches of the arts with an unusual turn of phrase. I had spoken to every other British musician and it was clear that Bowie was different; his dialogue had an intellectual quality that set him apart. Few musicians were as challenging. Many could only express themselves through music, while others were making such a mess of their lives that one never knew what might happen next. One interview was cancelled when the musician died of an overdose, and there were several where the interviewee was so far gone on heroin that we agreed to meet another day. By contrast, Bowie was polished and polite.

We had first met early in 1964 when Bowie was with The King Bees. Then I saw his first television interview on the BBC's *Tonight*, and watched him performing live with The Manish Boys, supporting Gene Pitney, Gerry and The Pacemakers, The Kinks and Marianne Faithfull. We bumped into each other again when he was with The Lower Third, whom I interviewed at their manager Ralph Horton's basement, but I did not begin interviewing Bowie in depth until July 1967, by which time he was launched upon a solo career, managed by Kenneth Pitt. We had two further long conversations before I saw him again this fourth time.

Pitt was a friend of my father and we frequently met for lunch or talked on the phone. He was a witty, literate, cultivated man with broad tastes, and his relationship with Bowie ran far deeper than the usual manager/artist bonding. Even before Bowie's father died, Pitt became virtually a surrogate parent and was deeply hurt when Bowie went on to leave him. And yet, over the next 15 years when we continued to talk frequently, Pitt remained in close contact with Bowie's mother and never ceased praising his gifts; he always knew far more about Bowie's career and private life than ever appeared in the press.

Bowie, Pitt and I shared a love of live entertainment. This bond unexpectedly extended my interview. Instead of ending when it should have done, our conversation became relaxed and animated and lasted five hours, triggered by the discovery that our fathers both lost money in the entertainment business.

My father had run through a small legacy leasing theatres and presenting variety shows; Bowie's father had lost a similar sum trying to make his first wife a star. Finding we had this in common, we started talking about our families, our childhoods and artistes we had seen in the dying days of music hall, especially the comedians. Bowie loved these, and we shared memories of Jimmy

Wheeler, Max Wall, Nat Jackley, Albert Modley, Frankie Howerd and Wilson, Keppel and Betty. He said he was envious that my parents had taken me as a young boy to see Laurel and Hardy at the Aston Hippodrome.

'What were they like?' he asked. 'Did they sing *The Trail Of The Lonesome Pine*? Was the house full?'

'Yes, against a backcloth of a log cabin with a pine tree. The house was half-empty. We went first house, Monday night. They were a bit over the hill by then, but it was still magic ...'

We were talking about the mid-50s, the early days of commercial television, when the London impresarios tried to save music hall by bringing in the new wave of American singing stars to top the bill on provincial tours, including Frankie Laine, The Platters, Guy Mitchell, Johnnie Ray and even Bill Haley and The Comets.

'We didn't see many of them in south London,' said Bowie.

As we continued to reminisce, Bowie surprised me again by saying he had never been totally sure about becoming an entertainer, thought most rock 'n' roll records were rubbish, and looked upon himself first and foremost as a writer. 'I often thought of becoming a journalist,' he said, adding with a grin as if we were playing a parlour game, 'Let me interview you. What made *you* become a writer?'

I told him about my training on a provincial evening newspaper, my years at the *New Musical Express*, the overseas music papers I represented in London, and how writers such as Dylan Thomas, Keith Waterhouse and John Osborne had all gone on from journalism to write poetry and novels or work in the theatre.

'Do you have any heroes of your own?' asked Bowie.

'Oh, yes – but not necessarily in rock 'n' roll. I write about rock 'n' roll because I love the music, but I've always seen it as a new art form, with all other forms equally valid ...' When I said I had twice hitchhiked long distances to see Paul Robeson, the nature of our conversation palpably changed again.

'You *saw* Paul Robeson?' he said, with just a touch of awe. 'What was he like?'

We went on to discuss Robeson's appearance at Stratford in *Othello* and his solo concert tours with his pianist Lawrence Brown, and how we both admired the dignity with which Robeson sustained his stand against racial prejudice. 'His concert perform-ance was something I shall never forget,' I said. 'They were alone on stage with a plain black backcloth, Brown seated at the piano and Robeson standing – no props, no microphones, and yet his voice seemed to roll around the theatre. You felt as if he was singing just for you, and the simplicity let you listen to every word ...'

'I wish I'd seen Paul Robeson,' Bowie said, with genuine feeling, asking whether I had ever seen anyone else with such impact. This led on to a discussion of French chansons, and the musicians who also worked with the simplest stage effects so as not to distract from their songs. I spoke of Juliette Greco, whom I had seen three times, who used a black backcloth, an accompanist, a piano, white spotlights, and who dressed wholly in black, with no jewellery or decoration. 'You just listened to the songs,' I said. 'There was nothing to distract you from her interpretation.'

'We've got a lot to learn, haven't we?' said Bowie, as this strangely intimate conversation continued to broaden out. We talked about our schooldays, whether we had missed much by not going to university, our first jobs, the works of Kurt Weill and Bertolt Brecht, reading Kerouac, Sartre and Orwell, and looking back on Paris in the 50s and Berlin in the 30s as times and places that we were sorry to have missed. One moment we would be talking about Oscar Wilde's short stories; next, the glassware of Galle or Lalique, or the designs of Charles Ricketts, Aubrey Beardsley or Walter Crane.

'Do you think rock 'n' roll is going to last?' Bowie asked.

'I have never had the slightest doubt,' I said.

'No, neither have I,' Bowie replied.

'Not all of it,' I added, suggesting that at least 90 per cent of it was garbage.

'Only 90 per cent?' grinned Bowie.

'Well, perhaps 98. My point is that during an artist's lifetime he'll be lucky to produce half a dozen enduring pieces of work. The rest will be forgotten, and his reputation will rest upon those; they may be derivative, but each will contain something distinctly their own, something new and original. The best of rock 'n' roll is going to last like the best of Shakespeare or Mozart ... At the heart of rock 'n' roll there's a simple form that an artist can use to express himself like a poet with a sonnet or an artist with a sheet of blank canvas.' Bowie asked if I had ever put that in writing. I told him no, because it was too soon.

'Why?' he queried.

'Neither the music papers nor the national press are ready to take the music seriously yet.'

'What do you think you'll be doing in ten or twenty years' time?' asked Bowie.

'Writing – and you?'

'I might be writing, too. I think of myself more as a writer than a musician,' he said. 'I shall be a millionaire by the time I'm 30,' he repeated with quiet conviction, 'and I'll spend the rest of my life doing other things.'

'Suppose you're not a millionaire by the age of 30?' I replied.

'But I will be,' he said, smiling but firm. By the way he said it, I saw the possibility that he might not make it had barely crossed his mind. 'I'll either be successful in this business, in which case I'll make all the money I need ... or I'll fail and still end up doing something else.'

By then we had been speaking for two or three hours, and I could sense him turning the conversation around to serve some unspoken purpose. 'You've interviewed a lot of people that I've never met,' he said. 'What advice would you have for someone like me coming into the business?' I paused before answering, anxious not to say anything that might appear disloyal to Kenneth Pitt.

'Get yourself a good lawyer, a good accountant and go into tax exile as soon as you can,' I said.

'As well as a manager?' asked Bowie.

'Gosh, yes. The functions are different. I have nothing against Ken. He is honest, which is rare enough in this business, but there will always be situations where you need a clear professional opinion on contract law, copyright and, separately, on money ...'

'Why tax exile?'

I told him how I knew which musicians arranged for their overseas earnings, primarily those from the United States, to be channelled through Switzerland, the Channel Islands, the Bahamas or the Cayman Islands to avoid Britain's high rates of taxation. 'Usually, they're not breaking the law – but sometimes they are,' I said, expressing the view that rather than engage in subterfuge it was better for an artist to settle in a new home of his own choosing. 'That's what I would have done if I'd earned their money,' I continued, adding, 'It never does a real writer any harm to go into exile, whether for tax reasons or to get away from their own familiar landscape. In fact, I think it makes them. Hemingway,

Joyce, Beckett, Lawrence and Graves are good examples. It's
often easier for a writer to understand his background if he's not
living in it every day.'

We continued talking around this theme, then Bowie asked, 'Do
you have any other advice?'

'Yes,' I said, 'and I shouldn't really tell you this – but never let
a journalist or a photographer into your home. It's not that they'll
start pinching the silver, but they see too much. They form an
impression of the way you live which may not be the one you
want to project, or it becomes an intrusion ... and the photographs
haunt you for the rest of your life.'

Bowie laughed at this. 'Do you mean that?' he asked, looking
puzzled.

'Absolutely,' I replied. 'John Lennon made a great mistake
letting journalists into his home, because they then felt they
understood him – and no creative artist or musician should fall
into that trap.' And I told Bowie how Tony Secunda – a manager
who was a great friend of mine – always advised his artistes to
hold something back, and leave the press wanting more.

'Ken doesn't tell me that,' he said.

'All managers are different. Some think short term, some think
long term. I like Ken a lot, wouldn't say a word against him, but
the business is changing. When I first started interviewing
musicians, they all expected their careers to last maybe two or
three years, and then thought they'd be going back home, perhaps
with enough money to buy a house or open a shop. Ringo Starr
used to tell everyone he hoped to make enough money to open a
hairdressing salon, but it's all changing. I honestly believe the
music is going to last.'

'You won't be using any of this when you write your article?'
asked Bowie, perhaps anxious that he had said too much (although
there was nothing to indicate then that he was about to leave
Kenneth Pitt, and was already rethinking his own long-term
career).

'No, no – I'd never get away with it,' I replied, thinking of all
the issues we had covered, telling him how Secunda once told me
that he coached musicians before their interviews to make sure
they never talked about politics, religion, literature or anything
intellectual. 'Remember your audience,' Secunda used to say.
'They're not intellectuals. They're not interested in stuff like that,

and it's their pocket money that pays your wages. Keep it simple, and never go over their heads.'

\* \* \* \* \*

After that long conversation in November 1969, there were several more. He invited me down to the BBC Paris Cinema in Lower Regent Street, the night he first performed with Mick Ronson (February 1970); met me again to discuss his marriage (May 1970); saw me at the Chrysalis offices after signing a new publishing contract (October 1970), and gave me a full account of his first visit to the United States and the launching of his group Arnold Corns (February 1971). Later we had three more lengthy conversations, the first covering his deals with GEM, Defries and RCA, his visit to New York to sign the RCA contract, when he also met Lou Reed, Iggy Pop and Andy Warhol (September 1971); the next, the release of his fourth LP *Hunky Dory*, when we also talked about his marriage and holiday in Cyprus (December 1971); and the third at the Royal Ballroom in Tottenham when he broke off from rehearsals with his new group The Spiders from Mars to tell me about their long-term plans, the recording of his fifth album *The Rise And Fall Of Ziggy Stardust And The Spiders From Mars* (January 1972). As we finished that final interview, Bowie said something strange as we shook hands and parted. 'You won't be needing anything more from me after this,' he said. I wondered what he meant, but understood a few weeks later when the Ziggy hype began.

These conversations, which form an integral part of this book, happened long ago. They were intellectual and career-orientated, yet also deeply personal. I glimpsed a finely balanced mind, able to tackle abstract ideas through structural forms. I also became aware of something even deeper, a sense of nervousness and alienation, which became particularly apparent that one evening when a planned interview developed into something else. He told me that night of his unusual family background, which will be explored in the first two chapters, and which was played down in my first book on him: *The David Bowie Story*.

'There's a lot of madness in my family,' said Bowie, when our conversation was drawing close to the bone.

'You mean eccentricity?' I asked, treading carefully, for this was the first time he had mentioned it and no other rock musician had ever admitted anything quite like this. Minor crimes, sexual adventures or family disputes were all part of the currency, but this was something else.

'No, madness – real fucking madness,' said Bowie, with more of a snort than a high-pitched laugh which I can remember still. 'It worries me sometimes, because I don't know whether it's in my genes and if I'll end up that way, too.'

I reminded him of Dylan Thomas's observation that madness and genius were closely related, especially in the arts. 'I'm no genius,' said Bowie, with that dismissive, well-formed grin he still uses to dissemble a situation, or discourage an interviewer from asking the next obvious question. Then he went on to tell me that through two generations, female members of the family on his mother's side tended to end up in mental institutions. Having thought about this carefully, I think it is probably fair to say that this may be a genetic fault, causing schizophrenia, paranoid schizophrenia or forms of depression, but it is not necessarily a disability in every manifestation. There is considerable evidence for a similar genetic fault in the families of William Burroughs and James Joyce. Dylan Thomas observed traits of what he described as eccentricity in Paul Verlaine, John Clare, Edgar Allan Poe, John Donne, William Blake, Swinburne, Oscar Wilde, James Thomson, Keats, Schumann and Baudelaire.

In the case of Bowie's family, his maternal grandmother started behaving strangely in late middle age. She became reluctant to leave the house, causing her husband Jimmy to go off drinking alone, often heavily. Mrs Burns retreated into a private world that her family could not share, writing poetry. With her husband's death, she became schizophrenic and her condition worsened until she needed hospital treatment.

That this was a genuine illness, possibly hereditary on the female side of the family, is clear from what happened to four of her five daughters. The eldest, Bowie's mother Peggy, had three illegitimate children by different men, and Bowie's half-brother, Terry, spent 19 years in mental institutions before committing suicide. Another daughter, Una, lived with a Canadian soldier during the war and had a baby, not knowing he already had a wife and four children in Canada. When the relationship ended, Una had a mental breakdown and was admitted to hospital. A third daughter, Nora, had several wartime affairs, including one with a Polish refugee who took her back to Poland. Eventually, the Burns family scraped up enough money to bring her home and she was diagnosed as a manic depressive, given a lobotomy and sent to live in a mental hospital in Yorkshire. The fourth daughter, Vivienne, fell in love with an American serviceman, and emigrated to the United States as a GI bride, only to discover that she too was schizophrenic.

Bowie told me much of this himself the night we had that long conversation, and Pitt gave me extra details, but I decided not to go into this too deeply in *The David Bowie Story* (1973), knowing that Bowie still hoped Terry's problems might go into remission and that his mother Mrs Jones was still in daily contact with Pitt. There was also a possibility that Bowie and Pitt might resume their working relationship, and I did not want to impede that, knowing they were genuinely fond of each other.

\*    \*    \*    \*    \*

In 1972 with a new manager, a better record deal, and an upmarket publishing contract, Bowie relaunched himself with a new persona, Ziggy Stardust – and stopped giving personal interviews. By extravagant claims and embroidered stories, he managed to persuade the press to accept him by his own evaluation, and I knew the image was false. The Ziggy hype was maintained with borrowed money and record company advances that had not been earned, and by 1973 I knew the money was running out, with debts to be paid and creditors knocking at the door. I also knew the bisexual imagery was largely false, and that Bowie was known to his friends as a hetero stud.

'Why don't you write a book?' said Secunda, who found me an agent and a publisher for *The David Bowie Story*. There was no market in those days for books that told the truth about the music business, so I only revealed a fraction of what I knew. In any case, the publisher told me that he wanted the book to appeal to a teenage readership, that I must be sure 'not to go over their heads', and limit myself to no more than 60,000 words. That was a problem: my material gathered from personal interviews with Bowie over a five-year period was enough for almost twice that, and I had even more from Pitt, who continued to give Bowie advice long after their business relationship ceased. Then there was a wealth of secondary background material from my interviews with Secunda, Marc Bolan, Steve Took, Mickey Finn,

Ralph Horton, Tony Defries, Les Conn, Tony Hatch, Dave
Cousins, Mick Ronson, Trevor Bolder, Woody Woodmansey,
Peter Noone, Lulu, Mott The Hoople, Steve Howe, Dick James,
Mickie Most, Denny Cordell, Brian Eno, David Platz, Tony
Visconti, Herbie Flowers, Freddi Buretti, Mary Hopkin, Rick
Wakeman, Peter Frampton and Bowie's wife and father.

In the end, I decided not to spill the beans but wrote a fairly
sympathetic study of Bowie. Some aspects of his character were
played down, especially in relation to his first marriage, for it is
dangerous territory for a writer, predicting what will happen to a
couple even when one knows they are no longer sleeping together.
Likewise, *The David Bowie Story* steered clear of drugs, and I also
avoided commenting on the more intellectual content of Bowie's
work. So there's been a lot left unsaid for the past twenty years.

*    *    *    *    *

The boy proved father of the man, and I can picture him now,
leaning forward, speaking softly and looking intently into my eyes
as he said he would be a millionaire by the time he was 30, and
would then devote his life to other pursuits.

And by the time he was 30, Bowie had recorded 12 albums and
25 singles, performed to vast audiences in many countries, made
his first film, *The Man Who Fell To Earth*, and, upon John
Lennon's advice, he had also taken total control of his career,
dispensing with managers, setting up his own group of companies
in Switzerland, and left himself totally free to pursue his other
interests in art, music, theatre and cinema.

At the same time, by projecting a series of different images of
himself – as Ziggy Stardust, Aladdin Sane, Diamond Dog, The
Thin White Duke and The Man Who Fell – Bowie defined his self
with more variety than any of his contemporaries.

Bowie did not retire by the time he was 30. He still needed
money to make himself totally secure – and achieved that by
waiting until he was free from Defries and then capitalizing on all
his achievements to date, signing a £10m three-album deal with
EMI America and earning at least £50m from his 1983, 1987 and
1990 world tours. Bowie handled all this with considerable style,
more like a 30s film star than a contemporary musician,
consolidating the value of his copyrights and creating a personal
fortune that is probably around £300m. He has avoided high levels

of taxation by operating through Switzerland and other tax havens, notably Jersey and the Virgin Islands, and now largely divides his life between homes in Lausanne, New York and Los Angeles, the new house he is building in Tuscany and the London town house he has bought in Chelsea. He has been equally adroit in his private life. None of his lovers has kissed 'n' told, apart from his former wife, about whom he now speaks with withering contempt. His immediate family, personal friends, hired musicians and company employees are all forbidden to talk to any journalist or biographer.

Inevitably, this makes it difficult for anyone to write about him – and Bowie is well aware of that. Much of my material was gathered in the early days when there were no such prohibitions, but I have also had to rely on secondary sources detailed in the Notes and Bibliography. I also owe a special debt to Tony Secunda. We remained friends until he died, and while I was finishing this book I went out to see him and his wife Franki at their home in Tiburon, just across the bay from San Francisco. As always, Tony helped me get the balancing right and those who know the underlying rhythms and friendships of the music business will sense his influence throughout this book.

George Tremlett
Laugharne, West Wales
August 1996

1

## 'Ask about Terry ... and he'll open out a bit'

When David Bowie was 12, a teacher asked what he wanted to be when he grew up. 'The British Elvis.' This was an unusual answer back in 1959 when the real Elvis was in Germany, driving US Army tanks, and many parents thought rock 'n' roll was on the way out.

There was a widespread belief, fanned by the press and rent-a-quote clergy, that rock 'n' roll had been a passing teenage phenomenon that ended with the burning of 'obscene' records and Fleet Street driving Jerry Lee Lewis and his teenage bride out of Britain. Newspapers carried articles demanding a return to family values, the banning of 'decadent' music, and suggesting that rock 'n' roll damaged the brain. What none of them knew, any more than we did, was that rock 'n' roll had established a largely *male* underground following across the land. Teenage girls might howl and scream, tear their hair and inflict unmentionable damage upon cinema seats when Cliff Richard came to town, but their brothers were tuning in to the real stuff which could only be heard on the US Forces Radio Network in Europe.

All over Britain, young teenage groups were moving on from skiffle to guitars, bass and drums, sometimes even piano and saxophone, hoping to sound like Little Richard, Chuck Berry, Gene Vincent, Eddie Cochran or Buddy Holly. In Liverpool alone, there were over 600 groups. Meanwhile, down in Bromley, young David Jones swivelled his hips, bent his knees and combed his quiff, dreaming of a glorious future swathed in lurex as he practised on his white acrylic plastic saxophone in front of a mirror.

The Jones family lived in a small terraced house at 4 Plaistow Grove, almost next door to Sundridge Park railway station. The bedrooms were tiny, and there was no bathroom, only a tin bath in the kitchen. Most of the time, Bowie – as I shall call David Jones throughout this book – lived alone with his parents, although his family was larger than this as I shall show in the next chapter.

Sometimes, his father would bring home 78 r.p.m. records to play on an old wind-up gramophone. The first record Bowie ever felt he really owned was Fats Domino's *Blueberry Hill*, but his real idol was Little Richard – and there was no point telling a teacher that in 1959. Little Richard was stunningly camp with shining glittery suits, dripping sweat and streaming make-up as he screamed effortlessly through several octaves. But within two short years, Little Richard's career seemed over as he went off to worship the Lord in his own peculiar way.

But it was never the music alone, nor only American music, that captured Bowie or the other musicians – Lennon, McCartney or Jagger – then in their youth. Their influences came from every root of contemporary culture, from music hall to Chicago blues, from Parisian chansons to Hollywood musicals, the artistry of Brecht and Weill, right through twentieth-century literature to Burroughs, Hesse or Moorcock.

In the days when musicians were taught to conceal their intelligence, we used to discuss all this when the interviews were over, notebooks shut and wine flowing. It was quite a surprise to learn Lennon shared a teenage passion for Juliette Greco, for the chanson was always a minority taste, and no less startling to hear young Bowie discussing Bertolt Brecht. This was something one could never write about in music papers or teenage magazines and so became one of the unexplored wells of rock 'n' roll.

Nowadays, when Bowie records a song-sequence such as *Baal* (1981), his conceptual album *The Buddha of Suburbia* (1993) or inspired pieces of music like *I Have Not Been To Oxford Town* on his latest album *Outside* (1995), the once-radical writers of the music press who have moved on to the daily papers accuse him of pretension. This is misplaced. The Bowie of 1995 may be more polished than the Bowie of 1967–72, but it's surprising how little he changes and how well defined his parameters remain. What he writes about now he talked about then.

*     *     *     *     *

Three men shaped Bowie's character – his father, elder brother Terry and Kenneth Pitt. And then a fourth gave him the confidence to play that character to the full – Tony Defries. I met Bowie's father only briefly and his brother not at all, but knew Pitt well when he was trying to launch Bowie's career, with Bowie living in his apartment, right through to the 80s when he remained in daily contact with Bowie's mother – even during periods when she and her son were barely talking and Bowie was trying to come to terms with fame, a rotten marriage, cocaine and an ever-present fear that the family streak of insanity might surface in some unpredictable way.

Bowie's father and brother, so I learned from Pitt, pulled in different directions. They disliked each other, yet both loved David, who veered between them while always anxious not to arouse his father's disapproval. The problem lay in the parentage. As I said in the Introduction, Bowie's mother had three illegitimate children by different men, and his father could never reconcile himself to this, despite being married before himself and being also the father of an illegitimate child by another woman. Jones lavished attention upon his own child but treated his stepson coldly. To make matters worse, Mrs Jones settled for a quiet life, going along with whatever he said and recoiling from physical contact with her children as they reached maturity.

In *Alias David Bowie* (1986), Peter and Leni Gillman go into this with some anecdotal detail, but they relied upon Bowie's Aunt Pat for their information. She has taken it upon herself to act as family go-between, writing letters to the press when she has a grievance, and her comments distressed Bowie when the book came out. I would not wish to rely upon her as a source, doubting whether anyone outside his immediate family would ever understand the pain that enveloped him as a child when one relative after another required psychiatric treatment. That pain is traceable in much of his writing.

\*     \*     \*     \*     \*

Outwardly, he seemed to develop like any other suburban middle-class child, always polite and neatly dressed when he arrived for morning lessons at Burnt Ash Primary School, joining the Wolf Cubs at seven with George Underwood and Geoffrey MacCormack, who remain close to him to this day; earning badges to stitch on his Cubs jumper, going off to summer camps and singing with them both in the St Mary's Church choir. Underwood became a graphic artist, designing LP sleeves for Marc Bolan and Procol

Harum and much of Bowie's artwork, while MacCormack worked as a backing singer on six of Bowie's albums, sometimes calling himself Warren Peace and travelling with Bowie on tour as friend and companion, someone to lean on in the wee small hours of the night.

As he moved on to Bromley Technical High School in 1958 at the age of 11, Bowie's only real interests were woodwork and art. He was tall for his age, slim and athletic, and nearly six foot by his mid-teens and weighing a little under nine stone. 'I can eat like a horse without putting on weight. It doesn't matter how much I drink,' he told me. However, there was nothing weak or spindly about his frame. Stripped of clothes, Bowie displayed taut, sinewy muscles and barely an ounce of fat.

As he described it to me, Bowie knew little of his family's troubles as a young child, growing up in a secure home with a mother who was always there when he came back from school and a safely dependable father in continuous employment. But while he never felt the pressures of a broken home or the anxieties of one without money, there was always an underlying tension.

For much of his childhood, Bowie was brought up as if he were an only child – which he wasn't, for his half-brother Terry, half-sister and these insane aunts drifted in and out of his life with their children, husbands or lovers, while his mad granny remained head of her branch of the family until she died in his mid-teens. They came and went without explanation, staying overnight, temporarily becoming part of his world or disappearing into institutions.

There was only one person whom he loved and looked up to, apart from his father, and that was Terry. Nine years older than Bowie, Terry had darker hair and more rounded, almost Mediterranean features, but similar natural gifts of charm, high intelligence and the ability to express himself well and imaginatively, all of which he lost as the family disease took hold. Terry became withdrawn, sitting silently in crowded rooms, only rarely revealing flashes of his former personality. This happened gradually, which only made it worse, for there were times when I first knew him when Bowie thought Terry might get better.

'Has he talked to you yet about Terry?' Pitt asked me one evening, with a hesitant laugh.

'No.'

'Well, you should get him talking and then he'll open out. Terry's the key,' said Pitt.

* * * * *

Mrs Jones's maiden name was Margaret Mary Burns. Her family called her Peggy. She was a vivacious, outgoing woman who loved horses, riding and dancing in her teens, and continued to live with her parents in Meadow Road, Southborough, Kent, well into her 20s. Her father, Jimmy Burns, who died six months before Bowie was born, won the Military Medal in the First World War, but returned home unable to find a job. For three years, he busked the Tunbridge Wells town centre, with his cap on the pavement to catch coins dropped by passers-by. Later, Burns worked as a lorry driver and tractor driver and laid electric cables, becoming a hard drinker in his later years when his home life was undermined by the family illness. His wife thought she had married beneath herself, for he was a rough and ready working man of Irish Catholic origin whereas she considered herself a peg or two up the social scale, her father having been of slightly higher military rank.

After working as a children's nanny for several wealthy families between Southborough and Tunbridge Wells, Peggy found herself a job at the Culverden Park Arms Hotel where she fell in love with a young Frenchman, Jack Isaac Rosenberg, whose father was a wealthy furrier in Paris. They were both 24 years old. Jack was a pot boy, just as handsome as she was attractive, and with them both living in, the inevitable happened.

Rosenberg said he would marry her, but for some reason he disappeared, with Peggy left literally holding the baby; a boy – Terry, born November 1937. However, this was not quite the end of the story, for Peggy kept in touch with his parents, who offered to bring Terry up themselves, while Rosenberg reappeared occasionally, offering money and expressing willingness to be more than just an absent father. Peggy would not part with her son, but could not provide a separate home for him, so Terry was largely brought up by her parents until her mother's illness made that impossible.

During the Second World War, Peggy moved to West London with her sister Vivienne to work at a munitions factory in Hayes, where an affair with a married man led to the birth of her second child, Myra Ann, who was handed over to foster parents at three months and later adopted. 'I don't know what happened to her,'

Bowie told me, adding somewhat improbably, 'The last thing I'd heard she'd married an Egyptian.'

When the War ended, Peggy returned to Southborough. Terry was now eight or nine years old. She worked as a waitress at the Ritz Cinema restaurant in Tunbridge Wells, where John Jones used to call for lunch when visiting the local branch of Dr Barnardo's. Peggy was 32 years old, still unmarried, and Jones was settling back into civilian life after wartime service with the Royal Fusiliers in Libya, Sicily and Italy. Jones was married, and his wife was looking after Annette, his daughter by another woman. With these different children and broken relationships swirling around them, the couple became lovers, found themselves expecting a child – Bowie – and married nine months later when Jones's divorce came through. They never had another child.

Gradually, Terry was drawn back into his mother's life – so far as his stepfather would allow. Some time during 1948, Terry was brought back into their home at 40 Stansfield Road, Brixton, but only because Peggy's sister Una moved back to their mother's house at Southborough with her own illegitimate daughter Kristine, which meant there was no longer any room there for Terry. The situation became even more disturbed when Una developed chronic schizophrenia, requiring full-time institutional treatment. Kristine was abandoned, left with foster parents, intermittently brought home and then abandoned again – just as Mrs Burns was showing signs of the same illness that was tearing her family apart.

This was all known to me back in 1973, when I wrote *The David Bowie Story*, but Bowie believed Terry might recover, and I did not think it right to lay out all the evidence so that anyone could see the poor man did not stand a chance.

Even then, the story had the seeds of appalling tragedy; but back in 1973 Terry was not beyond the brink. He had been receiving treatment since 1963 and became a full-time patient at the Cane Hill mental institution on the Bromley-Croydon borders in 1969, but was still well enough to spend weekends at Bowie's home and they both believed his condition might be curable.

Partly from Bowie and also from Pitt, I learned how Bowie had always yearned for Terry's affection, how Terry cradled him in his arms as a child, held the toddler's hand as they went walking, taught him ball games and always came back with presents. If

Terry was staying in the house at night, Bowie would creep into his room and say, 'Can I come in your bed, Terry?'

Jones was jealous of this bond between the two boys. He would isolate Terry within the house, quickly showing disapproval, and later – when Bowie was eight or nine – refused point-blank to help Terry stay on at school beyond the minimum leaving age. This was deeply unkind, for Terry was blessed with an enquiring mind and might have had a happier life.

\*     \*     \*     \*     \*

On Bowie's insistence, his mother has given no interviews in 20 years apart from co-operating in a radio biography that he authorized. But that she spoke about his childhood. She recalled that on the day he was born – 8 January 1947 – the midwife turned to her and said, 'This child has been on this earth before', and also remembered Bowie first putting on make-up when he was three years old. Bowie found some lipstick, eye-liner and face powder, and, said his mother, 'decided it would be a good idea to plaster his face with it. When I finally found him, he looked for all the world like a clown. I told him that he shouldn't wear make-up, but he said, "You do, Mummy." I agreed, but pointed out that it wasn't for little boys.'[1]

Bowie told me that when he first went to school shortly before his fifth birthday, he peed on the floor, with nerves – but that's not how she remembers it. Mrs Jones says he was an independent little boy who told her on the first day that he now knew his way to school, and there was no need for her to accompany him again. She dressed him up for the school Nativity play. 'I made him a robe and a head-dress and his father made him a crook. He ... absolutely loved it, and it was then that we began to realize there was something in David ... [he would] fling himself about to music. In those days, we thought he might be a ballet dancer.'

When Bowie was six years old, they moved out to Bromley, first to Canon Road, Bickley, and then to Clarence Road, Widmore, before eventually buying the smaller house at Plaistow Grove. Why they should have moved three times in two years has not been explained, although Bowie told me that when he was eight his parents sent him and Terry to stay at an uncle's ancient farmhouse in Yorkshire. He described open fields around the house, silence at nightfall, sheep and cattle, and even a monks' hole where Catholic priests hid to escape persecution. 'I never felt really happy there,' he said, explaining that he was a city child. 'I've never been impressionable, so I didn't get used to it.' These moves coincided with bouts of mental illness within the family, so the brothers may have been sent away to protect them, but moving from a small house to two larger ones only to return to a small terraced cottage suggests deeper problems. Probably Jones wanted to provide his family with a better standard of living but found he could not afford it.

Whatever the explanation, the home was unsettled and this was exacerbated by the way Terry never seemed part of the family. When they moved from Stansfield Road, Mr and Mrs Jones left Terry behind, lodging with a neighbour, ostensibly so that he would find it easier travelling to school. Later, he stayed with his grandmother and with other relatives, and for one brief period, less than six months in all, he moved into Plaistow Grove while waiting for his call-up papers. National Service was compulsory then, but a recruit could opt for a three-year engagement rather than the mandatory two and receive better pay, hope of promotion and a better than evens chance of an overseas posting. Terry signed on for three years with the Royal Air Force and was sent to Malta and Libya.

Over the next four or five years, when on RAF leave or later working for Amalgamated Press, Terry acquired a different status in Bowie's life. Maturing between the ages of 18 and 23, he was the older brother, who would turn up to take the young teenager up to Soho, to see the latest movies, to hang around jazz clubs or catch a concert by a visiting musician. 'It was Terry, Terry, Terry all the time,' said Pitt, who heard Bowie relive those years. Terry would pay the fares, buy the drinks and eye the prostitutes standing in doorways.

'Yes, it was Terry who started everything for me,' Bowie told me. 'Terry was into all the Beat writers, Jack Kerouac, Allen Ginsberg, Gregory Corso, Lawrence Ferlinghetti, William Burroughs and John Clellon Holmes, and he'd come back home to Bromley with the latest paperbacks tucked away in a coat pocket.

'He was into everything, reading up the early drug writers, Buddhism, poetry, rock and jazz, especially the saxophone players John Coltrane and Eric Dolphy.... His mind was open to anything.... He was rebelling in his own way and later travelled twice around the world as a merchant seaman while I was still dressing up every day in school uniform ... that had a very big impact on me.'

Terry's influence was all the greater because Bowie spent eight months away from school, choosing what books to read and which music to listen to, after injuring his eye in a fight with Underwood: Bowie had 'taken' Underwood's girlfriend. Whether that meant he fucked her or not I do not know, but Bowie did tell me that he lost his virginity at the age of 14 and also told me of an occasion that same year when he had been in bed with a girl and escaped down a drainpipe when her parents came home – and his fight with Underwood came later.

They fought one lunch-break. Underwood punched Bowie in the eyes, and a large ring he was wearing caused the damage. The school secretary took Bowie to her office and applied a cold compress, and the headmaster drove him to hospital for immediate dressing. He was left in extreme pain with a black left eye. Two days later the eye 'exploded' (the word he uses, although it should not be taken too literally) and his father drove him to the London Eye Hospital where doctors found the sphincter muscles were damaged. The injury proved permanent, despite several operations, leaving Bowie with a pupil that remains open, neither dilating nor contracting with light. His vision is blurred. Colours fuse into brown in the middle distance. 'The only other person I've seen with eyes like this is Little Richard,' he says[2] – but he's certainly made the most of it. Those distinctive eyes, with their different colours (one greener than the other) create a staring effect that has defined his facial image throughout his career, appearing prominently in his artwork.

Reading in hospital, Bowie acquired a far deeper knowledge of contemporary European and American literature, music and the arts than he would have found in a school curriculum. He began educating himself, having been told where to look by Terry.

Many years later, in an interview published in *Rolling Stone*,[3] Bowie said he started drawing up plans for his future, thinking: 'Who knows? Maybe I'm insane, too. It runs in my family but I always had a repulsive sort of need to be something more than human. I felt very, very puny as a human. I thought, "Fuck that, I want to be a Superman." ... I took a look at my thoughts, my appearance, my expressions, my mannerisms and idiosyncracies and didn't like them. So I stripped myself down, chucked things out and replaced them with a completely new personality. When I heard someone say something intelligent, I used it later as if it were my own. When I saw a quality in someone that I liked, I took it. I still do that. It's just like a car, replacing parts.'

\*    \*    \*    \*    \*

As we saw, Bowie later stressed that rock 'n' roll was never his deciding influence. He was already looking beyond music, absorbing other aspects of contemporary culture, including a passion for American ball games. He wrote to the US Embassy, asking for information about baseball because there were no books available in English shops; this led to an invitation to the Embassy, where he was given a guided tour, plus a baseball, hat and gloves. He began devouring the Beat writers from San Francisco and soaking up the traditions of decadence from Paris and Berlin, absorbing such poets as Rimbaud and Baudelaire, combining all this with an interest in Buddhism.

'It was a book I read that changed my ideas when I was about 14,' he said[4] about Jack Kerouac's *On The Road*, 'outlining what would now be the hippie way.... I was a serious Buddhist for about four years and very impressionable. It made me think that the human complex is such an inadequate form of existence. Physically, it doesn't function properly and mentally it's unstable. One must question one's existence and when you do it leaves you with an incredible loneliness ... Buddhism made me feel very keen on creativity. An outlet for it was the theatre mime group and playing tenor sax.'

John Jones did nothing to discourage Bowie's burgeoning interest in the contemporary arts. Peggy might 'hope David would find himself a steady job', endlessly worrying about his future prospects, but Jones was once a rebel himself and could see his own inner conflicts reappearing in his son. 'Don't worry about David,' he would say to her, 'he'll be alright.'

But this diversity of interests did not reduce Bowie's enthusiasm for rock 'n' roll. He was there, right at the beginning, when it mattered. The Rolling Stones, Eric Clapton, Rod Stewart and The Who were hanging around The Marquee, the Crawdaddy and Eel Pie Island, and Bowie started going to these venues with Underwood and MacCormack (who played rhythm guitar in his own school group, George and The Dragons, and later was with Bowie in The Kon-rads). Bowie was already playing saxophone, having studied privately with the jazz musician Ronnie Ross, who just happened to live in Orpington, a mile or two away from Plaistow Grove.

Ever capricious, Bowie's tastes would change suddenly and he would be off in a new musical direction: modern jazz, rhythm 'n' blues, The Mods, Soul or rock 'n' roll. Sometimes his hair was long, sometimes short. He would switch from group to group, calling himself Dave Jay one week, Davie Jones another (and several other names long forgotten), joining The Hooker Brothers to play rhythm 'n' blues and The King Bees with Underwood.

Some writers have struggled to put all this in a logical sequence. 'I wouldn't bother if I were you,' said Bowie, when I suggested his progression seemed unnaturally complex. 'A lot of these things happened when I was still at school, and some of them only lasted a few nights. I've always missed a few out whenever anyone's asked me and there's probably some I can't remember. The Hooker Brothers lasted a few weeks because we had a regular booking at the Bromel Club at the Bromley Court Hotel, but if I didn't have somewhere to play one night I'd be travelling around, listening to music, carrying my saxophone with me, just in case a group invited me to join them on stage … that happened a lot in those days. You'd go up on stage and if it went well they'd ask you to stay for another number, and if that was OK you might be there for the night – or longer … but I wouldn't like to put all that in any order, for there was none.'

2

# 'I want to be a saxophonist
# in a modern jazz quartet'

Terry Burns may have been the shaping influence, inspiring Bowie with ideas that remain his mainspring, but it was John Jones, an honest, meticulous Yorkshireman, who gave his son clear values and a moral attitude that remains visibly with him to this day.

'He was always anxious that David should do the right thing,' said Pitt, who came to have a close day-to-day personal understanding with Mr and Mrs Jones. (There were sound legal reasons for this, besides the quite natural one that Pitt was the kind of man who would want his relationship with Bowie underpinned in this way.)

Jones cut a deceptive figure. His hair was thinning and receding at the temples, and he chose to wear heavily framed spectacles that diminished his appearance. He was thin-lipped with piercing eyes, features emphasized by off-the-peg suits, chain-store shirts and neatly patterned neckties. Few would have looked at him twice in a bus queue, and yet there was a quality in his manner that set him apart. He spoke decisively, as Yorkshiremen often do, but was also courteous and precise which befitted a man who spent his working days pleading the cause of the children's charity, Dr Barnardo's. Something else lingered in the memory, after even the briefest of meetings, for he was firmer than many public relations officers, combining this with an anxiety to please that suggested doubts or tension. It was neither diffidence nor confidence.

'My father used to be in the theatre,' Bowie told me during our long conversation in November 1969, going on to say that Jones put on shows before the war. I responded that this was precisely what my own father had done in the 50s when he inherited some money from his mother and began presenting provincial variety shows and pantomimes before taking a lease on the Pier Pavilion in South Shields. When Bowie heard that he made no money from this, he related the similar tale of how John Jones inherited £3,000

on his 21st birthday, only to lose it all in little more than a year
trying to make his first wife a star.

When I came to write *The David Bowie Story*, this clue sent me
searching through the registers of births, marriages and deaths at
Somerset House where I discovered Jones was born at 41
Sepulchre Street, Doncaster, on 21 November 1912. Where and
when and why he became known as John Jones, I do not know, for
his real name was Haywood Stenton Jones. His father, Robert
Haywood Jones, described himself on his marriage certificate as
'A Gentleman'. This was a phrase usually used by wealthy men of
independent means. He was, in fact, a boot and shoe manufacturer.
His wife, Zillah Hannah Jones, was the daughter of a foreman
miller.

Jones's parents died when he was a child. He was brought up by
relatives and educated at a public school in Skipton, which may
explain that unusual mannerism and his softly spoken civility. On
his 21st birthday Jones inherited the £3,000 which his parents had
placed in trust. Had it been invested on the usual basis that it
would double in value every seven years, the sum would have now
grown to over £700,000. Jones had, in fact, become a wealthy
young man with all the benefits of a public school education
behind him, but Bowie told me a conventional career held no
attractions for him, for he fell in love with a singer.

'Who was this singer David's father married?' I asked Pitt on
the phone the following day.

'He told you about her! The interview must have gone well,'
said Pitt. 'She was The Viennese Nightingale.'

And so it was, bit by bit, through the odd comment from Bowie,
straight answers from Pitt to direct questions, and even more
research at Somerset House, that I learned the extraordinary story
of the young Yorkshireman without any parents who came down
to London in 1933, bought himself a sports car, became a raffish
young man about the bars, and fell in with a group of theatricals
who included a one-time circus clown, Jim Sullivan, who was
down on his luck. Pitt was far too loyal to Bowie to volunteer
information that might prove embarrassing. I had to know what
questions to ask: 'Was she from Vienna?' 'Good God, no – she
was Irish.'

It took me a while to unravel the tale. Eventually, I learned –
having established from Somerset House that her real name was
Hilda Louise Sullivan – that The Viennese Nightingale was the

daughter of this Irish circus clown, James Patrick Sullivan, and an Italian acrobat who died in a circus ring when one of her tricks went wrong. Hilda, the baby nightingale, was brought up by a grandmother in France and duly became an entertainer, accompanying herself on piano, in the night clubs and café bars of Vienna. With the rise of Fascism in the 30s she fled the country and travelled to London. By then, by a strange coincidence, her father was working as a caretaker in the same building where I had researched the family's background, Somerset House. He lived in a basement flat that went with the job.

Another story, told by the Gillmans, has it that Jones met The Viennese Nightingale when he accompanied her father to Charing Cross Station to meet her off the boat train from Vienna.[1] According to their version, there were already Nazi thugs on the streets of Vienna by the time she left for London and Jones 'asked me to go and have a cup of tea with him at the Lyons Corner House in The Strand, and he fell madly in love with me'. The Gillmans discovered her still performing in the Irish pubs and clubs of North London 50 years later, calling herself Cherie.

Hilda left an Italian lover behind in Vienna, a wealthy young banker, promising to return, and was initially none too keen on the dry, taciturn Yorkshireman Jones. 'Nothing made him laugh. You never saw his lips move and you never saw him smile,' she said. Nevertheless, he was keenly persuasive and due to inherit the £3,000. Less than a month after he received the money, Hilda married him – on 19 December 1933.

Another clue to this romantic drama can be found in their wedding certificate. Jones falsely claimed to be two years older than his true age, and one can only suppose he was so anxious to overcome her resistance that he tried to convince her he was more experienced than he really was. The money might have convinced her. Jones bought her stage costumes, clothes and make-up to maintain her image off stage as well as on, and helped finance a touring revue called *11.30 p.m. Saturday Night*, so that The Viennese Nightingale would have star billing. The show was booked for separate weeks in Dudley, Croydon and Chelsea – and then collapsed without reaching the West End.

With nearly all his money gone in little more than a month, Jones attempted to retrieve his financial situation by opening a London drinking club in Charlotte Street. This soon turned into another disaster, for he did not have the personality for running a private club. He would not mix with the customers, or share their jokes and badinage. Thieves began using the club and another partner cheated him. His fortune vanishing fast, John Jones turned to drink and became an alcoholic. Within a few months, the club closed. He lost every penny and was destitute, briefly living rough, until he picked up a poorly paid job as a porter at the Russell Hotel in Bloomsbury. This enabled him to climb back on his feet again, finding longer-term employment a few months later with Dr Barnardo's Homes. Jones joined their staff in September 1935, working from offices at Stepney Causeway in the East End of London. As for The Viennese Nightingale, she remained in the entertainment business – but only as a cinema usherette.

For some men, setbacks like these are the spur that drives them on to make a fortune, learning from their mistakes and making the most of each subsequent opportunity. John Jones was not one of them. The experience scarred him. He became excessively cautious, always careful with money, particular about his appearance and pernickety in his ways. Jones was also wary of drink, although at what stage all these habits coalesced to form the later man is by no means clear. When the war ended, he returned to Dr Barnardo's, met Peggy and married her on 12 September 1947, a month after his divorce came through. He was then 34 years old, she was 33. In 1950, he was appointed Secretary to the Dr Barnardo's Management Committee and given charge of a small administrative office. In 1956, Jones was made Chief Publicity Officer, the post he kept until he died 13 years later. This brought him back in touch with the entertainment business on another level, inviting stars to visit children's homes, seeking help in raising funds or making appeals for toys at Christmas.

And so it was, during the same period that Terry was introducing him to Kerouac and modern jazz, that young Bowie also found himself being taken around Dr Barnardo's homes when stars were making personal appearances, or visiting the small London suburban venues where the Tommy Steeles, Adam Faiths, Marty Wildes and Cliff Richards were taking their first raw steps towards stardom.

'You didn't collect any autographs?' asked Bowie with surprise, when we were talking about our first interest in music. 'I did. My father gave me an autograph album. Whenever anyone came to Dr Barnardo's he would take me along and I'd ask for their autographs.' (Bowie still had that album in 1969, and I would now expect it to be among his archives in Switzerland where he keeps all his old costumes, instruments, theatre programmes, concert posters, tickets, commissioned artwork, LPs, singles, compact discs, films, videos, letters, photographs and other personal memorabilia, all lovingly preserved like a living museum. Bowie is a natural collector. He rarely throws anything away.)

\* \* \* \* \*

After his eight-month confinement to bed, it was too late for Bowie to settle into the usual O-level curriculum, though he did produce one essay of stunning verbal power describing the thoughts of a man awaiting execution (which suggests he may have been reading Arthur Koestler or Jean-Paul Sartre in his hospital bed), and never wrote anything like it again. School failed him and he left Bromley Technical High in July 1963 with passes in only Woodwork and Art. His success in those subjects was due to the art teacher Owen Frampton, an off-beat character none too bothered by school rules, who encouraged his boys to experiment in sculpture, pottery, lino-cutting or watercolours, until they found a form through which they could express themselves. Frampton found Bowie a job on leaving school, after the teenager told the School Careers Officer: 'I want to be a saxophonist in a modern jazz quartet.' (Faced with this challenge, the Careers Officer offered him a work in a factory making harps which he declined).\* The job was with The Design Group in Old Bond Street, where Bowie started as a trainee commercial artist in July 1963, aged 16 and a half, managing to combine this with a Saturday job in Vic Furlong's record shop in Bromley and evening gigs playing saxophone.

'I gave it up after less than six months,' Bowie told me, explaining that he was already travelling from gig to gig with different groups most nights of the week, and already realized that music and day jobs do not mix.

When I asked him about all this in 1967, shortly after the event, Bowie told me he didn't think he appeared with The Hooker

---

\* Ironically, Frampton's son Peter, who was three years younger than Bowie, became a pop star well before he did. Frampton was hailed in the press as The Face of 1968 when lead singer with The Herd, who had three hit singles in 1967 and 1968, and then went on to form Humble Pie with Steve Marriott of The Small Faces, before working with such top musicians as George Harrison, Harry Nilsson, Billy Preston and Ringo Starr. His own double-LP *Frampton Comes Alive* sold 15m copies.

Brothers more than three or four times; furthermore, The King Bees were a group of young musicians – Bobby Allen, Dave Howard and Roger Black – whom he met in a Bromley barber's shop while waiting to have his hair cut. They appeared a few times at local youth clubs, but that was all – until Bowie cheekily wrote to the washing machine millionaire John Bloom in April 1964, offering him the chance to finance their future career.

'I told him that all he had to do was advance us several hundred pounds to buy new equipment. What had we got to lose? If he said "Yes", we would have had him and his money behind us. If he said "No", we would be no worse off than we were already.'

At that time I was working on the *New Musical Express*, and we heard about the Bloom fiasco a few hours afterwards. It was a matter of much amusement in the *NME* office because its owner, Maurice Kinn, was part of a show-business party set that revolved around Alma Cogan, The Beverley Sisters and a handful of Jewish agents who had a virtual monopoly of British TV and theatre bookings. London pop music was a small world in those days and when The Beatles hit town, their manager Brian Epstein quickly popped them into dinner jackets and took them round this circuit, which smacked more of Rotary Clubs and Freemasonry than the everyday world of rock 'n' roll.

I described our vantage-point to Bowie and he grimaced. 'It was all very embarrassing,' he said. 'We were asked to play one of Bloom's parties. This was a posh affair with many guests wearing evening dress. No one prepared us for that, and we turned up in jeans and T-shirts, ready to play rhythm 'n' blues. We worked hard, but many of them ignored us and carried on talking as if we weren't there. It wasn't our fault, really. They should have known what sort of party they wanted and booked a more conventional band.'

The booking was arranged by Les Conn, to whom Bloom sent Bowie's letter. Conn was a music publisher, managed Marc Bolan, and later became a talent scout for Dick James Music. When The King Bees recorded their first single, released in June 1964, for Vocalion, Conn was credited with writing the A-side. This meant he would receive the songwriting royalties, but these would not have amounted to much. Only 3,500 copies were pressed, and not many actually sold. An original copy of this first Bowie single, with the Vocalion label, is now worth hundreds of pounds.

One oft-told story has it that Conn took Bowie and Bolan down to Dick James Music, hoping to persuade James to sign them to writing contracts which would have given them a weekly allowance to live on. James, who died in 1986 shortly after losing a High Court case brought by Elton John over this same kind of agreement, was always looking for new talent. He had a good ear for hit songs and liked to sign up young songwriters for a tiny 'wage' (in Elton John's case £10 a week) on terms that gave him the rights to anything they wrote. The story is that James, a plump man given to sitting behind a vast desk with his jacket off, shirt sleeves rolled up, the light shining on his egg-bald head and a huge cigar clenched between his teeth, took one look at Bowie and Bolan and snapped: 'Get those long-haired gits out of my office!'[2]

This anecdote never had the ring of truth: Dick James (real name Isaac Vapnick) was too wily to miss the chance of signing up two young songwriters for a pittance. The Gillmans managed to see Mr Vapnick shortly before he died, and asked him how he let Bowie and Bolan slip through his fingers. 'I wouldn't dream of addressing anyone like that,' he insisted.[3] When they added that Les Conn claimed to have broken off his business relationships with Dick James Music because of this snub, James said of his former talent scout, 'No one in my organization would have tried to stop him leaving.'

Conn also tried to interest the independent record producer Mickie Most. This also came to nothing, although Most did produce one single for George Underwood, using the name Calvin James – *Some Things You Never Get Used To*/*Remember* (Columbia, April 1965).

While Underwood was taking this stab as a solo singer, Bowie continued to drift from group to group with his saxophone, hoping for a spontaneous jam or the chance to earn a few pounds. He would still play occasionally with The King Bees, even though they recorded without him, and also spent, from September 1964, several months with The Manish Boys, alternating from group to group, depending upon which one had a booking. Some nights he would also turn up at The Marquee, to jam with bands such as The Who (then known as The High Numbers), The T-Bones and, on at least one occasion, Sonny Boy Williamson. 'It was all much looser then,' Bowie told me. 'Bands would let you jam with them, and if you were any good you'd stay on for another number, and if it turned into a good night you'd just carry on playing ...'

The Manish Boys had three brief brushes with stardom: they

were booked as the opening act for six nights of a tour by Gene
Pitney, The Kinks and Gerry and The Pacemakers in December
1964; they recorded one single, replaced in March 1965 – *I Pity
The Fool/Take My Tip* (the B side was Bowie's first recorded
song. *see* Appendix); and they made a desperate attempt to
promote that with banal publicity stunts. Or, rather, Bowie did, as
their lead singer.

Having done no conventional work for nearly a year, Bowie's
hair was now flowing over his shoulders, long and blonde, and
constantly washed to preserve its sheen. Any woman would have
been proud of it, and in an attempt to boost the fortunes of The
Manish Boys Bowie claimed to have formed a society known as
The International League for the Preservation of Animal Filament
to campaign on behalf of long-haired pop stars. This society was
first mentioned in the press early in November 1964 after John
Jones phoned former Dr Barnardo's boy Leslie Thomas, now a
successful novelist but then writing a music column for the
London *Evening News*. Jones asked if he would care to include an
item about his son's new society, which was how the *Evening
News* came to publish a story on 2 November 1964 in which
Bowie, still known as David Jones, was described as the 'founder
and president' and quoted as saying the League was really for the
protection of 'pop musicians and those who wear their hair long'.
Those with 'the courage to wear their hair down to their shoulders'
went through hell, he went on. 'It's time we united to stand up for
our curls ... everybody makes jokes about you on a bus, and if you
go past navvies digging in the road, it's murder!'

The story was spotted by a researcher for the nightly BBC TV
news programme *Tonight*, and Bowie was invited to appear on it
on 12 November after being filmed with various long-haired
members of The King Bees, The Manish Boys, plus Screaming
Lord Sutch and session musician Jimmy Page, later of Led
Zeppelin. By then Bowie's society – which, so far as I know,
never had a meeting or a membership – had changed its name to
The Society for the Prevention of Cruelty to Long Haired Men. On
*Tonight*, looking more than a little winsome, Bowie declared: 'For
the last two years we've had comments like "Darling" and "Can I
carry your handbag?" ... and it just has to stop.' For this television
appearance, Bowie was paid five guineas.

Four months later, in March 1965, with a single on the verge of
release another opportunity to exploit Bowie hair arose. The

Manish Boys were booked to appear on an abysmal BBC-2 pop programme, *Gadzooks! It's All Happening* (8 March). Someone, possibly John Jones, again phoned the *Daily Mirror* to say producer Barry Langford would only allow them to appear if they had their hair cut.

This was several days ahead of the programme, which left Les Conn and John Jones plenty of time to develop the stunt, which rapidly grew into one of those crazy, early-60s pop stories so beloved by the national press. First shot went to the *Daily Mirror* which headlined its 3 March story 'ROW OVER DAVY'S HAIR' and told how Bowie was insisting, 'I have no intention of having my hair cut' while Langford, identified as 39, claimed there could be no compromise, as 'Kids today just don't want this long hair business any more.'

On 4 March, the *Daily Mail* reported that The Manish Boys had *definitely* been dropped from the TV programme, quoting Bowie saying: 'I wouldn't have my hair cut for the Prime Minister, let alone the BBC.'

This ludicrous false story was then taken up by nearly every national newspaper, as the *Daily Mirror* reported on 6 March that The Manish Boys would be allowed to appear on *Gadzooks! It's All Happening* after all, provided their fee was given to charity if viewers complained about the length of their hair; then the *Evening News* published a photograph on 8 March of Bowie having his hair cut for the show.

The British national press preferred garbage of this kind, rather than real news of the growing music industry, because it could be written in-house by a staff reporter at no extra cost to the news desk budget. Langford and Bowie played their parts to perfection, and both the TV programme and The Manish Boys received the publicity they craved. But the press are far more easily deceived than the record-buying public. The record was another flop, and within days of the TV broadcast, Bowie left the group, not through any dislike for their music, but through sheer angst. The other members of the group wanted it to be called The Manish Boys. He insisted it should be Davy Jones *and* The Manish Boys. There was no stopping him. Bowie was determined to become a solo star.

3

## 'He had to make the rounds ...'
## the way a cat sprays'

Before leaving The Manish Boys, Bowie became a regular at the La Giaconda coffee bar in Denmark Street, just across the road from Dick James Music and a few doors away from the *New Musical Express*. Musicians, writers, pluggers, publishers, salesmen of instruments, PR men and con-men used to meet there for morning coffee, a ritual that took up most of the day. Often, we slid from table to table, picking up gossip or racing tips (there's a lot of betting in the music business) or, in the case of young musicians, bookings along the way.

The 60s music was like a vigorous street market and was a sleazy, corrupt business. Many top groups were unable to play the records issued in their name but actually recorded by session musicians. Hiring studio time was expensive, and even good musicians came cheap – so a producer or publisher would book a studio, hire session guitarists, bass and drums for a standard Musicians Union fee; lay down a backbeat; bring in saxophones, trumpet or lead guitar for an overdub, and then the singer to record the vocal track. This was how top session musicians such as drummer Alan White or guitarist Jimmy Page made their money. Rights in the recording were owned by whoever paid the session fees. And if the record was a success, he would form a group, sometimes at a few hours' notice, to go out on the road.

By 1964/5, Bowie and Marc Bolan were regulars at La Giaconda, sitting by the window, looking up and down the street, eagerly searching for trade. It was thus Bowie made his next move.

Ralph Horton had come down from Birmingham with The Moody Blues, who were managed by Tony Secunda. Horton was their road manager, that is he drove their van, carried instruments and amplifiers in and out of ballrooms and studios, and fetched fish and chips if they felt hungry. Most road managers stank of stale sweat, wore dirty jeans and worn leather jackets, had greasy hair and were in desperate need of a shave. Horton was anxious to rise above this. He wanted to wear suits, have his hair cut and become a proper manager, since managers were becoming as glamorous as rock 'n' roll stars. Brian Epstein was a national celebrity, and so, almost, was Andrew Loog Oldham who managed The Rolling Stones. But Horton did not look the part. He was pasty-faced, bespectacled and seemed to be out of his depth – and he had no money. His first job with a Birmingham agency collapsed when the firm went bankrupt. Horton then found employment as a booker at King's Agency in Denmark Street, sleeping on a bunk in a back room when not travelling with The Moody Blues. This arrangement came to grief when the group temporarily imploded upon the departure of their singer Denny Laine.

But Horton kept going – and found The Lower Third, who came from Margate. They comprised Dennis Taylor (lead guitar), Graham Rivens (bass guitar) and Phil Lancaster (drums). When Bowie told Horton in La Giaconda that he was leaving The Manish Boys, Horton promptly lined him up as the new singer with The Lower Third. The attraction was regular bookings, for Horton's flatmate, Kenny Bell, who also worked at King's Agency, found groups every week to perform at venues along the south coast.

Superficially, Bowie's career seemed to gather momentum. With Bell's help, they appeared on the same bill as better-known groups such as Johnny Kidd and The Pirates or The Pretty Things. Bowie was also writing songs and in September 1965 secured a miserable contract with Hal Shaper at Sparta Music that guaranteed him £10 when one of his songs was recorded and 50 per cent of any subsequent royalties. And when The Manish Boys went their separate ways it was Bowie, ever keen to keep good contacts, who stayed in touch with their producer Shel Talmy. These links proved useful. Talmy, who produced hits for The Who and The Kinks, booked studio time and hired session pianist Nicky Hopkins while Bowie wrote *You've Got A Habit Of Leaving* – which sounded very much like The Who's *Anyway, Anyhow, Anywhere* – and the B-side, *Baby Loves That Way*.

This first Davie Jones and The Lower Third single was released by Parlophone, together with a typical 60s profile supposed to define a group's image: our Davie was born on 1 January 1946 (untrue), sang and played harmonica (what about saxophone and guitar?), disliked 'in crowds' (he did not know any), admired Sammy Davis Jnr, loved rump steak (he was almost vegetarian), and enjoyed drinking barley wine and vodka (hopefully not at the same time). Despite this, and similarly banal profiles of The Lower Third (whose tastes ranged from kinky boots to John Steinbeck), the single was ignored and they found themselves with neither a producer nor a recording contract. This gave Horton a chance to prove himself.

Back in Birmingham, Horton had known Denny Laine before he joined The Moody Blues. Denny's first group, Denny Laine and The Diplomats, made one record for Pye with producer Tony Hatch. This gave Horton an introduction, although had he been more experienced he would never have taken Bowie to either Hatch or Pye.

A gifted pianist and composer, Hatch's forte was romantic songs with melody and rhythm, which he produced for Petula Clark, sometimes writing them with his wife, the singer Jackie Trent; it was always a good team, producing *Downtown* and *I Couldn't Live Without Your Love*. But he wasn't rock 'n' roll and neither were Pye.

In late 1965, when he first recorded Bowie with The Lower Third, Hatch was riding high on *Downtown*, which sold three million copies. In the studio, Hatch handed Bowie the tambourine used on the *Downtown* session, saying 'I hope this brings you luck.' It did not. Bowie made three singles with Hatch during 1965/6 (*see* Appendix), the first with The Lower Third and the other two with session musicians – and they all flopped. 'It wasn't the right time for him,' says Hatch. Once again Bowie found himself without a producer or recording contract.

Horton, however, was optimistic. Hoping to make his fortune, he gave up his day job with King's Agency, ordered printed letterheads and set up in business at 79a Warwick Square, the basement flat near Victoria Station that he shared with Bell. Horton had total faith in Bowie, but paying the rent was a constant problem and bailiffs were repeatedly beating a path down the steps to the basement which stank of chip grease, cat shit and stale sperm. Life was a daily juggling act, holding off the creditors while trying to raise enough cash to buy the petrol for The Lower Third to drive to their gigs in the ancient second-hand ambulance that they used for transport. Mattresses were kept in the back, and rather than travel home to Plaistow, Bowie would frequently park in a side street, more often than not with a girl in the back.

With money so tight, Horton either had to find a sleeping partner or borrow. He tried both. First, for reasons Pitt never understood, he phoned Pitt on 15 September 1966, asking if he could call. He arrived a few days later with a new set of photographs, having persuaded the band to clean themselves up to look more like The Who, The Move or The Small Faces, cutting their hair and kitting them out with what looked like Marks and Spencer shirts and the slim, floral ties then in fashion.

'I think I've gone about as far as I can go,' said Horton, admitting he was short of money and would need more to launch Davie Jones and The Lower Third now that they had a recording contract.

'I'm not too sure about the name,' said Pitt, who knew of two or three other David Joneses, including one about to begin a career with The Monkees. Pitt was also none too sure that he wanted to work with another group, having recently represented Manfred Mann and The Kinks. 'I think I'd be happier working with a solo artist with long-term potential, someone like Tommy Steele who might go from pop music into films or television,' he said.

'In that case, Davie's your man,' said Horton. 'He wants to act and dance in films and musicals.'

'Let's leave it until the New Year,' cautioned Pitt. So they did, with Horton writing shortly afterwards to say Davie's name had been changed to DAVID BOWIE. It was Bowie who chose it, taking his surname from Jim Bowie, the Texan who invented the Bowie knife and died at the Battle of the Alamo.

\*   \*   \*   \*   \*

Without telling Pitt, Horton also approached Harold Taylor, owner of The Guardian Bank, which was registered in Guernsey with offices in Bristol and London. Taylor lived near Wimbledon Common, which was where Horton and Bowie went for a loan. 'I don't know much about the pop music business,' said Taylor, recommending them instead to his neighbour Raymond Cook, a central heating engineer, who ran his own company, Petray Heating Ltd, and lived upstairs. They explained that they now had a record deal with Pye, and subsequently entered into an agreement with Cook – still without informing Pitt, who later had to pick up the pieces.[1] This agreement was signed on 15 November 1965 and was described by Pitt as 'an amazingly inept, do-it-yourself document,* the like of which usually tempts lawyers to do something illegal'. It stated:

> That Ralph Horton manager of David Bowie (David Robert Jones) will pay to Raymond Cook ten per cent of the artiste's earnings provided that the artiste's earnings total more than one hundred pounds per month. If the artiste's earnings do not total more than one hundred pounds per month then no such remuneration is payable. The length of the agreement will be for a period of three years upon the signing of this agreement and a further continuance of two years will take effect should the option clauses on the management contract between the artiste and Ralph Horton be exercised ...

In return, Raymond Cook was to 'supply to the artist care of Ralph Horton a financial investment the amount of which will be verbally agreed between the two parties'. In other words, Bowie had agreed to sign away ten per cent of his earnings in the hope of receiving an unspecified sum of money to further his career.

Once the document was signed, Cook began shelling out cash, paying off some of Horton's debts, advancing him the odd £25 for cash expenses, giving him another £25 to buy a microphone, and then £410 to purchase amplifiers and speakers so that Bowie and The Lower Third could make more ambitious public appearances, notably their first 'overseas tour', always a highlight in any group's career. In their case it meant driving their rackety old ambulance down to Dover, catching the cross-Channel ferry, and then travelling up to Paris to perform at the Palladium Club in Montmartre and for two nights at the Golf Drouet Club over the 1965/6 New Year.

*    *    *    *    *

Like most managers and publicists, Pitt usually had several irons in the fire. In the 50s, he launched The Singing Gypsy, Danny Purches, who contrived to look like a gypsy by wearing a ring in one ear and a silk head scarf while rubbing his face with hedgehog

* Reproduced on p. 41 of *The Pitt Report*.

grease. Pitt also acted as London representative or publicist for Nana Mouskouri, Nina and Frederick, Leonard Cohen, Rod McKuen, Judy Garland, Anthony Newley and Bob Dylan, when he first visited London in April 1965.

Having realized when working with bands that he made no more money and endured far more hassle with a four- or five-man group, Pitt now believed he would be happier working with solo artistes. That autumn of 1965, he was representing Crispian St Peters, a fine-sounding new singer who recorded a cover version of We Five's American hit *You Were On My Mind*. It took Pitt just a few days to realize that Crispian was not going to top the bill at the London Palladium, however good his voice. Once he began meeting the press, Crispian talked too much, claiming to be a finer songwriter than John Lennon or Paul McCartney and a better singer than Elvis Presley. The laughter could be heard from Billingsgate to Bangkok. As if he had not done enough to self-destruct, Crispian also began losing hair quickly – and the world was not ready for balding pop stars.

By now, money was pouring out of Raymond Cook's bank account as David Bowie and The Lower Third prepared for their trip to Paris in December 1965. As things turned out, events early in January 1966 proved crucial.

\*     \*     \*     \*     \*

The single *Can't Help Thinking About Me* was released in January 1966, with a reception at the Victoria Tavern in Strathearn Place, off Marble Arch. The Lower Third were thoroughly pissed off when told to return to London from Paris for the event the hard way, in their ambulance, while David flew back with Horton on the pretext that there was 'important business' to attend to in London. They may have thought it 'important' to travel back early to see Vicky Wickham at Rediffusion Television, but she was only the floor manager for *Ready, Steady, Go!*, not the producer, and they could easily have seen her at some other time. And they were none too pleased by the reception. There was a standing buffet and oodles of booze, all paid for by Cook, which was fine: but Horton and Bell were steering Bowie around the room on his own, introducing him to journalists and treating him as a star. The press seemed to be kept away from *them*. What was far more significant, looking back, was that even then, before he was earning enough money to buy his own trousers, there were people willing to look upon Bowie as a future star.

For The Lower Third, this single was a record produced with their new singer; for Bowie it was one recorded with his new backing group. The label said it all. Both songs were performed by David Bowie and The Lower Third, with Bowie also given the songwriting credits. He was the star; they were not. With the group already starting to grumble, the crunch came a fortnight later. They had few bookings, other than The Bromel Club on Bowie's home turf. He expected many of his friends to be in the audience. Just before they were due to go on, Horton announced: 'There's no money for you tonight!' explaining he wanted some himself as he was overdue with his rent.

The disgruntled musicians put their heads together while Bowie burst into tears. 'We had a quick discussion about it,' Graham Rivens informed Pitt, 'and then told Ralph it was a question of "no pay, no play". Ralph suggested we went to a nearby pub to think it over, but when we came back we were of the same mind. Ralph still refused to pay us, so we packed up and left. David cried, but it made no difference. We had had enough.'

This anecdote, relayed in *The Pitt Report*, has the ring of truth, for Bowie always burst into tears whenever anything went wrong – if an audience disliked him, a girlfriend upset him, or if something happened to disturb his equilibrium. 'I've always been like that,' he told me, 'ever since I was a child ... it's nothing to be ashamed of, it's just the way I am. Artists often cry. It's in their nature.' Pitt learned to handle him gently. 'David is very sensitive,' he told me, more than once. But was it more than that? Was he, as the Gillmans suggest in *Alias David Bowie*, emotionally imbalanced, a practising bisexual, possibly experiencing homosexual relationships, besides sleeping with any girl who was willing?

Here we tread upon unsure ground. Bowie has talked so often of his sexuality that he would have a hard job suing anyone for libel, and yet his admissions hardly amount to a convincing truth.

In a notorious interview with *Playboy* which I am sure Bowie now regrets (and which I never believed to be true, knowing he was doped up with cocaine when he gave it), Bowie claimed to have first become aware of his homosexual inclinations at the age of 14: 'It didn't really matter who or what it was with, as long as it was a sexual experience. So it was some very pretty boy in class in some school or other that I took home and neatly fucked on my bed upstairs.' Later, he was to have a fleeting homosexual relationship with Lindsay Kemp, who taught him mime. Secunda told me Bolan also admitted having 'a thing going' with Bowie, but throughout this whole period – from his mid-teens to stardom – Bowie was also rampantly heterosexual.

More recently, Bowie's witty response to any questions has been to say that he was always a 'closet heterosexual' and that it was all his management's fault for creating his gay image. I believe that to be true, for Bowie was an accomplished seducer in his teens. I have already mentioned the occasion when he shinned down a drainpipe to escape a girl's parents. The singer Dana Gillespie met Bowie when she was 14 and says he saw her brushing her hair in a mirror at The Marquee, walked over, took the brush from her hand, carried on brushing and said, 'Can I take you home tonight?' Her reply was 'Absolutely,' and she smuggled him upstairs past her parents' bedroom and the affair continued some months.

Bowie frequently had two or three affairs running in parallel. Natasha Korniloff, whom he met with Lindsay Kemp's mime company and who later designed many of his stage costumes, described their love-making as 'a wonderful experience' while another lover, journalist Mary Finnegan, said Bowie was 'physically quite gorgeous ... he just loved making love.'

This is confirmed by his first wife, Angie, who has written two books about their marriage, saying 'His pride in the size and staying power of his sexual equipment was quite obviously justified ... he used sex the way a cat sprays, to mark his territory.'

Bowie never seemed genuinely bisexual to me, but he was attractive to the gays cruising around the London music business, being tall and slim, with sleek flowing hair, pastel coloured clothes and a shoulder bag swinging near his hip (other than when he passed through his Mod and Bob Dylan phases). He was an attractive piece of meat, but had anyone said so he would have decked them with his handbag.

*  *  *  *  *

In these learning years, Bowie drifted, from group to group as much as from bed to bed. He was lazy and languid, aimlessly wandering until situations arose when he would suddenly assert himself with a strength that could be upsetting. He always regarded himself as a solo singer working with a backing group, and inevitably left them behind.

With his Pye single to promote, some bookings in hand and Cook willing to produce another £250 for Horton to push *Can't Help Thinking About Me* into the charts, Bowie moved quickly to find a new backing group: this time they were only that from the start.

An advertisement was placed in *Melody Maker*, inviting musicians to audition for a new group that would 'accompany a singer' who had a record 'in the charts and climbing' (it was at No. 34). Similar wording was frequently used when producers or publishers holding the rights to a record found themselves with a hit on their hands, and there were always musicians looking for a weekly wage.

Those who phoned through to Bell, Horton or even Bowie at 79a Warwick Square were asked, 'What's your image?' or 'Are you a Mod or a Rocker?'

'I'm a bit of both,' said bass player Derek Fearnley, who was promptly called for an audition. Guitarist John Hutchinson heard about the job when he wandered in to The Marquee to see if there was any work available, and he recommended a friend from Yorkshire, organist Derek Boyes. The fourth recruit was John Eager, a drummer from Harrow. Bowie decided to call them The Buzz.

They began rehearsing on 7 February 1966, nearly a month after Bowie's 19th birthday. They appeared together for the first time at Leicester University on the 10th, with a booking at The Marquee the following night. This time, there could be no dispute about the musicians' status. They were each paid a weekly wage of £12, plus travelling expenses – and the standard Musicians Union session rate of £9 when they recorded Bowie's next single, *Good Morning Girl/Do Anything You Say*. Even so, it is by no means clear that The Buzz earned enough to cover their wages, for they only had four or five gigs in February, seven the following month and an appearance with Bowie on *Ready, Steady Go!* on 4 March when Bowie probably did not earn enough to pay for his tailored white suit.

This lack of financial return was worrying Raymond Cook, who was fast discovering that investing in pop stars is far more risky than installing radiators. After shelling out more than £3,000 in four months, he could see no chance of getting his money back. And refused Horton the cash to push the single further up the chart. With that, the record stopped selling. And Horton decided it was time for him to see Ken Pitt again.

4

# Rock, Warhol and The Velvets

By the time Horton made his next approach to Pitt, Bowie's second Pye single was ready for release. 'I'd like to bring you up to date with all David's news,' said Horton, giving no indication that financial crises plagued him on every front.

They met on 5 April 1966, with Horton bringing a copy of the new single, *Do Anything You Say* (*see* Appendix). David Bowie and The Buzz were out of town gigging. Much more important for Bowie than far-flung provincial dates was the regular Sunday afternoon fixture he had secured at The Marquee from 10 April. This was billed in The Marquee's weekly advertisement in *Melody Maker* as 'THE BOWIE SHOWBOAT' – every Sunday from 3 p.m. to 6 p.m., featuring him with the group, Top Ten Discs and Guests. These shows had a sponsor, the pirate station Radio London, and Bowie made sure of an audience by bringing up school friends from Bromley. Every week, his mother would be in the front row, wearing a straw hat and clapping her hands like a southern Baptist.

Pitt saw the second of these shows on 17 April. He stood at the back, leaning against a wall, and watched Bowie intently, quite clearly fronting and not part of a band, dressed in a tight-fitting, biscuit-coloured sweater, buttoned at his shoulder, with slacks. Looking quite unlike any other group of the day, for there were no jeans, T-shirts or leather jackets, David Bowie and The Buzz worked through an unusual set that combined rhythm 'n' blues and rock 'n' roll standards with his own songs *Do Anything You Say*, *Good Morning Girl*, *Can't Help Thinking About Me*, *And I Say To Myself*, and a new number, *London Boys*. Bowie closed with *You'll Never Walk Alone*, the showstopper from *Carousel*.

'It was a stunning performance for someone who had never had a hit record,' Pitt told me shortly afterwards. 'I was looking for someone who could come out of the pop world and be a star as opposed to a guitar cowboy. Up to that time, the only person who had done that successfully was Tommy Steele, but now he had moved on to stage shows and films. I felt he had left a gap behind him and the time was ripe for someone else to make the same transition from singing with a group to becoming a TV personality, a West End stage star, what we used to call an "all round entertainer" .... when I saw David that afternoon I thought he was someone who might be groomed in just the way I had in mind – from the way he moved on stage, by the way he held himself in front of an audience, and even his eyes .... Even then, I thought the songs he was writing were remarkable, outstanding for someone of his age and of quite different quality to much of the material other groups were writing.'

This was what Pitt told me early in 1967. His words have been frequently cited by writers on Bowie, but a problem lies in the way his comments about Tommy Steele have been misinterpreted. Steele was always an attractive, folksy, middle-of-the-road, family entertainer and I have never thought Pitt saw Bowie like that. What Pitt spotted was a raw talent that could be refined, shaped and trained, which was how a good manager would guide an artist's career. He could see Bowie had the potential to become a world star.

Pitt's show business career stretched back 20 years. He left the Army in 1946 to work in the design department at J. Arthur Rank, having studied at the Slade before the war. His diplomatic skills were noticed and he was soon transferred to the Publicity Department, escorting stars when they made personal appearances. In the early 50s he worked in Hollywood, sharing a flat with James Dean, later returning to London as British representative for such stars as Judy Garland, Louis Armstrong, Frank Sinatra, Frankie Laine, Duke Ellington and Jerry Lee Lewis, during that ill-fated first British tour when the press forced Lewis out of Britain on discovering that his third wife was only 13 years old. Pitt tried to defuse the situation by giving her a Bible to hold in public, and Lewis was sufficiently impressed by these signs of coolness under pressure to invite him to handle press arrangements when he returned to Britain in 1962. By then, Pitt had a reputation for being reliable in a crisis, a man who did not flap.

Some of this was known to Horton, who repeatedly said, 'You can open doors that are always closed to me.'

'I wouldn't say that,' answered Pitt, who was naturally self-effacing, as he invited Horton and Bowie back to his apartment after that first night at The Marquee.

\*    \*    \*    \*    \*

Although he added years to his age (as his father had done in 1933) David Bowie was only a little past his 19th birthday and still living at home with his parents in Plaistow Grove. There were still two years to go before he could make any formal decisions himself, and John Jones was keeping meticulous records of Bowie's income and expenditure. Pitt learned that Bowie's income during his year with The Lower Third totalled £2,204, against which he was able to offset his expenses, making his net income for the year negligible. He was not earning enough to pay income tax.

However, Bowie had total faith in himself and Pitt could see he was bubbly, cheerful and laughed easily. 'I was delighted to find he had a sense of humour,' he told me. They talked all around the problems Horton was facing, without Horton admitting that the bailiffs were at the door. It was more of a general conversation, about what should happen next to advance Bowie's career, and whether Pitt could handle publicity, contracts, accounts and negotiations with agents or record companies more easily than Horton. During the conversation, Bowie turned to Horton and said: 'Let's do a deal with Ken.'

So it was agreed that Pitt would look after day-to-day administration, leaving Horton to act more like an aide-de-camp, travelling with Bowie wherever he went, dealing with problems at that level and mediating with TV directors, theatre managers, record producers and so on.

Within two or three days, the bills started arriving through Pitt's letterbox, often accompanied by a short note from Horton explaining why they had to be paid urgently: the telephone was about to be cut off; the electricity was being disconnected because Horton, a trained electrical engineer, by-passed the meter with some clever wiring; the ambulance kept breaking down, which meant Pitt had to buy another for £125. On 25 April, Horton wrote: 'I have just looked at my diary and remembered this Court Order, and as you can see £22 2s 6d must be paid before 10.30 a.m. tomorrow morning.' The order had been secured by Roneo Ltd, who supplied Horton with duplicating equipment and stationery. Another judgement was issued by Croydon County Court because Horton failed to pay for a few copies of Bowie's own records ordered from Pye for promotional purposes, and now the bailiffs were planning to raid the Warwick Square basement on Pye's behalf – even though Bowie was due back in their recording studio with Hatch to make his next record. Pitt was able to divert seizure of Horton's few goods by asking Pye to offset the cost of the records against Bowie's royalties.

In his first month, says Pitt in *The Pitt Report*, he estimated that his expenditure totalled £630 3s 7d while Bowie's income from his few performances added up to £147 10s. There were to be many months worse than that.

Even so, there were signs that Bowie's career was steadily moving ahead. On some occasions at The Marquee, Bowie and The Buzz were booked to support The High Numbers, who were on the point of changing their name to The Who. In Bognor Regis, they appeared alongside Long John Baldry and his backing group Bluesology, with a young lad named Elton John on piano. And in August 1966, Radio London agreed to sponsor another six performances of The Bowie Showboat.

Bowie was interviewed that month for the first time on radio, for the station was keen to publicize its Marquee promotion. He told the interviewer that he was planning to write a musical with Tony Hatch (a project that came to nothing, although several songs written by Bowie for the musical were included in his first album). Asked if he would be able to carry on with his pop career, Bowie replied: 'I hope so. I'd like to get into cabaret, obviously,' but would not be drawn on his ideas for changing his act. 'You don't see yourself as another Tommy Steele?' probed the interviewer. 'No, not at all. No!' 'Just the first original David Bowie?' the questioning continued. 'I hope so,' responded Bowie.

But despite such advantageous publicity, as a recording artist, Bowie was making no headway – and Pitt would have realized Pye was totally the wrong company. Pye ruined the career of The Searchers (John Lennon reckoned them 'the best group that ever came out of Liverpool'); failed to spot the potential of another group on their books, Status Quo; amazingly signed up Lennon's runaway father, dubbed by his son The Ignoble Alf; and now allowed Bowie, arguably the most influential artiste of the post-Beatles era, to slip through their fingers.

*Do Anything You Say/Good Morning Girl* flopped – and so did

Bowie's next, *I Dig Everything/I'm Not Losing Sleep*, issued on 19 August 1966. Without hits, Bowie was driven to accept the cheapest jobs in the marketplace. Some nights he performed in youth clubs, public houses and village halls, earning barely enough to cover the petrol – and nowhere near enough to pay the group.

On 6 September, Bowie went to see Pitt, unhappy because of his lack of progress and because Pye were refusing to issue *London Boys*, which he rightly believed to be one of his best songs. 'I thought it was a remarkable song, and in it David had brilliantly evoked the atmosphere of his generation and London,' says Pitt.[1]

In September Hatch agreed to release Bowie from his Pye contract; he then rerecorded *London Boys* and two other songs, *Rubber Band* and *Please Mr Gravedigger*, which Pitt took to Decca, where Tony Hall and Denny Cordell were setting up a new label, Deram, specifically to develop new talent. After some haggling, they agreed Bowie could record an album of his own songs with the producer Mike Vernon while Deram released *Rubber Band* and *London Boys* as a single. Pitt also discussed a publishing agreement with David Platz at Essex Music, who already had Pete Townshend and Marc Bolan under contract and offered Bowie an advance against royalties of £1,000. 'This was less than I was hoping for,' says Pitt, who asked for time to think about it while he left for New York early in November 1966, where he thought he might be able to pick up a better deal.

Unexpectedly, Crispian St Peters was currently No. 1 in every American chart with *Pied Piper* (which peaked at No. 5 in Britain), and Pitt was out there reaping the proceeds before flying on to Australia and New Zealand. He was also hoping to meet Andy Warhol, who was planning to enter the music business with a new group, The Velvet Underground, which Pitt foresightedly wanted to represent in Britain. Warhol was as yet still relatively unknown in rock terms. He was more of a curiosity, an avant garde artist made famous by his screen prints and first erotic films. Nonetheless by 1966 Warhol was experimenting with 'mixed media', films and art and rock 'n' roll running side by side, at the Café Bizarre in New York City.

'The pop idea, after all, was that anybody could do anything,' said Warhol,[2] '… we all wanted to break out into every creative thing we could. That's why when we met The Velvet Underground at the end of 1965, we were all for getting into the music scene, too.'

Warhol had already tried forming his own rock 'n' roll group, with himself 'singing badly', but soon decided to concentrate instead on fusing lights with music, after meeting Lou Reed at the Café Bizarre. Warhol was drawn to The Velvet Underground as much by their image (they were named after a sado-masochistic paperback[3] that an early member, Tony Conrad, found on the sidewalk in the Bowery) as their music. Their repertoire ranged from Chuck Berry to their own songs, such as *Venus In Furs*, *Heroin* and *Waiting For The Man*, mainly written by Lou Reed and centred on previously unmentionable themes – sado-masochism, drugs, transvestism and homosexuality.

Reed was also keenly experimenting with what he called Metal Machine Music, which became the title of an album ten years later, and was the forerunner of Bowie's own experiments with Tin Machine.

Warhol persuaded them to bring in Nico, whom he knew through Brian Jones of The Rolling Stones, a frequent visitor to the Warhol Factory. By the time Pitt heard of the venture Warhol was already starting to appear with them in presentations that were billed 'ANDY WARHOL and his EXPLODING PLASTIC INEVITABLE SHOW featuring the NEW sound of the VELVET UNDERGROUND'.

At this point, the group's first album, *The Velvet Underground And Nico*, was near completion,[4] produced by Andy Warhol who also designed the famous banana motif for the sleeve and associated artwork – posters, advertisements, etc. – and there was talk of them presenting a sensational stage show. This would have matched their high-blasting heavy metal sound with a light show that combined images of bull whips, drug needles and sexual accessories with extracts from such Warhol films as *Blow Job*, *Kiss*, *Whips*, *Eat*, *Harlot* and *Banana*.

Pitt was taken to Warhol's studio, The Factory, then situated on the upper storeys of a former industrial building on East 47th Street, which could only be reached by travelling in a wire mesh cage lift on the outside of the building.

As we entered the studio I saw to our left a group of people manipulating their hands to make shadow pictures on a large suspended sheet. They seemed to be making a film. Over to the right a girl was seated at a typewriter and she looked up as we passed by. She was the now legendary Nico.... The general decor seemed to be silver, on all the walls and on the ceiling, from which lights and all movement reflected. Andy Warhol, whose hair was also silver, was standing at a table arranging pieces of paper. Suspended from the ceiling above his head was an enormous yellow banana. He was everything I had expected ... the shades, the polo-neck, the mask. I cannot recall what was said or even that we said anything at all. Having been introduced and it having been proved to each other that we existed seemed to be all that was required to set the seal of approval to our plans ...

Pitt met Lou Reed and was given a copy of the first Velvet Underground LP; this he gave to Bowie when he returned to London, thus introducing him to musical ideas that have remained part of his armoury ever since: the timbre of Reed's voice, the songwriting style, the fusion of art forms and the willingness to ignore conventional boundaries. Their music became an obsession for Bowie, just as Anthony Newley's had been a few years earlier, and several of Reed's songs – *Waiting For The Man* from that first album and especially *White Light, White Heat* from their second – became a constant part of Bowie's stage act.

Meanwhile, Pitt spent a further three days in New York, seeking to better the Essex Music offer for Bowie's songs and agreeing that London Records should release *Rubber Band* in the United States (which they did, but with *There Is A Happy Land* instead of *London Boys* on the B-side, objecting like Pye to the homosexual undertone of its lyrics). Pitt also continued to negotiate arrangements for The Velvet Underground's first visit to Britain. On the morning of 13 November, his final day, Pitt received an offer of $30,000 for Bowie's songs, as an advance against royalties, with $10,000 paid on signature of contract and similar sums in each of the following two years. Then he caught a plane to Australia.

In Melbourne, Pitt received one letter from Horton saying, 'We are broke with a capital B. It looks now as though I will have to go bankrupt ...' and then another saying that he and Bowie had decided to sack The Buzz as there was not enough money coming in to pay their wages, and that Bowie would now be concentrating on writing rather than performing 'because there is absolutely no money in the ballroom business at present'.

Pitt arrived back in England to discover that in his absence Horton and Bowie had signed a deal with Essex Music, not for the £1,000 offered before he went away, but for an advance of just £500. The contract was dated 7 December and required all monies to be paid to Horton. Bowie and his father had also signed it.

Pitt was furious, but decided to say nothing before establishing who had done what, and to whom the money had gone. After speaking to Bowie's father, Pitt learned that Horton kept £200 for himself and gave £200 to Bowie, plus a further £100 which Bowie had been advised was an advance from Decca for his musical arrangements. John Jones was mortified when he learned that by rushing through the Essex deal, Bowie lost the chance of a $30,000 contract, telling Pitt he had agreed to sign because he understood Pitt had settled the terms before leaving for America. 'No, no, no – I told Essex Music that I wanted time to think about it,' Pitt replied. Jones asked if Pitt was going to tell Bowie about the US offer. Pitt thought not, saying Bowie would be 'very depressed' if he did. Jones agreed: 'It would crush him.'

Legally, Horton was still Bowie's sole manager. Everything Pitt had done, including spending £1,500 of his own money, had been on a basis of trust and without a contract, although his solicitors had drawn one up before he left for New York. However, Horton had not signed it and Pitt realized the time had come either for a formal agreement or a parting of the ways. Before he had taken this any further, Bowie phoned and said, 'Ken, I'm worried about Ralph. May I come up and talk about it?'

Pitt sensed Bowie was being careful, satisfying himself that Pitt was willing to handle his affairs before broaching the matter with Horton. 'David, I would be very pleased to look after it all for you,' said Pitt, and away Bowie went to see if Horton was willing to tear up their management contract.

'I'll say this for Ralph, he was very good about that,' Pitt told me. 'He let David go without any bother, when he could quite easily have made things difficult.'

\*   \*   \*   \*   \*

Bowie's *Rubber Band/London Boys* single was released by Deram on 2 December 1966, with Bowie playing guitar and saxophones.

He was by then hard at work on his first album. Both single and album revealed a whimsical streak was running through Bowie's writing. Bowie's music sounded old fashioned compared with the maturer contemporary sounds of The Beach Boys' *Good Vibrations* album, Jimi Hendrix (on his first London stage appearances) and the newly emerging Pink Floyd. Meanwhile, the clubs were agog with rumours about The Beatles' sessions at Abbey Road, where EMI allowed them unlimited time to record their next LP, *Sergeant Pepper's Lonely Hearts Club Band*.

No one knew it, but popular music was changing for ever. Rock was becoming a serious form. The first major festival, Monterey, was but months away, rock was about to get its own newspaper, *Rolling Stone*, yet Bowie's twee little songs belonged more naturally to another time, to music hall or the West End stage. *Rubber Band* was a bouncy number about a soldier returning from the First World War and losing his sweetheart to the leader of a brass band. It earned a few radio plays but no TV appearances and hardly any reviews. The best appeared in *Disc*, a music paper noted more for photos than editorial content. Even that didn't think it was a hit, though it showed 'how David Bowie has progressed himself into being a name to reckon with, certainly as far as songwriting is concerned'. David Bowie had changed: 'a different voice – distinctly reminiscent of a young Tony Newley – has emerged'. Perceptively, *Disc* also said *London Boys*, the B side, 'would have been a much more impressive topside'.

Bowie's debt to Anthony Newley was real. Newley's career could be seen as one route to the London Palladium. It began with Newley playing the Artful Dodger in David Lean's 1948 film *Oliver Twist* and developed through what was then known as pop music with Newley having seven Top Ten hits between 1959 and 1961, before creating *Stop The World I Want To Get Off*, a vehicle for himself both on the London stage and on Broadway, and then *The Strange World Of Gurney Slade*, an offbeat forerunner to Monty Python or Rowan Atkinson's *Mr Bean*. It was all very much his own work, blending pop with theatre, old-style showbiz and contemporary humour – but belonged to another generation that rock was leaving behind.

Bowie continued in similar vein with *Over The Wall We Go*, a tongue-in-cheek topical song inspired by a recent rash of prison escapes, released in January 1967. He did not record this himself, but joined in on the backing vocals when it was recorded by

Oscar, a new singer launched by the Australian entrepreneur Robert Stigwood.[5] Likewise, Bowie's next single *The Laughing Gnome* (April 1967) and his songs for his first LP *David Bowie* (June 1967) showed him looking backwards rather than forwards, still larding his lyrics with whimsy, and writing quaint little numbers with such titles as *Little Bombardier*, *Come And Buy My Toys*, *Uncle Arthur* or *Love You Till Tuesday* that gave no hint of what was to come.

5

# Terry comes home

The need to secure his parents' consent to every contract brought Pitt closer to Bowie's background. Sometimes, he would settle matters on the phone with John Jones. At others, Pitt drove down to Plaistow Grove and sat across the living room fireplace, answering the worries of Mr and Mrs Jones, and explaining how he thought their son's career might develop. In those early stages, Pitt remained unaware of the insanity running through the maternal side of the family. Terry's name was never mentioned, and if either of them thought of telling Pitt about Horton's dealings with Cook, they clearly thought better of it.

Pitt began to see that Bowie enjoyed a rare understanding with his father, to whom he would naturally turn rather than to his mother. 'David and his father were devoted to each other, although their attitudes to life were very different, and I would say that this was much the most important relationship in his life, to that time,' Pitt told me, adding that he could see that Bowie was 'never that close to his mother'. 'His father was a very nice man, a real gentleman, a very nice person indeed.... He was genteel and eloquent ... and always concerned that David should behave properly in every situation. He was meticulous and this carried through into every area of his daily life.'

As Pitt came to know them better, Mr and Mrs Jones began to open out. With art the only school subject to which Bowie seemed naturally drawn, they encouraged him to study graphic design and to think of a career in advertising. 'They both admitted being none too keen on him going into music, but were not oppressive about it,' said Pitt. 'As soon as they saw this was where his heart lay, they gave him support, encouraging him to practise, going to see nearly all his shows and taking a close interest in every aspect of the work he did.

'Perhaps it was because of his own background, but his father's anxieties kept coming through. Whenever there was an offer to consider ... John would be on the phone, saying, "Now tell me what you think, Ken? Do you think David is doing the right thing?"'

In this, Bowie's background was different from many other musicians who left homes often far from London for bedsitter areas of Notting Hill, Paddington, Earls Court or West Kensington, with their continually changing, multi-racial sub-culture. Bowie experienced none of this. His opinions were literary-based rather than street-based, and with Plaistow Grove only minutes away from central London by train he continued to live at home, with his mother washing his clothes and preparing meals whenever she could persuade him to eat, and his father sticking the stamps in his National Insurance card, looking after his bank account, and dealing with any tricky questions from the Inland Revenue or the Department of Health and Social Security. Mr Jones advised his son to take out an insurance policy, which he did – at a time when most musicians were only taking chances.

Some nights, when travelling back from a distant gig, Bowie might rough it temporarily; but he always had a home to go to and he was never in debt. Mr Jones saw to that. Borrowing money was anathema to him.

Pitt observed that Jones 'realized he had bred an unusual son – but coped bravely with it.... John would often ask me what sort of potential I thought David had, what ideas I had for his future, and I know David did not agree with some of those ideas.... David's career would have turned out differently had his father lived ... John would have continued to be the moderating influence David has needed, though there was certainly nothing of the artist, or, indeed, anything creative about his father.'

\*     \*     \*     \*     \*

Some kind of bonding process drew Bowie and Pitt together during those early months of 1967. The Gillmans suggest a homosexual chemistry, but I suspect their relationship had other, more subtle dimensions. Having seen them together on several occasions, with Pitt behaving more like an uncle than a conventional manager, I suspect Bowie was looking to this older man not as a father-substitute, but as someone who could provide the width, depth and balance of judgement that comes with maturity in any profession. Bowie, desperate to become a star, was seeking guidance. Pitt was searching for the answer to every manager's dream, an artist with many talents who would evolve naturally.

'What intrigued me most about David was the range of his interests ... literature, art, poetry, philosophy and every form of music,' said Pitt. Having studied at the Slade School of Art, he could 'identify with the ideas David was grappling with'.

That conversation took place in Pitt's apartment in Manchester Street, with its stripped pine floors and Victorian furnishings, all chosen long before they became fashionable again. I sat on the same *chaise-longue*, edged in rosewood and trimmed with holly-green velvet, that Bowie sat back in when he and Pitt talked through the basis upon which they would work together.

'The very first time he came here on his own, David walked straight over to that bookcase and knew who all the authors were,' said Pitt, who had a collection of Oscar Wilde first editions, books illustrated by Gordon Craig and Charles Ricketts, and the works of Aubrey Beardsley, to whom he is related. 'No other would-be pop star would have been able to look along the shelves of a bookcase like that, talking knowledgeably about Oscar Wilde or Antoine de Saint-Exupéry ... pop music wasn't attracting intelligent people then, like it did later ...

'He ran his fingers along the spines, lingering over the better editions, clearly knowing which they were, and saying, "Oh, you've got that one" and "Oh, that one, too." He was obviously interested in books and art, and I think it was this common interest that strengthened our relationship because it was when he was reading one of my books on graphic drawing that he suddenly turned to Ralph and said, "Let's do a deal with Ken." The thing that made such an impact upon me, there and then, was that here was a young singer and songwriter who was interesting in so many other ways, because he had a mind as well.'

This may have been true, and I am sure it was, but Bowie was too much for Pitt to handle. Neither of them faced up to this for several years, and it distressed Pitt when Bowie eventually left him. Bowie was malleable up to a point. He might seem receptive to other people's ideas, but had the disquieting habit, unusual in so young a man, of maintaining an intellectual distance. 'He could be very cold,' says Pitt. My own judgement is that Pitt gave himself wholly to the relationship, but Bowie never did, retaining a sense of distance and doubting Pitt's objectives (which was just as well, in the long run).

In saying that he saw Bowie as an 'all-round entertainer', Pitt gives the game away. They were working towards different ends. Having been unsuccessful at every turn, Bowie was prepared to sublimate himself, but only so far. That coldness concealed a stubborn streak and a strong sense of his own worth.

'Have you thought of cabaret?' Pitt enquired, not once but repeatedly, assuring the young man that if he prepared a suitable night club act he might be able to find him West End bookings at around £100–£150 a week. This was quite respectable money in 1967, especially if Bowie was willing to keep costs down by accompanying himself on guitar or using an in-house backing group. Pitt also discussed the possibility with Bowie's father, who was enthusiastic, and away Bowie went to sort through his songs and select a few suitable for such an act, interwoven with standards familiar to any night club audience – *You'll Never Walk Alone*, *Trains And Boats And Planes* or Anthony Newley's show-stopper, *What Kind Of Fool Am I?* – but when the crunch came, and he had to decide whether to accept an offer, Bowie refused to cross that bridge. It was the same with pantomime. Pitt was sure that if Bowie learned dance and the skills of stagecraft, he would be able to find work every Christmas in traditional productions, such as *Aladdin*, *Puss In Boots* or *Babes In The Wood*: ten or twelve weeks' steady income. I can just imagine Pitt pointing out that Cliff Richard and The Shadows willingly appeared in pantomime most years – and Bowie reminding him that neither The Beatles nor The Rolling Stones would touch it with a barge pole, even when offered the chance.

Bowie was right. He could sense that rock was synonymous with change. As he put it more than 20 years later, 'With the advent of the Stones and the other rebels of rock one could see that a new approach was being taken, but there was still a good stiff stream of Tin Pan Alley biz'[1] – and it was this that Bowie was resisting.

Pitt may be partly to blame for the type of songs that Bowie continued to write. Some numbers on that first Decca album would have fitted comfortably within a stage musical or a Christmas pantomime. That was also true of *The Laughing Gnome* and his later, back-to-childhood song *When I'm Five*, a charming song about a little boy who wants to grow up and marry his mummy.

The conventional view among rock 'n' roll writers is that Bowie made a terrible mistake recording songs like this. When the rereleased *The Laughing Gnome* was a hit six years later, Charles Shaar-Murray and Roy Carr called it 'the most embarrassing example of Bowie juvenilia,[2] comparing it to The Chipmunks and The Smurfs. I have never seen anything wrong in an artiste writing for children or sharing a joke with an audience. Bowie was young, experimenting in what was still a new genre, and now looks back upon these records as 'fumblings about how to bring theatricality to pop music or rock. It stems from the very English thing, the idea of music hall and vaudeville ... which is still very popular with the Mums and Dads.... I would probably have gone on to all that, pantomimes, musicals and that sort of thing, if I hadn't been so stubborn and hard-headed about doing something that had to do with Art.'[3]

\*     \*     \*     \*     \*

Pitt, then, was pulling in one direction while Bowie was drawn to another – but for nearly three years this was not so apparent; Bowie tended to follow Pitt's advice, with his father's encouragement. Acting more like a friend than a mentor, Pitt encouraged Bowie to start going to the theatre, starting down-market with a West End show starring Cilla Black and Frankie Howerd, and that year's London Palladium pantomime starring Cliff Richard and The Shadows, but moving on to straight drama, musicals and art exhibitions, before going on to dinner in the West End.

This also set Bowie apart from other musicians. Few had time to go to the theatre or develop other cultural interests. Having borrowed so much to establish themselves (The Who told me they were over £300,000 in debt), with record companies not yet paying advances, they mostly had to work every night, if their agents could pick up the bookings, travelling constantly to maintain a cash flow to meet their hire purchase payments and payroll costs. Once he dispensed with The Buzz, Bowie escaped all that; he became a solitary performer, hiring musicians only when he needed to, and free to write, record or audition for small parts in films and television. As he still had his room at Plaistow Grove, with neither rent to pay nor a wife and family to maintain, Bowie could live frugally. 'He was never broke in the sense that so many other musicians have been, and he was never in debt, either,' Pitt told me.

And then his sense of stability changed. Terry came home. Where he had been is unclear, for Bowie told me that after leaving the RAF and returning home to civilian life, Terry chose to sign up with the Merchant Navy, travelling twice around the world, whereas the Gillmans claim that Terry returned to his old clerical job at Amalgamated Press, forged a close friendship with the family of one of his workmates and moved with them down to Cornwall. Later, they say he returned to London and moved in with his Aunt Pat and her husband Tony Antoniou. They had a house in Ealing where Terry found a job in a bakery. The dates given in the various accounts do not tally, and it is possible that Terry managed to do all Bowie says he did, and that the Gillmans are correct as well, for several years are unaccounted for.

Whatever the explanation, Terry clearly lost touch with his family until he was nearly 30 years old, when he returned to Ealing only to find the house had been sold. He then went to see his mother in Plaistow Grove who told him the Antonious were now in Australia, hoping to start a new life, with Tony setting up in business with his brother as a garage mechanic and taxi driver. On being told this, Terry vanished, walking off to the Chislehurst Caves where the Gillmans claim he saw a vision of Christ and 'a simultaneous vision of heaven and hell'.[4] They say Terry began blindly walking

until he reached the countryside beyond Orpington. There he collapsed beneath a hedge. He spent the next eight days living rough, begging or stealing food from farms, and sleeping rough in outhouses or under trees. Finally, he stumbled into a greengrocer's and asked for an orange. Seeing Terry's dishevelled and bewildered state, the greengrocer called the police. The police took Terry back to Plaistow Grove, where Peggy railed at him for coming back in such a state. Terry shouted back at Peggy, and there was a furious row. David was at home, and witnessed the whole episode.... His father, John Jones, showed a remarkable change of attitude. John was now stricken with remorse for his former jealousy towards Terry, and told him that he was welcome to stay at Plaistow Grove. Thereafter Terry would spend the week having treatment at Farnborough

Hospital, and stay at Plaistow Grove at weekends…. Terry's
return to Plaistow Grove was followed by David's departure.

This account cannot be authenticated, for the Gillmans did not
meet Bowie, Terry or their mother. However, they also claim
Bowie 'did not tell Pitt that Terry was mentally ill; nor was he to
do so in the three years that Pitt remained his manager'[5] – and I
happen to know this part of the story is untrue, for Bowie openly
discussed Terry with Pitt in my presence, and was no less open in
talking about his brother to me.

Whatever it was that happened to make Bowie feel uncomfortable at home, he went to Pitt and started pouring out his woes. 'I
suppose you had better move in here,' said Pitt, looking at his
pale, strained, tearful face.[6] And so, on Sunday 11 June 1967,
Bowie left home. He packed all his treasured possession into the
back of his father's tiny Fiat 500 and drove with him up to
Manchester Street. After his father had gone, Bowie told Pitt: 'Dad
liked the flat. He said it's very masculine.'

                    *    *    *    *    *

If there was a bisexual period in Bowie's life, it probably began
now – but that is not to assume he and Pitt necessarily had a
homosexual relationship. Bowie was still only 20 years old, below
the age for homosexual consent, and it would have been dangerous
for either of them to have admitted a relationship, even if they had
one. It was certainly an issue Pitt was sensitive to. Pitt openly
advocated homosexual law reform, joining the Conservative
Campaign for Homosexual Equality – and when they were both
living at Manchester Street, they would walk around naked, Bowie
with 'his big dick swaying from side to side'.[7]

Once, when Pitt emerged from the bathroom without any
clothes on, Bowie is said to have mimed the act of measuring his
penis with a tape-measure, saying with mock awe, 'Ye Gods!' –
and Pitt also papered over the kitchen window so that Bowie's
nakedness could not be seen by neighbours. How much closer the
relationship became, Pitt refused to say, in his own book, to the
Gillmans, or to anyone else, although he does agree that it was
'strong and affectionate'. I suspect it was largely Bowie who
controlled the relationship. 'He had a way of sitting in a chair and
looking at you with a certain intensity,' says Pitt. 'He managed to

look at you as though his eyes were slightly closed but then you realized that they were in fact wide open and you got the impression that, as you were talking to him, he was analysing and dissecting every word you said and forming an opinion in his mind ...'

My own impression, having observed Bowie and Pitt together at Manchester Street, is that they probably did have a sexual relationship – but one that was never as important to Bowie as it was to Pitt. I believe Pitt genuinely loved him, but Bowie was always a chancer – and within days of him moving into the apartment Pitt was left in no doubt that Bowie would happily sleep with women as well.

Still thinking of Bowie's long-term career, Pitt took him to meet Michael Armstrong, an actor hoping to stage his own musical satire based on *Orpheus In The Underworld*, for which he needed someone to write the music and play Orpheus. Armstrong had bought the *David Bowie* LP and liked Bowie's 'wicked humour', so he contacted Pitt, asking whether Bowie might consider writing the music for his production. When they met, Armstrong explained that his Orpheus would be a young pop star torn apart alive by his fans. Pitt thought that Bowie would want to play Orpheus as well as write the music. They met to discuss the project in more detail on 27 June,[8] and then Bowie went off with Pitt to a party at the new Chappell recording studios in New Bond Street, where he drank far too much. As the party ended, Pitt saw him sitting in a corner, well the worse for wear, with a young girl on his lap. Later still, Pitt heard Bowie with the girl in his bedroom at Manchester Street. When Bowie went to the bathroom and started vomiting, Pitt thought he ought to tell her the party was over. As she vanished down the stairs, Bowie ran after her but Pitt grabbed his arm before he reached the street.

'You're too bloody possessive,' said Bowie.

\* \* \* \* \*

Whether he was gay or bisexual, or happily promiscuous, Bowie was never part of the rock 'n' roll gay scene, and neither was Pitt, who led a more sedate life, visiting the theatre, dining out, or driving down to his country cottage at Robertsbridge, where his friend and next-door neighbour was Malcolm Muggeridge.

There was a fairly grubby gay scene at the time, involving

booze, drugs and rent boys at three addresses in Kensington, Fulham and Marylebone, which well-established artists and managers would avoid, and Bowie was never a part of it.

In 1967/8, Bowie had neither the money nor the inclination to drift into rock's wilder fringes. He might have worn bells and kaftans, firing sticks of incense in his room at Manchester Street, and smoking the occasional spliff – but, in the language of the time, he was 'clean'. So far as Mr and Mrs Jones could tell, Pitt was looking after him well – and between them all, there existed a genuine desire to see him succeed.

\*   \*   \*   \*   \*

Pitt was solicitous. Boxes of each new release – the *David Bowie* LP and *The Laughing Gnome* and *Love You Till Tuesday* singles – were ordered from Deram, and Pitt worked away at his mailing list, sending copies to friends on the music papers and elsewhere in the entertainment industry, to theatre bookers, TV and radio producers, disc jockeys, pirate radio stations, and so on. Always there would be a covering letter urging them to listen to the future star. Where it might help, Pitt also included a press release that he had written himself with a brief résumé of Bowie's career and photographs suitable for publication. This was not a hard sell. Managers worked like this in the mid-60s – and I was on his mailing list.

An abstemious man, avoiding the pubs and clubs where journalists and PR men met at lunchtimes, Pitt worked around the offices, calling personally on music papers and publishers, agents and bookers, up and down the Soho backstreets, and through every floor of the BBC, ATV and Rediffusion, knowing that just one booking on a TV show of the calibre of *Top Of The Pops*, *Thank Your Lucky Stars* or *Ready, Steady, Go!* might be enough to give a record lift-off. That was the current theory: television led to record sales, which led to *more* TV and radio, *more* record sales, press coverage, and – BINGO!

But it didn't happen like that for Kenneth Pitt and David Bowie in 1967, and neither they nor his parents knew what should happen next. Pitt kept them fully informed. On 28 June John Jones wrote to thank him for all the documentation, and to suggest sending promotional material to 'our two local papers, *Bromley Times* and *Bromley Advertiser*' which were 'both always willing to write about David'. As always, Jones was attentive to money matters. Thanking Pitt for recommending an accountant he went on: 'I have this week heard from him that David is unlikely to have to pay any income tax until 1969 – well worth the modest £23 he has charged.' He continued to worry about Bowie's precarious finances: 'do you think there is any chance of Decca sending in the money for the arrangements fairly soon?' The money in David's account was beginning to look 'pretty sickly and he begins to get a little despondent when he feels he is down to his last few pounds. Of course, I would never allow him to be without a few shillings in his pocket although he would hate to think that I was advancing money to him.'

John Jones was continuing to look after his son's finances, helping him out when necessary, and keeping an eye on his career's progress, long after Bowie left home. My understanding is that Pitt continued to be in daily contact, discussing every twist and turn, until Jones died in August 1969. Bowie always had these twin props, Pitt and his father – and never needed to borrow a penny from anyone else. But, kind though they were, his career was floundering.

*The Laughing Gnome* was widely seen as nothing more than a novelty record, a humorous one-off that would have done little for its creator if it had been a hit. With *Love You Till Tuesday* (released in July 1967), Bowie came up with a much more subtle song, produced by Mike Vernon and engineered by Gus Dudgeon. This single had everything going for it but the spirit of the moment. Flower Power had arrived. The children of the world dressed in kaftans and beads, with daisies and forget-me-nots in their hair. They sang *All You Need Is Love*, and nothing else mattered at all, least of all a song with a coded lyric suggesting love seldom lasted.

Bowie's originality was not in doubt, but why was he failing to think about the potential market for his songs? The music paper critics responded favourably but cautiously to the single. 'It's nice to be able to report,' said Penny Valentine in *Disc*, 'that he's getting a bit closer to commercial success – though whether he'll ever have it as long as he goes on turning out such wonderfully weird stuff is hard to say.' Peter Jones, in *Record Mirror*, called it 'a stand-out single', and *Melody Maker's* Chris Welch declared Bowie to be 'one of the few really original solo singers operating in the theatre of British pop. He writes very unusual material, he's

good-looking, and while his voice has Anthony Newley connotations, it matters little while he makes fine songs like this ilk.' The
single, he wrote, was 'very funny', deserving 'instant recognition'.

It was to be nearly two years before Bowie released another
record, but Pitt was sufficiently impressed by *Love You Till
Tuesday* to spend those two years, and nearly £10,000 of his own
money, planning a film around it. He hoped to recoup the money
by selling the film to the German TV Channel ZDF, and then
using it as a promotional calling card, a filmed showcase for
Bowie's talents, that would be far more effective than LPs, photos
or press kits in persuading British TV producers to book Bowie for
their programmes. In 1967 there were no video machines or
camcorders readily available; in planning to use *Love You Till
Tuesday* in this way, Pitt and Bowie were ahead of their time.

Pitt needed no reminding of the parallels with Anthony
Newley's career. Newley also started off in pop music with Decca,
recording two No. 1 singles – *Why* and *Do You Mind* – and four
other Top Ten entries before turning to the legitimate stage. Pitt
could envisage Bowie taking a similar route, using *Love You Till
Tuesday* as the vehicle to set him on his way. Pitt had worked with
Newley on *The Small World Of Sammy Lee* and still had some
studio out-takes in a cupboard at Manchester Street. Pitt told me:

> When David saw them, he was very impressed, There's no
> denying that he was heavily into Newley at the time, and he
> loved the *Gurney Slade* TV series.... In the short time that I'd
> known him, we'd really been going through it. To begin with,
> he had a scruffy period when he wouldn't change his clothes
> and my secretary kept telling me how worried she was that he
> wasn't eating ... and then we had a Bob Dylan period, when he
> dressed in black and went all introvert, which is fatal in show
> business ... then he went hippie, like everyone else, wearing
> beads and bangles ... and now we were back to Newley, whom
> he'd been listening to before in 1960 and 1961.
>
> David had never met Newley, but felt a certain rapport for
> him through his films and TV series – and on the first few times
> he came to see me David photo-copied various letters I had
> from Newley and took them back to Bromley to show his
> father. David was always coming under different influences,
> and I used to tease him about it sometimes. Anyway, this
> Newley thing was really serious – and if you listen to *Love You*

*Till Tuesday* it could be Anthony Newley. The likeness in his phrasing and intonation is incredible.

Bowie was keen on making the *Love You Till Tuesday* film, but none too sure it would ever happen, so while Pitt busied himself with all the arrangements, Bowie began to drift again. Pitt heard that Lindsay Kemp was using the *David Bowie* LP as background music. Intrigued, and not a little flattered that someone in another art form was taking up his work, Bowie went to see Kemp presenting a one-man show in Covent Garden. Afterwards, he went backstage where Kemp invited him to write more music specifically for his mime shows. 'I said I would if he would lead me into the mysteries of mime,' said Bowie.[9] 'So I became his pupil. He was the master and I was the student. I was into ballet and mime and I got into the company and wrote some of the plays with him, and realized Lindsay Kemp was a living Pierrot. Everything in his life was tragic and dramatic and straight theatrical. So the stage was, for him, just an extension of his own life ...'

Like many of Bowie's descriptions of the influences upon his career, this may be overdone. What happened was that Bowie started going to Kemp's mime classes at the Dance Centre in Floral Street, Covent Garden, paying 7s 6d per lesson. This led to him being invited back to Kemp's nearby flat and the beginning of another short-lived homosexual liaison.

Kemp was a man of broader talents than most people Bowie met in the music business. He was descended from the clown William Kemp who played for Shakespeare and Jonson and made his own small mark in theatrical history by performing a morris dance from London to Norwich and writing an account of it, *Kemp's Nine Daies Wonder* (1660). Lindsay Kemp was a broad Scot, born on the Isle of Lewis, who learned dance with the Ballet Rambert and mime with Marcel Marceau before launching his own troupe at the Edinburgh Festival in 1964. Like Bowie, he tended to exaggerate their relationship, suggesting in a Belgian TV interview in 1981 that 'David worked for my company for three or four years.... I once heard him on the radio singing something and it sounded as if it could have been me singing.... My voice, of course, is my body, but if I had a voice that came from my chest, it might have sounded something like David Bowie. In other words, I identified myself with David Bowie like I identified myself with

Picasso and Jean Genet ... it was a voice that attracted me like a
siren. I was Ulysses, attracted by the song of Circe. It was
inevitable that we came together. We found each other and we
began to work together.'

Their relationship began in the summer of 1967, and – despite
what Kemp says – was all over, in a day-to-day sense, by shortly
after Christmas. Pitt continued as Bowie's manager throughout
this period, helping to place his songs with other artistes, lining
him up for a Dutch TV show in November and the BBC radio
programme *Top Gear* on 18 December, but was seldom sure of
Bowie's movements.

Bowie still had a room at Manchester Street, but was free to
come and go. He spent some time with Marc Bolan and Tony
Visconti, an American producer whom he met at Deram, sharing
an interest in Buddhism, but even more with Kemp, who asked
him to write some songs for his next production *Pierrot In
Turquoise*. Between visiting Kemp, Bowie would also slip down
to Greenwich where Kemp's costumier and set designer, Natasha
Korniloff, was creating a new front cloth for *Pierrot In Turquoise*,
laying the huge cloth across the floor of her attic flat and painting
in the show's title and images of Kemp, Bowie and the third
member of its cast, Jack Birkett.

'I'll tell you something about David,' says Korniloff,[10] a short,
bubbly, vibrant woman, born of an English mother and a Russian
father, who spent her childhood in India and Africa. 'He's not an
acquisitive person at all. He doesn't care for possessions very
much. He's always either hungry or tired or cold, or any
combination of the three, and if you can satisfy his immediate
demands, like put another coat on him or feed him something, of
which he will eat only a bit, or make him a little nest to sleep in,
he's absolutely and totally happy. Then he wakes up and goes to
work ...'

Soon, Bowie was sleeping with her as well. If she, or any of his
other lovers, or Pitt, wanted to know where he was going next,
Bowie would disarm them all by saying, 'I must go down to
Bromley to see my parents.' How many lovers there were, or who
they were, is uncertain and hardly matters, for none of these
relationships was meant to last.

'When we first met, there was a great deal of affection,' says
Kemp.[11] 'There was a great deal of love and a great deal of
admiration and respect as well ... when love and emotion, and

passion, and sexual passion are mixed with respect, then that's the most ideal kind of relationship for me. We weren't lovers from the beginning – it took about 30 seconds … of course, he wasn't always there because frequently there were notes from his mother to say he had earache or something, but later on I realized, of course, that those notes had been faked, the same as the notes that I had sent to school from my mother…. He stabbed me in the back several times with other ladies.'

This bisexual affair ended in farce when Kemp took *Pierrot In Turquoise* to The New Theatre, Oxford, on 28 December 1967, and then to the millionaire Nicky Sekers's private theatre at Rose Hill, Cumberland, between 3 and 5 January 1968. Natasha Korniloff drove up in a rented van with the front cloth and costumes, staying with Bowie, Kemp, Jack Birkett, their accompanist Michael Garrett and the director Craig San Roque and his wife in a nearby farmhouse. That night, Bowie and Kemp went off to bed together – then Kemp awoke some hours later to find Bowie had gone. He looked outside his bedroom door, and there across the landing were Bowie's shoes – outside Korniloff's door.

'What do you think you're doing?' said a distressed Kemp, confronting Korniloff the following morning. 'He's my boyfriend!'

'No, no, no – he's not. He's mine!' insisted an equally anxious Korniloff.

That afternoon Kemp cut his wrists and was rushed to hospital. Bowie, as always, burst into tears – and Korniloff took an overdose of sleeping pills.

If there was still a lingering feeling in Kemp's heart that he might win Bowie back, that was shattered just days later when Bowie walked off again – this time with a girl named Hermione Farthingale on his arm.

6

# Almost a Buddhist monk

Bowie met Hermione Farthingale when they were both attending classes at the Dance Centre in Covent Garden – he, mime and she, ballet. This was during the autumn of 1967, which was the most important formative period of his early career. That was not so obvious at the time. 'David could be very trying,' was how Pitt described this growing process. Sometimes, they would not see each other for several days, having reached an understanding that Bowie would phone in at least once a day to see whether there was anything he needed to attend to at the flat.

'I could never get him to settle down and actually finish anything,' says Pitt. 'I would put an idea to him, and David would respond enthusiastically. "Great! Great!" he would say – and then nothing would ever get done.'

Apart from the daily phone calls, which might come at any time, Pitt had no idea where Bowie was. He knew about the mime classes, but Bowie chose not to say he sometimes stayed overnight at Kemp's apartment; Natasha Korniloff was a totally unknown name, and there was no reason for Bowie to mention his more casual pick-ups.

Pitt was not a moralist. Bowie's room was always available, ready for him to return to at any time. In any case, Pitt knew there was another reason for these absences. Bowie had to earn money somewhere to avoid borrowing from his father. 'I know David had one or two little jobs on the side that he didn't like to talk about, not even to me,' says Pitt. One of them was in a friend's stationery shop in Carey Street, where Bowie operated a photocopying machine for local businessmen. He also occasionally washed dishes and cleaned houses, but was careful not to let it be known that he was willing to work like this if he had to, lest anyone assume he was starting to compromise or, even worse, failing in his chosen career.

The other new influence upon his life was the young American record producer Tony Visconti, who divided his days between Essex Music and Deram, and was already producing Marc Bolan's records. Bowie and Bolan were both contracted to Essex Music, and whatever one did the other tried – right through to sexuality and management style. For a time, Bolan also lived in Manchester Street, just across the road from Pitt – who turned down an invitation to become his manager, as well.

Bowie has never admitted a sexual relationship with Bolan, but Bolan talked freely enough about this to Secunda; I suspect they were both willing to hop from bed to bed if it would help their careers. After being rejected by Pitt, who thought him 'too crude', Bolan turned to another homosexual manager, Simon Napier-Bell.

'He saw a manager almost in terms of someone to live with,' says Napier-Bell,[1] using words that suggest Bolan may well have been trying to develop the same kind of artist-manager relationship that Bowie enjoyed with Pitt. Napier-Bell suggests Bolan wanted him to be a patron or Svengali-figure: 'I remember him complaining once that he couldn't come round and sit in my flat all day when he wanted ... [he wanted someone] who would help him, guide him, be a partner, talk with him, provide a home, give him some money *and* be a manager ...

'He used to come round on the early morning bus from his parents' prefab in Wimbledon and get in bed with me in the morning ... it was of no more consequence than smoking a joint together. I think Marc had a whole series of people with whom he went around having very intimate but very nice, easy relationships ...'

Visconti moved to an apartment in Lexham Gardens. Bolan started rehearsing there with Steve Peregrine Took, and before long this was another axis in Bowie's tangled life that was also largely unknown to Pitt.

David Platz listened to Visconti's first recordings with Bolan and told him: 'Since you seem to be the expert with these strange people, I'd like you to see what you can do with David Bowie.... We've had him under contract for over a year, but we don't quite know what to do with him. Every time he writes something, he comes up with a different style.'

Visconti first met Bowie in the music room at Essex Music and found him 'a nice, well-mannered Englishman. He wasn't the bizarre person that he was made out to be ... he liked the fact that I was American and within 15 minutes we were sharing stories and experiences. We became very close in a very short space of time.'²

Their backgrounds and experiences could not have been much more different. Although he later grew it longer, Visconti's hair was neatly cropped. He looked like a young Sicilian with dark, Mediterranean features and a tall, lean physique that came from practising karate and other martial arts. Born in Brooklyn in 1944, Visconti grew up on the fringes of the New York music business. He studied classical guitar from the age of 11 and at 13 a friend used to sneak him into Aretha Franklin's recording sessions. By the time he was 16, Visconti was playing with teenage groups and picking up session work and from this he moved naturally into the professional side of the business, finding a job with Howie Richmond, the US affiliate of Essex Music, and soon becoming a house producer at just the same time Denny Cordell was working with Essex in London, setting up the Deram label and producing records with Joe Cocker, The Move and Procol Harum.

Visiting New York, Cordell was impressed by the way Visconti kept costs down by carefully planning his use of studio time, and promptly invited him over to London to be his assistant. The timing was fortuitous. London was the place to be for any young musician in 1967/8, with The Beatles and The Rolling Stones holding court in the London clubs and thousands of young Americans moving to Europe to avoid being sent to Vietnam. Harry Nilsson, Jimi Hendrix, P. J. Proby and The Walker Brothers all settled in London, and no one was quite sure whether they were making music or avoiding the Army. To the conservative ex-Army officer Pitt, Visconti was 'just another typical draft-dodging American anarchist' – an unfortunate attitude to have, for Visconti soon became Bowie's producer.

Although he had only been in London a few weeks, Visconti soon demonstrated that he knew how to find the best session musicians, hiring John McLaughlin and Alan White for Bowie's first session – the same John McLaughlin who went on to record with Miles Davis, Buddy Miles and Chick Corea before forming The Mahavishnu Orchestra; and the same Alan White later recruited by John Lennon for The Plastic Ono Band before joining Yes.

Bowie recorded two strongly commercial songs that day, *Let Me Sleep Beside You* and *Karma Man*. One had an openly sexual theme about an older woman searching for love, and the other reflected his interest in Buddhism. By any criteria, they deserved to take their chance in the marketplace – but Deram was bound to Decca, who were notoriously reluctant to take chances.

\*   \*   \*   \*   \*

It may seem incredible now, but popular music was largely controlled by two large companies, EMI and Decca, whose senior management found it all a bit of a nuisance. EMI was primarily a manufacturer of electrical goods and lighting equipment. Its chairman, Sir Joseph Lockwood, an ageing bachelor, was an international expert on the manufacture of animal feed and flour milling, whose books had been translated into many languages. He lived in some style in Cheshire, was a member of the Reform Club and listed his interests in *Who's Who* as walking and fishing.

EMI's main interest in music was that those little black vinyl discs gave them a way of making use of petroleum by-products, and it was fairly well known that Sir Joseph only became aware of his company's most striking product when The Queen went up to him at a reception in St James's Palace and asked, 'How are The Beatles?'

It was the same story over at Decca, where Sir Edward Lewis led a company famous for its pioneering work in radar, electronics and armaments technology, much of it contracted by the Ministry of Defence.

For both companies, pop music was a minor interest. In Decca, it was left to a committee that met on Monday mornings to decide which records would be released and, according to Pitt who was invited to be present on one occasion, their meetings 'had to be seen to be believed', with men in suits sitting around a table, some apparently asleep and others reading newspapers, making it all too clear that they would rather not 'listen to all this jangle'.[3] 'It was a lamentable performance and I believe that the seeds of Decca's eventual demise were sown during those unhappy Mondays.'

Decca turned down The Beatles and lost The Rolling Stones – and on 18 September 1967, they rejected *Let Me Sleep Beside You* and *Karma Man*, suggesting Bowie's lyrics were too explicit. Letters from Pitt went unanswered, and an alternative single – coupling *When I Live My Dream* with *Karma Man* – was also turned down.

In the States, publisher Howie Richmond was doing all he could to promote Bowie's songs, releasing the *David Bowie* LP on the London label, together with a single, *Love You Till Tuesday/Did You Ever Have A Dream?*, and distributing a 32-page booklet of Bowie's lyrics and music to over 500 American disc jockeys. Even in London, Essex Music were trying to develop Bowie's career as a songwriter, inviting him to write the English lyrics for a catalogue of Israeli songs, and also the lyrics for the French number *Comme d'Habitude* by Claude François, Gilles Thibault and Jacques Revaux.

For just a moment, Bowie thought his breakthrough had come. He was visiting his mother and heard the song on the radio – but he'd lost out. The French publishers, who owned the copyright, insisted that the song should be recorded by an established star, and what he heard was the Frank Sinatra version of *Comme d'Habitude* – now called *My Way*, with lyrics by Paul Anka.

\*   \*   \*   \*   \*

It is easy to see now that Bowie was hovering on the brink of fame, with publishers in both Britain and the United States, a manager and a producer who all believed in him. The problems with Decca were soluble. All he had to do was get the product right, and then it would be easy enough to find a distributor – but it did not feel like that then. In the autumn of 1967 and the early months of 1968, with an indifferent record company and no commercial bargaining power, Bowie was visibly and physically shaken. With 11 failed singles and an unsuccessful album now behind him, he felt his chances of fame slipping away.

One day, he complained to Pitt of severe stomach pains. Pitt sent him to see his own doctor who arranged for X-rays to be taken. So far as the doctors could tell, there was nothing the matter with him, so the probability must be that after three years of failure, interspersed by moments of raised hope before the release of each record, the strain was beginning to tell. Bowie was usually impassive, taking care not to reveal what he was really thinking, but the thought must have been passing through his mind that the end was near. He had failed. His dreams were falling apart.

Once again, Pitt sought to persuade him to work on a cabaret act, believing this would bring in regular money while he worked on other projects, but Bowie still refused – and it was then that he went off to Cumberland with Lindsay Kemp and Natasha Korniloff.

*   *   *   *   *

One more strand needs to be brought into this narrative, linking the oddly disparate paths Bowie was following: Buddhism, shared with Visconti and pursued during those months when he was drifting away from Pitt's tutelage. They were still artist and manager, on the phone each day even when there was no work to be done, but already they were sliding apart.

Pitt's faith in Bowie was total, but he believed fame would be found down another route and was continually pressing Bowie to follow up different opportunities. Bowie would not perform in cabaret, so Pitt encouraged him to try other ideas: writing a television play *The Champion Flower Grower*, drawing upon his family's Yorkshire background, and a musical *Ernie Johnson*; meeting Franco Zeffirelli, who wanted someone to write the music for his new cinema film version of *Romeo and Juliet*; and auditioning for roles in the films *The Virgin Soldiers*, *Triple Echo*, *Sunday, Bloody Sunday*, *Alain* and *Oh! What A Lovely War*. Any one of them could have given him the break he was looking for, and he awaited them all with high expectation – but they came to nothing.[4]

Instead, Bowie was spending more and more time either with Lindsay Kemp or Natasha Korniloff, or at Visconti's flat, playing music, talking Buddhism and smoking the occasional joint. He did not have the money for expensive habits, but liked the way Buddhism could combine with diet, drugs, yoga and sexual athleticism to form an alternative lifestyle.

Buddhism first caught his imagination at Bromley Technical High School, partly through reading Jack Kerouac, when he was also learning saxophone and playing modern jazz. During that conversation to which I refer in the Introduction, Bowie told me he started off with two Pelican paperbacks by Christmas Humphreys, *Zen Buddhism* (1949) and *Buddhism* (1951), and then returned to Buddhism more deeply in the mid-60s, shortly after meeting Pitt. This was when he and Bolan both modelled themselves on Bob Dylan, dressing all in black and making a conscious effort not to smile. I was reminded of this when reading a feature in *Disc* in which Bowie said he was now studying Buddhism seriously, was reading a history of Tibet, and thinking of learning to speak Chinese.

'I want to go to Tibet,' he said. 'It's a fascinating place, you know. I'd like to take a holiday and have a look inside the monasteries. The Tibetan monks, Lamas, bury themselves inside mountains for weeks and only eat every three days ...'

When he explained Buddhism to me, Bowie knelt down on the floor and arranged his cigarettes around a table lighter. 'You see,' he said, 'the lighter is your mind and those cigarettes are your experiences. Those experiences may be emotional, mental or physical, but the idea is to remove those experiences and be left with just that bit in the middle [the lighter]. It's a difficult thing to accept unless you actually realize it is inside you. I'm only just beginning to ...'

Bowie and Visconti joined the Tibet Society. They used to spend much of their spare time at the Society's office in Hampstead, becoming friendly with a Tibetan monk, Chimi Youngdong Rimpoche, who fled to England with three other monks when the Chinese invaded Tibet. The other three settled in Scotland, while Chimi chose to stay in London, liaising with London Buddhists and helping raise financial support.

At the time I was doubtful about Bowie's involvement, knowing of his tendency to romanticize and invent stories about himself. When I told Pitt of Bowie's references to Buddhism, he was dismissive, equating this with Bowie's other phases when he dressed like a Mod, or even a hippie, complete with bangles, beads and Afghan coat. 'I managed to cope with most things when I worked with David – except for Buddha,' said Pitt. Largely upon his advice, I toned down my references to Bowie's Buddhism interests when writing *The David Bowie Story*. The Gillmans discount this part of his life completely, but I have since learned several other details that suggest Bowie may have been telling me the truth all along.

During my first discussion of Buddhism with Bowie, in September 1967, I didn't realize that he had only just joined the Tibet Society, and what I took to be naïvety in the way he expressed himself was, in fact, a description of Tibetan beliefs that he was only just beginning to absorb. When we next discussed this 18 months later, Bowie told me he had been to the Scottish monastery ... and I did not realize that this period coincided with mime, Lindsay Kemp, Natasha Korniloff, his leaving Decca, Pitt's search for a new record deal and a period of general instability in his life.

It was only later, much later, that I perceived there were several periods during those 18 months when Pitt lost touch with Bowie, and Bowie could quite easily have gone to Scotland for two or three weeks or even more, for I learned that Visconti and Bowie both became keen Buddhist students late in 1967 and it was Lindsay Kemp who persuaded Bowie not to take the drastic step of becoming a novitiate monk which would have meant him retreating to the monastery, shaving his head, taking a seven-month vow of silence and spending three years, three months and three days in isolation, rising each day at 3.45 a.m. after only five hours' sleep, with his days spent largely in prayer and meditation.

This is where the significance of *Pierrot In Turquoise* falls into place, for Kemp created the mime play with Bowie modelling its characters Cloud, Harlequin and Pierrot on the classic clowns of the *commedia dell'arte*, and choosing the colour turquoise as what Kemp describes as 'the British symbol of everlastingness'.

Traditionally, the mineral turquoise was also said to be a 'lucky stone', the birth-stone for December with the ability to change colour to reflect an owner's mind. Bowie was later to call his own multi-media group Turquoise, with Tibetan allusions in his songs which, as will be shown in later chapters, he usually did not explain. Kemp made comments in an interview with Kerry Juby[5] that underlines the relevance of Bowie's comments to me.

> David claims I saved him – not from Buddhism, not from everlastingness, but from being a Tibetan monk. I do remember saying to him, 'Look, you can give yourself to God but to me as well, and to the public. You don't have to leave any of us out ...'
>
> I didn't really teach him to be a mime artist but to be more of himself on the outside.... I enabled him to free the angel and the demon that he is on the inside ... dance is a way of allowing and encouraging ourselves to escape through our fingertips, eyelids, lungs and tips of tongues. He already did it with his tongue, but up to that period his fingers were a bit stiff.

These comments, and the factual confirmation that the Buddhists were engaged in precisely what Bowie told me they were doing, tends to confirm that Buddhism was far more significant in

Bowie's development as an an artist than he has since chosen to admit. The Buddhists were led by Chimi Youngdong Rimpoche's contemporary Lama Yeshe, who established the Samye Ling Tibetan Centre (named after Samye Ling, the oldest Tibetan Buddhist monastery, destroyed by the Chinese) on a bleak mountainous site, bought for £3,000, at Eskdalemuir, 14 miles north of Lockerbie. With the help of an architect and largely their own labour, the Buddhists built a temple that is 'the largest and most splendid of its kind in the Western world',[6] with 'a gigantic gilded Buddha flanked by two carved dragons and hundreds of miniature Buddhas'.

Bowie tried to tell me all this in 1967 and 1969. I was frankly disbelieving when he told me that he slept upright in a traditional wooden box, eating only two modest meals each day and observing periods of intense silence, and when he further described how his tutors shaved their heads, wore saffron robes and sat in a slightly elevated position, on tables with short legs, answering questions.

'I just sit there, asking questions, and he usually answers them with another question,' said Bowie. 'You can't show people what Buddhism is. You can only show them the way towards it. Buddhism is really a process of self-discovery, of discovering the truth for oneself…. Chimi Youngdong Rimpoche gave me the best advice I have ever been given, "to try to make each moment of one's life one of the happiest, and if it is not to try to find out why"…. I was a tremendously earnest Buddhist at that time, and yet very unhappy.

'I had studied their literature and their philosophy, meditated for long periods, and stayed at their monastery in Scotland. I was within a month of having my head shaved, taking my vows and becoming a monk. Yet, I had this uneasy feeling inside me that Buddhism wasn't right for me. It was a very crucial time, a worrying time, because I had already gone a long way towards Buddhism…. I never became involved in any of the forms of Buddhism linked to yoga, although that did interest me. I was studying Mayana Buddhism, which is more oral. You have to study carefully through tuition, reading and meditation. For a time, I was vegetarian – even to the point where I would never wear anything leather, not even leather shoes or belts, on the principle that this was part of what was once another living being. This was all very important to me until I suddenly realized how close I was to having my head shaved and taking the vows of abstinence. I decided that wasn't for me, but I was actually studying mime with Lindsay Kemp by then, and he was so earthly that I learned from him that people are much more important to me than ideas ...'

\*     \*     \*     \*     \*

At the same time as this near-commitment and sudden change of mind, Bowie was also preparing for *Pierrot In Turquoise*, though Pitt saw his role as 'little more than an extension to his mime classes ... he received no payment, it having been agreed that if there was anything left after expenses had been met then it would be shared between the company, but, of course, there was nothing left over'.[7] Nonetheless he thought that Bowie 'was doing what he enjoyed most and making steady progress'.

Pitt was right. A Scottish group, The Beatstalkers, who were also Pitt's clients, released three recordings of Bowie's songs; a Belgian singer, Dee Dee, released another, *Love Is Always*; and a group named Slender Plenty issued their version of *Silver Treetop School For Boys*. The teenage magazines *Jackie*, *Diana* and *Fab 208* published his photograph in colour poster form; he spent four days in Holland to promote his music, appearing on the Dutch TV show *Fan Club*; and, even more significantly, was invited to present five songs in live performance on the BBC radio programme *Top Gear*.

This last booking was particularly important, for it led to Bowie appearing several more times on BBC Radio; this time it was with session musicians hired through the BBC and an agency for £7 an hour. Visconti chose John McLaughlin, together with bass player Herbie Flowers and drummer Barry Morgan, who later formed Blue Mink and continued to work with Bowie through the 70s; two more whose names have been forgotten, and also Marc Bolan's partner Steve Peregrine Took, who provided backing vocals. For this one occasion, they were billed as The Tony Visconti Orchestra. Bootleg LPs based on this appearance on *Top Gear* now fetch high prices among Bowie collectors, for he can be heard experimenting with ideas far removed from his later work. His five songs were *Karma Man* and *Silly Boy Blue*, reflecting his interest in Buddhism; *Let Me Sleep Beside You*, the song rejected by Decca; *In The Heat Of The Morning* and *When I'm Five*, a delightful children's song describing the ways a four-year-old hopes to be able to wash his face and hands all by himself and 'chew and spit tobacco/Like my Grandpa Jones': an interesting allusion, clearly based on something his father told him – 'Grandpa Jones' died many, many years before Bowie was born.

*Silly Boy Blue*, which Bowie recorded for his Deram LP and also featured in *Pierrot In Turquoise*, was one of his earliest songs with an Eastern influence, written long *before* he met Visconti, and so this, too, underlines the significance of his conversation with me about Buddhism. The lyric refers to the Chinese invasion of Tibet, describing 'a child of Tibet' and 'the mountains of Lhasa' and referring to the Buddhist belief in reincarnation: 'You'll never leave your body now/You've got to wait to die'.

Had Bowie been better known, this song might well have given him a hit single. Its potential was spotted by other artistes. Billy Fury recorded it for release as a single in Britain; in the US it was recorded by Elephant's Memory, who later worked with John Lennon.

Nine weeks later, David Dore, Assistant to the Light Entertainment Booking Manager at the BBC, wrote to Pitt saying that a BBC panel had listened to the *Top Gear* broadcast: Bowie's performance received 'favourable reports' causing his name to be added to 'the list of artists available for broadcasting generally'. While this did not mean an immediate offer of more radio work, other producers were now free to book him; which they did, sporadically, between 1968 and 1971.

*     *     *     *     *

Bowie's career may have been moving steadily forward, but only the tiniest sums of money were coming through. For *Top Gear*, his fee was £10.50. He earned nothing for his first performance in *Pierrot In Turquoise* at the Oxford New Theatre, and only £40 for his three nights at The Rose Hill Theatre in Whitehaven, Cumberland. Apart from his income from Essex Music, Bowie earned only £322 in 1967 – prompting Pitt to tell his father that he would 'never make any money the way he wants to, sitting on his backside strumming a guitar'.

Fortunately, even if their terms were not the best, Essex Music continued to demonstrate confidence in Bowie, agreeing a new two-year contract in December 1967 that would earn him £1,500 in 1968 and £2,000 in 1969, paid quarterly and enough to cover his immediate costs. The first cheque came through before Christmas and his visits to Oxford and Whitehaven, encouraging John Jones to write that his son could now 'concentrate on the cabaret act without undue financial worry.... With the cabaret act very much in his thoughts I feel that we can look forward to the coming year being more successful than the last.'

But Bowie was not going to give in to this pressure to become a cabaret artist, either from his father or from Pitt. Not then. He drew up a list of songs that he might be willing to perform in cabaret, and that was as far as he would go – and before Pitt could push him any further, he disappeared again, this time with a woman.

When the Lindsay Kemp troupe returned to London in early January 1968, he and Bowie probably repaired their relationship, for Bowie continued to attend mime classes at the Dance Centre. Dancers often found work through the Centre, which also functioned as an agency, and every day when he came in to lead a class Kemp would pop his head around the office door and ask, 'Anything for me today?'

This day, there was. The producer of *The Pistol Shot*, a forthcoming BBC TV play, needed a choreographer and dancers for a minuet scene, complete with eighteenth-century costume. Kemp was hired and suggested Bowie should partner Hermione Farthingale. They went to the audition at the BBC studios on Shepherds Bush Green, and afterwards, as they all walked to the Tube station, Bowie and Hermione quickened their pace and talked animatedly, but Kemp was 'trailing behind about ten paces, sulking'.[8] As they neared the station, Bowie glanced back over his shoulder and said, 'I'll give you a ring later' – and disappeared through the ticket barrier and down the escalator.

'David Bowie just walked out of my life,' said Kemp. 'I couldn't believe that anyone could love me and a lady equally.... He'd already stabbed me in the heart several times before that with other ladies, but at least this time there was a lady that I liked immensely.'

Bowie was, as usual, secretive. If he said he was going somewhere – to see his mother, Pitt, Kemp, Bolan, Visconti, Korniloff, Essex Music or the photocopying shop – he would usually end up somewhere else. Now he vanished again – with Hermione Farthingale.

Despite this, Pitt would still receive daily phone calls, and some days Bowie would walk in unexpectedly. He still had his key to Manchester Street, and could let himself in to the apartment at any time. But their relationship was cooling, and it was to remain like this, distant, until Bowie's father died 18 months later.

One day when Bowie phoned, Pitt told him a German TV producer was willing to pay him £280 plus expenses to appear on the TV show *4–3–2–1 Musik für junge Leute*. He flew to Hamburg on 26 February accompanied by Mrs Joan Barclay of Decca, filmed three numbers the following day – *Love You Till Tuesday, Did You Ever Have A Dream?* and *Please Mr Gravedigger* – and returned to London on 29 February.

Meanwhile, Pitt arranged for him to meet the Broadway producer Harold Prince, who was visiting London. When Bowie failed to phone, Pitt contacted his parents; they hadn't seen him. Pitt then called Mrs Barclay. 'We said "Goodbye" to each other at Heathrow,' she said. 'He told me he was going to see his fiancée.'

'His what?' asked Pitt.

'His fiancée. Why, hasn't he got one?'

'Not to my knowledge,' said Pitt, who did not meet Hermione until *Pierrot In Turquoise* opened at the Mercury Theatre, Notting Hill Gate, some days later. Even then, it was some time before Pitt was told the couple had moved to 22 Clareville Grove, South Kensington, where they rented a cramped attic bedsitter barely large enough to accommodate their bed.

7

# 'OK. So I'm doing cabaret.'
# When do we start?'

Early 1968 saw Ken Pitt and John Jones continuing to insist Bowie would make more money if only he would try his hand at cabaret, and he at last gave way – but with no great enthusiasm. By this point, his life was revolving around Bolan, Visconti and Hermione; *they* all urged him not to compromise.

'You must never compromise your musical principles,' urged Visconti, committed to the two budding stars, Bowie and Bolan, who were sharing his enthusiasm for the teachings of Chimi Youngdong Rimpoche, exchanging ideas, attending sessions together, yet still eyeing each other warily. They were like a family, with Visconti and his girlfriend Liz living at Lexham Gardens and Bowie and Hermione in their bedsitter just three or four minutes' walk away, by Gloucester Road Tube station. When Bolan fell in love with June Child that spring, the 'family' found themselves with transport – for June owned a battered mini-van and was happy to drive them anywhere.

At first, Marc and June lived in the van, keeping a mattress in the back and parking it on Wimbledon Common – having both walked out on other partners, they had nowhere else to live. But June soon found a proper bed. She was highly efficient, working at Blackhill Enterprises (the company set up by Peter Jenner and Andrew King that staged the first Free Festivals in Hyde Park) and it took her less than a week to find a flat in Blenheim Crescent, off Ladbroke Grove, which became another cornerstone in Bowie's life.

Music and ideas overflowed. They were all highly literate, enjoying a Bohemian lifestyle and yet comfortably aware that this was just a phase. Bowie was reading more voraciously than ever. In one of his few interviews during this period, he told Barbara Marilyn Deane of the *Chelsea News*: 'My only ambition is to be in the position to get out before I am 30 ...' (which he also said to me). His recommended authors were Brendan Behan, e. e. cummings, Jean-Paul Sartre and Keith Waterhouse. His taste in music ranged from The Fugs (a mid-60s band that fused rock with the Beat poet tradition, whose LP Pitt also brought back from New York) to Ray Davies of The Kinks, the jazz musicians Stan Kenton and Gary McFarland and the 'Big Band' sound of Glenn Miller. Rock 'n' roll was not mentioned at all.

The practicalities of the music business were not neglected; in this area, Visconti was a hard-headed disciplinarian who made sure sessions were properly planned, studios booked, musicians hired and all appointments kept.

When Bolan recorded *Deborah*, his first single with Visconti, Bowie was there, too, and can be heard in the background, clapping his hands, underlining the rhythm. Bowie also attended some of the sessions when Bolan was completing his first LP, *My People Were Fair And Had Sky In Their Hair, But Now They're Content To Wear Stars On Their Brows*. Once that was finished, Visconti booked time at the Decca studios in West Hampstead to record Bowie's next single, *In The Heat Of The Morning* and *London Bye Ta Ta*, the first in similar vein to his album and the other, with a wry lyric and Jamaican phrasing, describing how London had changed since his childhood. A month later, these were again turned down by Decca's 'Monday meeting'.

Despite these rejections, Bowie went ahead with his second appearance on *Top Gear*, whose presenter, John Peel, regularly featured Bolan's group, Tyrannosaurus Rex. The programme was recorded at the BBC Piccadilly studio on 13 May 1968 and broadcast twice, on 26 May and 20 June, with Bowie playing the two songs turned down by Decca, together with *Karma Man* and *When I'm Five*.

Three weeks later, he tried a completely new approach, presenting *Silly Boy Blue* in mime, accompanied by the record, in a one-night show at the Royal Festival Hall, London, on Whit Monday, 3 June, with Tyrannosaurus Rex topping the bill, supported by Stefan Grossman and Roy Harper, and with John Peel as compere.

Bowie, who was paid £20 and allotted 12 minutes, dressed in costume and used this appearance to attack the Chinese invasion of Tibet, prompting an American in the audience to stand up and shout, 'No politics!' 'David liked that,' says Pitt. 'He was always pleased to get a definite response from an audience.' His performance was also well received by the *International Times*, which noted: 'David Bowie ... received the longest and loudest applause of all the performers and he deserved it. It was a pity that he didn't have a longer set.'

Adventurous though this was, Bowie was still not earning a living and Pitt kept on telling him that if he wanted to make good money he ought to adapt his stage presentation to cabaret. 'I wasn't trying to get him to give up his own music or abandon his ideas,' says Pitt. 'It was a question of finding an audience ... he needed money to live, and I thought that if he had a cabaret act I would be able to find him steady work at around £100–£150 a week, which would have solved a lot of his problems and left him free to write songs and record without money worries pressing down on him all the time.'

The day after his appearance at the Festival Hall, Bowie began rehearsals for his cabaret act – or so Pitt thought. He spent three days working on the structure, choosing songs, deciding how to relate them to his props, selecting numbers of his own and resolving which ones to use with a backing track, and which to perform acoustically. The numbers he chose were his own *Love You Till Tuesday*, *The Laughing Gnome*, *When I'm Five*, *When I Live My Dream* and *Even A Fool Learns To Love*, interspersed with The Beatles' *When I'm Sixty-Four*, *Yellow Submarine* and *All You Need Is Love*, the Roger McGough poem *At Lunch-Time – A Story Of Love* with several other standards that could be worked into the act as and when required, including his old favourite *You'll Never Walk Alone*, Anthony Newley's *What Kind Of Fool Am I?*, the Al Jolson show-stopper *Sonny*, the 60s Burt Bacharach classic *Trains And Boats And Planes* and *Life Is A Circus* by the American band Djin, a song Visconti first heard in the States.

Bowie may have *seemed* enthusiastic, but his heart was still not committed – and once again he disappeared, avoiding all mention of cabaret when phoning Pitt.

In mid-July 1968, John Jones wrote to Pitt enclosing Bowie's income tax forms and commenting that his son's 'earnings from show business do not give him sufficient income to pay for his own Social Security stamp'. This comment clearly stung, for Pitt replied that in the 1967/8 tax year Bowie's gross income had been £2,223 0s 8d, with a net income of £1,405 3s 3d after allowable expenses. 'From these figures,' wrote Pitt, 'under his first year with me he netted roughly £27 a week, which is of course subject to tax,' adding that had David 'persisted with his work in the cabaret field he would have reached £100 a week'. Bowie happened to be visiting his parents when Pitt's letter arrived, and clearly father and son discussed its contents, with Jones urging Bowie to follow his manager's advice, for he phoned Pitt immediately afterwards[1] and said, 'OK. So I'm doing cabaret. When do we start?'

Having pressed him to take this step for so many months, Pitt suggested they met the following day. They agreed to use Beatles cut-outs as props, with a gnome glove puppet for a routine with *The Laughing Gnome*. When Bowie said he did not know how to link the songs with dialogue, Pitt offered to write a script. 'My attempt to humour him seemed to have the right effect,' he says.[2] 'Those were warm summer days and he derived comfort from leaving off his clothes, sometimes sitting cross-legged on the floor encircled by blaring hi-fi speakers, sometimes just loping around the flat, naked, his long, weighty penis swaying from side to side like the pendulum of a grandfather clock.'

Once he felt the cabaret act was ready, Pitt arranged two auditions, the first for the agent Sidney Rose in Pitt's own office, and the second for two more agents, Harry Dawson and Michael Black, at the Astor Club, where Dawson had an office. According to Pitt, they watched 'as if transfixed, astounded at this display of competence', with Black saying at the end of the twenty-seven-minute set, 'Where did you find him? He's better than Cliff Richard.'

As Bowie was beginning to pack away his props and guitar, Dawson told Pitt: 'The boy's tremendous! It's a marvellous act! But where can you book it? It's too good.' This was typical agents' talk, the kind of patter they adopt when faced with something new – and Pitt must have known as well as they did that the typical West End cabaret audience consists of drunks and deadbeats groping secretaries, Arabs, hookers and out-of-town businessmen looking for pussy. Bowie knew that, too – which was why he dragged his feet for so long. One look at Bowie's face told Pitt that Dawson's comment was overheard. Neither of them mentioned cabaret again.

*     *     *     *     *

Bowie and Pitt still worked together after that, but now saw even less of each other. Bowie no longer relied upon his judgement, and Pitt became aware that Bowie's circle of friends regarded managers as an expensive anomaly. There was still no formal estrangement, just a steady growing apart, more apparent to those around them than to themselves. Pitt was scarcely consulted about Bowie's next venture, a trio called Turquoise formed with Hermione and guitarist Tony Hill from the group Misunderstood. How many performances they gave together is not known, for Bowie was now picking up occasional gigs on a word-of-mouth basis, pocketing the money, such as it was, without paying an agent's percentage.

'It's all anarchy,' Pitt told me at the time, and no doubt he thought it was, but the situation also reflected Bowie's growing loss of faith in Pitt's judgement.

While Pitt was in Poland with Crispian St Peters in August and in Germany with The Beatstalkers in September, Bowie abandoned the name Turquoise, replaced Tony Hill with John Hutchinson (who had been in The Buzz) and changed the group's name to Feathers. Pitt thought he was floundering – but Bowie was now gradually putting together the kind of act which would eventually astonish the world. It lacked the solid rhythm section that would underpin his future work, but Bowie was now trying to combine mime with music, interworking poetry with his own songs, interpreting other songwriters, notably Jacques Brel's *Next* and *Port Of Amsterdam* and Lou Reed's *Waiting For The Man* and *White Light, White Heat* (which he was to use throughout the 70s) and also presenting his own mime sequence *The Mask*.

Feathers made their debut at The Round House on 14 September 1968, earning £15 – and according to Pitt made only three further appearances, earning £6 at the Hampstead Country Club on 17 November, nothing at all for their show at the Arts Laboratory in Drury Lane on 6 December, and £50 from Sussex University the next day. They were almost certainly more active than this, earning money that Pitt never knew about. Feathers certainly appeared at the Wigmore Hall and The Middle Earth, and probably at art colleges and other venues on the newly established college circuit that was beginning to thrive by then, linking together the polytechnics, art colleges, universities and colleges of further education. This was all part of the counter-culture that evolved after the Summer of Love, featuring such new bands as King Crimson, Ten Years After, Jethro Tull, Led

Zeppelin and Blodwyn Pig. It was a world Pitt did not know, with
its own venues, newspapers and magazines, a network of cafés and
squats in different cities, and a free-and-easy approach to sex,
drugs and fashion. The centre of gravity was shifting again. Pitt
did not know this – but Bowie did. Bolan was a key figure in this
fast-developing underworld, while June Child helped new groups
find gigs through her work at Blackhill Enterprises.

*     *     *     *     *

That autumn of 1968, Lindsay Kemp invited Bowie and Hermione
to join him in Scotland for a season in the pantomime *Puss In
Boots*.

'I can't,' said Bowie, 'but how much are you offering?'

'It's gone up since last time,' said Kemp, recalling Bowie's
paltry pay for *Pierrot In Turquoise*. 'I think we could manage £25
a week ...'

Bowie was earning enough to turn that down, but from where?
And what other reasons did Bowie have for declining? There were
some paid appearances: £80 plus fares for a return to the German
TV show *Musik für junge Leute* (September); six days' work as an
extra in *The Virgin Soldiers* – at standard Equity rates, totalling
£40 (October). November saw Bowie's third German TV appearance, on *Für Jeden etwas Musik*, for £220 plus expenses; and over
the Christmas period, when he might have been in *Puss In Boots*,
he was in Cornwall, at The Magician's Workshop in Falmouth for
two nights, receiving £50 plus expenses.

Meanwhile, it must be said, Pitt was still thinking long-term –
he wanted Bowie to make another LP, booked the Purcell Room at
the Festival Hall a year in advance for an appearance to promote it
and was now reaching the stage when his cherished *Love You Till
Tuesday* film would go into production. This was a gamble, for
there was no commitment from the German television company –
Pitt was taking all the risk. A former employee of his, Malcolm
Thomson, was now in the film industry with his own company,
Thomasso Films Ltd, and Pitt commissioned him to draft a script
and prepare a shooting schedule and budget. This was all agreed
and *Love You Till Tuesday* was ready to go into production near
the end of January 1969. Even so, Bowie was still doubtful that it
would happen.

Meanwhile, Bowie earned another £25 making a TV commercial for a new Lyons Maid ice cream product called LUV. He had to run up and down the stairs of a London bus as he sang and part-danced to a jingle:

> LUV LUV LUV
> Let me give it all to you
> Let me know that some day
> You'll do the same for me
> LUV LUV LUV

The words seem ludicrous in print, but at the time Bowie and Pitt were happy to be offered work – and Pitt even phoned me to say what time the commercial would be shown on Thames Television, and I duly tuned in to watch. Bowie received residual fees every time the advertisement was repeated, and so received over £150 over the weeks that followed.

Pitt was sure the *Love You Till Tuesday* film would convince TV producers and theatre directors Bowie possessed the breadth and depth to handle starring roles. He and Bowie discussed the structure of the film in detail with Malcolm Thomson, approving the script and choosing songs to demonstrate Bowie's vocal range. As well as the title song, they chose *Sell Me A Coat*, *Rubber Band* and *When I Live My Dream* from the *David Bowie* album, together with *Let Me Sleep Beside You*, the A-side rejected by Decca, and a song Bowie had recently written for Feathers, *Ching-a-Ling*, interspersing these with his mime sequence *The Mask* and the children's song *When I'm Five*.

'I think we need another strong song,' Pitt told Bowie.

'I'll see what I can do,' said Bowie, returning to Manchester Street only days later with his 12-string guitar. In the meantime, he holed up at Clareville Grove, toying around with a new machine called a stylophone that was being marketed as 'a pocket electronic organ with a new concept in sound'. Advertisements for the stylophone appeared in the *New Musical Express* with the endorsement of Rolf Harris and the claim that it was so easy to play that a baby could master it in 15 minutes. Bowie used one, supplementing its sound with a 12-string guitar played by John Hutchinson and devising a lyric with vocal parts for them both. One would be an astronaut drifting into space and the other his link with earth, Ground Control. The idea was inspired by Stanley

Kubrick's film *2001: A Space Odyssey*, which was packing hippies into London cinemas after word spread that the final vivid scene of the floating astronaut provoked a wonderful trip if watched smoking a joint.

Almost as a private joke, Bowie called his song *Space Oddity*, a deliberate play on words, and as he settled down on the *chaise-longue* at Manchester Street with the 12-string across his lap, he began to sing: 'Ground Control to Major Tom'. Neither Pitt nor Thomson had a clue what the song was all about, for it was deceptively simple. As with all the best songs, there was a strong riff and a haunting melody. This could have been a story about an astronaut lost in space, wanting to tell his wife he loved her one last time, and yet by no means sure he wished to return. The only clue that it might also be about something else was Major Tom's cry that he was 'floating in a most peculiar way'.

*Love You Till Tuesday* commenced production on 26 January with one day's filming on Hampstead Heath for *When I Live My Dream*. All seemed well between Bowie and Hermione, with the neatly blue-grey-suited singer gazing intently into his fiancée's eyes, but by the time filming resumed on 1 February at the Clarence Studios in Greenwich, the crew could sense something wrong. Hermione filmed *Ching-a-Ling*, with Bowie and John Hutchinson sitting on cushions, set well apart in the studio, the camera switching from one to the other, as they each sang separate verses; but in between filming these sequences shouting could be heard from Bowie's dressing room and when they filmed *Sell Me A Coat* the couple stood apart, with Bowie casting her a sudden cold glance. 'Can you feel the atmosphere?' Thomson asked Pitt, who saw no more of Hermione after that.

What happened, Bowie would never say; but it is clear from the songs *Letter To Hermione* and *An Occasional Dream*, which he recorded for his second album, that *she* walked out on *him*, having fallen in love with another man. Hermione later disappeared, apparently to the United States, where she is thought to have changed her name – perhaps after marrying someone else. Pitt believed she chose to break the news to Bowie that day at Clarence Studios, for he went back to Clareville Grove, removed his possessions and moved back, temporarily, into his old room at Pitt's apartment.

'We had a perfect love – so perfect that it burned out in two years,' Bowie said long afterwards. 'We were too close, thought

alike and spent all the time in a room sitting on the corner of the
bed. She was a brilliant dancer and I was a struggling musician ...'
'I, too, was disappointed because she was a likeable girl,' says Pitt.
'I think she would have been a great help to David in both his
home and his career, but his lifestyle was not hers. When she went,
leaving him bruised and insecure, he was at the mercy of the first
predator to appear on the scene ...'

Bowie took particular pride in the mime sequence, *The Mask*,
describing how an actor finds a mask in a junk shop, takes it home
to his parents (who had Yorkshire accents!), eventually allowing
the mask to take over, acquiring a life of its own, with him dying
on stage at the London Palladium, apparently strangled by his alter
ego.

*     *     *     *     *

One of Hermione Farthingale's final appearances with Feathers
was with The Who at The Round House, a former engine shed in
Camden Town, converted into a theatre-in-the round. That was in
late January or early February 1969.

In the audience that night was the American record producer
Lou Reizner who was hoping to sign Bowie to Mercury Records,
his side-kick Calvin Mark Lee; and Reizner's girlfriend, Angie or
Angela Barnett, who had never been to a concert before. Her first
impression was of a 'lean, blond, enigmatic figure in a pastel-
striped sweater and mustard-coloured sailor's flares and a voice so
compelling that no one could turn a head ... every move, every
gyration quickened the pulse'.[3]

In another account, published 12 years later,[4] she said Bowie
was 'very pretty' with his hair 'cut and permed in tight little curls
around that fallen angel's face'. Hermione, she wrote, had
'delicate, tea rose features and lush, gorgeous copper-burgundy
hair. As tall as David, 5ft 10in, she was also lithe, graceful and
physically charismatic.... David had designed the act around her
talents. I think he really loved her, or, at least, really needed her.'

With Hermione gone, Bowie moved back into Manchester
Street and on 15 February Pitt travelled with him to Birmingham
where Bowie was due to begin a brief tour with Tyrannosaurus
Rex, working as a duo with John Hutchinson. Pitt 'watched the
show from the back of the hall', contrasting Bowie's performance
with Bolan's. It was the first time he had seen them performing

together on the same bill; this brought out the contrast between them: 'Marc was always shallow and crude, so far as I could see, whereas you could never say that about David.'

Manager and artiste also resumed their theatre outings, seeing *Hair* and Roy Dotrice's one-man show based on the writings of the seventeenth-century diarist John Aubrey, which, Pitt told me, Bowie considered to be 'real theatre'.

After three more college gigs with John Hutchinson, Feathers fluttered to an end. Hutchinson was fed up. With a wife and child to support, he could not afford to carry on gigging for as little as £15–£20 a night, and went back to Scarborough and his old job as a draughtsman. Once again, Bowie was on his own.

\*   \*   \*   \*   \*

Strangely, neither Bowie nor Pitt saw the potential in *Space Oddity*. The song evolved in various forms, initially as a demo tape and then in the filming of the sequence for *Love You Till Tuesday* in which Bowie played both Ground Control (in a white T-shirt with the words emblazoned in red) and Major Tom (in a silver lurex 'space suit' with what looked suspiciously like a motorcycle helmet for his spaceman's headgear). It all seemed amateurish, with Major Tom floating off into space through a studio door – but the melody had an instantly memorable quality, and Pitt noticed the film crew were chuckling about Major Tom and humming the tune.

The silver suit came from Dandie Fashions in the King's Road, Chelsea, which was where Bowie first met Calvin Mark Lee, a Chinese American who arrived at Chelsea College in 1962 to begin a three-year PhD course in molecular chemistry. Lee abandoned chemistry after achieving his doctorate and turned to rock 'n' roll, not as a musician but as a groupie, working at Dandie Fashions by day and gatecrashing the party circuit by night, hanging around such late-night clubs as The Speakeasy and The Bag Of Nails, and becoming friendly with Reizner. Lee, who became Bowie's constant companion, was appointed Assistant European Director of Mercury Records. Reizner hoped that in his party-going Lee would either find new talent or poach musicians away from other companies.

Little of this was known to Pitt, who complained to me that Bowie was spending far too much time, with 'this revolting

Chinese American who dresses all in black, with long black hair down to his arse and a silver love-jewel stuck to his forehead'. In his book, Pitt regards Lee as 'the first of the predators.'[5] This may have been true, but with Lee as his companion Bowie briefly became a rock 'n' roll barfly, joining the nightly round of London parties where record companies and PR men launched new LPs or artists, circulating for the first time among fellow musicians, making new friendships, and hearing the new, heavier sounds that were becoming popular. He was being drawn into the underground world of free festivals and arts laboratories, but Visconti felt this new enthusiasm was at odds with *Space Oddity*, and refused point-blank to record it.

Visconti wanted him to concentrate on one style of writing: 'I felt that it was his undoing that he was writing in so many different styles. I remember that when he threw *Space Oddity* at me, I hated it.... I still don't like *Space Oddity* all that much, although when I hear it now I realize that I'm listening to a classic recording.... I guess I was too idealistic in those days and felt he should be more faithful to his own style. This is where we differed on this point. In those days he would do anything to get a hit record.'[6]

Using his knowledge of the company, Bowie wrote a letter to Pitt suggesting whom to contact at Mercury, and Pitt agreed terms for a new recording contract that guaranteed Bowie £20 a week for six weeks while he worked on a new LP with Visconti, plus £1,250 as an advance against royalties. Mercury also agreed to pay all the production costs and Visconti's fees, so the £1,250 was money in the bank. Still determined not to record *Space Oddity*, Visconti asked his partner, Gus Dudgeon, if he would like to produce the session instead.

Dudgeon, who engineered the *David Bowie* album, listened to the demo tape. 'You're mad,' he told Visconti. 'This song is great' – and so a separate budget was agreed with Mercury for the one session, at which *Space Oddity* and *The Wild Eyed Boy From Freecloud* were recorded for release as a single. Dudgeon hired the session musicians Rick Wakeman (Mellotron), Mick Wayne (guitar), Herbie Flowers (bass) and Terry Cox (drums), plus 14 orchestral musicians used on an arrangement by Paul Buckmaster for violins, violas, cellos and bass – all at the standard Musicians Union rate of £9. Total session costs, including studio time, voice dubbing, reductions and tape, were just under £500.

    The *Space Oddity* single was released on 11 July 1969, nine
days ahead of the date when the US Apollo space mission was due
to land on the moon. This was no coincidence. From their head
office in Chicago, Mercury's National Product Manager wrote a
personal letter to Bowie, saying 'with the moon shot coming up in
less than ten days, you know time is of the essence. To meet this
challenge we have pulled out every stop to get the record out
quickly.' Copies of the single were airmailed to every disc jockey
in the United States, and Bowie was put on stand-by to fly to
Chicago at 24 hours' notice should the record suddenly start to
take off. Unfortunately, it was not the US hit everyone was hoping
for.

8

# 'It's paranoid schizophrenia, so they say'

Mary Angela Barnett was young, tough and aggressive – and a great organizer, one of life's natural prefects. Officially still a student at Kingston Polytechnic, she also helped run a travel agency in Paddington, was busily buzzing around the music business with Reizner and Lee and managed to pack a surprisingly volatile life into a few short years. Having clung to her virginity until the age of 18, she was now rapidly making up for lost time.

Angie was born at Xeros on the northern coast of Cyprus, but carried a US passport. Her family were everything Bowie's were not – wealthy, worldly and practising Catholics. Her father, Colonel George Milton Barnett, a highly decorated US Army veteran, led a force of guerrilla fighters against the Japanese in the Philippines during the Second World War, later described in his book *Three Fields To Cross*. In peace-time, Colonel Barnett retired early to take up a position as senior engineer with the American-owned Cyprus Mining Company at Xeros.

Angie enjoyed a comfortably privileged childhood. The family lived in a large, old, red and white Colonial house between the mountains and the sea, employing domestic staff and enjoying a busy social life within the expatriate community. The mine's staff was cosmopolitan, with engineers from America, Canada and Australia, and there was also a large British base nearby where the retired Army colonel was always welcome. Born of British parents, he was tall, lean and imposing, with a military bearing and a neatly trimmed moustache. Angie's mother, Mrs Helene Marie Barnett, was tiny, only 5ft 2ins tall, born of Polish immigrants to the US, but more naturally outgoing, vivacious and artistic. The couple's only other child, Milton John, was already in his teens by the time Angie was born in 1950 and is now a mining engineer in New Guinea.

At the age of nine, Angie was sent to a school in Switzerland, St

George's at Clarens near Montreux, where she found herself
surrounded by girls from 53 countries. She became Head Girl,
claimed to be the school's organizational genius, and left with
eight O-levels and four A-levels in English, French, History and
the History of Art. From there, her parents sent her to the
Connecticut College for Women, where she joined the dramatic
society, learned about stage lighting, and was expelled after a
lesbian affair with a fellow pupil. Appalled, her parents sent Angie
to London – initially with her mother as chaperone – and she
enrolled as a student at Kingston, studying for a degree in
economics and business studies.

Through an uncle who was a Lebanese wrestler, a fellow
student found Angie a job at the Nomad Travel Club in Sussex
Gardens, Paddington, where she was working by day and living in
an upstairs room by night when she met Bowie. There was nothing
romantic about it. Three Mexican musicians slept in the room
above. A pair of female bartenders shared the room next door,
working in a disco below the Travel Club.

Angie met Reizner in a lift at Leonard's, the hairdressers, while
still studying at Kingston, and through going out with him met
musicians, actors and Calvin Mark Lee, who would often drop in
at Nomad when business was slack and talk for hours. Soon she
was also calling at his flat in Sloane Street, where the walls were
covered with photographs of people Lee either slept with, or
hoped to, both men and women. Bowie was among them. Lee was
trying to persuade Mercury to sign Bowie, and in case he needed a
little encouragement Bowie was happy to satisfy him in every
way. 'I always wanted to help him,' says Lee.[1] 'Maybe, he needed
something at the time, which was fine with me ... one doesn't
mind being used if there's a feeling the other way. In fact, one
wants to be used because that offers a tie ... [but] you lose people
if you start possessing them.'

No one could ever accuse Calvin Mark Lee of that. He was
willing to share himself with anyone – and to share Bowie, too.
None of this surprised Angie, once she knew them both, for she
saw gays 'going gaga' for Bowie, once they started going around
together,[2] and soon had no doubt that 'sex – given, promised,
implied, even strategically withheld ... was a very significant
factor in his rise through the gay mafia of the London music
business. That soft intensity of his, the way he was able to suggest

profound intimacy simply by looking at you straight in the eye, was a potent weapon, and he used it often and well.'

*     *     *     *     *

'You ought to meet him, he's marvellous, he's going to be a star,' Lee kept telling her, eventually arranging for the three of them to meet up for a Chinese meal in Soho. The date was Wednesday 9 April 1969. Marc Bolan's management were launching a new group that night, King Crimson, and the idea was that Lee, Angie and Bowie should all go on to see them perform at The Speakeasy, the top London club of the moment.

She and Lee were both dressed up for the occasion, wearing three-piece velvet suits, hers pink and his purple; Bowie sported stone-washed sailor trousers, buttoned up the front, with a light blue and mustard striped woollen sweater. After finishing their meal, they walked to The Speakeasy, down the stairs to the basement, where they sat in a corner, 'both feeling pretty bored', so Bowie told me afterwards.

As usual, the music press journalists were standing at the bar with their backs to the stage and the tiny dance floor was empty when the group started to jam and Donovan joined them to sing a Buddy Holly medley.

'Can you jive?' asked Bowie.

'Yes,' said Angie – so they did. Afterwards Bowie started to talk about his music and Lindsay Kemp, while she told him of her plans to be an actress or go into stage management. Meanwhile, Angie was worried that if she took David to bed, 'Calvin might freak', since she assumed that they had slept together. So she carefully observed 'the signals Calvin was giving out. Yes, he approved.... so we went back to Paddington together, and what was going to happen happened. I got fucked.'[3]

The greater shock came next morning when Bowie leapt out of bed, pulled on his clothes and headed for the door. 'Where are you going?' cried Angie.[4] 'You can't leave me....' Insisting that he had work to do, Bowie left – and she hurtled down the stairs after him, falling over herself, and landing in a heap at his feet. Bowie stepped over her, said 'I'll call you tomorrow' – and was gone.

A whole week went by before Bowie made the promised phone call. Angie did not know it, but within days of his romance with Hermione ending, Bowie moved in with the journalist Mary

Finnigan at 24 Foxgrove Road, Beckenham, and was sleeping with
her as well.

'I'd come home from work and there would be a candle-lit meal
ready for me,' Finnigan later told the *News Of The World*: 'The
room would be all warm, there would be incense burning and a
joint rolled ready to smoke.... The atmosphere was so heady and
sensual, it was inevitable we'd end up in bed. David seemed to
love the ritual. He was not the kind of man who had to make love
every night, but when it happened it lasted for hours and hours....
It was so electric and tingly, I never knew what was going to
happen next.... I found him incredibly attractive, right from the
start.... He was slim with this pale, pale skin, but he was very well
endowed ...'

Mary had gone away for a few days, and Bowie was not one to
be lonely for long, especially when under the weather. He phoned
Angie, his voice indistinct, said, 'I've been down with flu', and
asked whether she would mind calling a minicab and coming
down to Beckenham right away.

'I don't want to see a doctor,' he said, so Angie bought him
aspirin, put him back to bed and fed him with soup, fruit and
sympathy. He played her demo tapes, talked about his childhood
and told her how Terry introduced him to jazz, American writers
and poetry. Bowie also told her that something happened to Terry
while he was in the Royal Air Force: 'It's paranoid schizophrenia,
so they say. That's how they've diagnosed Terry ... and it runs
through the family on my mother's side. Sometimes, when I'm
pissed or stoned, I can almost feel it in me.'[5]

There was never any suggestion, then or later, that his
admissions shocked her, for Angie talked of her lesbian affair in
Connecticut and her male lovers since enrolling at Kingston. They
were drawing closer, sharing more of their inner selves, and if he
was not falling in love with her – as he told me repeatedly that
year and the next he was not – she was with him. But Angie was
under few illusions. 'I don't know how much love David felt – I
suspect very little,' she says. 'My main (and powerful) appeal to
him was my potential as a nurse, cook, creative ally and business
advisor ...'

By the time Mary Finnigan returned, she could tell another
woman had been sleeping in her home. A poem to Angie was also
left on a chair. 'I was a bit put out for two or three days,' says
Mary, who later accepted the situation, drawing closer to Angie

when she learned they had both gone to the same Swiss school and could talk to each other in French, much to Bowie's annoyance.

*     *     *     *     *

Angie became what she said – nurse, cook, mentor and eventually wife, though I am none too sure of her creative input or value as a business advisor. Her main skill, so far as I could see, lay in her drive and sense of direction. Whenever the couple arrived anywhere, Angie's shrill, assertive and demanding voice could be heard clearing the way seconds before Bowie entered a room – she was like a human snowplough.

Giving up her job at Nomad and walking out on Reizner, she moved her possessions in to Bowie's room at 24 Foxgrove Road and began accompanying him everywhere, sitting through the recording session for *Space Oddity* and *The Wild Eyed Boy From Freecloud* at Trident Studios on 20 June, and through all those that followed over the next six weeks while Bowie recorded his first LP with Visconti, which, like his first LP, was titled *David Bowie* in Britain – though in the United States, it was *Man Of Words, Man Of Music*. They became inseparable, with Angie the buffer between Bowie and the world. Not everyone liked her, for she was sharp rather than witty, and ever-persistent, claiming a knowledge of business – and in particular, the music business – that she did not possess.

Before they actually moved into Foxgrove Road together, Mrs Jones found Angie in his bedroom at Plaistow Grove – naked. She immediately phoned Pitt and complained furiously, as she often did. Pitt confirms that when Bowie persuaded Mary Finnigan to allow Angie to move in with him, it caused his parents 'considerable anguish and Mary to be severely censured by them for seemingly encouraging the couple to live together. Angela had not endeared herself to them ...'[6]

*     *     *     *     *

*Space Oddity* was not an immediate hit, despite its timing, and the willingness of Bowie's friends at Blackhill Enterprises to play it to the crowd of over 250,000 that gathered in Hyde Park on 5 July for The Rolling Stones' free concert. Fifteen days later, Bowie was sitting around the television set at Foxgrove Road with Angie,

Mary and a group of friends, watching the Apollo moon landing. As background music, the BBC played *Space Oddity* and the sound of 'Ground Control to Major Tom' echoed through the Finnigan living room. Angie did not know whether to laugh, scream or cry and became hysterical as the joints were passed around. Bowie, as he often does when something important happens, sat there calmly, saying little, taking everything in – but it still needed an extra push, a bribe of £140 which Pitt freely admits he paid,[7] to get the record into the *New Musical Express* chart.

Confident that the record was going to become a hit, Mercury started paying Bowie the agreed £20 a week to begin work on his first LP for them, with the first sessions held at Trident Studios on 16 July.

This was not the only money Bowie was earning and he was not totally penniless. Bowie continued to pick up gigs, making a lunch-time appearance at The Three Horseshoes in Hampstead on 6 May, supporting Tim Hollier in concert at the Wigmore Hall on 22 May, guesting on The Strawbs' BBC-2 series *Colour Me Pop* on 10 June (it was broadcast four days later), and was still earning cash when he needed to at the photocopying firm in Carey Street.

There was a growing feeling within the music business that, perhaps, his time had come. Penny Valentine, who praised his earlier records, wrote in *Disc and Music Echo* that it was 'going to be a huge hit – and knock everyone senseless'. She went on: 'I listened spellbound throughout, panting to know the outcome of poor Major Tom and his trip into the outer hemisphere.' Praising 'some really clever lyrics', she continued: 'the sound is amazing. Mr Bowie sounds like The Bee Gees on their best record – *New York Mining Disaster*' while the backing was 'like a cross between The Moody Blues, The Beatles and Simon and Garfunkel'.

Pitt featured the review in a half-page advertisement in the trade paper *Record Retailer*, urged Howie Richmond to make use of it in the States, and began finalizing arrangements for Bowie's appearance at song festivals in Malta and Italy at the end of July.

In Malta, Bowie was representing the United Kingdom. The contest was staged at the Hilton Hotel in Sliema, with entrants from 15 countries. It was an annual event but an amateurish one, according to Pitt, who was unimpressed when told to take backing tapes in case anything went wrong with the Festival's orchestra. Instead, Pitt arranged for a top conductor, Norrie Paramor (producer of many of Cliff Richard's records), to go with them when Bowie and Pitt left for Malta on 24 July. With his own conductor and wearing the grey suit bought for filming *Love You Till Tuesday*, Bowie looked polished as he sang *When I Live My Dream*, and Pitt thought 'he presented it well, walking up to Norrie as the ballad ended and shaking his hand ... a good, professional touch'. Bowie came second and was presented with a statuette, 'which he was very pleased with at the time. It was the first time David had won an award,' noted Pitt.

Afterwards, all the artistes appearing at Malta flew to Monsummano-Terme in Pistoia for the Italian Song Festival, only to find there was no band, no musical accompaniment and no one who could read music. Pitt saw the humour in all this, but Bowie did not, phoning Angie to complain about the suit and the dull mediocrity of the two festivals. She immediately flew over, using the return half of her ticket home to Cyprus, and booked into the room at the festival hotel in Monsummano-Terme that Pitt had reserved for Bowie and himself.

'David was thrilled, Ken wasn't,' she says.[8] Worse was to come. Knowing how much Bowie disliked the suit, Angie had travelled to Italy via the Kensington Antique Market where she bought him a cream balloon-sleeved Victorian silk shirt, with very tight black satin trousers, equipping herself with a romantic white Victorian lace dress – and it was in those clothes, not the hated suit, that Bowie made his entrance with his hair held back by a velvet bow, and Angie on his arm, flowers in her hair. The crowd gasped as they swept down the grand, curving, ceremonial staircase. This was not surprising. Angie's dress was see-through.

\*     \*     \*     \*     \*

Bowie was anxious to return to London on Sunday 3 August, having agreed to perform that night at the Beckenham Arts Laboratory. While he was in Italy, his father phoned Mary Finnigan to ask when he would be back, and she didn't remember to tell Bowie until the interval. 'He said he wasn't well,' she said.

Bowie's face went ashen. 'Why didn't you tell me earlier?' he screamed, realizing that his father would never have left the message without good reason: Jones avoided personal small talk. Quickly finishing his set, Bowie rushed home to Plaistow Grove, still carrying the statuette he won in Malta.

John Jones was not a strong man. He suffered from stomach
ulcers, and his body was weakened by several operations. A few
days earlier, he had collapsed in the street and the family doctor
diagnosed a lung infection, lumbar pneumonia. Bowie found him
in bed, being nursed by Peggy, looking weak and emaciated. He
showed him the statuette. 'I always know you'd succeed in the
end,' said his father.

Jones died on 5 August. 'David was very shaken, but calm,' Pitt
told me. 'He was crying a bit, which was understandable … his
father was an extraordinarily tidy man, so it was possible to get
things straight very quickly. I went down when David asked me,
and the thing I remember most clearly was David turning to me, as
we stood by the desk looking at John's dentures, and David
saying, "I know it sounds a silly question, Ken, but what do I do
about his teeth?"'

'Just drop them in the wastepaper basket and forget about it,'
said Pitt. As he told me of these events, Pitt walked over to the
office, which adjoined his living room in Manchester Street, and
produced a file of letters exchanged between them, together with
financial records and early photographs. He let me copy them,
some of which have already been used in this book. They showed
how much Bowie's parents trusted him to look after their son. This
is typical: 'We are convinced that with your help and guidance
David will in due course achieve the success his ability and hard
work deserves.'

When Bowie phoned Angie at her parents' home in Cyprus to
tell her of his father's death, Col. Barnett immediately gave her the
money to fly back to London. She arrived at Plaistow Grove to
find Peggy diminished and Bowie already becoming more of a
man around the house, looking after the funeral arrangements and
trying to care for his mother, which was not easy with neighbours
and aunts coming in and out. 'I remember the following weeks
quite clearly, because they were among the most difficult of my
life,' she says.[9]

As there were only two bedrooms at Plaistow Grove, and Peggy
hated the thought of her son sleeping with a woman to whom he
was not married, Bowie slept in one room and Angie slept in the
other, sharing a bed with his mother. Angie found this 'odious' but
cooperated in an endeavour to keep the peace; Peggy was
'extremely depressed and incapable – both bereaved and incompe-
tent, since John had handled virtually everything for her' – and as

for David: 'He was grieving for a father he'd really loved and depended on, but he was also angry and having a hard time with that … he hated the idea of having to take care of his mother … [and] couldn't reconcile himself to the manner of his father's passing. Peggy had waited too long before summoning a doctor, and in the end John Jones had asphyxiated alone in an upstairs room, trying to get to an oxygen tank just outside his reach … the two [were] pecking at each other like psychotic vultures in that closed little house while I bounced around in the middle…. [Peggy] turned on me the way she must have turned on Terry, and I began to understand what drove David to distraction about her.'[9]

9

# 'Can you deal with the fact
that I'm not in love with you?'

Nevertheless, life seemed to go on as before. Bowie and Angie were staying at Plaistow Grove, but still had their room at Mary Finnigan's. Socially, their lives continued to revolve around Beckenham Arts Laboratory and plans for a Free Festival. Bowie threw himself back into work, writing and recording songs for his next LP. *Space Oddity* only gradually built a sales momentum, but its success led to better-paid gigs.

Superficially, nothing changed but the pace; in reality, everything had. Bowie was being forced to rely more upon his own resources. 'He came to depend upon me in new ways,' was how Angie saw it. She says in *Backstage Passes* that she offered her man a deal. They were sitting in his bedroom at Plaistow Grove, the room where he slept as a child, and she offered to stay with him – 'to accomplish his goal ... to make him a star' – on the understanding they would then repeat the trick, propelling *her* into a life of stageshows and movies.

'Can you deal with the fact that I'm not in love with you?' asked Bowie.

It sounds cruel and hard, but I can vouch that this was the basis of their relationship, agreed from the beginning, before they married, for I put the necessary questions to him in Pitt's apartment that autumn. With *Space Oddity* at last becoming a hit, a magazine commissioned me to write an article about Bowie's 'romance', as they put it.

Phoning Pitt to arrange the interview, I asked: 'Do you think David will be willing to talk about Angie?'

'Try him,' said Pitt. 'He's always told me he likes talking to you, so see what he says ... but let me warn you. He's not in love with her. She's making the running.'

'Are you in love with her?' I asked Bowie. He threw back his head, laughing.

'Love?' he asked. 'Getting a bit old fashioned today, aren't we, George?' That threw me for a moment and I explained that the magazine specifically commissioned the feature, which made him laugh even more.

'Well, you can call it love if you want to,' he said, 'but that's not the word I'd use ...' and then went on to tell me how they met and Angie's family background. Six months later, after their wedding at Bromley register office, I put the question again and received a similar response. 'She's an American citizen, and if I hadn't married her she'd have had to leave the country ... that's why we did it. But for that I don't think we'd have got married at all. Those bits of paper mean nothing to me.'

\*     \*     \*     \*     \*

Many opportunities came Bowie's way that autumn of 1969.

For months, he, Angie, Mary Finnigan and their friends at the Beckenham Arts Laboratory had been planning their own Free Festival. Its aims were modest – more like village fête than Woodstock.

The Festival was staged at the Beckenham Recreation Ground on Saturday 16 August with the Mayor and councillors present in all their glory – and the police unable to tell which was which: hash, hamburgers or patchouli oil. There was something for everyone, an adventure playground with an assault course, a Buddhist monk selling pamphlets, joss sticks and bric-à-brac for the Tibet Society and stalls packed with jewellery, ceramics, home-made candles, herbs and spices, vegetarian food, hippie clothes and rare Californian psychedelic posters imported and sold by Calvin Mark Lee, who donated the proceeds to the Arts Laboratory. Angie ran the hamburger stall, a smile on her face all day. And then there was the music – not just Bowie playing *Space Oddity* and songs from his Deram LP, but also Junior's Eyes, Bridget St John, Gas Works, Sun, The Strawbs, Miscarriage, Amory Kane, Keith Christmas and others less well known, all compered by John Peel.

It was a fine day, the sun shone, they all had a marvellous time – except Bowie. He looked pretty enough in a blue silk shirt with his hair permed, but he scowled as he strode through the park, snarling, 'You bunch of materialistic arseholes' as he strode past the grinning Angie, cheerfully counting the takings. 'He was extremely rude to a lot of people, some of whom vowed they would never speak to him again,' said Mary Finnigan. That was not how Bowie remembered the day at all. 'We had a marvellous day,' he told me, explaining how the Arts Laboratory was taking shape, inspiring his song *Memory Of A Free Festival*, and comparing its spirit to Glastonbury Fayre.

Much to the annoyance of his Aunt Pat, who once again decided to become the family intermediary, Bowie took possession of his father's car, the Fiat 500, and with his amplifiers strapped to the roof and Angie driving, began gigging far afield. *Space Oddity* entered every chart in the last week of September and first week of October, and he was booked to appear on *Top Of The Pops* on 9 October.

With the record breaking fast, Andrew Loog Oldham, who had moved on from The Rolling Stones to manage Humble Pie, booked Bowie to support them on a short British tour of major provincial venues. This opened at Coventry Theatre on 8 October and took up most of the month. A London gig was fitted in on the 21st at the Queen Elizabeth Hall. Bowie was paid £50 a night, almost three times the fee he earned six months earlier supporting Tyrannosaurus Rex, but the audiences did not like his 20-minute acoustic set, wanting rock 'n' roll, not a pretty boy sitting alone on a chair in the spotlight, playing guitar. For the first time in his life, Bowie faced booing and whistling, which he found unsettling.

Between the Humble Pie dates, Bowie picked up several others – £110 for a night in Exeter, £125 for another in Birmingham, with daytime radio spots slotted in, then £280 for another appearance on *Musik für junge Leute* in Germany, and £120 for a twin-booking at the end of the month, in Gravesend and Gillingham. This brought his live appearance income for the month, after paying agent's and manager's percentages, to just over £1,000 – more than he had earned in the whole of the previous year.

This sudden change in circumstances, with his income from live shows supplementing the £1,250 advance from Mercury and their weekly £20 payments, encouraged Bowie and Angie to move away from Plaistow Grove and Foxgrove Road; neither looking after his mother nor a ménage-à-trois brought them peace of mind.

It was Angie who found their next home, with a suitably imposing address for a would-be rock star – Haddon Hall, a sprawling 30-roomed red-brick Victorian pile with a mass of chimneys and a mock-Gothic tower at 42 Southend Road, Beckenham (demolished in 1981 to make way for a block of flats).

With extensive gardens and a view across the local golf course, Haddon Hall was built in 1851 by a tycoon who made his fortune mass-producing candles. Its main door opened on to a vast central hallway, 40 feet wide and 60 feet long, with sweeping staircases, moulded ceilings, ornate tiled fireplaces, a huge stained-glass window at the far end, and doors wherever one looked. Such places could always be rented cheaply, for no normal tenant would contemplate furnishing costs or heating on this scale. Bowie rented the ground-floor flat for £8 a week, and for that acquired a massive living room nearly 50 feet long, complete with minstrels' gallery where friends could sleep on mattresses, a huge dining room, a music room, a bedroom, kitchen and bathroom.

They moved in towards the end of October, after Angie convinced the landlord she was of independent means and he had no need to worry about her long-haired boyfriend being unable to pay the rent. (The poor man was to have many problems getting his rent over the next five years. In 1976, he sued Bowie for unpaid rent and damage to the property. The local council also had difficulties collecting property taxes, and eventually caught up with Bowie in 1978, serving him with a demand when he returned to Britain for a concert tour.)

I spent several hours with Bowie on 17 November and he described the work then in progress. Visconti and his girlfriend Liz – who later moved into an adjoining flat – together with several friends from the Arts Laboratory, were cleaning out the ground floor which stank of cats, since the last tenant had had 27 of them. A small army set to with water buckets and bleach before removing old wallpaper and stripping off layers of paint from the stairs, floors, doors and door-frames to reveal the original woodwork, giving Haddon Hall back its original Victorian feel.

'It's like starting afresh with a blank canvas,' said Bowie, explaining that his greatest expense was laying down a cheap industrial carpet underlay. The bedroom was being painted pink with a silver ceiling, the floors covered with loose Indian carpets that could be picked up cheaply second-hand for £10 or £20, and he had found a vast Regency bed in a junk shop, lying in pieces: 'It's fabulous, like a huge coffin with a canopy.' In the living room was a 12-foot teak sideboard, 'made in Burma and hand-carved, that was the main feature at a Maples furniture exhibition in 1936.

I bought that, complete with a catalogue for the exhibition showing the sideboard in all its glory ... and I'm having floor-length draped curtains made for all the windows, just to show everything off.'

Pitt, listening in, added: 'Whenever he's had some money, he's bought something collectable ... another piece of glassware, pewter or a vase, or Victorian children's books with illustrations by Arthur Rackham, Randolph Caldecott or Kate Greenaway ... they're all over the flat now at Haddon Hall.'

In every room, there were vases, bowls, jugs, jardinières, bottles, ashtrays and paperweights, all in coloured glass. 'I've had a passion for art nouveau glassware, ever since I was learning art at school,' said Bowie, 'and when I started to earn money I promised myself that I'd build up a good collection as soon as I could afford it. Galle glass from the Nanay factory in France, and also Lalique and Daum ... and I've paintings by Montenegro, who designed ballet sets for Nijinsky; fashion designs by Erté, and a fairy scene – an island of fairies – drawn by one of my favourite Victorian artists, Phil May.'

Their new home was not always as peaceful as it sounded. As soon as Visconti moved in, Angie found herself a job as a secretary, leaving Liz his girlfriend to do all the cooking, which she hated. 'So it was totally unsuccessful as a commune,' says Visconti,[1] recalling that they each gave money to Angie towards the housekeeping costs. One week she came back with a Chinese take-away meal for Bowie and herself, and two tins of baked beans for them. Visconti adds that there was 'nothing but animosity flying about everywhere ... and when they started being very open about their sex lives, that's when it got really heavy'.

There was no hint that day at Manchester Street of any tensions between Bowie and Pitt. They were talking in the same close, friendly way I had observed in the past, and our conversation turned to The Velvet Underground, Lou Reed, Iggy Pop and The Fugs, whose music Bowie was now playing 'all the time'. Bowie said Lou Reed was doing something new: 'it's literature, music, politics, all bound together.... I've never felt of myself as rock 'n' roll before, because a lot of that old stuff I didn't relate to at all. There's melody and rhythm, but the lyrics don't say anything. Now, Lou Reed is bringing in original lyrics – and you shouldn't miss Iggy Pop. No one's writing about him here, yet – but he's great. Crazy, outrageous, but great ... it's all happening in

America now. Everything was centred here a couple of years ago, but that's now changed.'

Bowie went on to explain how his own writing was changing, and it is clear to me now that his father's death profoundly changed him, leading to a sense of isolation or withdrawal that became even more apparent in his later albums. Bowie, seeing less of his mother and much less of Pitt, was becoming reliant to a degree on Calvin Mark Lee and Angie, but not as much as they would like. Terry was also back in his life again, living at Cane Hill during the week and Haddon Hall at the weekends.

On a creative level, Bowie was gathering around himself a core of musicians; notably Visconti, who was to produce nine of his albums; the engineer Ken Scott, who produced *Hunky Dory*, *Ziggy Stardust*, *Aladdin Sane* and *Pin-Ups*; guitarists Mick Wayne and Tim Renwick; cellist and arranger Paul Buckmaster; pianist Rick Wakeman; bass player Herbie Flowers; and drummers Terry Cox and John Cambridge.

'Have you listened to my new album yet?' he asked me. 'It's the best thing I've done so far. There are some tracks on there I'm really proud of ... *The Wild Eyed Boy From Freecloud* is one of the best. It's about a boy who falls in love with the mountain where he lives. The people in his village think he's mad and they're determined to kill him, to hang him, but the mountain protects him and kills the village. That was the B-side of *Space Oddity*, but no one ever heard it.... We've also rerecorded *Space Oddity*. It's a bit longer and in stereo, and I prefer this version.'

Bowie confirmed that *Letter To Hermione* and *An Occasional Dream* were both written after the end of his affair with Hermione – 'that's me in a maudlin or romantic mood. I'd written her a letter, and then decided not to post it. *Letter To Hermione* is what I wished I'd said. I was in love with her, and it took me months to get over it. She walked out on me, and I suppose that was what hurt as much as anything else, that feeling of rejection.... *God Knows I'm Good* is more like my earlier songs. It's the story of a shoplifter who gets arrested and can't believe it.... *Memory Of A Free Festival* is my writing now.... *Unwashed And Somewhat Slightly Dazed* describes how I felt in the weeks after my father died.' He insisted that the best song on the album was *Cygnet Committee*, which he would have preferred as a single but the record company objected: 'They say it's too long, nine-and-a-half minutes as opposed to the usual three ... but that's a song in which

I had something I wanted to say, it's me looking at the hippie movement, saying how it started off so well but went wrong when the hippies became just like everyone else, materialistic and selfish.' I noticed afterwards, when I checked through my notes, that he avoided mentioning one track, *Janine*, which Visconti preferred. Even stranger, he rarely played the song again.

As we were finishing the interview, Bowie asked if I was going to his show on 20 November at the Purcell Room – the venue Pitt had booked a year in advance (although I was not aware of that then). Bowie said he thought it was just the right size of hall to present his latest songs with Junior's Eyes as accompaniment. 'It's the first time I've worked with a backing group for ages,' he said.

'I'm sorry,' I replied, 'no one's told me about it. Had I known earlier I'd have come' – not realizing I would be missing Bowie's most important concert, a real turning point. For the first time, he played the kind of songs that were to establish his reputation three years later, songs with biting imagery that said more than they seemed to; songs with subtle lyrics that worked on different levels of interpretation, suggesting an underlying sense of alienation. His performance was clearly planned with care, and Bowie was distressed to learn afterwards that there were hardly any critics in the audience.

'The show was marvellous,' said Pitt when I phoned him the following day, 'but David was very disappointed at the lack of response. He thought this was going to be the night that would establish his reputation.' Bowie blamed Pitt for the lack of press coverage – while Pitt blamed Angie and Calvin Mark Lee, who insisted on organizing the event their way, drawing up their own invitation list.

This concert came at a crucial moment in Bowie's career when he was feeling torn between the steady, conventional, safe managerial skills of Pitt, to whom he remained under contract, and his highly ambitious wife-to-be who was energetically trying to propel him forwards. Pitt went back to his dressing room after the concert to congratulate Bowie upon his performance. 'Which papers were here tonight, Ken?' asked Bowie.

'So far as I can see, very few,' said Pitt. 'One or two from the music papers, but none from the dailies.'

The only significant press comment came in the *Observer*, where Tony Palmer wrote:

He gave a sizzling concert in London's Purcell Room which was mostly ignored by the national press, presumably because they thought pop and Purcell were incompatible ... on stage, he is quite devastatingly beautiful. With his loofah hair and blue eyes, he pads around like every schoolgirl's wonder movie star. He smiles; you melt. He winks; you disintegrate. He apologizes that his repertoire is mostly his own songs, which he admits sound all very much the same.

It's all relaxed, chatty, informal and you forgive him his husky voice, his strained top notes and his careless intonation. You slump back, allowing this contemporary minstrel to dazzle you with niceness. Then, suddenly, he tears into you with a violent, passionate, angry, stamping song about fear and despair ... when he turns his eye to the absurdities of technological society he is razor-sharp in his observations.[2]

Pitt agreed: 'the best performance David had ever given,' he told me. But that was no consolation for Bowie, who was desperately anxious to convince the world that he was not going to become another one-hit wonder. According to Pitt, after the concert Bowie 'became very angry and swore' and rushed off into the night. So far as Pitt knows, Bowie ended his relationship with Calvin Mark Lee that evening. 'His name was never again mentioned and I hoped that David had learned a lesson.'[3] Within a few weeks, Bowie was also to say he no longer wanted Pitt to handle his affairs, but for the moment Pitt did not see that rift coming.

Meanwhile, there was another newsworthy booking in the diary – a charity concert at the London Palladium on 30 November in the presence of Princess Margaret, to raise funds for the Invalid Children's Aid Association. Dusty Springfield, Tiny Tim, The Settlers, The Mojos and Marmalade were also on the bill.

Bowie was due to be presented to the Princess, and this caused another rift involving Pitt – this time with Angie. In *Backstage Passes*,[4] Angie says she went off to Cyprus 'in a huff' after a dispute with Pitt over who should accompany Bowie to the presentation of the Ivor Novello Awards, him or her – but as the awards were not presented until 10 May the following year her angst was obviously over whether or not she should be at the Palladium, standing by her man, meeting the Princess.

Angie says 'the fact that Ken chose to exclude me from his boy's achievement bothered me greatly. I wasn't, I was told, welcome at the awards ceremony.... I went over the top about that, verging into hysterics and causing more than dust to fly at Haddon Hall ... but all my raging won me nothing.'

Later, contradicting other accounts of their relationship, Angie says she left for Cyprus in November 1969 and did not receive a letter or a postcard from Bowie for three or four weeks because of a postal strike. The mail arrived all at once, together with a Christmas card saying, 'This year we will marry.' Her immediate reaction was, 'That's just what I don't fucking need!'[5] – but Bowie phoned the following day, said he had written *The Prettiest Star* just for her, and played it over the phone. And she said 'Yes'.

'This is the third plane ticket I've bought for that man,' said her father, who nevertheless promised them £2,000 as a wedding present.

While Angie was away, Bowie continued working closely with Pitt, dining out, flying to Dublin for an appearance on Radio Telefis Eireann, attending the world premiere of Peter Maxwell Davies's *Vesalii Icones*, recording an Italian lyric to the *Space Oddity* music, *Ragazza Solo, Ragazza Solo*. Pitt was also trying to secure another contract from Essex Music who were reluctant to agree a new advance. Despite the success of *Space Oddity* and the release of his two LPs, Essex had still not recouped their previous advances and were unwilling to agree new terms – which was unlucky for them. Had they done so, Essex would have secured publishing rights to Bowie's first three major albums, *The Man Who Sold The World*, *Hunky Dory* and *The Rise And Fall Of Ziggy Stardust*.

On another front, Pitt found Bowie a new agent, NEMS, who started lining up gigs for January, February and March 1970, between recording sessions for the new single, *The Prettiest Star*, and new version of *London Bye Ta Ta*, which Bowie recorded on 8 January 1970 – his 23rd birthday – with Bolan playing lead guitar. That night, Bowie also performed a solo acoustic set at The Speakeasy, his first booking arranged through NEMS. He was paid £100. This was reviewed by a journalist from the gay magazine *Jeremy*, who was writing an illustrated feature on Bowie at Pitt's suggestion. Noting that the girls in the audience out-numbered the boys four to one, he observed:

It's just not David's scene. The disco stops and a single sharp spot stabs its way through layers of multi-coloured light show.

It's David's turn. Perched precariously on two boxes – a luminous elfin surrounded by an aureole of curls – he looks very vulnerable. He works hard…. Throughout the act there is a spattering of applause. Groupies parade. People keep right on talking. No one seems involved. The reaction is disturbingly muted. It's all over and David joins us at the bar. The elfin face looks puzzled. 'I can't believe it. The manager says I got a good reception. If that's what happens when they like you – what happens when they hate you?' A marauding groupie gropes him in the crush. 'Who was it? I ought to get a fee for that …'[6]

Bowie's set included songs by Jacques Brel, numbers from his LP and poems by Mason Williams, with Visconti on bass and John Cambridge of Junior's Eyes on drums. 'I'm going electric,' he jokingly told Pitt, for Bob Dylan had gone electric four years earlier in a famous cross-over from folk to rock, losing his more traditional following along the way. 'We're going to dress up and be totally outrageous. It'll be one big hype.'

'That's a good name. Why don't you call yourselves Hype?' said Pitt – and the new group was born. That February, advertisements started appearing in the music press for Bowie's appearances with his 'New Electric Group' – at The Marquee on 3 February, on John Peel's new BBC radio programme *The Sunday Show* on 5 February, and at Basildon Arts Centre later that month.

Bowie's mind changed daily, as it always did when he was planning something new – and so did the line-up for the band. At one stage it included Rick Wakeman. Tim Renwick was briefly recruited, with Bowie thinking a lead guitarist would leave him free to concentrate on vocals. 'I know someone from Hull,' said Cambridge, recommending Mick Ronson – 'a brilliant guitarist' – who had toured France, Germany and North Africa with different groups. 'OK – bring him down,' said Bowie, and Cambridge went to Hull where he found Ronson working for the local Parks Department, mowing lawns, pruning hedges. The son of a storeman, he left school at 15 with no academic achievements. Ronson moved from group to group – Voice, The Wanted and The Rats – which travelled far and wide in search of gigs and usually folded up when the money ran out, the van blew up or the bailiffs moved in.

But when Cambridge told Ronson Bowie wanted to meet him, the reply was not ecstatic. 'I've been through all that before,' he

said, having been to France with one group only to find the club
that booked them had closed; he had also been ordered out of
Algeria.

'David's just had a hit record, writes all his own songs – and
he's released two albums,' said Cambridge. 'This could be it ...'

So Ronson chucked in his job for the third or fourth time, and
travelled back to London with Cambridge. He first met Bowie at
The Marquee on 3 February, a gig that Bowie accepted on the
basis that he would receive 60 per cent of the ticket money.
Unfortunately, only 129 people turned up and Bowie's share of the
'gate' was £34 4s, out of which he gave half to the support group,
£7 to Visconti for playing bass, £6 to a van driver for carrying the
instruments and a £1 16s booking fee – which left him with a little
over £2 to share with Renwick and Cambridge. 'We usually do
better than that,' said Bowie, as he drove Ronson back to Haddon
Hall.

Two nights later, Ronson joined them at the BBC Paris Cinema,
Lower Regent Street, recording an hour-long edition of *The
Sunday Show* – the first time Bowie was ever asked to perform a
show of this length. I was the only writer there. I met Bowie at
Manchester Street and took a taxi down to the Paris, joining
Ronson, Visconti and Cambridge in the empty theatre. It did not
sound like the beginning of a brave new world, but there was
something that left an indelible imprint on my mind. Bowie was
undeniably in charge, up front, leading the group, issuing
instructions and taking total responsibility for their music. Even
Visconti was being told what to do, and accepting it.

Bowie opened the set with *Port Of Amsterdam*, the first of four
acoustic numbers and a brave choice for 1970, following this with
*God Knows I'm Good*, *Buzz The Fuzz* and *Karma Man*, before
bringing in Ronson, Visconti and Cambridge for their first song
together, *London Bye Ta Ta*. He followed this with *An Occasional
Dream*, one of his love songs for Hermione Farthingale, before
introducing another new song, *The Width Of A Circle*. This was its
earliest form, only two verses; he expanded it to an eight-minute
number by the time he recorded it as the intro to his album *The
Man Who Sold The World* the following year.

Ronson's hard-edged guitar was heard to better effect on *The
Prettiest Star*, where he played a similar arrangement to Bolan's,
and also on *Unwashed And Somewhat Slightly Dazed* and an
extended version of *Space Oddity*. On a session such as this, as in

his later live stage versions, Bowie would frequently take the basic
theme of a song, perhaps the riff or maybe just the riff and a verse,
expanding that semi-spontaneously to maybe two or three times its
original length, playing to the mood of his audience, which was
more of a jazz tradition than rock 'n' roll. That night, he
developed *Space Oddity* and then the two numbers that particularly pleased him from his latest LP, *The Cygnet Committee* and
*The Wild Eyed Boy From Freecloud*, and a favourite by the
American Biff Rose, *Fill Your Heart*, that was later featured on
the *Hunky Dory* LP.

It was a strong selection of songs, and unusually adventurous
for such a live BBC show, for there was not one conventional
three-minute pop song among them. Visconti's enthusiasm was
almost tangible; he was champing at the bit, suggesting technical
changes while they rehearsed, repositioning microphones, coming
in with ideas for the use of bass or drums, and yet clearly bowing
to Bowie as the ultimate arbiter. This was a fascinating process to
observe: Bowie was not a star, he was still a struggling musician,
earning a pittance – yet here he was, totally in command, directing
the shape of the programme with far more authority than many
better-known musicians.

\*     \*     \*     \*     \*

During autumn 1969 and spring 1970, I must have phoned Pitt at
least once a week. Our conversations were usually solely about
Bowie, for his other projects were of little interest in the territories
where the column appeared. Pitt was always honest with me. He
was having problems with Bowie and made little attempt to
conceal it. This all came to a head after Angie returned from
Cyprus and before she married Bowie.

Until then, Bowie's plans for the 'New Electric Group' seemed
to be going well, and then he had several other projects on the go.
At the end of January, he and Angie went to Scotland to film a
guest spot on *Cairngorm Ski Night* for Grampian Television in
Aberdeen, appear in concert at Aberdeen University, and record a
short mime piece with Lindsay Kemp, based on *Pierrot In
Turquoise*, for Scottish Television in Edinburgh. In February,
there was the hour-long radio show already mentioned and his first
gigs with Hype.

On 14 February, Bowie was presented with a gold disc in a

leather case as the Brightest New Hope at the annual *Disc And Music Echo* Valentine Awards. The ceremony was staged at the Café Royal in Regent Street. Other awards were won by The Beatles, Lulu, Cilla Black and Cliff Richard, and Bowie chose to dress for the occasion, wearing a shiny, six-buttoned, double-breasted, putty-coloured suit, with a flowery shirt and a mass of curls framing his face. He looked happy and his relationship with Pitt must still have been good, for when the award was presented to him by the disc jockey Tony Blackburn, Bowie walked across the room to Pitt, in full view of the audience, and said, 'This is for you.'

Nine days later, on 22 February, Bowie paraded his new band for the first time at The Round House in Camden Town – a gig that he accepted for just £10 expenses so that Hype could work to a live audience and test their reaction. If Pitt still nursed any hopes that Bowie might develop a cabaret act, they must have been shattered that night.

'We're going to have a totally different stage act,' Bowie told me when we met at the Paris Cinema. 'There'll be costumes and mime, all sorts of songs, not just rock 'n' roll ... in fact, there may not be much rock 'n' roll at all. It's going to be very theatrical.' In the intervening fortnight, Angie and the other musicians' girl-friends were hard at work at Haddon Hall, making a set of costumes. 'I'm not quite sure what they're doing, but I know David's got something up his sleeve,' Pitt told me.

That night at The Round House, supporting the Californian folk rock band Country Joe McDonald and The Fish, Bowie pressed his 'outrage' button hard – and came out on stage dressed as a Space Star, wearing a draped cape of turquoise silk and silver netting over an all-white suit; Visconti was Hypeman, wearing a leotard and wide-framed collarpiece; Ronson, Gangsterman, with a double-breasted suit in gold velour; and Cambridge, Cowboy, in tight-fitting jeans, high boots and fringed jacket.

'Putting that show together had been a blast,' says Angie,[7] but the audience was baffled. Pitt thought they had overdone it, and Bolan, who was there, thought the presentation did not work at all. This was not the first time Bowie fired from too many cylinders at once, and a stronger manager – or a manager in a stronger position – would have told him firmly that he should be concentrating on his follow-up single, *The Prettiest Star*, rather than camping it up like a bunch of drama students let loose in a theatre wardrobe. Pitt

was no longer able to do that. In most day-to-day matters, Bowie
was allowing Angie to make the decisions and Pitt had the feeling
that whatever he said or did she would overrule him.

One day, Bowie phoned and asked Pitt, 'Can't I get some more
TV commercials?' – so Pitt found him a day's work making a
commercial to promote Wall's Sausages for a fee of 92 guineas
plus repeat fees. With monies for repeats, that one day's work
would probably have earned Bowie at least £500 and quite
possibly nearer £1,000, for Wall's advertised frequently. However,
when Pitt told Bowie about this, and other jobs for the same week
that would have brought him in another £450, Bowie said angrily,
'I don't want to do television commercials.' And that was that; no
reason given. It was clear to Pitt that Bowie was listening to the
advice of others, notably Angie, and that he could not be relied
upon to hold the same opinion from one day to the next. To me, he
said: 'David's being very capricious, but I don't think it's his
fault ...'

Bowie appeared again with Hype at the Regent Street Polytechnic on 7 March, but Gavin Petrie, a critic for *Disc and Music
Echo*, wrote that the show was 'a disaster': Ronson's guitar was so
loud, 'not only did he block out David's singing but also
completely overpowered John Cambridge's drums.... That magic
that makes for greatness is there but suppressed, sometimes
hidden.' Still, Petrie was optimistic: 'If my ears recover I expect to
see David plus Hype in a few months' time ... shining through.'

However irritating, these were small problems, the kind a sound
engineer can correct in minutes. Much more serious was the lack
of any co-ordinated thrust behind Bowie's career just when he
really needed it. Pitt was being marginalized. Angie was out of her
depth. NEMS were lining up gigs in far-flung places, when Bowie
should have been plugging *The Prettiest Star* for all it was worth,
and Mercury Records, a relatively new label in London terms,
were failing to throw what little muscle they had behind the new
single. There were quite possibly personal reasons for this, since
Reizner was none too keen on signing Bowie after losing his
girlfriend to him – and so Bowie's contract was signed with the
head office in Chicago, at Calvin Mark Lee's instigation, and not
with the Mercury office in London.

Releasing a follow-up single when an artist has had just one hit
record requires careful plugging, perhaps a bribe or two to get the
record played on the right radio programmes and personal

appearances on television, and substantial investment in media
advertising – and Bowie was not getting this. The fundamental
problem was that at the Arts Laboratory and Haddon Hall, he was
surrounded by naïve amateurs – and they were on the verge of
taking control.

\*    \*    \*    \*    \*

Mercury released *The Prettiest Star/London Bye Ta Ta* on 6 March
1970. It was a strongly commercial single and in its first fortnight
received fairly good reviews: 'a very strong follow-up' (*Music
Business Weekly*); 'Chart cert' (*Record Mirror*); 'lovely, gentle …
a hit indeed' (*Disc and Music Echo*). But it had hardly any radio
plays and sold less than 800 copies. Record shops were not
stocking it, and if the single was not readily available and the song
could not be heard on radio, there could be only one possible
outcome: it flopped.

That widened the distance between Bowie and Pitt, but still they
continued to see each other, with Pitt going to the Royal Albert
Hall on 12 March when Bowie appeared in another charity
concert, this time for mentally handicapped children. After the
show, Pitt walked with Bowie and Angie along Kensington Road,
Knightsbridge and Piccadilly, heading for Piccadilly Circus
underground station. They went down the steps, bought tickets and
were saying farewells when Bowie said: 'By the way … we're
going to get married.'

'Congratulations,' Pitt replied.

'Well, we're happy,' said Bowie, and as they were parting
Angie opened a carrier bag to show Pitt something they had
bought that day. He cannot remember what it was, but such was
their impracticality it was probably something decorative rather
than functional – a vase, a painting or a mask of Buddha.

'Is that for your bottom drawer?' asked Pitt, possibly face-
tiously, although his remark could have been an innocent joke.

'You pig!' she spat, as Bowie laughed, grabbed her by the arm
and whisked her off to their train.

# 10

# 'I want to have a go at managing myself'

Bowie had moved into Haddon Hall hoping to escape from his mother. While his father was still alive, he kept in touch with them both, often calling back home to Plaistow Grove, but now he was nursing a grievance that she failed to get his father to a doctor in time – and there was always that memory of an indignant childhood.

Some might call it motherly love, but her demands never stopped – work harder, dress smarter, wash more often, stop wasting time, do your homework, get ready for Cubs, don't be late, come straight home – there was no end to it. Mrs Jones wanted the best for her son, and kept him to the mark with a constant stream of sharp, jabbing imperatives.

There is often a thin dividing line in parenthood between a natural setting of standards and an infuriating attention to detail, and although Mrs Jones may have tried her hardest – rearing a son who was notably smart and courteous – the way she did it drove him nuts and he was forever trying to avoid her. The need to escape had driven him to move into Pitt's apartment, which became his easy road to independence, and to urge Angie to find them a home of their own.

Pitt had to listen to Mrs Jones's daily telephone diatribes against Angie after finding her naked in her son's bedroom: slut ... whore ... tart ... cow ... filthy bitch.

'What's she like?' I asked Pitt in all innocence, only to be answered by more peals of laughter.

'You've got a mother, haven't you?'

'Well, yes....'

'There are mothers and mothers ... she is a very formidable example. You should never underestimate mothers,' said Pitt, who was devoted to his own.

With the death of her husband, Mrs Jones withdrew into herself.

Her grief was genuine; furthermore, John Jones was the kind of man who took every major domestic decision, shielding his wife from the everyday realities of a world built on money. This made the shock of his dying all the harder to bear. She became very lonely, lost in silent thought.

'Let's take the dog for a walk.... Shall I put the kettle on? ... What shall we have for supper?' Angie would say, to break the silence or avoid the tensions of grief. But it was no good trying to be reasonable, especially with Bowie away at the studios working on his album while Angie was left alone with her in the house, or sleeping in his room while they shared the bed in the other. Soon, Angie moved out – unable to stand the tensions any longer – and that made their search for a flat even more urgent.

After they moved into Haddon Hall, Angie went home to Cyprus, in November 1969, and returned in January 1970, when their love nest began to expand, with friends and musicians moving into every room: as well as Tony Visconti and his girlfriend, there were John Cambridge; Mick Ronson; two road managers; friends who made costumes and dresses; musicians passing through; callers from the Arts Laboratory, arriving to share a bottle of plonk or a joint, to play some music or have a game of darts.

'The first thing we must do is install a telephone,' said Angie.

'I don't think that's a good idea,' said Bowie, knowing exactly what would happen. But Angie insisted, only to find the phone ringing every other day with another diatribe from Mrs Jones. 'You've only moved there to get away from me,' she would whine. 'You've left me on my own to die ... after everything I've done for David.... You're ruining his life, you bitch,' and so on, after which Angie would put the phone down and start crying, and Mrs Jones would put her hat and coat on, march round to the house, and berate them yet again for 'living in sin'.

\*     \*     \*     \*     \*

The phone rang at Pitt's apartment. 'Has David told you he's getting married?' asked Mrs Jones.

'He did mention that after we left the Albert Hall the other night ...'

'Has he told you when?'

'No.'

'Well, I hear he's getting married in the morning,' said Mrs Jones, who said she had been round to the local registry office herself to check the time and date. 'Are you going?' she went on.

'If David wanted me to go to his wedding, he'd have invited me,' said Pitt.

The date was Friday 20 March, and when Mrs Jones went round to Haddon Hall to ask her son about his wedding plans she found no one. Angie received her £2,000 wedding present from her father, and they drove up to Kensington Antique Market to buy some wedding clothes.

'This isn't going to be a conventional marriage,' said Bowie, who told her again that he was not in love with her.[1] Rather, this was a relationship that solved problems for both of them – as the wife of a British citizen, Angie would face no more problems with the Home Office Immigration Department. As the husband of an American citizen, Bowie would not be denied a Green Card when he wanted to work in the United States. They might live together as man and wife – and, no doubt, go through phases of being rather more loving than others – but there was no question of them observing the traditional values of marriage.

That afternoon at Kensington Market, Bowie bought himself a pair of tight, black satin trousers, a cream satin shirt with flared sleeves and a blue-and-tan floral pattern, and an Afghan goatskin coat. His bride-to-be chose a Victorian-style silk dress in brown and purple silk, with attractive fringing, and then they jumped back into the tiny Fiat … and drove off to another woman's bed. They went to Bloomsbury to see a young artist and model called Clare whom they met through Calvin Mark Lee.

In her second book, Angie describes Clare as 'a gorgeous dark-haired actress' and says they 'got tipsy, fell into bed together, romped *à trois* until we all passed out, then woke late and rushed in a panic to the registry office'.[2] She says they 'struggled into the kitchen to regain our strength with honey and yoghourt for breakfast. We exchanged glances, the three of us, like kids who had done something very naughty but we were left feeling just great inside.'[3]

Meanwhile, Mrs Peggy Jones was determined not to miss the big occasion – and phoned the *Beckenham Journal* and the *Beckenham and Penge Advertiser* to make sure they knew where and when to send their reporters and photographers.

Bowie and Angie arrived a few minutes late, with their good

friend Clare and John Cambridge who were to be their witnesses,
and their other house guests at Haddon Hall. 'You'll be late,' said
Mrs Jones pushing forward. 'Late for your own wedding! There
you are, I told you they'd be late,' she said, turning to the
Registrar who had been looking a little anxious.

Inside, when it was Cambridge's moment to sign the wedding
register Mrs Jones pushed forward again, seized the pen and
signed the book instead of him. Cambridge looked at Bowie, who
shrugged his shoulders with a half-smile, as his mother linked her
arms between the bride and groom and said, 'Don't worry – I've
called the press!' No way was Mrs Jones going to miss her son's
wedding – or let it go off half-cock.

That evening, while the celebrations overflowed at the local pub
The Three Tuns and later at Haddon Hall, Mrs Jones phoned Pitt
to tell him what had happened. 'It was a lovely wedding,' she said.
'Why didn't you come?'

'I don't think David wanted me there,' said Pitt, who told me
what had happened the following Monday. By then, I suspect he
knew he would not be managing Bowie's affairs much longer,
although another fortnight passed before he gave me his explanation.

What he did not know was that Bowie was now blaming him for
telling his mother about the wedding,* and that senior executives
at Mercury Records and Philips, all personal friends of Pitt's, had
been helping Bowie find a way of breaking his management
contract. Angie claims Bowie had wanted to leave Pitt for months,
but that Bowie's habit was 'to whine a lot and resist, passive-
aggressively, never really speaking up for himself or taking charge
of a situation.... What he actually did wish for, I think, was his
father. The roles in the relationship between David and Ken were
all messed up along *those* lines. David wanted a father figure as
uncritically supportive as his real-life Daddy ...'[4] She also
suggests that sex 'was a significant component of the deal between
Ken and David', but has little hard information to confirm which
course this sexual aspect took, suspecting that if Bowie 'let Ken do
a number on him' this was probably early on. By now, she
believed, 'Ken really wished the best for David, really worked

* He hadn't. Pitt told me that Mrs Jones went down to the local registry office for several
weeks, rightly expecting their intended marriage to be 'posted' – and it was. No one had
told her. She discovered it for herself.

hard for him, and really loved him' – which was how I saw their relationship.

Close though they were, rather than face the choice he wished to make, Bowie began avoiding Manchester Street and refusing to reply to phone calls – until Pitt made the great error of seeming to be a party to Mrs Jones's visit to the registry office. 'Wrong move, Ken darling,' commented Angie, 'you just allied yourself with Private Enemy Number One in David's mind.'[5]

Four or five days after the wedding, there was another dispute between Pitt and Bowie: fundamentally trivial, it showed that neither was responding to the other. Urged to find more bookings for Hype through NEMS, Pitt agreed they would appear in Scarborough on 2 April – only to be told by an angry Bowie that he was already booked that day for a recording session with Visconti.

'My records are important to me,' cried Bowie petulantly. 'I'm not going to cancel the session.'

'Why didn't you tell me?' asked Pitt. 'Or ask Tony to phone me with the dates he wanted reserved? That's the way these things are done ...'

The situation was becoming hopeless, and when Pitt went down to the BBC Playhouse Theatre in Northumberland Avenue, where Bowie was recording two appearances on the radio series *Sounds Of The Seventies* on 25 March, he was virtually frozen out by Bowie and the other musicians. At that moment, says Pitt, he knew 'something was afoot'.

It was. Bowie had been to see Ralph Mace, the Artistes and Repertoires Manager at Philips, and his boss Olav Wyper, the company's General Manager, saying he was unhappy with the way his career was going, and asking for their help in finding new management. Being anxious not to come between artiste and manager, Wyper referred him to a choice of three solicitors who might be able to advise Bowie on how his contract could be terminated.

On 31 March, Bowie phoned and asked if he could see Pitt. They met that afternoon at Manchester Street. 'He seemed to be in a good mood,' says Pitt.[6] 'We talked about this and that, and then he came to the point of the visit ...' Bowie sat on the edge of the *chaise-longue*, where he had perched himself so often before, and said, 'Ken, I want to have a go at managing myself ...'

When Pitt enquired what was the matter, Bowie said he was

worried that he and Hype were spending too much time gigging, and not enough recording, which was the very opposite of what he had said only days before. 'For the time being, perhaps you should accept no more bookings then,' said Pitt, knowing Mercury were willing to again pay Bowie £20 a week while he worked on his next LP with Visconti, *The Man Who Sold The World*, with the group all receiving session fees.

'Just one more thing, Ken,' said Bowie as he was preparing to leave. 'Do you think you could let me have some money in advance?' Without a word of complaint, Pitt took out his chequebook and gave him £200.

When I asked Pitt what he thought was the true reason for Bowie's decision, during a conversation three days later, he seemed bitter. 'David hasn't been the same since he became involved with that Arts Laboratory down in Beckenham and then moved into Haddon Hall,' he said, adding, 'I think his father's death has a lot to do with it. His father was a rock, someone to rely on … and now David is hanging around with these long-haired, left-wing hippies and anarchists, who never wash, don't change their clothes, and think the world stinks…. Marc Bolan and Tony Visconti: they're the worst. They keep filling his head with these ideas that managers are parasites, all determined to rip artistes off and do nothing for their money. They … put down any kind of Establishment figure – which is how they see me. So far as they're concerned, the manager is someone who steals £10 out of every £100 the artist earns, and you can't argue with people who think like that…. They would never think of the manager as the person who made the record sessions and the recording contracts possible.'

Pitt told me he had gone to Trident Studios early in January, the night Bowie recorded *The Prettiest Star* with Bolan playing lead guitar. In the control room he met June Child, who married Bolan three weeks later (on 30 January) and was already part of their circle.

'You're David's Mr Ten Per Cent, aren't you?' were her opening words.

'I don't work that cheaply,' Pitt replied.

'That's how they all think,' Pitt told me. 'It's sad, because David was never like that before. He was always very trusting.'

\*     \*     \*     \*     \*

At the time they parted, David Bowie and The Hype had three bookings left in the diary – at the Stockport Poco Club (27 April), Scarborough Penthouse (21 May) and the Jesus College May Ball at Cambridge University (16 June). Between these dates, time had been set aside to complete *The Man Who Sold The World* and record an extended version of *Memory Of A Free Festival* from Bowie's first Mercury LP, which was released as a double-sided single in both Britain and the United States in June. Bowie was also due to take part in the Ivor Novello Awards telecast on 10 May.

'I was now fairly confident that David's career lay set on a firm foundation,' Pitt says in *The Pitt Report*,[7] adding that he was also discussing plans for Bowie to make a film with Tony Palmer, and appear at the Harrogate Festival in a stage adaptation of Sir Walter Scott's *The Fair Maid Of Perth*, narrating the production, writing the music and performing in a mime sequence. I spoke to Pitt several times that month, and he seemed confident Bowie would be back, picking up the pieces and working with him again, once he found managing his own affairs was not as easy as it sounded. Then on 27 April he received a letter from Bowie: 'I have been advised that you have not performed your part of our Agreement by using your past [sic] endeavours to further my career thereunder.'

His use of the word 'past' instead of 'best' convinced Pitt that Bowie was being primed by someone else. The letter went on to say that Bowie no longer considered him his personal manager, and required his confirmation, within seven days, that he would no longer act in that capacity, an abrupt form of legalese that was not part of Bowie's normal vocabulary.

Pitt replied that he could not give that undertaking, 'but if you care to make an appointment to see me I shall be pleased to discuss with you the ways and means by which we might end our professional relationship'. There was no answer to that letter. Instead, Pitt received a phone call from Godfrey Davis and Batt, a firm of solicitors, arranging an appointment for him to see Mr David Bowie and Mr Anthony Defries. A time and date was agreed: 5 p.m. on Thursday 7 May.

\*   \*   \*   \*   \*

Bowie had nearly finished *The Man Who Sold The World* and The

Hype were no longer working together. The group lasted less than four months in its original form, with Visconti deciding to concentrate upon his work as a producer rather than continue as bass player, John Cambridge departing after one of those flare-ups that often happen in a recording studio when the sound does not come right, and Ronson returning home to Hull, with the thought that if he could not make enough money in London he might as well re-form The Rats.

Meanwhile, Bowie was doing what all musicians tend to do when engaged in disputes with their managers or record companies – nothing, or nothing that would require a contract.

His agreement with Pitt was signed in April 1967, and although it ran initially for only one year it gave Pitt the right to exercise a renewal clause in each of the following four years. (There was a similar clause in Bowie's contract with Mercury Records.) This may sound arcane. The relationship between manager or record company and an artiste is not unlike a marriage contract. Once either party moves in with someone else, the 'marriage' is effectively over, with only the property settlement to be resolved. Bowie and Defries were coming to discuss such a settlement.

Tony Defries never described himself as a solicitor, although some people may have assumed he was. His parents ran their own business in Shepherd's Bush, selling antiques and junk and restoring furniture. Tony, their fourth child, was always delicate with an asthmatic condition. He avoided games, achieved little at school, and it was largely through them that he managed to find a job with Martin Boston, a firm of solicitors with offices in Wigmore Street. Defries found himself in the right office at the right time. Until the British rock 'n' roll boom started in the early 60s, there were few London lawyers specializing in music business law. Once one mentioned the names of Oscar Beuselinck and David Jacobs, it was hard to think of anyone else – yet there was a new breed of wheeler-dealers who needed independent advice. Of these, Mickie Most was phenomenally successful. Initially an artiste himself in the late 50s Most then worked in South Africa as a solo singer. On his return in late 1962, The Beatles were breaking and Most, realizing he was not cut out to be a solo singer, saw a future in producing records. He found The Animals from Newcastle upon Tyne and produced their first single, *House Of The Rising Sun*, a world-wide No. 1 hit in 1964. Subsequent successes included recording Herman's Hermits,

Donovan and Lulu amongst others, and forming his own record company, RAK.

By the time Mickie Most went to Martin Boston's for advice, Defries had already spent nearly ten years with the company, without qualifying as a solicitor but trusted within the office to handle divorce and litigation paperwork. Most wanted someone to help him with The Animals, who were engaged in disputes with each other, with their management and with Most himself. Defries got the job and spent two years at it, dealing with Most nearly every day and negotiating with the New York accountant Allen Klein, another wheeler-dealer who was handling Donovan's affairs and later represented The Rolling Stones and The Beatles.

Having learned what it takes to be a good rock 'n' roll hustler Defries left Martin Boston to become a freelance 'legal adviser'. Defries spent part of his time working with the music accountant Laurence Myers, who also represented The Animals, and part at the offices of Godfrey Davis and Batt, another firm of solicitors taking on music business work. Their offices were in Cavendish Square – and they were one of the three firms recommended to Bowie by Olav Wyper.

Defries was then 26 years old, self-confident, personable, always neatly attired (if a bit flashy), with his curly black hair trimmed short and greased back – and the most enormous nose, a nose of Pete Townshend proportions that some said was larger than Cyrano de Bergerac's. Angie liked his 'refreshing lack of Englishness' and was largely responsible for pushing Bowie into his arms. 'He didn't consider it his job to tell you why you couldn't do what you wanted to do…. He just looked at the problem, then solved it.'[8]

When Bowie and Defries arrived at Manchester Street on 7 May, Pitt made a real effort to accommodate them both. He thought there was still a chance that after a few weeks his boy would be back. (For years Pitt would never rule out this possibility. 'Stranger things have happened,' he would say to me.) Bowie perched on his usual seat, the *chaise-longue*, his 'shiny eyes fixed on the wall in front of him',[9] not saying a word, probably having heard Defries say the words he would soon use so often: 'Don't worry – leave everything to me.'

Pitt agreed there was no point continuing with their management agreement if Bowie was unhappy with it, but as he had dipped deeply into his own pocket to fund Bowie's career, not

least in financing the film *Love You Till Tuesday*,\* Pitt thought he
ought to be compensated for his loss of earnings. Defries seemed
to accept this, but said that as he had no figures to work from he
would need time to think about it. Generally speaking, though, he
opined, this compensation should be based on Bowie's earnings to
date, which had, of course, been minimal – which was largely why
they were sitting there. 'Had he then asked me if I had a sum in
mind, I would have said £2,000, a modest sum that would have
satisfied me, but he did not ask and the meeting ended, along with
my management of David Bowie,' wrote Pitt. As they left, Bowie
shook Pitt's hand and said, 'Thank you, Ken' – which suggests
Defries prepared him for a tougher meeting. Pitt could have
threatened him with an injunction.

Pitt was scathing about them both when I phoned him three
days later. 'David's made a great mistake,' he said. 'He's very
naïve … and he's also trusting, innocent and easily led. This man
Defries is a shyster. He has no right to pretend to be a lawyer. He
has no qualifications…. It's all going to end in tears, and I dread to
think what's going to happen to David in the meantime. He's
surrounding himself now with people who are doing him no good
at all.'

Despite Pitt's bitterness, his feelings of rejection and betrayal, I
had the impression that there was some truth in what he said. I
kept in touch with him over the next 12 years and Pitt always felt
it possible Bowie might return. He kept in constant touch with Mrs
Jones (not knowing how much harm this had done him), with
David Platz at Essex Music, and with friends throughout the music
business whose lives touched Bowie's in one way or another. He
always knew where Bowie was, what he was doing and what his
plans were; and this insight had an irony of its own, for everything
Bowie now did was directly related to his years with Pitt: he
formed a stage act, bringing back Mick Ronson and the other Rats
to be his backing group; he brought back Lindsay Kemp to help
him plan that act, and Natasha Korniloff to design the sets and
costumes; he continued to work with Visconti and Scott as his
producers, and the whole of his new persona, seen first in *The Man
Who Sold The World* and then more clearly in *Hunky Dory* and
*The Rise And Fall Of Ziggy Stardust And The Spiders From Mars*,

\* The film *Love You Till Tuesday* lay in Pitt's cupboard for years until he licensed the
video rights; it is released on video from time to time.

came so clearly through Lou Reed, The Velvet Underground, Iggy
Pop and Andy Warhol, all of whom he discovered through Pitt,
acquiring their sense of alienation and detachment, and matching
this with the deeper sense of literary purpose that also came
through Pitt, who was always in, but never of, the world of rock
'n' roll.

\*    \*    \*    \*    \*

Initially, Bowie may have wanted to manage his own affairs. The
rift wasn't due solely to Pitt's attempts to turn him into a cabaret
performer, or his alleged tip-off to Mrs Jones about the wedding.
Many other factors were niggling away. Pitt had been just as
doubtful as Visconti about *Space Oddity*, seeing the song as too
much of a gimmick to enhance Bowie's long-term reputation as a
songwriter; and then *The Prettiest Star* proved a disaster and
NEMS were finding it hard to line up enough gigs to keep The
Hype in business. 'If you went out on your own with an acoustic
guitar, you would still get £100–£125 a night – so why split it with
three other people?' argued Pitt when Bowie first broached the
matter, once again saying what Bowie did not want to hear.

For once, I believe Angie assessed the situation well when she
said that Bowie 'possessed the unfortunate character defect of
needing everything he did to be his own idea, even when most of
his ideas really came from other people'. In Defries, Bowie found
just the right person to foster this illusion. Although still a young
man, Defries was at heart an old-style Jewish fixer. Like the
previous generation of agents and managers, he was street-wise
rather than well-read, a hard-nosed bullshitter more than a
gentleman – and that suited Bowie. He did not need anyone to tell
him how the business worked, or to introduce him to diverse
cultural interests. What he needed was someone who could make
him a star without questioning his judgement, for David Bowie
was now a fully formed artiste.

11

# The man with the big cigar

David Bowie lay doggo for over a year, writing no songs and recording no music – so far as anyone knew. He gave no interviews, following the usual music business practice of saying nothing and doing nothing when a contract is about to run out. In saying, 'There's nothing to worry about. Leave it all to me,' Defries was also playing a traditional role.

Inevitably, their relationship changed. At their first meeting, Bowie sat in Defries's office, emotionally bereft, scruffy and unwashed, looking as he often would in moments of stress – totally dependent upon the person on the other side of the desk. Ever the office tactician, Defries let him sit there while he looked through papers, answered phone calls and received messages. 'How can I help you?' he asked, once the tea had arrived, and the principle was firmly established that this was *his* office and Bowie could wait until *he* was ready.

Bowie poured out his heart, complaining about Pitt's failure to find him work he wanted, Mercury's lack of promotion, and the hopeless state of his career. While this went on, Defries listened, walked around the room, returned to his desk, shuffled through papers, walked around again, and then gazed through a window down into the street, waiting for Bowie to stop, and then a bit longer while Bowie sat waiting, wondering about his response.

'Yes, you do have a problem,' said Defries, emphasizing that this might not be the one that he thought he had, but the fact that Mercury Records were a company of little consequence with no major artistes on their books who did not know how to handle a rising star. 'The real problem is one of control – they control you, whereas you, as an artiste, should be in control of your own work,' argued Defries, saying that if the staff at Mercury were any good they would be out in the business making money for themselves; the only way to deal with second-rate people was to have control, and that meant changing the basis of the relationship between the artiste and the record company.

Defries knew this was just what Bowie wanted to hear. Anyone who read the trade papers would have known that the leading artistes were trying to gain greater control of their affairs, forming their own publishing and recording companies, and bringing in lawyers and accountants as employees to handle the minutiae of copyright control previously dealt with by old-style music publishing houses.

'Look what happened to The Beatles and The Rolling Stones,' said Defries. Both groups lost millions of pounds by signing away their rights to other companies over which they had no control. 'You have to have control,' he reiterated. This was music to Bowie's ears and he willingly gave Defries what he needed to know, the terms of his contracts with Essex Music, Kenneth Pitt and Mercury Records – and his expectations from those contracts.

Bowie's timing in seeking to place his career in new hands was good. A new agreement had been proposed to Essex Music shortly before Christmas 1969 by which they would have received the rights to three years of Bowie's work in return for an advance against royalties of £5,000, but the terms were never agreed – which was how Essex lost the rights to the first Mercury LP *David Bowie, The Man Who Saved The World, Hunky Dory* and *The Rise And Fall Of Ziggy Stardust And The Spiders From Mars*. Bowie was already free to sign elsewhere.

His contractual situation with Pitt and Mercury was more complicated, because both had the right to exercise option clauses to extend the term of the contracts. 'You should expect them to do that, if only to protect their position,' warned Defries, advising Bowie to lie low and do nothing that might exacerbate the situation. 'You don't have to do anything you don't want to do,' said Defries. 'You're an artiste and you must be allowed to create, to work at your art.... The role of a manager is to make that possible for you, to take all your worries off your shoulders.'

Bowie left in tears. 'I was so relieved that somebody was so strong about things,' he said. 'I was always stronger than everybody else around me, more determined and wanting to do more things, and everybody else was mousy and didn't want to take any risks ... and there was this pillar of strength. It was like everything was going to be different.'[1]

What Bowie may not have known, for Defries had no reason to

tell him, was that Defries was planning to go into artistes' management in partnership with Laurence Myers. Bowie's first meeting with Defries was at Godfrey Davis and Batt, but Defries soon moved to the Regent Street offices where Myers ran the Gem Toby Organisation, which embraced accountancy, legal services, music publishing, artistes' management and, eventually, their own GTO record label.

Gem Toby also represented the songwriter and producer Mike Leander, Gary Glitter, The Glitter Band and The New Seekers. It was housed in a plush suite with heavily glazed windows and deep piled carpets to block out all sound, furniture far too expensive for anyone's needs and Gold Discs on every wall. One visit was enough to make one think, Who's paying for all this? – but Bowie was too naïve to ask.

'You are an artiste' were the words that rang in his ears and, naturally, Angie started inviting their new ally down to Sunday lunch at Haddon Hall, where they would be joined by Dana Gillespie, who was appearing in *Catch My Soul*, the stage musical based on *Othello*. Soon, lunchtime with Defries became their Sunday routine and in the afternoons they would sit around the garden, mapping out the future, sharing their dreams.

'Leave everything to me,' he said, again and again: when advising Bowie on the letter to Pitt once it had been agreed he needed a manager rather than a lawyer; when Bowie had agreed they should try to regain the rights to his Mercury LPs and find a better-known record company and a new publisher; when he insisted that the artiste left free to create should never have to attend auditions or make TV commercials about Wall's Sausages.

'You would be better off staying at home, writing songs, creating music – and it's my job to see that you are free to do that,' argued Defries. When the Bowies said they were short of money, a wad of notes would appear from his pocket. 'A manager should take care of things for you,' he said – and did. Initially, it was small sums of ready cash, but as the outline of Bowie's future became clearer, their financial relationship was put upon a formal footing.

Bowie was delighted when Defries secured a new publishing deal, persuading Chrysalis to pay £5,000 upfront against royalties due on whatever songs Bowie wrote over the next five years, being a minimum of 100 songs, 70 of them recorded. This was a good deal for Chrysalis, giving them rights to both Mercury LPs

(because Essex had not signed a third contract) and most of the
songs on the *Hunky Dory*, *Ziggy Stardust*, *Aladdin Sane* and
*Diamond Dogs* LPs, which earned extra royalties when released as
singles, reissued on compilation LPs, or rerecorded on Bowie's
live albums.

After Gem had been paid their 20 per cent commission this gave
Bowie an immediate £4,000 – the largest sum he had ever
handled, an excuse to go hunting out antiques, glass and furniture
and to provide floor-length curtains for every room at Haddon
Hall. Bowie was even more pleased when Defries agreed to pay
him £400 a month for living expenses, directly into his bank
account, and arranged an overdraft facility. What Bowie never
seemed to realize, or perhaps never thought about, was that these
people were not giving him money through love or affection, but
were making a shrewd, calculated long-term investment, and
Defries was keeping a precise record of every penny spent.

\*     \*     \*     \*     \*

With £400 coming in each month and only £8 rent to pay each
week, the Bowies were as happy as lambs in spring. Bowie bought
two ancient Riley motor cars to restore, parked them outside
Haddon Hall and began dabbling with their engines; the music
room became a studio, packed with instruments and recording
equipment acquired through Essex Music; a grand piano was
moved into the lounge; and the Bowies began stalking the
Kensington markets, those that dealt in high camp fashion and
antiques, and also The Sombrero, where there existed a market in
flesh.

'Do you know The Sombrero?' Pitt asked during one of our
Monday conversations.

'I've been lunching there once or twice a week for years,' I
replied. 'You can get a good plate of spaghetti, a sweet and a
coffee for under ten bob.'

'There's more than spaghetti on offer at night,' said Pitt,
explaining that The Sombrero had become a pick-up point for
gays, rent boys and prostitutes. 'I wouldn't tell anyone you go
there regularly if I were you.'

By day The Sombrero was a pleasant restaurant decorated in
sombre colours with splashes of red. By night the curtains were
drawn, the lights dimmed and down a curving staircase lay one of

London's first discos, playing rhythm 'n' blues to a blasé crowd of gays strutting on a glass dance floor, lit from beneath in changing pastel colours. It was a nighttime mecca for a melange of art students, boutique assistants, hairdressers, models ... and the Bowies. Angie thought The Sombrero 'had a sizzle to it'.[2]

Perhaps it did, but the sizzle was decidedly down-market, louche rather than luxurious – and the Bowies took to calling late at night, circling the dance floor, enjoying their occasional jive and sometimes taking pick-ups back to Haddon Hall, juiced up with amphetamines and hash.

Visconti found their personal lives 'very bizarre ... always turbulent and very strange'.[3] He might be from New York City, but Visconti was conventional at heart and listened in horror as the Bowies returned, sometimes at four o'clock in the morning, giggling, laughing and often drunk, shrieking as they collapsed into bed with lovers of either sex.

In *Backstage Passes*, Angie recalls their friends – the rent boy Mickey King who was bayonetted after attempting to blackmail an Army officer; the 'incredibly gorgeous' Mandi who sold herself to visiting Arabs and spent the money on speed, and, dearest of all, a shirt-maker whom they knew as Freddi Burretti.

Freddi was tall and winsome with blond, curling hair and a hint of hauteur and appeared every night on the dance floor with his friends Daniella and Antonello upon each arm, and soon became another fixture at Haddon Hall, advising the Bowies on their clothes. As with all Bowie's flights of caprice, there was a touch of originality in all this. No other British musician had ever had his own personal live-in fashion designer – but soon Bowie was urging Freddi to change his name to Rudi Valentino and become a singer, creating a group for him (Arnold Corns), promising to write him songs, and giving the poor man the Defries treatment: 'Leave it all to me and I will make you a star.' Or, at least, this was what Bowie said, telling me at the time: 'Rudi Valentino will be a bigger star than Mick Jagger, who is finished.' Only later did I discover that the vocals for the three songs recorded by 'Arnold Corns' – *Moonage Daydream*, *Hang On To Yourself* and *Man In The Middle* – were actually by David Bowie, and the whole jaunt was a blind with Bowie unable to issue records in his own name while still under contract to Mercury. Bowie told me the other members of Arnold Corns were previously in a group known as

Runk – and that was a blind, too, for Bowie was actually on the verge of creating The Spiders from Mars.

\* \* \* \* \*

On completing *The Man Who Sold The World* in May 1970, Ronson and Woodmansey returned home to Hull, never expecting to hear from Bowie again. 'We hadn't been making any money and I thought it was all over,' said Ronson. They re-formed The Rats with bass player Trevor Bolder, whose father ran a record shop in Hull, and, changing their name to Ronno, recorded one single, *The Fourth Hour Of My Sleep*. 'When that failed, I thought this is the end,' said Ronson. 'It made me miserably depressed, and then one night the phone rang and there was David on the line, sounding chipper and ready to go. "What are you staying up there for?" he said. "There's nothing doing in Hull, is there? Why don't you come back here? I've got some sessions to do and you can stay with us.... Catch the next train down and we'll meet you at King's Cross."' Ronson, Woodmansey and Bolder moved into Haddon Hall, with session fees being paid by Chrysalis, and Defries giving them a weekly allowance – £30 for Ronson, £20 for Woodmansey and £15 for Bolder.

Meanwhile, to fulfil the terms of his Mercury contract, Bowie recorded *Holy, Holy, Holy* which was released as a single in Britain in January 1971 with *Black Country Rock* as its B-side. He appeared on Granada TV to promote it, playing acoustic guitar. In the US, Mercury released another LP track, *All The Madmen*, as a single, and also the album itself, six months before it became available in Britain.

After nearly nine months in seclusion, Bowie was becoming restless. Everyone was telling him he would be a star. He had new management, a new publishing deal and his own backing group, but what would he look like, what would his image be? His acolytes from The Sombrero were moving into Haddon Hall with the musicians, with this strange Victorian folly becoming home to an admiring menage that revolved around his every whim. Buretti would be in one room with Daniella, Antonello and Angie, pinning up tucks and stitching away with their sewing machines; the kitchen bubbled away with stews and spaghetti; and there was soon a resident hairdresser and before going out, the Bowies

would be styled for every occasion, their faces adorned with make-up, their hair blow-waved and sprayed in many colours.

When the time came to choose a sleeve for the new album, Mercury were astonished to receive a set of colour transparencies from the Haddon Hall art-house in which Bowie looked more like a woman than a man, wearing a long, flowery silk dress bought from Mr Fish for £300, reclining casually on a *chaise-longue*, draped in blue silk, his blond hair flowing around his shoulders towards his breast, a rose in one hand and the Queen of Diamonds in the other, with playing cards scattered across the carpet. (This was too much for the Mercury head office in Chicago, who released the LP in the US with another design chosen by Bowie. As a joke, he asked a friend, Mick Weller, to draw a cartoon that was the very opposite of the original; Weller came up with a design showing a butch cowboy walking past the Cane Hill mental institution, and another of Bowie looking like a native American. Mercury chose a monochrome photo, instead.)

\*    \*    \*    \*    \*

Mercury invited Bowie to the US at the end of January 1971, and initially it was thought he would recover his expenses by performing at clubs in the major cities, but those plans came to nothing. Having married an American citizen, Bowie was able to work in the States, but Ronson, Woodmansey and Bolder needed work permits. Rather than miss the opportunity, Bowie went to the States alone, packing his bags with a strange array of dresses and feminine make-up. When his plane landed at Washington International Airport on 27 January, Mercury's Publicity Director Ron Oberman was waiting on the tarmac.

All the other passengers disembarked, and after a gap of several minutes there was still no sign of Bowie. After 45 minutes, he emerged, his freshly brushed hair falling across his shoulders, wearing what looked like a woman's dress and appearing a little shaken. When he began to put on his women's clothes, straighten his dress, brush his hair and apply make-up, one of the cabin crew alerted the US immigration authorities. Strict rules were applied in those days – no homosexuals, no drug-users and no Communists. Bowie was subjected to heavy questioning and a body search before being allowed off the plane.

'I had a wonderful time,' Bowie told me when he came back.

'The LP has been selling well and there have been lots of radio plays.... It's gone Top Ten in some cities, but not nationally.... They're ready for something new over there. The Americans are open-minded to all kinds of music.'

In reality, his visit was low-key – but it gave Bowie a new sense of perspective. Since first reading Kerouac and discovering Little Richard, Bowie had been obsessed by America, even to the point of wearing American clothes and following baseball. He had always known this was where he would have to go to make his name, and now here he was in Washington, meeting Oberman's parents, being introduced to their friends, and taken around radio stations in Washington, New York and Chicago.

Those who met him were intrigued. His music set him apart, and now his imagery, mincing and prancing, playing the game – more like Lauren Bacall than a sweaty rocker. His first important interview was with John Mendelsohn of *Rolling Stone*, who was told that his readers should 'make up their minds about me when I begin getting adverse publicity – when I'm found in bed with Raquel Welch's husband'. Scything through all the imagery, Mendelsohn commented, 'Bowie's music offers an experience that is as intriguing as it is chilling, but only to the listener sufficiently together to withstand its schizophrenia.'

That last word said it all. There always seemed to be an undertone of schizophrenia in everything Bowie did, here as everywhere else. He flirted with the gays in San Francisco, but never responded to their advances. Provided with a woman for the night, he would retreat to bed with a spring in his step, always the closet heterosexual if the truth be known; but what did it matter? He would be wearing a dress in the morning.

In Los Angeles, his schedule was planned by Rodney Bingenheimer, Mercury's West Coast promotion man, an all-night creature who liked nothing more than floating around the LA discos with a drink in his hand. He arranged for Bowie to stay at a mansion in the Hollywood Hills owned by Tom Ayers (a manager, and a record producer for RCA) which came complete with an Olympic-sized swimming pool and Ayers's Cadillac Convertible. Bowie saw Los Angeles in style, his hair trailing in the breeze – and knew what he was doing.

Rock music should be 'tarted up, made into a prostitute, a parody of itself,' Bowie told *Rolling Stone*. 'It should be the clown, the Pierrot medium ...' And who better to play the part?

Bowie's aim was to be outrageous, to affix himself in the public
memory by out-shocking everyone else, a familiar ploy in rock 'n'
roll since Elvis first waggled his crotch, but effective always,
especially with a perfect foil like Bingenheimer, whose grovelling
demeanour, skinny physique and rotten teeth made them look like
Powerhouse and Pimp. 'He wasn't coming on like a girl,'
Bingenheimer observed.[4] 'He was grabbing girls right and left ...
picking up girls hitch-hiking in the street.'

Lou Siegel, Mercury's publicist in Los Angeles, was in no
doubt that Bowie 'was doing this act for effect and aware of the
effect he was producing.... He was smart, determined to make it,
worked hard, and did whatever was necessary.'[5] It did not bother
Siegel that when he took Bowie out to a restaurant, the waiter
refused to serve them, believing Bowie to be a transvestite. This
was all part of the game. More good copy.

*   *   *   *   *

In the long run, just as Bowie expected, it was not the radio
interviews or meeting the press that made this first US visit
successful, but the new friendships, meeting people who were
willing to go out of their way to help him advance his career.
Through Bingenheimer, he played the field at the Whisky A Go
Go, partied around the Hollywood Hills and picked up movie
gossip. Through Ayers, he met Gene Vincent and the Andy
Warhol superstar Ultra Violet, who were both recording albums
for RCA with Ayers as their producer. Bowie told him of his
interest in Lou Reed, Iggy Pop and Warhol. 'You really should be
with RCA,' said Ayers, telling him Reed was also being signed to
the label. 'I love it here.... They're very supportive and they don't
interfere at all. The only thing they've got is Elvis. You'll get
world-wide coverage, tour support and a lot of money.'[6]

Ayers arranged for Bowie to meet Greylun Landon, head of
publicity for RCA on the West Coast, who had worked with
Presley since the 50s. Landon was impressed by Bowie's quiet
confidence and gentle manners. 'He's very bizarre,' said Landon,
'but I think he's going to be the Bob Dylan of the 70s.' Relaying
this to Bowie, Ayers added: 'You have a real shot there.' So he
had, but there were problems to be resolved: Mercury were
entitled to one more album under their contract; Ronson was

thinking his group Ronno might record in their own right; and who was going to produce Bowie's records?

Those late-night comings-and-goings at Haddon Hall had been too much for Visconti; furthermore, he disliked Defries. 'I didn't mind what they did in their bedroom,' said Visconti, 'but there were people trying to get into our bedroom as well.'[7] So Visconti moved out, and quit as Bowie's producer when Bowie signed with Defries.

Initially, when Defries was seen as 'the show business lawyer', Visconti was willing for Defries to act for him as well, writing letters to people who owed him money, but the relationship changed when Visconti thought Bowie was becoming far too trusting. 'David was in a state at that time, saying he had signed these things years ago and here was Defries saying he could get him out of anything,' said Visconti during the Kerry Juby radio series, adding that what happened thereafter made him 'very suspicious'.

The crunch came when Pitt's contract with Bowie lapsed and Defries felt able to produce his own management contract for Bowie to sign, suggesting that Visconti also be contracted just as he was becoming a highly rated producer working with Marc Bolan as well as Bowie. There was a suspicion in Visconti's mind that Defries was trying to acquire a percentage of all his earnings, and he thought the terms of Bowie's contract were 'crazy'. As they stood in Regent Street after meeting Defries at the Gem offices, Visconti told Bowie bluntly: 'He's trying to rip you off.'

This was not how Bowie saw his relationship with Defries, in whom he now had the same blind confidence that he had once shown in Pitt; a confidence that was reinforced by the monthly funding he received from Defries when they were not bound together by any form of contract. 'He's not like that at all,' said Bowie. 'You've got him all wrong ...'

'Well, it's your decision,' said Visconti. 'But if you're going with Defries, I'm not going with you ...'

\*     \*     \*     \*     \*

There was one other factor that may have influenced Bowie's judgement: the success of Marc Bolan. Their friendship had endured six or seven years but, as I have mentioned before, it was always competitive, with their careers and personal lives running in a curious, off-beat parallel. Each would attend the other's studio sessions more than either cared to admit, and when not working spent hours at each other's apartments playing music, following Buddhism, discussing art and politics, gazing into crystal balls and fantasizing about their futures.

When one married, so did the other – but they both had a taste for black women, too. Angie Bowie describes this as her husband's 'strong preference for women of African extraction'.[8] Bolan put it more bluntly, but with a touch of self-mockery, when he told me with a wicked grin, 'I've always wanted a little black pussy to call my own.'

It was a genuinely creative friendship, and my view has long been that Bolan was one of the more under-rated British rock stars. I used to see Bolan regularly, enjoying his company as much as Bowie's. Both were far more political than they liked to appear (which was easy for me to identify with), and their interests in the arts and literature were original and innovative, with Bolan as keen as Bowie to keep abreast of new ideas, no matter where they came from. We would have good conversations about European cinema, artists such as Schiele, Erté or Modigliani, or books that we might have read.

In 1970/1, Bolan and his everchanging group T. Rex suddenly captured teenage hearts with *Ride A White Swan*, following this immediately – while Bowie was in America – with the No. 1 hit *Hot Love* and then *Get It On* and *Jeepster*. Bolan was doing something that Bowie was increasingly reluctant to attempt, playing it simple and banging the gong in the teenage market, which have always been dangerous quicksands. Visconti was making it happen, and Bolan was responding to his success by working harder than ever, souped up with amphetamines, going into the studio whenever he had a spare few hours and recording new songs on the hoof. Bolan would have wanted first call on Visconti, and it was not in his nature to share him.

And then there was another problem, too. Bowie was sometimes unreliable, missing appointments or turning up late for sessions – especially when he would rather be in bed with Angie or someone else. This happened particularly on *The Man Who Sold The World* sessions and drove Visconti to distraction. 'They would be cuddling and cooing and wooing,' he says.[9] 'I suppose if you were either one of them it would be nice but I'd go out and say to them, "David, it's time for us to do a vocal now" and Angie would say,

"Oh, Davey Wavey, do you have to leave me now?" to which he would reply, "Oh, Angie Pangie, I suppose I do".... It was absolutely nauseating to be involved with. The album didn't go smoothly at all.... On the last day of the mix, I remember telling David, "I've had it. I can't work like this any more. I'm through. I've got Marc Bolan who wants to record day and night and is keen to go, and I might as well put my energies into him because you really don't want to work very hard."' So there was that undertone, as well, with Visconti torn between the two – and suspecting Defries of trying to gain a slice of his Bolan income.

But Bowie was willing to replace Visconti rather than lose Defries, and signed several contracts with him during 1971. How Pitt came to know the terms of these contracts, I do not know; but he did, and discussed them with me. I made no mention of any of this in *The David Bowie Story*, either, for there was no way of knowing then whether his information was correct or his denunciation of Defries justified.

'The man's a bastard,' he told me, using a word I would not have expected from him. 'He's got David by the balls and he'll destroy him ...' The first part of that sentence was true. The second was not.

Bowie came back to Britain, convinced he should sign with RCA Records, and determined not to be eclipsed by Bolan. 'They were both jealous of each other and it ran deep,' says Tony Secunda, who heard of this rivalry from the other side. Bowie brought The Rats back down from Hull again, working with more concentration than ever before. Defries would only call him up to town when there was decisions to be talked through, or papers to sign.

In essence, the sequence of events thereafter was very simple. Irwin Steinberg and Robin McBride flew to London intending to offer Bowie a new contract with Mercury. Under his existing agreement, Bowie was due to deliver this third album and they met Bowie and Defries for lunch at the Londonderry Hotel. After all the usual polite preliminaries, they outlined their proposal, stressing how much faith they had in Bowie, and their willingness to help him in his career.

'No,' said Defries. 'There will be no contract – and no third album!'

Astonished by this summary rejection, Steinberg and McBride turned to Bowie whose eyes did not meet theirs. Steinberg then said, 'Unless you let us have that third album, we won't release from you from the contract.'

'If you want to have the third album, we'll give you crap,' Defries said, invoking the same tactic that The Rolling Stones had used against Decca. Steinberg and McBride were horrified to discover there was nothing in their contract to say Bowie could not deliver them an off-key choral version of *The Star-Spangled Banner*, if that was what he wanted. Totally out-manoeuvred, Steinberg and McBride said they would discharge Bowie from all his contractual obligations, and also let Bowie have back the rights to his two Mercury albums, if he would repay the monies spent by Mercury in promoting his career. This was eventually calculated to be $17,884.41 under a termination contract dated 27 September 1971.

Meanwhile, through Gem's American lawyers, Laurence Myers arranged for Defries to meet Dennis Katz, head of Artistes and Repertoire at RCA Records. Defries arrived there with acetates of Bowie's latest recordings, and it was agreed that Bowie should record three new albums; RCA subsequently agreed to advance the monies so that rights to the two Mercury LPs could be bought back. Under his RCA agreement, Bowie was required to deliver the three new albums within two years. As he had already finished *Hunky Dory* and was now working on *Ziggy Stardust*, this meant RCA would pay upfront for both albums. They were due to pay an advance of $37,500 for each album, against a royalty of 11 per cent, with half ordinarily due when recording started and the other half on delivery of the finished recording. In this situation, RCA agreed to pay the $37,500 for *Hunky Dory* and also the $18,750 due for *Ziggy Stardust* in one lump sum when contracts were signed in September. They also agreed to advance a further $20,000 so that Bowie could buy back the two Mercury LPs.

While the fine print for these contracts was being agreed between lawyers for both sides, a separate recording agreement was drawn up between Bowie and Gem, dated 1 August 1971 and running for six years. On 12 August 1971, Bowie also signed a management contract with Defries. This was backdated to April 1970 and contained no clause specifying when it would end: in other words, he was bound to Defries in perpetuity.

By the time the Mercury termination contract and the contracts with RCA were due to be signed, there were other documents for Bowie's signature. Rights in the two Mercury LPs were returned to him, and he then assigned them to Gem. As he now had a recording agreement with Gem his contracts with RCA were also through Gem. RCA paid Gem a total of $76,250. In return, Gem agreed to license his two past and three future LPs to RCA – and used the money, quite properly, to reimburse Mercury and recoup those monthly sums Defries credited to Bowie's bank account, and the monies spent by Gem enabling him to record his songs.

Under the deals Defries had agreed for him so far, Chrysalis had the rights to publish his songs, and Gem had the rights to his recordings, which would now be distributed by RCA. Bowie was happy. Once the money had been received from RCA, he was told his debts to Defries had been paid and he was given £4,000. That money was his, for him to spend, however he wished. He was almost a star ...

12

# The debts start mounting

David Bowie bubbled with energy all through the summer of 1971. His music was good and he knew it. He was recording dozens of songs, making demos in his own music room or at the Radio Luxembourg studios where Chrysalis booked him time. Meanwhile, the Bowies had a new game to play – Mummies and Daddies.

Bowie warmed to being a father as the date grew nearer, although he and Angie would still arrive at The Sombrero late at night, with her belly 'the size of the Goodyear blimp'.[1] She was aware of his other lovers, or at least some of them, and must have accepted it, for there were no separations on that score. Bowie continued to be cold, 'frigid' being the word she sometimes uses, but they were affectionate enough on the surface, with Bowie going along to the antenatal clinic when she went for her monthly check-ups.

Their son was born at Bromley Hospital on 28 May 1971. It was a difficult birth. He was a large baby – 8lb 8oz – and having narrow hips, Angie cracked her pelvis in delivery, after being in labour for 36 hours. They called the baby Duncan Zowie Heywood Jones, and his birth prompted Bowie to write one of his most affectionate songs, *Kooks*, which dances along like a lullaby with Bowie warning Zowie his parents are: 'a couple of Kooks/ Hung up on romancing'.

So far I have barely touched on the content of Bowie's songs, for a reason. Many songwriters evolve as they master technique. Others are born with a gift and spend their lives finding ways to express it, and that's how I have always seen David Bowie. One cannot look at his output and trot out the same tired clichés, saying this album is 'worse' or that 'better', and trying to establish some mythological progression between them all. Even Bowie's early songs are expressed with an intricacy usually missing in rock music.

Take a song like *She's Got Medals*, recorded for his first album in 1967. It might appear a fairly conventional song, but there is a subtlety in the lyric that is not immediately obvious. This is a song about a girl 'whose mother called her Mary', but who changed her name to Tommy: 'She went and joined the Army/passed a medical – don't ask me how it's done'. As a man, she wears a trench coat, khaki and hobnailed boots, plays 'a good game of darts' and is often first at the bar to buy a round of drinks – but when she finds herself at the Front, 'he' becomes 'she' again, buying herself silk dresses, changing her name to Eileen, and successfully deserting the Army in this guise. Back in London, she re-establishes herself as a woman, with no one aware of her past. The title of the song is also the chorus, a double-entendre with 'She's got medals' being a slang euphemism for male genitals in one part of the song, and a simile for courage in another.

Or take another song from the same album, *Please Mr Gravedigger*, which opens to the sound of bombs falling and the toll of a church bell. This is a neat exercise in irony, with a similar theme to that in Dylan Thomas's poem, *Among Those Killed In The Dawn Raid Was A Man Aged A Hundred*: the bombs are killing those who are dying anyway. In Bowie's lyric, the bombs are falling on a graveyard in Lambeth (his birthplace, Brixton, is in Lambeth) where, amidst rain, thunder and tolling bells, the singer tells the gravedigger: 'Don't be ashamed/as you dig little holes/for the dead and the maimed', and then tells us why he is there, standing by the grave of a ten-year-old child: 'I was the man who took her life away', and now he knows that he is going to die, as well.

At any point in Bowie's early career, there are songs with lyrics as advanced as these; advanced in the sense that in storytelling and use of either imagery or allegory, they were far ahead of what other songwriters of the day were trying to achieve within the format of the contemporary pop song. Bowie was seldom whimsical, like Harry Nilsson or Randy Newman, and, in my view unlike Pete Townshend, usually wrote songs with more than one obvious meaning.

Even work from his Anthony Newley phases – such as *Maids Of Bond Street* or *The Laughing Gnome* – should not be written off as being too derivative, for there is nearly always an undercurrent idea, a trick with words, a hidden pun, or an unusual blend of lyrics and harmony that sets them apart.

*The Laughing Gnome*, recorded with producer Mike Vernon and released by Deram in 1967, has often been ridiculed. Roy Carr and Charles Shaar Murray, two of the better music writers, dismiss it as 'undoubtedly the most embarrassing example of Bowie juvenilia', adding that 'the most generous assessment' of it would be to 'consider it as Bowie's equivalent to The Beatles' *Yellow Submarine*'.[2] They make the right comparison – Lennon and McCartney drew upon the music hall tradition as much as Bowie: in their childhoods, as in mine, the touring shows at the Liverpool Empire were the main form of live entertainment – but with a sneer that offends. Where Bowie differs is that he takes an idea that seems simple and then gives it a twist, introducing puns, jokes and similes. He gives his laughing gnome a roasted toadstool and a glass of dandelion wine, before putting him on the train to Eastbourne – only to find that by some unexplained magic the gnome is sitting on the end of his bed next morning when he wakes up. 'Haven't you got a gnome to go to?' sings the punning songwriter, accusing the gnome of behaving like a Rolling Gnome. The story ends with the annoying gnome dancing away to the tune: 'I'm a laughing gnome and you can't catch me'.* There were no word-plays like that on *Yellow Submarine*. Several of Bowie's early songs, particularly *Love You Till Tuesday*, *Silly Boy Blue*, *Rubber Band*, *Sell Me A Coat* and *London Boys*, possess something more than juvenilia, and each leads in its own way to the sudden flowering of Bowie's talent between 1969 and 1971.

*     *     *     *     *

There is a general assumption in many of the books about Bowie that his career took shape with the success of *The Rise And Fall Of Ziggy Stardust And The Spiders From Mars*, which caused a sensation in 1972, coinciding as it did with his new stage act, a British tour and Defries's ploy of treating Bowie like a star before he was one. Roy Carr and Charles Shaar Murray go back a little

---

* On Bowie's tour with Tin Machine in 1991 and 1992, a small group in every audience shouted 'Sing us *The Laughing Gnome*' between numbers. This also happened on other tours. On each occasion, Bowie feigns deafness or smiles bleakly. I suspect that if he stopped the show, sang *The Laughing Gnome* and asked the audience to join in the chorus, complete with 'Chipmunk' sounds, there would be nightly standing ovations and calls for an encore.

further, and suggest 'the story really starts' with the release of *The Man Who Sold The World* in 1971. My view is that Bowie was a fully formed creative artist well before this: the first Mercury LP, recorded in late summer 1969, is the starting-point for anyone studying Bowie.

In *Cygnet Committee*, he rejects the overall hippie ideal that first drew him to the Arts Laboratory, but plucks from their philosophy the transient *Memory Of A Free Festival* and the Eastern storytelling of *The Wild Eyed Boy From Freecloud* (both of which he later rerecorded in more substantial form). In their underlying ideas, these are songs that prepare one for *The Man Who Sold The World*, where he began working with the nucleus of a backing group, augmented by Ralph Mace, the Artistes and Repertoire Manager at Mercury, who had an interest in synthesizers. His Moog underlines the lyrical darkness of the eight-minute opening track, *The Width Of A Circle*, and others such as *All The Madmen, Running Gun Blues, The Supermen* and the title track, which show the real Bowie of private conversation and intellectual thought embracing the rock medium properly for the first time. These are strong songs – and one can understand him wanting the rights back from Mercury.

In *The Width Of A Circle*, we find him exploring schizophrenia in ways that could be autobiographical, for he notes that in the past all his roads have been straight and narrow but now he has come across a monster 'and the monster was me'. When he the songwriter asks for help, 'a simple black bird/who was as happy as can be' laughs himself insane and recommends Khalil Gibran, in gentle mockery of prevailing hippie ethos, in which the writings of this Lebanese mystic had become required reading. Bowie says he cried for all the other mystics, realizing he would 'never go down to the gods again', a refrain that Bowie repeats again and again, with the phrase 'Do it again' wavering in counter-point. What does all this mean? Aha – that's the secret. When we had that long conversation referred to in the Introduction, I expressed my belief that in all great art explanation lies in the mind of the beholder, and that no one meaning may necessarily be correct. This was a theory we discussed at length, with Bowie arguing that an artiste should always hold something back; as in this instance. In *The Width Of A Circle* he masters the technique of *suggestion*.

With *All The Madmen*, he looks at the insanity of the world around him, comparing his own situation in life with those of others: 'Day after day/they send my friends away/to mansions cold and grey'. This I take to refer to the Cane Hill mental institution, where his half-brother was already living. His implication is that the world is a mad place, and while it is tempting to escape it temporarily through drugs, 'it's pointless to be high/'cos it's such a long way down'. Clear drug references run throughout this song, which escaped the music paper critics, who were looking for simpler explanations. His only truly personal comment is: 'Don't set me free/I'm as helpless as can be/my libido's split on me/ gimme some good lobotomy.' Here I believe he is looking at mental illness as both patient and observer, sounding lighthearted when he sings it, but making the point that because his libido is split – a suggestion that he already thinks himself bisexual – others may think him in need of psychiatric treatment, too. He may even be making the point that bisexuality and schizophrenia could be considered twin conditions.

In *Running Gun Blues*, Bowie uses the deceptive simplicity of the traditional three-minute pop song (it actually runs for 3 minutes 11 seconds), with conventional melody and riff, to argue that War destroys Man. Bowie makes his point through telling the story of a Vietnam veteran who develops a taste for killing and finds he cannot control it.

There are some tracks that do not work for me, notably *Black Country Rock, Saviour Machine* and *She Shook Me Cold*, but overall there is a developing pattern between the two Mercury albums and what came next and there can be little doubt that David Bowie was already fully rounded as both writer and performer before he made the switch from Pitt to Defries, from Mercury to RCA, and from Essex to Chrysalis.

\*    \*    \*    \*    \*

During the 18 months that Bowie waited, relying upon Defries to sort out his problems, his writing methods changed. In the past, when studio time had to be carefully calculated and all costs kept within a budget, Bowie would often have finished lyrics and musical arrangements written for the session musicians before going into the studio. This may be why so many of his earlier songs sound over-orchestrated. Now, he had his own music room at Haddon Hall where he would work on songs with Ronson, Woodmansey and Bolder, or just Ronson alone, producing demo tapes of near studio quality. This meant he was putting more of his own personal stamp upon each song, becoming his own musical arranger.

One can hear this new authority on *The Man Who Sold The World*, and it comes through even more markedly on the LPs that followed, *Hunky Dory, Ziggy Stardust* and *Aladdin Sane*. I interviewed Bowie again at length just before *Hunky Dory* was released and he told me had written and recorded enough songs for five albums, but he was still as ill-prepared as everyone else around him for the sudden fame that came with the next LP, *Ziggy Stardust*. I can say that with some certainty, for I also interviewed him again at the Royal Ballroom in Tottenham High Road in the third week of January 1972 when he was rehearsing a stage act with Ronson, Woodmansey and Bolder. Even as late as that, several months after completing *Ziggy Stardust*, Bowie told me he and Defries had still not chosen a name for his backing group, and neither had they decided whether he and the group should go out on the road in costume or in jeans and T-shirts. 'That's a big decision,' Bowie told me, 'because once you've made your choice you're stuck with it.'

Whether he was ready or not, Bowie *had* to start gigging that spring. The RCA money had run out and he needed the cash. The wages for Ronson, Bolder and Woodmansey were being debited from his account with Gem, as were his recording costs, the costs of instruments and equipment, costumes and travel, and his own monthly allowance for living expenses. His debts were rising by at least £5–6,000 a month, and by the end of that year were to rise even more – although by then there was regular income. By June, he owed Gem nearly £30,000, and although he would eventually spend far more on the back of *Ziggy Stardust*, it was clearly beginning to trouble him. When we spoke at the Royal Ballroom, he was unusually tetchy about the cost of costumes.

Choosing the name may also have been a question of money. How *could* they call themselves The Spiders from Mars if they still looked like The Rats from Hull?

Whatever the reason, Bowie began touring the usual circuit for nearly successful groups that February – the Toby Jug at Tolworth, High Wycombe Town Hall, Imperial College, London, and so on. Posters at every venue billed him simply as 'DAVID BOWIE' with no mention of any backing band. When he appeared at the Dunstable Civic Hall on 21 June, the promoter also added the extraordinary description that he was 'THE FLAME OF THE HOME COUNTIES', which all tends to underline my argument that although he may have told me that he had recorded enough material for five albums, and now had all the resources of RCA behind him, David Bowie was working within very tight finances as he awaited the release of these first two RCA albums.

\*   \*   \*   \*   \*

*Hunky Dory* was the first to be released (although it only became a hit album after the success of *Ziggy Stardust*) and continued in a similar vein to *The Man Who Sold The World*. It opened with an outstanding track, *Changes*, in which Bowie once again explored subtle questions of identity within the pop format ('I turned to face me/But I've never caught a glimpse/of how the others/must see the faker'), continuing with a well-developed simile between time and water and 'the stream of warm impermanence' with which he equates life – all life is transitory – and noting that other young people's lives are slipping away, he asserts 'Time may change me/ but I can't trace time'.

Either Bowie or Defries offered the next track, *Oh, You Pretty Things* to producer Mickie Most as a possible song for Peter Noone, who had a hit with it six months before *Hunky Dory* was released. The lyric was far too subtle for the boy-faced star of Herman's Hermits, with its underlying notions of bisexuality, hints of uncertain personality, and a refrain about the 'pretty things' who are driving their mamas and papas insane. Still, Noone did stamp his own personality on the song in one respect, changing the line 'the earth is a bitch' to 'the earth is a beast', with which he must have felt more comfortable.

*Andy Warhol* has lyrics of rare ingenuity – so rare that Warhol was upset when Bowie played it to him. In several lines, Bowie appears to be mocking Warhol's appearance, suggesting that instead of drugs he must be taking cement mix and that in substance he may be no more than his image: 'Andy Warhol looks a scream/Hang him on my wall/Andy Warhol, Silver Screen/Can't tell them apart at all' – which came dangerously close to *lèse-majesté*.

*Song For Bob Dylan* takes up the theme that Dylan should return to the style of music and writing with which he first found an audience, with Bowie saying 'you gave your soul to every bedsit room', including his own, for the lyric indicates Bowie must have had a portrait of Dylan on his bedroom wall at Plaistow Grove, and that in his own early approach to music he was inspired by this American songwriter with 'a voice like sand and glue'. However, Bowie argues that Dylan has since lost his way and ends with the wish that he would 'Give us back our unity/Give us back our family'. This suggests Bowie believed that the liberal ideas and attitudes of Dylan's early writing would only become accepted again when Dylan himself returned to those roots. Bowie was stepping beyond the ritualized boundaries of the pop song to express an argument, pleading for what Dylan stands for as much as for the singer himself.

All the tracks on *Hunky Dory* contain something original, a personal insight, from the *Eight Line Poem* with its conclusion 'the key to the city is in the sun/that pins the branches to the sky' to the song that he wrote for his son, *Kooks*, and what I believe to be Bowie's third song about the end of his affair with Hermione Farthingale, *Life On Mars?*. The title gives few clues to the song, for this is actually a haunting refrain about the end of 'a God-awful small affair' between a girl with mousy hair and the lover her parents cannot stand, thickened with personal allusions that Bowie has never made any attempt to explain. My understanding is that he was particularly hurt when Hermione left Feathers, and also left him, having not only fallen for someone else, but also been offered a small role in the Harry Secombe film *The Song Of Norway*, which he was convinced lay far beneath her talents. In *Life On Mars?*, the girl is 'hooked to the silver screen' and Bowie expresses his contempt for her choice: 'the film is a saddening bore/for she's lived it ten times or more', and goes on to compare the world she is prepared to live in with others that he would prefer, with allusions to John Lennon, America and the need to avoid living one's life like other people. In this he uses as an image the package tour trade: 'the mice in their million hordes/ from Ibiza to the Norfolk Broads'.

Although I think I know what the song is all about, it is all the more effective for not being certain. Bowie bares his wounds but not his soul, giving *Life On Mars?* that extra element of mystery, especially when he compares the world that she wants to move to with what he has to offer, saying that in his the sailors fight in the dance halls and lawyers beat up the wrong man, but nevertheless: 'Oh man! Look at these cavemen go', a repeated line that suggests his reference to 'cavemen' is probably a private joke, perhaps a name she called him when they argued over her decision to leave.

*Queen Bitch* confirms the influence of Lou Reed in Bowie's life, for it's a wry, New York song, a look down the wild side from the eleventh floor of his hotel at the gays cruising below on the sidewalk where the Queen Bitch is 'trying hard to pull sister Flo'; and how he wishes, he says, that he was down there on the sidewalk with them rather than in his cot, gazing at the hotel wall.

*Quicksand* is the only political song on *Hunky Dory*, with Bowie comparing the appeal of different heroes, leaders or charismatic figures from Aleister Crowley to Himmler, Garbo, Churchill and Brigitte Bardot, a muddled selection of names with no natural thread between them, suggesting he had not thought through the idea clearly enough. His message was plain: avoid following leaders, for they lead you through quicksands, but it needed to be put with more subtlety than this.

The final track, *The Bewlay Brothers*, was straight from the heart. Bowie has refused to explain the song, but the fact that he chose its title for one of his own publishing companies suggests its importance to him – almost certainly because it concerns his half-brother Terry. But why 'Bewlay' brothers? Or is it meant to be pronounced as BOWlay or BEAUlay with, perhaps, a matching of the names Bowie and Newley, as in Anthony Newley? So far as one can tell, this was not a family name and there are no clues within the lyric. When asked about its origin, Bowie said, 'I can't imagine what the person who wrote that had on his mind at the time.' Roy Carr and Charles Shaar Murray say he also described it as '*Star Trek* in a leather jacket',[3] which is equally unhelpful.

If Bowie was a poet, writing with his library and reference books all around him, one might be tempted to draw parallels between the chapels of Beulah or the ancient word 'bewray', meaning to reveal involuntarily, but he isn't that obtuse, is he? Carr and Shaar Murray suggest the Bewlay Brothers may be a reference to the older gods of ancient mythology, but I am not sure they are right – and neither are they. Even the music critic Wilfrid Mellers, in a characteristically overblown analysis written especially for *The Bowie Companion*,[4] admits that 'the subversive meanings of this song can only be difficult to decipher', commenting: 'The music is a shade nightmarish as the Bewlay Brothers, "real cool traders" and "kings of oblivion", float lyrically up to F-sharp while the original ostinato is reiterated at the original pitch, again subsiding on an interrupted cadence in C instead of D ...'

Mellers, who was widely ridiculed when he wrote in a similar vein about The Beatles, was clearly baffled, while the Gillmans argue there is a homosexual theme to the song, suggesting that 'I was Stone and he was wax/So he could scream, and still relax' was 'a precise description for successful homosexual intercourse'.[5] This I do not believe, for it does not explain other equally compelling imagery: 'the grim face on the Cathedral floor' or 'it was stalking time for the Moonboys' or 'you thought we were the fakers'.

Significantly, most Bowie biographers miss *The Bewlay Brothers* out altogether, rather than face the challenge – so let me try. My theory is that the lyric describes the relationship between Bowie and his half-brother, describing how they dressed up in clothes that were not theirs, either metaphorically or in a physical sense, to hold a seance, i.e. when they were 'stalking the Moonboys' and were trying to communicate with the dead – and that the experiment went terribly wrong at a time when Terry's incipient insanity was only just becoming clear. There are several lines that make me think this may be the explanation. When Bowie refers to 'shooting up pie in the sky' he may be mixing his metaphors, suggesting that shooting up (taking heroin) leads not to self-discovery, but 'pie in the sky' nonsense. I have two other reasons for thinking my conclusion may be correct. When Bowie and I had that long heart-to-heart conversation referred to in the Introduction he asked me whether I had ever tried to communicate with 'the other world' using a ouija board. I said no. 'Don't,' he replied. 'It can mess you up, especially if you're taking drugs ...'

He also asked me whether I had taken heroin, and I replied that I had a medical reason for not taking any of the drugs then being experimented with by many young British musicians, also mentioning that I had seen musicians after they had taken heroin, and knew several who had died. 'Don't ever try it,' he said. 'Heroin is bad news. You shouldn't try it at all, not even once. Believe me, don't ...' and as he said this, he leant forward and looked straight into my eyes.

I am not saying I know what *The Bewlay Brothers* means in its entirety, for Bowie himself may not know that, either, but my disclosures possibly explain why the 'kings of oblivion' 'were so turned on in the mind-warp pavilion'.

13

# From *Pork* to New York

*Hunky Dory* was eventually seen as a major album, but RCA Records chose to release it in Britain on 17 December 1971, just a week before Christmas. It was bad timing, too late for the usual pre-Christmas sales rush, too late for inclusion in radio schedules over the holiday period, and too late to ensure reviews in the music papers before the country turned its mind to turkeys, gifts and Christmas crackers.

'What are your record company playing at?' I asked Bowie when we met at the Royal Ballroom.

'God knows,' said Bowie, clearly distressed that by late January 1972 his album could not be found in record shops, whose managers always begin de-stocking as soon as the holiday season is over. Bowie had been badly let down. *Hunky Dory* was finished before Defries negotiated the distribution deal with RCA, which was how RCA Records came to pay both parts of the advance for the album when the contract was formally signed in New York in September 1971. RCA should have had the record in the shops by the end of October if they wanted to secure maximum promotion.

Four of the album's songs were first performed on *John Peel's Sunday Concert* on BBC Radio seven months earlier, on 5 June 1971. These were the newly written *Kooks*, *Song For Bob Dylan*, *Andy Warhol* and *Queen Bitch*. This was Bowie's first public appearance with Ronson, Bolder and Woodmansey. He was accompanied on vocals by MacCormack, Underwood and Dana Gillespie. Their harmony gave the songs a substantially different sound, which was why the *Ziggy 2* bootleg, based on tapes of the show, became so successful. It was also Bowie's first experiment with a harder rock 'n' roll format, both for his own songs and in reworking Chuck Berry's *Almost Grown* and *It Ain't Easy* by The Kinks.

In this concert, and through his eight live recordings for the

BBC over the following year (which ceased with the success of *Ziggy Stardust*), Bowie moved further into the rock format, but there was still something missing.

\* \* \* \* \*

Whenever Bowie committed himself to some new cause, he gave his heart to it – for as long as the passion lasted. He could be remarkably capricious, especially with people – devoted to them one day, ignoring them the next – but never wavered in his enthusiasm for Lou Reed, The Velvet Underground and Andy Warhol. In Bowie's mind, they had taken over from Bob Dylan as rock's prime influence, especially Warhol with his sense of theatre, mastery of image and ability to hold centre stage. Bowie's obsession dated back to Pitt's return from New York with the first Velvet Underground LP, which he played constantly, day after day, putting the needle back to the beginning the moment it finished, absorbing the structural sounds and the harshness of Reed's lyrics.

In July 1971, after finishing *Ziggy Stardust* in just two weeks, Bowie heard that several 'stars' from Warhol's 'Factory' were coming to London to present his stage show *Pork* at The Round House in Camden Town. They weren't stars at all. Hardly anyone in London had ever heard of them, and *Pork* was a slice of underground theatre with decidedly limited appeal, based on Warhol's tape recordings.

In 1964, Warhol began tape-recording conversations of 'friends'. These were mainly the unknown artists, models, transsexuals, transvestites, junkies, gays and drag queens who adorned his studio and enlivened the bars and night-clubs he frequented in New York City. 'I was curious about all these new people I was meeting who could stay up for weeks at a time without ever going to sleep,' wrote Warhol in *From A To B And Back Again*. 'I thought, "*These* people are so imaginative. I just want to know what they do ..."' Warhol ended up with hours of conversation about sex lives, love affairs, drink and drugs habits, and 200 of these tapes were boiled down into a stage production with physical movements to accompany the conversations – on-stage douching, simulated masturbation and portrayals of oral, anal and genital sex, both male and female, between one sex and both.

The cast brought to London was led by Tony Zanetta, the actor playing Warhol, with his hair and eyebrows bleached, and that charismatic gaze of dull, dazed, pasty-faced indifference. The other six members looked equally bizarre, even if they did all come from 'irreproachably narrow, lower middle-class backgrounds'.[1] There was Wayne County, a drag queen who looked as if she had been applying make-up in mid-Atlantic during a Force Ten gale; Leee Black Childers (he always spelt his name that way), who wore mascara and bleached his hair; two nude boys with pastel-coloured genitals who called themselves The Pepsodent Twins; Cherry Vanilla, who played the heroine Amanda Pork, and usually introduced herself by baring her breasts and saying, 'Hi – I'm the Pork from New York'; and the enormously full-breasted Geri Miller.

To save money, they all booked into a flat in Earls Court with stage manager Jaime DeCarlo Lotts Andrews, and spent their days and nights scouring bars, boutiques and late-night shows. Before leaving New York, Childers had read the piece on Bowie in *Rolling Stone*. 'Hey, here's that guy who wears a dress,' he said, noticing an advertisement in the *New Musical Express* for Bowie's 28 July appearance at the Hampstead Country Club, where he was planning to try out some new songs, accompanied by Ronson on lead guitar and Wakeman on piano.

Only 20 people turned up for the show, so Bowie sat them around in a semi-circle, perched himself on a chair and gave what was, in effect, a one-man show, knowing that Childers, Cherry Vanilla and Wayne County had phoned for tickets. As they walked in, Bowie said, 'We have some celebrities in the audience tonight' and asked them to take a bow. Cherry Vanilla opened her blouse and waved her nipples while Wayne County, a walking absurdity in an ill-fitting dress, bowed with the grace of a Southern belle. Bowie made a fuss of them in the bar afterwards, listening to their Warhol gossip, and exchanging phone numbers. 'Was he wearing a dress?' asked the others when the trio returned to Earls Court.

'No,' said County, who had been expecting Bowie to be far more outrageous. 'Floppy pants and a brocade jacket. He had stringy hair, much too little blue eye-shadow, and didn't look at all like Lauren Bacall.[2] He was just a folkie, just another folkie.'

What fascinated them most was that Bowie had a wife and was accompanied by Dana Gillespie, and they described how Angie sat herself down in the middle of the semi-circle, loudly drawing attention to herself throughout Bowie's set. 'The consensus was,' says Zanetta,[3] 'that of the two Bowies, Angie was definitely the more masculine.'

Bowie not only attended the *Pork* first night, but went back again and again during its month-long run, entranced by what he thought was a chic blend of camp vulgarity, street humour and outrageousness. The more shocking it was, the more he liked it – and thought he was drawing closer to Warhol who was only just beginning to attract attention within British rock 'n' roll. This was the year (1971) that Warhol designed the sleeve for The Rolling Stones' *Sticky Fingers* LP and the logo for their new record label, and after his early connection with The Velvet Underground this helped make Warhol irresistible – and therefore all-things-Warhol, too. As with all Bowie's obsessions, it was total. His friends were told they had to see *Pork*, as well, and after the show he would invite the cast down to The Sombrero.

'We were all perceived as Warhol stars,' says Zanetta.[4] 'We somehow connected. For a long time I was confused as to exactly why. Part of it I think was because I was playing Andy and the attraction was to Warhol, the way of Warhol. I was the key to Warhol, or something like that…. It was a lot about role-playing, and David was lured in the same way…. He was coming from the same base as we were. Which is basically an inability to be oneself and constructing a new personality in which one could act out one's fantasies and desires.' Outside observers saw through that. They could see that the cast of *Pork* and the sideshow at The Sombrero were all part of the same charade, unknown poseurs trying to be outrageous for all they were worth. But not Bowie. For him, they were stars.

The Bowies believed *Pork* would lead them to Warhol, and who better to frank their ticket than Zanetta? They reasoned that Warhol must know his clone. Zanetta was invited down to Haddon Hall, taken on a tour of the mansion and told grandly that with the success of Bowie's records they would 'do it all up'. (Bowie used to pretend the house was his, and once told me he bought it.)

'Andy would look at me during rehearsals and I'd look at him,' Zanetta told the Bowies.[5] 'We'd stare at each other. I used these moments to look for any detail that I could add to my performance…. We were each other's mirrors … even his friends treat me like I'm Andy.'

'How wonderful,' said Bowie, playing Zanetta the *Hunky Dory* tapes, telling him of his next album and his new creation, Ziggy Stardust, and saying how much he hoped to meet Warhol and Lou Reed when he went to New York for the formal signing of his RCA contract.

*     *     *     *     *

Success in lining up his first contracts was doing wonders for Defries. Wherever he went, Defries now wore a coat of racoon fur that made him look like a furry animal, with his white pasty face, hair grown fuzzy and thick, gold jewellery and a thick black cigar clenched between his teeth. Pitt observed that Defries had 'metamorphosed into the last of the 60s swingers, complete with roll-top sweater, neck chains, hanging medallions and Afro hair-style'.[6]

'David is going to be bigger than The Beatles, bigger than Elvis,' Defries told everyone, including me, while carefully tutoring him in every tiny detail of what he perceived to be stardom, much of it learned from reading show business biographies. Bowie was told he must never carry *anything* – not a case or a briefcase, a suit of clothes or a guitar. He must never open doors or carry money in his pocket. A huge muscular black man with the bulk of a body-builder, Stuey George, was taken on as Bowie's bodyguard. Defries argued that if you lived like A Star, the world would treat you like A Star – and what better proof than the sight of this enormous black minder towering above Bowie whenever he left his home?

In this surreal world, every event had to be an occasion. When RCA said the contracts were ready for signature, Defries asked where they would hold the 'signing ceremony', as if this were as important as some international treaty – and duly told the Bowies they would be signing the contracts in New York, that RCA were sending air tickets, and that they would be booked in the same suite at the Plaza Hotel that The Beatles occupied when they first visited America in February 1964.

This was where Zanetta met them again, with Bowie, under strict instructions to play the role of The Star throughout his visit, wearing a full-sleeved Paisley shirt, cream-coloured bell-bottomed trousers, a leopard-skin style jacket, hat and cape, with yellow Italian shoes.

'This is Tony Zanetta, the actor who played Andy Warhol,' said Bowie, in case Defries had forgotten.

'Ah, yes – pity about Andy Warhol. Should be making much more money. His films aren't being handled properly.... Andy should be enormous, mass-marketed throughout the world. He needs distribution,' said Defries, half-suggesting that Zanetta might like to join the payroll there and then as liaison man between Bowie and Warhol. 'Get Warhol on the phone and arrange a meeting,' he went on, developing his own role in this scenario as the all-powerful manager whose wishes prevail.

\* \* \* \* \*

The RCA contract was signed on 9 September 1971, with Bowie suitably dressed for the occasion, wearing another ensemble, together with eye-liner, blue eye-shadow and mascara'd lashes. 'You don't have to do anything,' said Defries as the lift took them up to the ninth floor of the RCA building on 44th and 6th Street. 'Leave it all to me ...'

Defries discussed RCA's promotional plans with Artistes and Repertoire Manager Dennis Katz and his assistants Richard Robinson and Bob Ringe. Other executives came in to introduce themselves. A photographer arrived to capture the moment when the contract was signed. 'I've got a surprise for you tonight,' said Katz. 'I've booked a table at The Ginger Man and invited along Lou Reed. I know you like him. Lou's just signed with us, too, and I'm sure he'd like to meet you ...'

'That would be wonderful,' said Bowie, knowing Reed studied creative writing at Syracuse University under Delmore Schwartz, graduating with honours, and that he, too, suffered a crisis of identity in his late teens when his parents forced him to have a course of 24 electric shock treatments, fearing he might be homosexual.

Bowie changed again for dinner and spent much of the meal sizing up Reed, learning how Warhol frequently dined at this same restaurant, saying how often he included Reed's songs in his stage act, and mentioning that *Queen Bitch* was written in tribute to Reed. This was Bowie at his most persuasive, smiling, fluttering his eyelids, making no attempt to compete verbally for he could see that Reed, a constant speed-user, was far too fast for him.

At Max's Kansas City, Bowie was introduced to Danny Fields,

manager of Iggy Pop, who thanked him for mentioning Iggy in interviews. 'I love Iggy,' said Bowie, which prompted Fields to phone Iggy at his home. He arrived with a sudden demonic burst of energy, arms flailing and demanding attention, spitting out his sentences as fast as Lou Reed as he talked of shooting heroin and trying to wean himself off it with methadone.

'I'm cleaning myself out, man,' he told the Bowies, with a deep foghorn of a voice. 'Heroin was my main man, but now I'm getting my shit together.'

Bowie glanced at Defries, which was enough for the manager to know what was on his mind. This was pure theatre. Bowie was loving it, and did not want the night to end. 'Come round to the hotel around midday tomorrow and have breakfast with us,' said Defries, who was to find that Iggy never changed, whatever the time or the setting. Midnight or midday, wherever he was, Iggy was firing away on all cylinders, mind and mouth as one, telling a harrowing story of music and poverty, surviving on drugs, forever dependent on anyone willing to help him.

'Can't we do something for Iggy?' asked Bowie, triggering off another of the now familiar monologues on how to become a great star, getting the right deals, keeping control, advertising, merchandising and so on. 'Sounds terrific,' gabbled Iggy. 'You be my main man.'

The Bowie circus moved on to the Warhol Factory the following day, with Zanetta as herald. The Factory was now located in downtown New York, on the fifth floor at 33 Union Street West. With just two rooms, it looked more like an office than an artist's studio – except that the walls were papered with aluminium foil and all other surfaces painted white, reflecting the identical glass-topped desks, white telephones and IBM typewriters. The back room was used for painting and screening films.

Warhol had now switched from black leather to velvet, having told Truman Capote, 'Everyone's back to beautiful clothes. The hippie look is really gone.'[7] His working days were spent standing at a table, wearing his death's head mask, knowing as well as any rock 'n' roll manager that Mystique Sells Art. At the centre of his web, never paying anyone a penny if he could help it and quietly amassing an immense fortune, Warhol was also in total control, surrounded by nonentities.

Only the flicker of a smile appeared on his face as Bowie entered the room with Angie and Defries. They all *knew* why

Bowie was there. 'He'd homed in directly on the most happening of happening themes in American pop culture, which at the time meant simply one name: Warhol,' wrote Angie Bowie.[8] The meeting was in Warhol's interests, too, for he was trying to cross over into the rock 'n' roll mainstream, sensing the power of its audience.

As they walked in, Angie was aware of 'a bunch of incredibly pale people lounging around in various stages approaching coma, squeezing out the occasional nihilistic statement ... and I recall many moments of silent, relatively acute social discomfort before David took the initiative and played a tape of his song *Andy Warhol* to its subject.'

The moment the song finished, Warhol hurriedly left the room, without a trace of any reaction. Bowie and Defries waited some minutes, not realizing Warhol was distressed (for he was far more sensitive than he would let them know). Just as they were wondering what was going to happen next, Warhol came back, said, 'That was great, thank you very much' – which was not what he thought at all, though he wasn't going to let them know that – and then took out a polaroid camera. Without any explanation, Warhol started taking dozens of photos of Bowie, his face expressionless, not saying a word and not letting Bowie see any of the photos, until suddenly he noticed Bowie's delicately cut Italian-made yellow shoes. That broke the ice. 'Oh, my dear – those shoes,' said Warhol, dropping to his knees and starting to photograph Bowie's feet. 'What pretty shoes ... you have such nice shoes!'

Unwittingly Bowie had triggered off the inner man, for Warhol was 'a classic foot fetishist ... he found the ritual of kissing his lover's shoes particularly erotic. A surprisingly large number of people are said to have acquiesced to his requests.'[9]

Bowie had come closer to Warhol than he ever knew, but Warhol still would not say why he left the room so suddenly. There was no way the one poseur would let the other poseur know that words could hurt him, especially the lines 'Andy Warhol looks a scream'; and 'Andy Warhol silver screen/can't tell them apart at all'; and 'He'll think about paint/And he'll think about glue/What a jolly boring thing to do'.

According to Warhol's biographer Victor Bockris, the artist thought the song was 'horrible' because he was always sensitive about his appearance. That night, Bowie met Lou Reed again, this time at Max's Kansas City, told him of his visit to the Factory and how Warhol had 'nothing to say at all, absolutely nothing'.

'He was always the same with us,' said Reed, adding that when he was with The Velvet Underground they had thought of marketing an Andy Warhol doll. Its trick was that when you wound it up, the doll did nothing at all.

*   *   *   *   *

The visit to New York was a huge success. Bowie now knew the three figures who had dominated his thoughts and writing in recent years – Lou Reed, Iggy Pop and Andy Warhol. He had travelled around New York as an unknown visitor, walking the streets, absorbing the sounds and the smells of the living city, reading its newspapers, listening to its radio stations, watching TV, going to Radio City Music Hall, and being taken by RCA to watch Elvis Presley perform at Madison Square Garden. 'I was happy that he was happy. We were all happy, really,' says Angie.[10] 'RCA was treating us like stars, throwing parties for us and limo-ing us around the hot spots.' Shortly before they returned to Britain, Zanetta called to see them again at the Plaza. After eating dinner in their suite and watching more TV, Angie retired to bed. Bowie sat talking to Zanetta through the night, watching dawn break across the New York skyline. 'You know, this is going to be bigger than a new album or tour or anything like that,' said Bowie. 'I want to do everything and I feel that I can. I'm going to be huge and it's a little scary ...'

Several more parts of the Grand Design were now in place. Bowie went back to Haddon Hall and straight into the recording studios with Ronson, Bolder and Woodmansey. 'I'm ready to start the next album,' Bowie told Ken Scott. 'You're not going to like it. It's much more like Iggy Pop, more rock 'n' roll ...' And within a fortnight, from start to finish, he wrote and recorded *The Rise And Fall Of Ziggy Stardust And The Spiders From Mars*.

14

## 'I'm gay and always have been, even when I was David Jones'

A strange buzz occurs when a musician is about to become A Star. Managers, bookers, producers, publishers, promoters, publicists and disc jockeys all know it's going to happen. The press are often the last to hear, and the hapless artiste sits in the middle, wondering whether it's all coming true this time. Just such a buzz was in the air in the early months of 1972, which was hard to explain. Initial sales of *Hunky Dory* were poor. Few people bothered to buy Bowie's first RCA single *Changes/Andy Warhol*, and yet there was this definite, tangible sense of excitement. The Defries wind-up had started.

Rather than leave anything to chance, Defries himself phoned every newspaper and magazine that might be interested in rock music to tell them David Bowie was going out on tour with his new group. They were all invited to the Royal Ballroom in Tottenham High Road during the third week of January 1972, but few bothered to take up his invitation, for Bowie had not had a hit record since *Space Oddity* in 1969, and that was now viewed as a one-off gimmicky single of no great significance. So Bowie was going out on tour: Big Deal. Musicians tour every night of the year. That's how they make their living, especially those who cannot sell records.

'You'll come, won't you, George?' asked Defries, adding the extra flattering detail that 'David specially asked me to phone you 'cos you've been so good to him in the past ... he'd like to see you again.' So I went, which was how I came to see Bowie on the eve of his 'I am gay' announcement, the calculated publicity master-stroke that gave his career lift-off.

The Bowie bandwagon was now a multi-headed hydra: principally Bowie The Artiste and Defries The Manager, but with dozens of others, either members of his group, part of his travelling entourage or down at Haddon Hall, at Gem, Chrysalis or

RCA. There were people to answer the phone, carry the baggage, do his shopping, prepare his meals, arrange his diary, make his clothes (and wash, clean and dry the soiled ones) – and even a personal publicist, Dai Davies, who was brought up from Wales since Defries was wisely anxious not to give the job to anyone who might have friends elsewhere in the music business. When Davies suggested pay of £35 or £40 a week, Defries retorted 'You can't work for David Bowie for only £40 a week, that's not enough. It creates the wrong image. You must have 100 pounds a week!

\*   \*   \*   \*   \*

Minutes after receiving the call from Defries, I phoned Pitt, telling him that Defries had invited me along to the Royal Ballroom where Bowie was rehearsing his new stage act with his group.

'You're going, aren't you?'

'Of course,' I replied, mentioning how Defries sugared the invitation with flattery.

'That would be true,' said Pitt. 'David always said he enjoyed talking to you and learned a lot from you because you'd been around the business and met other musicians, when he hadn't.... Intellectually, you had a lot in common. I still hear about him all the time. They tell me this next record is going to be the one. RCA are very confident. They're investing a lot of money in David's career, but I don't understand what Defries is doing at all. I hear he's now got 30 people on the payroll with hardly any money coming in – and that can't last. He's signed up Dana Gillespie and Iggy Pop, but what's he going to do with them? If David really does make a break through with this next LP, he'll take up all Defries's time – and then he won't be able to give Dana Gillespie and Iggy Pop the attention they'll be wanting. I can see this all ending in tears ...'

\*   \*   \*   \*   \*

It was now mid-January 1972; ten months since my last interview with Bowie, when had we met at the Chrysalis office. Even then he was talking of his new stage act. And, here he was at the Royal Ballroom, looking slimmer than ever, grinning impishly with a small velvet cap perched on his head above tufts of hair, and wearing a light green jump suit.

'How's this stage act turning out?' I asked.

'Outrageous,' he said. 'Quite outrageous. But very theatrical. We haven't decided on the costumes yet, whether it'll be the same costumes every night, which means you have to carry lots of spares, or different ones every night – or whether we'll go out in jeans and T-shirts, which we could do – but there are too many bands doing that, really. It's time for something different. We're going to be different, costumed and choreographed, ideally – quite different to anything anyone else has tried to do before.'

His enthusiasm was infectious, but I couldn't help smiling at the young Dai Davies, who was hovering within earshot, anxious lest anything be said out of place. Bowie misinterpreted my smile. 'No, it will – really,' he said. 'This is going to be something new. No one has ever seen anything like this before ...'

Bowie went on to claim that his previous album, *The Man Who Sold The World*, sold over 100,000 copies in the United States, without him making a concert tour to promote it, and said how hopeful he was for *Hunky Dory* in the States. That drew another smile, with me commenting that on the first LP sleeve he had been compared with Lauren Bacall and now with this latest cover portrait, showing him in profile with his hair swept back from his cheeks and the original photograph lightly touched up by George Underwood to make him seem slightly out of focus, he could have been either Greta Garbo or Veronica Lake.

'You wait until you see the stage show,' said Bowie. 'This is going to be a very exciting show – and it's going to be entertainment. That's what's missing in pop music now – entertainment. There's not much outrageousness left any more – apart from me and Marc Bolan. The Beatles were outrageous at one time and so was Mick Jagger, but you can't remain at the top for five years and still be outrageous ... you become accepted and the impact has gone. Me? I'm fantastically outrageous,' he said, declining to explain what he meant. 'I like being outrageous. I believe people want to see you if you're being outrageous – and I'm old enough to remember Mick Jagger!'

Our conversation switched to the Arts Laboratory, his visit to New York, signing the contract with RCA, seeing Elvis Presley at Madison Square Garden, meeting Lou Reed, Iggy Pop and Andy Warhol, and his marriage to Angie and the birth of their son. 'We don't want to talk about that,' said Angie, who must have been 30 feet away but was still managing to hear every word, and now came across to where we were talking, standing above me.

'All right then,' I said.

'I think you should leave me right out of it,' said Angie, explaining that very few people knew they were married, and she could see no point in talking about their relationship. She seemed quite agitated and Bowie calmed her down by adding, 'Angie's got her own career mapped out, which she wants to pursue independently of mine, so d'you mind leaving all that out?'

I soon knew why the Bowies were being secretive. It was Wednesday, and on my way home I picked up a copy of *Melody Maker*, which was always available on the central London news-stands on Wednesday afternoon – and there was Bowie all over the front page, being given the star treatment even though it was well over two years since his success with *Space Oddity*. A large photograph covered the front page with an inset paragraph that read:

> DAVID BOWIE, rock's swishiest outrage: a self-confessed lover of effeminate clothes, Bowie, who has hardly performed in public since his *Space Oddity* hit of three years ago, is coming back in super-style. In the States critics have hailed him as the new Bob Dylan, and his *tour de force* album *Hunky Dory* looks set to enter the British charts. *Changes*, the single taken from it, was Tony Blackburn's Record of the Week recently. David will be appearing, suitably spiffy and with his three-piece band, at the Lanchester Festival on February 3. Breathless for more? Turn to page 19 ...

Inside, there was a two-page feature by Michael Watts, a young reporter who had recently joined *Melody Maker* from a provincial newspaper. They met at the Gem office, where Bowie arrived dressed to impress, wearing 'an elegant, patterned type of combat suit, very tight around the legs, with the shirt unbuttoned to reveal a full expanse of white torso. The trousers were turned up at the calves to allow a better glimpse of a huge pair of red plastic boots with at least three-inch rubber soles, and the hair was Vidal Sassooned into such impeccable shape that one held one's breath in case the slight breeze from the open window dared to ruffle it ...'

The headline to the article was 'OH YOU PRETTY THING' and it was a well-written profile, encapsulating Bowie's career to date and showing how the different influences he acknowledged now dovetailed to produce his own distinctive style and personality. Within it, there were two paragraphs that were to change Bowie's life:

David's present image is to come on like a swishy queen, a gorgeously effeminate boy. He's as camp as a row of tents, with his limp hand and trolling vocabulary. 'I'm gay,' he says, 'and always have been, even when I was David Jones.' But there's a sly jollity about how he says it, a secret smile at the corners of his mouth. He knows that in these times it's permissible to act like a male tart, and that to shock and outrage, which pop has always striven to do throughout its history, is a balls-breaking process.

And if he's not an outrage, he is, at the least, an amusement. The expression of his sexual ambivalence establishes a fascinating game: is he or isn't he? In a period of conflicting sexual identity he shrewdly exploits the confusion surrounding the male and female roles. 'Why are you wearing your girl's dress today?' I said to him (he has no monopoly on tongue-in-cheek humour). 'Oh dear,' he replied. 'You must understand that it's not a woman's. It's a man's dress.'

Watts mentioned Bowie's wife and son, which was probably unexpected (for Angie had been anxious I should not), and said Bowie 'supposes he's what people called bisexual ...' It was an intelligent article, almost an essay in musical style, describing how Bowie took his Cockney accent from Anthony Newley quite deliberately: 'He used to make his points with this broad Cockney accent and I decided that I'd use that now and again to drive a point home.' Watts also referred to the influence of Iggy Pop, Lou Reed, Warhol and Marc Bolan, the intelligence of Bowie's lyrics, Ronson's qualities as a lead guitarist, and Bowie's gift for parody – but little of this appeared in the press as other newspapers and magazines took up his story, with first *Disc and Music Echo* explaining 'WHY BOWIE IS FEELING BUTCH' and the *New Musical Express* quoting Bowie as saying 'I'M NOT ASHAMED OF WEARING DRESSES'. Then every tabloid newspaper and most of the broadsheets joined in the scrum, wanting to explain this shameless newcomer: Britain's first bisexual pop star.

Thereafter, *Gay News* chronicled Bowie's growing career, publishing front-cover photographs and reviews of his concerts, while he was given the full star treatment by the national press, with every writer taking whatever Bowie said at face value – they swallowed the Defries hype whole, accepting every claim: Bowie the penniless musician became Bowie The Famous Star, protected by his own personal bodyguard wherever he went. They described how his personal chauffeur drove him to and from his country home; how he had to live in secrecy at a secluded mansion to escape his fans' attention; how his manager, staff and musicians responded to his every whim; and how he had a bisexual wife who was every bit as outrageous as he was, sleeping with lovers of both sexes, while their personal publicist kept the press at bay.

'They've overdone it this time,' said Pitt when we spoke days after my interview and the first publication of Bowie's 'confession'.

'There's nothing wrong in being interviewed by the gay press, or admitting you're gay, if that's what you are, but it has to be done with taste,' said Pitt, arguing that this area of the press was largely ignored by publicists, which was why he said he organized the interview with *Jeremy* two years earlier. 'I wouldn't have wanted anything to appear like this ... it's vulgar,' Pitt continued, telling me that he happened to be in the RCA offices when the *Melody Maker* story broke. 'They were horrified. This wasn't the sort of publicity they were looking for at all ... they've discovered that they've taken on rather more than they'd bargained for.'

\*   \*   \*   \*   \*

No one could fault Bowie's timing, if this was the image he wanted, for Glam Rock had been Britain's bestselling pop music market for 18 months, since Marc Bolan leapt from *Ride A White Swan* into suits of multi-coloured satin, tapping his dainty feet in shiny dancers' shoes, wearing mascara and eye shadow and affixing glittery stickers to his cheeks and brow. This was the era of Sweet, Mud, Slade and Gary Glitter, who minced and stomped the ballroom circuit and *Top Of The Pops*, with no one wanting to mention Glam Rock's gay undercurrent – and now here was A Star with no pretences.

Overnight, the innocence of Glam Rock, with its sub-teen following, turned into something naughty – Fag Rock, Gay Rock, Camp Rock and The Parade of the Rock Queens. Underground magazines that made no attempt to appeal to a family readership called it Cock Rock. The American rock writer Victor Bockris says 1972 became 'the year of the transsexual tramp … all of a sudden almost everyone in rock 'n' roll wanted to be – or at least suggest the possibility of being – a raging queen' and he quotes Tom Hedley of *Esquire*:

> It was the homosexual time. The faggots were our new niggers. Homosexuality was chic. There was a kind of angry gayness going on and we were very open to making faggots and lesbians our brothers…. They were the most stylish people in town, they ran the galleries, they had the best clubs, they had the best dinners.

In the United States, Andy Warhol's Factory became part of this gay movement – but in rock it was all down to David Bowie, his timing, his sense of imagery and that one interview with *Melody Maker* which led, directly, to the success of *Ziggy Stardust*, his subsequent work with Lou Reed and Iggy Pop, and the emergence of other stars who were to eventually admit their homosexuality: Elton John and Freddie Mercury of Queen.

Inevitably, attention focused on Bowie's marriage. Was he gay or wasn't he? How could any woman live with him? Was Angie a lesbian? Perhaps to a degree that he did not anticipate, David Bowie became the original Mr Gender Bender – with no one daring to ask him: *Is it true?*

Angie Bowie maintained their image, driving him on in moments of doubt, her brash vulgarity in total harmony with the business drive of Tony Defries. Where Bowie tended to hesitate, Angie never did, willingly talking of her lesbian and other love affairs, whereas Bowie seldom would – probably because there were few names to mention. After being interviewed by Michael Watts, Bowie was nervous as he told her what he had said. She was the very opposite – delighted, excited, 'so thrilled, in fact, that I hooted'.[1] As he sat there, looking worried, she gabbled: 'David! You realize what you've done? You've fucking made it…. Marketing-wise, it was just perfect.'

And so it was: *but was it true?*

With Angie usually by his side, it was hard to believe Bowie was gay or his self-proclaimed bisexuality anything more than an occasional aberration. Even then, there were rumours that their marriage was little more than a sham. Bowie told me himself that he only married Angie to prevent her being deported when her visa expired, and she admits that he laid it on the line that he was not in love with her before and after their wedding. Sexually, they enjoyed each other for a while – but even that was a short-lived experience. She admits they 'were both very young and quite ignorant in sexual matters'[2] and that 'all he really knew how to do was pump, and all I really knew how to do was take it'.

So The Star made a public issue of being gay or bisexual, while his wife says he was ignorant of sex, knew nothing about oral sex or foreplay or how to bring her to orgasm, and often avoided sex altogether because he came out in a rash. At those times, he said 'it hurts too much to fuck' and she says his penis 'looked as if it had been massaged with sandpaper'.[3] This drives me to the conclusion that if David Bowie *was* bisexual, he was not having much fun.

True or not, it was the image that mattered and with Bowie now receiving constant coverage in the British press he continued to work at that, losing more weight, choosing even more flamboyant clothes and topping all this off with an equally bizarre hairstyle. This was another of Angie's contributions.

One day in February 1972, Angie walked into the Evelyn Paget salon in Beckenham High Street and told stylist Suzy Fussey, 'Honey, d'you know what I'd like? A white stripe, a red stripe and a blue stripe down the side of my head!' And then she sat excitedly in the chair, watching this transformation take place. According to Zanetta, this visit to the salon was planned as a form of audition; the Bowies felt they could not ask any of their gay hairdresser friends from The Sombrero to fashion their new hair styles for fear of causing jealousy. With Bowie now under strict instructions from Defries never to step outside Haddon Hall without costumes and make-up, Angie was given the job of finding someone who would come to the Hall and attend to The Star's coiffure.

'Do you like the way my hair's been cut?' asked Bowie when Suzy came round to see them.

'It's a bit boring,' said Suzy. 'Everybody's got a long shag.'

'What would you do?'

'I'd have short hair – because no one else has short hair.' Angie agreed, claiming in *Backstage Passes* that what happened that day, the creation of the Ziggy Stardust hairstyle, 'was the single most reverberant fashion statement of the 70s'.

'I don't want an ordinary short cut,' said Bowie, while Angie began thumbing through back issues of *Vogue* to find the combination of cuts that would give them what they were looking for, a pointy front suggested by a French edition of *Vogue* with styles from two German issues prompting the sides and the back, two long points of hair down the sides of Bowie's face, with the top and back cut short. By the time Suzy finished, they knew they were looking at something none of them had ever seen before.

'Lovely,' said Angie. 'Truly, truly lovely ... so now let's dye it red.' Bowie seemed nervous – it was, after all, his head – but Angie was confident 'Red is such a beautiful colour,' she said. 'You'll be so pleased ...' And so, indeed, he was – until he looked in the mirror next morning, found his head a mess and began to panic.

Angie phoned Suzy at the salon. 'You must do something! He's going crazy! He hates it!'

When Suzy Fussey returned to Haddon Hall, Angie sought to reassure her husband. 'You need a star's hair colour. Your hair should glow!' By the time Suzy had finished, it did. After applying peroxide she used a German dye called Red Hot Red, with added setting lotion applied to the front of his head so that Bowie's hair stood up in orange-red spikes.

That night, when the Bowies made their entrance at The Sombrero, the gays stood around clasping their hands in envy. The superlatives flowed while the Bowies sat at their table, quietly triumphant, knowing one more part of the image was now in place.

'Very good,' said Defries, when he saw Suzy Fussey's handiwork. 'Very marketable ... now what we ought to be planning is David Bowie Dolls, with red hair.' No one laughed. They knew he meant it.

Suzy Fussey gave up her job at the Evelyn Paget salon and moved into Haddon Hall. Besides the backing musicians, manager, minder, chauffeur, road managers, publishers, designers and clothes-makers, The Star now had his own personal, full-time hairdresser.

*    *    *    *    *

Night by night, through the spring 1972 series of college dates and
one-night concerts in provincial ballrooms, Bowie's image sharp-
ened: first the clothes, the hairstyle, and then a starker appearance
for the band, still without a name, whose live sound was becoming
tighter all the time. A momentum was growing in the press, with
Bowie having something new to say in every interview:

> I'm just an image person. I'm terribly conscious of images and I
> live in them.
>
> *New Musical Express*

> The dresses were made for me. They didn't have big boobs or
> anything like that. They were men's dresses. Sort of mediaeval
> type thing ... the only thing that saddens me is that less
> attention is given to the music. I am an outrageous dresser and I
> always have been.... I don't stay with one thing very long. I
> think I'm like a grasshopper. I really want to move on all the
> time.
>
> *New Musical Express*

> I don't think I'm outrageous. It's just a more exciting way of
> looking.
>
> *Daily Express*

> I've done a lot of pills ever since I was a kid. Thirteen or
> fourteen. But the first time I got stoned on grass was with John
> Paul Jones of Led Zeppelin many, many years ago. He was still
> a bass player on Herman's Hermits records.... I had done
> cocaine before, but never grass. I don't know why it should
> have happened in that order, probably because I knew a couple
> of merchant seamen who used to bring it back from the docks. I
> had been doing coke with them. And they loathed grass. So I
> watched in wonder while Jonesy rolled these three fat joints.
> And we got stoned on all of them. I became incredibly high and
> it turned into an in-fucking-credible hunger. I ate two loaves of
> bread.... I went downstairs to answer the phone and kept on
> walking right out into the street. I never went back. I just got
> intensely fascinated with the cracks in the pavement.
>
> *Melody Maker*

Inch by inch, his image was taking shape more earthily than his clothes or hairstyle, with Bowie carefully identifying himself with the drug habits and other experiences of the leading musicians of the day; proving he was one of the boys – but there was still no hit record. Following *Changes*, which I (wrongly) thought a hit as soon as I heard it, Bowie delivered a new song to RCA for release as a single. This was a deceptively simple song about a *Starman*, waiting in the sky who would 'like to come and meet us/but thinks he'd blow our minds'. Like so many of Bowie's songs, it could be interpreted several ways – as a whimsical lyric about a space traveller from another planet, or as a drug-induced fantasy – but there was no denying the strength of its melody line. When Dennis Katz, head of the Artistes and Repertoire Department at RCA in New York, heard *Starman* he immediately suggested that it should not only be released as a single, but also included in the *Ziggy Stardust* album. Another track was dropped to make way for it, Jacques Brel's *Port Of Amsterdam*. Katz was right. *Starman* complemented the other tracks on the album – which was not as fully cohesive as Bowie later chose to suggest; the storyline was unclear.

*Starman* was released on 28 April, coupled with another track from the album, *Suffragette City*. This gave Bowie an immediate chart entry, enabling Defries to secure him bookings on the long-running BBC TV show *Top Of The Pops* and an ITV programme, *Lift Off*. Out on the road, where Bowie and the group were fulfilling bookings made months before, the ticket prices were seldom more than 50p or 75p on the gate with Bowie still earning little more than £150 a night, but the mood was changing, fitting into a classic pattern of what the music business calls a 'breaking tour'. The same thing happened to The Beatles when they went out on tour early in 1963, starting as a secondary attraction and ending a bill-topping act.

Defries could barely contain himself. He was full of ideas for the future. With the release of the *Ziggy Stardust* LP at the beginning of June, he was convinced the floodgates would open – and he wanted to merchandise Ziggy Stardust products: Ziggy Stardust boots, hair treatments, jumpsuits, posters, books and stickers – even a Ziggy Stardust wind-up doll that would say 'Wham! Bam! Thank you, Ma'am!'

As the tour gathered momentum, Angie clung to Bowie like a limpet at every show, preventing him picking up women afterwards. According to Zanetta, Bowie found her presence inhibiting. And it seemed to Defries that the marriage was over.

*   *   *   *   *

There are few LPs that change the course of rock music. One might mention The Beatles' *Revolver* and *Sergeant Pepper's Lonely Hearts Club Band*, or The Who's *Tommy*, perhaps Simon and Garfunkel's *Bridge Over Troubled Water*, The Beach Boys' *Pet Sounds* or Bob Dylan's *Bringing It All Back Home*, but it's a short list, all in all, with many albums that seem important when first released, like those from Crosby, Stills and Nash or the Police usually failing the test of time. Among those few that really count, I would include *Hunky Dory* and *Ziggy Stardust*, which capture Bowie at his driving best, concentrating every skill, and desperate to succeed.

My own preference is for *Hunky Dory*, which brought a new use of vocabulary to the language of rock music, but *The Rise And Fall Of Ziggy Stardust And The Spiders From Mars* introduced something else altogether – rock as an integral part of the Arts. No one bothered to present *Tommy* as a full-dress theatrical or film production until David Bowie proved beyond all doubt that there was an audience for *intelligent* rock. With this one LP, and the razzmatazz that went with it, Bowie extended the boundaries of rock 'n' roll.

Bowie's best description of *Ziggy Stardust* was in a conversation with William Burroughs arranged and taped by Craig Copetas for *Rolling Stone*.[4] He explained that the opening track, *Five Years*, leads into the album on the premise that there are only

five years to go before the end of the earth. It has been announced that the world will end because of lack of natural resources. Ziggy is in a position where all the kids have access to things that they thought they wanted. The older people have lost all touch with reality and the kids are left on their own to plunder anything. Ziggy was in a rock 'n' roll band and the kids no longer want rock 'n' roll. There's no electricity to play it. Ziggy's adviser tells him to collect news and sing it, 'cause there is no news. So Ziggy does this and there is terrible news. *All The Young Dudes* is a song about this news. It is no hymn to the youth as people thought. It is completely the opposite.

In answer to a question from Burroughs, Bowie agreed that the world would not end with the exhaustion of natural resources, but civilization would collapse and the population shrink by as much as three-quarters:

This does not cause the end of the world for Ziggy. The end comes when the infinites arrive. They really are a black hole, but I've made them people because it would be very hard to explain a black hole on stage.... Ziggy is advised in a dream by the infinites to write the coming of a starman, so he writes *Starman*, which is the first news of hope that the people have heard. So they latch on to it immediately. The starmen that he is talking about are called the infinites, and they are black-hole jumpers. Ziggy has been talking about this amazing spaceman who will be coming down to save the earth. They arrive somewhere in Greenwich Village. They don't have a care in the world and are of no possible use to us. They just happened to stumble into our universe by black-hole jumping. Their whole life is travelling from universe to universe. In the stage show*, one of them resembles Brando, another one a Black New Yorker. I even have one called Queenie the Infinite Fox.

Now Ziggy starts to believe in all this himself and thinks himself a prophet of the future starman. He takes himself up to incredible spiritual heights and is kept alive by his disciples. When the infinites arrive, they take bits of Ziggy to make themselves real because in their original state they are anti-matter and cannot exist in our world. And they tear him to pieces on stage during the song *Rock 'n' Roll Suicide*. As soon as Ziggy dies on stage the infinites take his elements and make themselves visible. It is a science fiction fantasy of today ...

The problem with Bowie's analysis is that it barely fits the structure of the album; storyline and content do not marry, however innovatory *Ziggy Stardust* may be. What makes *Five Years* work is the simple drum-beat underlining his lyric, isolated and alone like a beating heart.

The song that follows, *Soul Love*, brings a total contrast – a gently lyrical tribute to various forms of love, the love of a mother

* At the time of this conversation with Burroughs, Bowie was working on plans to stage *The Rise And Fall Of Ziggy Stardust And The Spiders From Mars* as a London show, and also as a television production. Nothing came of either project.

for a dead child, the love of a brave man for an ideal, the love of a priest for his congregation, the love of Man for God, and the love of a boy and a girl for 'New words – that only they can share in'. This is, above all, the song of a compassionate man, and in its fusion of profound thoughts, simple words, rock 'n' roll rhythms and his own swinging, jazzy saxophone, lifts rock to a new plane.

Ziggy makes his entrance on the third song, *Moonage Daydream*, which Bowie first recorded the previous year as Arnold Corns, and now works through again with Ronson's feedback guitar underlining and then controlling the rhythm with dramatic force while Bowie tells us through which routes he came to rock 'n' roll, as an alligator (i.e. through the original rhythms, Bill Haley's *See You Later Alligator*) and via The Mamas and The Papas (through melody). As always, Bowie is sparing in his use of similes and allusions and unless you know rock 'n' roll the idea is lost that he's 'the space invader ... a rock 'n' rolling bitch/... busting up my brains for the words'.

Having introduced his central character, Bowie almost lost him. In the original structure of the album, the next song was due to be Jacques Brel's *Port Of Amsterdam*, which has no conceivable connection. The song that replaced it, *Starman*, brings in the (later) thought that the Starman may be waiting to come down to earth at just this juncture – although it's not easy to see how the next song, *It Ain't Easy* by Ray Davies of The Kinks, fits into Bowie's overall conception.

It is only on the second side of the album that the idea of Ziggy as the heroic rock figure takes proper shape, with *Lady Stardust* suggesting Ziggy might be partly feminine, singing 'his songs/of darkness and disgrace' and *Star* planting the thought that Ziggy chose fame after rejecting every other alternative. This leads into *Hang On To Yourself*, the first of the driving rock songs in which Bowie draws from Eddie Cochran's *Summertime Blues*, which he and Marc Bolan both raved over years before its 1970 revival by The Who. There were two lines in Cochran's song that touched a chord with every rock 'n' roll songwriter: 'I called my Congressman and he said quote/I'd like to help you, son, but you're too young to vote'. Now, by echoing its sound and with Ronson's use of buzz-saw guitar, Bowie tells us honestly 'the bitter comes out better on a stolen guitar' and that The Spiders from Mars know their roots. This all runs naturally into *Ziggy Stardust*, the song at the heart of the album, and *Suffragette City*, which charts his downfall, then *Rock 'n' Roll Suicide*, which explains how the broken rock star consoles himself with the thought 'oh no love! you're not alone' when there is still an audience out there, willing to respond to him, and give him their hands. Both on the album and in the finale of the stage act, *Rock 'n' Roll Suicide* ends with this final embrace, with Ziggy reaching out to the audience, fingertip to fingertip, crying 'you're not alone, gimme your hands' and then eventually 'you're wonderful, gimme your hands' as the final consummation of the relationship that always exists between rock star and fans, actor and audience.

Musically, despite its structural weaknesses, *The Rise And Fall Of Ziggy Stardust* was a *tour de force* – but it was Bowie's theatrical presentation that made it the most talked-about rock event since Woodstock. As his spring tour progressed, word travelled back to London that his audience was growing, but he was still playing small halls and his act was incomplete. With the show still not seen by the London critics, Defries pulled another clever publicity stroke – by inviting the American press to see it first, thereby letting The Star upstage the British critics.

\*    \*    \*    \*    \*

The album was released in Britain on 6 June 1972, but for the rest of that month Bowie continued touring out-of-town, making each night a rehearsal. News continued to filter back. At Croydon, over a thousand fans were turned away at the door because the hall was full – and at Dunstable the famous photograph was taken by Mick Rock, showing Bowie engaged in simulated fellatio with Ronson's guitar (the photograph was promptly distributed by Defries to every newspaper), but still there were no invitations to the London critics. Defries was treating the tour like a pre-London run.

On 8 July Bowie appeared at the London Festival Hall at a charity concert in aid of the Friends of the Earth, with all proceeds going to the Save the Whale campaign. Also on the bill were Lou Reed, making his first British appearance, Marmalade, the JSD Band and disc jockey Kenny Everett, but the occasion was Bowie's from the moment the loudspeakers began to play a Moog version of Beethoven's *The Song Of Joy*, the music chosen for the film *A Clockwork Orange*. As the darkened stage filled with musicians, a single spotlight picked him out – a startling vision in red with red spiky hair, bleached face, red and green skin-tight space suit, and thick-heeled red boots. 'Hello,' he said. 'I'm Ziggy Stardust – and these are The Spiders ...' as the spotlight then picked out Ronson, Bolder and Woodmansey. This was the moment. The group had a name. They really were Ziggy Stardust and The Spiders from Mars. Myth was replacing reality. A legend was born.

That night, costumed thus and in make-up, Bowie presented a stage act that went far beyond the album, performing The Velvet Underground songs with Lou Reed, Cream's *I Feel Free*, Brel's *Port Of Amsterdam* and songs from his own past albums. Ray Coleman, editor of *Melody Maker*, was in the audience and wrote:

### A STAR IS BORN

When a shooting star is heading for the peak, there is usually one concert at which it's possible to declare, 'That's it – he's made it'. For David Bowie, opportunity knocked loud and clear last Saturday at London's Royal Festival Hall – and he left the stage a true 1972-style pop giant, clutching flowers from a girl who ran up and hugged and kissed him while a throng of fans milled around the stage. It was an exhilarating sight.

Bowie is going to be an old-fashioned, charismatic idol, for his show is full of glitter, panache and pace. Dressed outrageously in the tightest multicoloured gear imaginable, Bowie is a flashback in many ways to the pop star theatrics of about ten years ago, carrying on a detached love affair with his audience, wooing them, yet never surrendering that vital aloofness that makes him slightly untouchable.

On Saturday, the magic was boosted by an unadvertised appearance by Lou Reed. The American jammed with David and his group, and although mutual admiration societies like this are often disappointing ego trips, an electrifying heat came across the stage as David and Lou roared into *White Light, White Heat, I'm Waiting For The Man* and *Sweet Jane*. Their obvious admiration for each other's style was great to watch....
But this concert still belonged to Bowie ... His music naturally comes mainly from the *Ziggy Stardust* hit album, but little on this record equals the canny *Changes* from the *Hunky Dory* set, or the classic *Space Oddity* ... Bowie came over powerfully, oozing with histrionic confidence ... obviously revelling in stardom, strutting from mike to mike, slaying us all with a

deadly mixture of fragility and desperate intensity, the undisputed king of camp rock.

This reaction was mirrored elsewhere: 'a remarkable performer' (the *Guardian*); 'probably the best rock musician in Britain now' (*Gay News*); 'T. S. Eliot with a rock 'n' roll beat' (*The Times*).

It may have been remarkable timing, or just good luck, but Bowie had no more stage appearances due until a ballroom booking at The Friars in Aylesbury the following Saturday – and Defries arranged for RCA to fly a small group of hand-picked American rock writers in from New York to witness it. RCA were happy to fund this freebie now Bowie had given them both a hit single and a hit album.

The Americans – including Lisa Robinson (*After Dark*), Lilian Roxon, author of the first rock encyclopaedia (*New York Daily News*), Bob Musel (United Press International), Ellen Willis (*The New Yorker*), Alan Rich (*New York*), Lenny Kaye (*Changes*), Henry Edwards, who later co-authored *Stardust* with Zanetta (*The New York Times*), and others from *Playboy*, *Creem* and Andy Warhol's *Interview* – had never seen anything like it – a red-haired rock star in high-heeled boots, his musicians dressed in sequinned shirts open to the waist and skin-tight pants, belting out gay and strangely intellectual songs from Bowie's *Queen Bitch* and *The Width Of A Circle* through to Lou Reed's *Waiting For The Man* and Brel's *Port Of Amsterdam*.

Next day, Defries introduced them to Bowie in an appropriate setting for a star – an ornate suite at the Dorchester Hotel, with the champagne flowing. Each was ushered in one by one for their own 15-minute personal interview with Bowie, who was dressed to inflame, with a dress open to the navel. 'Everything in his pants is absolutely real, sweetie,' called Angie as one wide-eyed writer entered the room, while Bowie told another, 'Call me Ziggy, Ziggy Stardust ...' How were they to know that the star was penniless, living in a rented flat, with barely anything to call his own?

15

# 'Act like stars to be
# treated like stars'

With the success of *Ziggy Stardust*, Tony Defries came totally into his own, master of all he purveyed. When he wasn't pulling master-strokes, it was nothing but deals – and Bowie left all this to him, revelling in his new role, The Star who made all things possible; the songwriter and producer whose magic touch turned donkeys into superstars.

It was an extraordinary turn of events, with no parallel in the history of rock, for Bowie, apparently backed by unlimited funds, began bestowing fame upon his favourites. This was accepted by the press at face value, even though it was widely suspected within the music business that everything was being done on credit. 'I don't know where the money's coming from, but good luck to them,' said Pitt.

This was where the harsh realities of rock 'n' roll economics came into play. Bowie still had those pre-*Ziggy Stardust* bookings to fulfil, at which the whole group worked for no more than £200 a night – nowhere near enough to cover their present expenses; and it could be two years before the *Ziggy Stardust* royalties came in. Meanwhile the wages had to be bankrolled and Bowie's debts continued to escalate.

A more realistic manager would have quailed, but Defries abounded with confidence and as *Ziggy Stardust* started to move in the record shops – 8,000 copies sold in the first week of release and sales mounting steadily thereafter – Defries pulled another series of masterstrokes: he created MainMan, opened his own offices, and, with press interest in David Bowie reaching a peak, made him invisible. Bowie became inaccessible.

\*     \*     \*     \*     \*

MainMan was the name Defries gave to his management

company, which was originally called Minnie Bell Ltd, an off-the-shelf trading company that Defries acquired in 1971 to enable him 'to employ authors and composers and to purchase copyrights of all kinds' with the full personal protection of the British Companies Acts.

Why he should have chosen to change the company's name to MainMan is by no means certain. The Gillmans claim that the title 'was taken from the unattractive phrase "the main man", with its connotations of autocracy, influence and power, then current in the entertainment industry. Its origins were even less appealing, for it was used as black slang for a drug dealer. Defries liked the conceit of formulating the name as MainMan.'[1] That may be so, but I rather doubt it, for 'You're my main man' was a generally jokey phrase much used at the time. It was part of Iggy Pop's street-speak and of Marc Bolan's daily vocabulary, too. He used the words in his song *Telegram Sam* ('Telegram Sam, Telegram Sam,/ You're my main man'), the first release on his own T. Rex Wax Co. label in January 1972, and the first No.1 in which Bolan secured all the rights, thanks to the deals negotiated for him by Secunda. When he recorded the song Bolan told Secunda: 'This one's for you – you're my main man, my Telegram Sam ...' and that's where I suspect Defries pinched the title for his company, although I wouldn't know whether it was his idea or Bowie's, for there was always this intense rivalry between them. Defries changed the name of Minnie Bell Ltd to MainMan Ltd on 30 June 1972, and right from the very start Bowie thought half the company was his.

\*    \*    \*    \*    \*

Over the previous six months, Defries's partner Laurence Myers became increasingly unhappy at the way Defries kept spending money. A prudent accountant, Myers thought Defries was taking too many financial risks. According to the Gillmans, and I have no reason to dispute their figures, Bowie's debt to Gem mounted steadily during early 1972 and by the summer he owed them £29,062.69, while Iggy Pop and Dana Gillespie, both taken on by Gem at Bowie's suggestion, had debts of £5,767 and about £2,000 respectively. Bowie also recommended a third act, Mott The Hoople, who were showing a surplus of £2,603.92, although they subsequently refused to sign a management contract. 'I was very aware that the meter was running,' Myers told the Gillmans, revealing that only 10,961 copies of *Hunky Dory* were sold in the first six months, 'and in the end it got to be a choice between Liberty prints for a new dress for David Bowie and new curtains for Laurence Myers's home'.

Myers told Defries he wanted to end their business relationship, and they agreed the first of several key deals that Defries accomplished that summer. Myers agreed to assign Gem's contracts with Bowie to MainMan Ltd, and in return said he wanted his investment back (i.e. the £29,062.69 plus half-a-million dollars from Bowie's future earnings if he proved to be as successful as Defries predicted). There was one other crucial element in the deal: MainMan Ltd became the owners of the copyright in the two LPs re-assigned from Mercury, and in all the recordings made under Bowie's contracts with RCA.

Bowie also signed a new contract with MainMan Ltd, agreeing his future earnings would be split 50:50 with the company. This may be how he came to believe he owned 50 per cent of MainMan, which he most certainly did not. The Companies House records showed that 99 of the £1 shares were owned by Defries, with the remaining single share allocated to Peter Gerber, an accountant recruited by Defries to work for MainMan. Within days, Defries also formed two other companies, one in the United States with the same name as the British company, MainMan, and a second British company, MainMan Artistes Ltd. Later still, he opened a Japanese company known as MainMan Tokyo, and two more American companies, MainMan East and MainMan West, to function on the East and West coasts.

All this happened at breakneck speed, with Defries moving what were now the MainMan staff into newly leased offices in Gunter Grove in West London, only days after the concert in Aylesbury, and by the time the party of American journalists arrived back in New York, Defries was planning to open offices there, as well.

This was the moment Defries chose to make Bowie invisible, banning all personal interviews and allowing only two photographers to take his photograph. One was Bowie's own 'personal photographer' Leee Black Childers, kitted out in full black leather suits with silver accessories, his hair bleached white and his face a mess of mascara. The other was Mick Rock. The music papers were outraged, for Bowie had wooed them well since *Hunky Dory*, responding to all their questions with brightly original quotes, playing the part so well that they had taken him to their hearts; and now Bowie was plucked away from them like a queen bee wrenched from a hive.

They should have realized – as all the other managers immediately did – that Defries was pulling one of the oldest tricks in the book. An artiste has to be accessible on the way up because publicity is hard to get if you are not famous, and every little helps – but there comes a moment when the skilful manager cuts off media access, and thereby changes the way the game is played. (Col. Tom Parker did it with Elvis Presley, Brian Epstein with The Beatles.) Thereafter interviews are carefully rationed, timed to coincide with the release of new LPs or films, and given only to those journalists who can be trusted not to ask awkward questions.

In Bowie's case, the timing seemed premature to older hands – but Defries had got it right, and Bowie was happy to follow his advice, being preoccupied in the latter part of 1972 by his projects with other artists: helping Mott The Hoople record his song *All The Young Dudes*, and then producing their LP with that same title; co-producing Lou Reed's LP *Transformer* with Mick Ronson, including the memorable single *Walk On The Wild Side*; and also remixing an album for Iggy Pop before co-writing all the songs for the one that followed it, *Raw Power*. Between these sessions, Bowie also recorded his own next single, *John I'm Only Dancing*, which was released on 1 September 1972.

Denied their usual access, the London music press nevertheless turned out in force for Bowie's next concerts at the Rainbow Theatre on 19 and 20 August. Defries talked up the shows in advance, inviting other stars to attend as Bowie's guests, while Bowie brought Lindsay Kemp down from Edinburgh to add a mime routine, and Natasha Korniloff to design new stage costumes, making him a hand-stitched elastic jump suit that exposed his crotch in all its glory. Bowie was leaving nothing to the imagination, or to chance.

Bowie's audience were becoming as odd as his stage act. There were hardcore homosexual cruisers, dressed in tight black leathers and silver jewellery, with their heads shaved bald and sporting greasy moustaches, and silky, feminine queens, plus a growing army of younger Ziggies, who were beginning to bleach, dye and blow-dry their hair and wear outrageous pant-suits, though seldom with Bowie's panache. They first turned out in noticeable numbers at the Rainbow and Bowie delighted them, putting on another histrionic show, with a stage set made of scaffolding, enough dry ice to enshroud the stage in fog, a suspended screen for photo-imagery, a troupe of dancers trained by Lindsay Kemp and calling themselves The Astronettes, and Kemp himself in a spotlight for the *Starman* routine, leering and louche, like a refugee from a Left Bank revue, with a cigarette drooping from his lips.

Not everyone liked it. Elton John was reported to have walked out half-way through, saying, 'David's blown it!' while Bryan Ferry said 'I don't think it's worked' – but the music papers loved it. 'Breathtaking,' reported *Record Mirror*, while Charles Shaar Murray told readers of the *New Musical Express* they had missed a 'thoroughly convincing demonstration of his ascendancy over any other soloist in rock today' – and that within only three months of the release of *Ziggy Stardust*.

Convincing it may have been, but Bowie was still seeing very little money for his efforts. His fees at the Rainbow were £1,000 for the first show and £1,250 for the second which was hurriedly arranged when promoter Mel Bush discovered how fast tickets were selling (and Defries realized he could ask for an extra 25 per cent). That would not have been enough to pay for the stage sets, the extra musicians hired for the night, rehearsal-time and performance fees for the dancers and Lindsay Kemp and The Spiders from Mars – and within a week Bowie was back on the road, *still* fulfilling old bookings in farflung places, even performing in jeans and T-shirts when he was far from London, with no journalists in the audience and not a photographer in the house.

The money was running out, but still Defries kept his nerve. His next big target was the American market with the release there of *Ziggy Stardust*. In between his promotional pushes at home, Defries whisked Bowie to New York for a weekend of fast-talking to convince RCA that now was the moment to back their judgement with hard cash. Having secured their backing, Defries smoothly swung into action.

During that short series of gigs after his Rainbow concerts, Bowie spent two nights at The Hard Rock, a newly opened Manchester venue. With all his entourage, Bowie was booked in to The Excelsior Hotel near Manchester Airport, where Defries invited them to a party after the second show, and then staged a 'business meeting' in a hired conference suite the following morning. Bowie and Defries sat at opposite ends of a long table with Ronson, Bolder, Woodmansey, the road managers, lighting engineers, hair stylist, dressers and three bodyguards seated around the table.

According to Zanetta, who was now starting to work for Defries in New York and was later appointed President of the American MainMan operation:

> Tony explained that in two weeks' time they would be in the United States, and as far as RCA was concerned, David was the biggest thing to come out of England since and possibly before The Beatles. Each and every member of the group had to look like a million dollars. They had to act like stars so that they would be treated like stars. They had to learn to spend money, and spend it in the right way. They were to go out and buy everything they needed for America. They were to buy all the new clothes they needed, all the necessary equipment – two of everything because they might need spares. They had to learn to spend. No one dared challenge Defries. They charged 50,000 dollars worth of new equipment for the eight American shows. Spending was part of their mission, and they were cushioned by the unreality that was at the core of the entire experience.

Defries left for New York, moving into a duplex apartment on the Upper East Side with Zanetta occupying the second bedroom, and the other rooms turned over to MainMan's embryonic American operation. Their immediate mission was to make Bowie's forthcoming eight-city US tour a media sensation – on credit. Meanwhile, having had a nasty flight back from Cyprus,* Bowie was travelling in stately style across the Atlantic on board the *Queen Elizabeth 2*. He and Angie travelled in one first-class cabin, with Underwood and his wife Birgit in another. Bowie insisted on tickets for the Underwoods to keep him company. They were booked in to The Plaza Hotel in New York together with Ronson, Bolder and Woodmansey, Bowie's personal hairdresser Suzy Fussey and the appointed tour photographer Mick Rock, their road managers and the three bodyguards, who had all been told that if

---

* This story has been told in many different forms. Bowie told me he had a bad flight returning to London after spending Christmas 1971 with Angie's parents in Cyprus. Zanetta suggests Bowie did not want to go back to Cyprus again, and feigned fear as an excuse, adding that Bowie claimed to have had a dream in which his father warned him never to fly again, saying he only had five years to live. I still think the most likely explanation is the first: it was a bad trip.

they needed anything while staying at The Plaza they should charge it down to account.

RCA, who seem to have underestimated the implications of allowing credit to Bowie's entourage, were making their own plans for the visit, knowing the *QE 2* would dock in New York on Sunday 17 September, with Bowie due to make his American stage debut five days later at the Cleveland Music Hall. RCA wanted to have one of their own men present on the tour and, after more coaxing by Defries, Gustl Breuer found himself called in to meet the RCA President Rocco Laginestra. After ten years with the Company, Breuer had risen to be Vice President of their Classical Division, Red Seal.

'Congratulations,' chorused the other dark-suited executives as Breuer walked into the room, for none of them was keen on the prospect of travelling around the United States in a Greyhound bus, accompanying this strange young Englishman wearing women's dresses and mascara.

'We've got just the job for you … you're going out on the road with David Bowie,' said Laginestra.

'What is a "David Bowie"?' asked the genuinely puzzled Breuer, a Jewish refugee from war-time Austria who often accompanied classical artistes on their American tours. If he could smooth the way for Artur Rubinstein and Leontyne Price, why not Bowie? – that was RCA's reasoning.

Hearing this response, a man in a raccoon overcoat pushed forward and embraced him. 'You're just the man,' said Defries, who was always happiest to have people working with him, such as Dai Davies and the cast of *Pork*, who had no loyalties elsewhere in the music business. So Breuer found himself standing on the quay when the *QE 2* docked in New York, accompanied by other RCA executives, Zanetta and another new recruit to the American MainMan operation, Cherry Vanilla, who started off as the receptionist and found herself running the 'Film Division' within a year.

As Bowie walked down the gangplank, Breuer stepped forward, introduced himself and explained that he was from RCA and would be accompanying Bowie on tour.

'Any relation to Josef Breuer?' asked Bowie, a wondrous sight with his carrot-red Ziggy hairstyle, as he extended his hand with a charming smile, knowing Josef Breuer had pioneered psycho-analysis and collaborated with Freud.

'Yes, I'm his grandson,' said Breuer, startled that the visiting rock star should ask him a question like that.

'That's very nice. We must talk,' said Bowie, disarming them all, as Breuer led the way to a limousine waiting to whisk them all to The Plaza Hotel, where Defries had arranged a welcoming party in the Oak Room.

\*   \*   \*   \*   \*

Whether it was Defries's idea or Bowie's does not really matter, but between them they agreed to recruit the former cast of *Pork* to run the American MainMan operation, and so Bowie launched himself in New York with a certain degree of artistic credit. With over-dressed actors and actresses sitting at typewriters and answering the phones, the idea was to give MainMan the same kind of buzz that a visitor found at Warhol's Factory. The more outrageous they looked, the better. The aim was to shock. There were leather-clad messengers, their faces painted like characters in a Fellini film, and girls dressed up like Ziggy Stardust, wearing the brightest of clothes and spiky red hair.

'It sounds a crazy set-up to me,' said Pitt, who was closely following events in New York, learning with growing astonishment how a rapidly expanding MainMan staff was being recruited to plan Bowie's concerts. 'David is staying at one of the most expensive hotels in New York, and I hear he hasn't got enough money in his pocket to buy a packet of cigarettes. He's broke, absolutely broke, and whenever he wants a smoke he has to charge another packet of cigarettes down to his room account. RCA will go mad when they get the bill. I can't see where it will end.'

Elsewhere in New York City, the William Morris Agency faced a dilemma of a different kind: how to arrange a tour schedule for a visiting British rock star who was still refusing to travel by plane. There was only one answer: set the dates far apart and allow plenty of time for bus travel between concerts – which was how David Bowie came to spend much of September, October and November 1972 travelling across the United States in a second-hand Greyhound bus, usually sitting at the back, several seats away from his wife, gazing out of the window at this new, unfamiliar landscape, writing lyrics and composing the songs that were to comprise his next album, *Aladdin Sane*.

*   *   *   *   *

If anyone in MainMan knew what they were doing, it was a well-kept secret. The Welshman Dai Davies, who had never been to America or worked on a rock tour, was sent down to Cleveland to help with the arrangements for the first concert on 22 September. As Davies was totally bewildered, Leee Black Childers was sent down too, dressed as usual in black from head to toe. 'This won't do,' they told the far more experienced promoter as they consulted Defries's check-list. 'It says in the contract that David is to be supplied with 6-foot piano ... this one is eight inches short!' When the promoter insisted that this was the finest piano in Cleveland, they phoned Defries. 'Cancel the show,' he barked, issuing what was to become a familiar command as the MainMan circus began to criss-cross the United States of America. It rarely came to that. Defries would usually relent in the end, but only after anyone who crossed his path had been left in no doubt that he was in control, the man who made every decision.

Not only was there no piano, there was also no pianist – and Bowie's extravagant stage show definitely required accompaniment. At his Rainbow concerts, he was accompanied by Matthew Fisher, formerly of Procol Harum, and in his studio sessions by Rick Wakeman, who declined the offer of a regular job with the band.

'I know someone,' said Ken Glancey at RCA, a keen jazz fan, mentioning the name of Mike Garson, a classically trained New York musician and piano teacher. When Defries phoned him, Garson said: 'I can't come now. I'm giving a piano lesson and the next one is waiting.'

'You must come,' said Defries, stressing how strongly he had been recommended. Eventually, Garson agreed, sending one of his students home and leaving the other looking after his baby daughter. At the RCA studios, Bowie sat in the control room while Ronson ran through the guitar chords to *Changes*. Garson started to play. After a few moments, Garson says it was only eight seconds, Ronson told him: 'You've got the gig.'

'How much do you want?' asked Defries, who, as always, took care of the money.

'Eight hundred dollars a week?' suggested Garson, intentionally underrating himself, thinking Ronson, Bolder and Woodmansey,

On the threshold of his solo career. Bowie released his first single with The Lower Third in August 1965, calling himself DAVY JONES – and sometimes DAVIE JONES. The single was *You've Got A Habit of Leaving*. By January, his name was changed to DAVID BOWIE – and they released their second and last single, *Can't Help Thinking About Me*. © Pictorial Press

Hermione Farthingale, the first woman to capture Bowie's heart. She is pictured here with Bowie and John Hutchinson in their group Feathers. Bowie wrote several songs for her and was devastated when she left him. The trio broke up soon after this photograph was taken. © Ray Stevenson/Retna

CH-ch-ch-ch-ch-changes . . . Bowie and his first wife Angie on their wedding day with his mother Mrs Margaret Jones, who discovered they were to marry by keeping an eye on the noticeboard at Bromley Register Office. Her hunch paid off, and when they found her on the doorstep on March 20th 1970 she was invited to join them. Without telling them, Mrs Jones had phoned the local newspaper who sent the photographer. © Pictorial Press

The Return of The Thin White
Duke, Bowie appearing at the
Congress Centrum Halle in
Hamburg, April 1976, performing
in Europe for the first time in three
years. Three days later, Bowie
moved into his new home in
Switzerland in almost total secrecy.
© Ellen Poppinga/K&K/Redferns

With yet another image
abandoned, Bowie returns to the
Congress Centrum Halle in May
1978, no longer The Thin White
Duke, but instead The Svelte
Lounge Lizard, wearing a snakeskin style long jacket. His costume
was specially designed for him by
his former lover Natasha Korniloff.
© Van Houten/Pictorial Press

David Bowie and Mick Jagger, firm friends for over twenty-five years, performing *Dancing In The Street*. The video was shown throughout the day during the Live Aid Concert (July 13th 1985), and their single was a No. 1 hit for a month. All royalties were donated to the Live Aid appeal. © Redferns

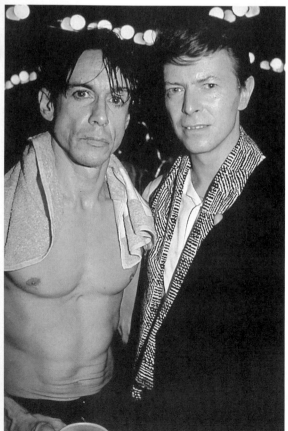

Another of Bowie's enduring friendships has been with Iggy Pop. They met in 1972. They have appeared on each other's LPs, shared a flat in Berlin, toured together and even been busted by the US police – and both have survived. © Jerry Busacca/Retna

Bowie meets his teenage idol
Little Richard at a Los Angeles
party to launch the *Tin Machine
II* album in 1991. Also
photographed with them is Tin
Machine bass player Tony
Sales. © Robert Matheu/Retna

Once he was the unknown
musician paying Warhol a
courtesy call. Now, more than
twenty years later, Bowie the
Actor is starring as Warhol in
the cinema movie *BASQUIAT*,
which was filmed in New York
in the summer of 1995. The film
was directed by Julian Schnabel.
© Bill Davila/Retna

DAVID BOWIE

stars in

NICOLAS ROEG'S

dramatic new film of

# THE MAN WHO FELL TO EARTH

by WALTER TEVIS

Pan

A characteristically obtuse Bowie joke. The front cover design for the paperback edition of THE MAN WHO FELL TO EARTH (Pan Books, 1976) is similar to the sleeve design for his LP *LOW*. The music he had written for the film was not used but could instead be heard on the *LOW* album. © Pan Books

Essex Music move in to capture Bowie's new feminine image when they re-published *THE LAUGHING GNOME* sheet music in 1973 to coincide with the re-release of the DERAM single. This was done without Bowie's co-operation, but the single sold over 250,000 copies in Britain and reached No. 6 in the Charts.

Frontcover of *Rolling Stone*, (main picture) and cutting from *New Musical Express*, both from 1976.

as established members of the group, would be on around two thousand dollars a week.

'Fine,' said Defries, looking a little dazed, but quickly recovering his composure. He agreed so quickly that Garson was half-kicking himself, wishing he had asked for more, never dreaming for a moment that he had been hired in desperation when the others were being paid the same money they had been receiving for the past year in Britain, £30 a week.

MainMan's publicity were still under instructions to deny all requests for interviews, but Bowie would answer questions readily enough if anyone broke through their cordon, and Defries himself agreed to be interviewed by Timothy Ferris for *Rolling Stone* as part of the build-up for this first American tour. They met at The Plaza Hotel. 'Bowie is setting a standard in rock 'n' roll which other people are going to have to get to if they want to stay around in the 70s,' said Defries.[2] 'I think he's very much a 70s artist. I think most of the artists who are with us at the moment are 60s artists, and Bowie, certainly to me, is going to be the major artist of the 70s. In 1975, he will be at his peak in music. What he does after that is going to depend on what his talents are in other fields…. I want to see him making feature films…. Bowie himself often says he is not a musician, and really isn't. To me, he has the potential to be a major force in films in the way he has been in music.'

The highlight of this American tour was intended to be Bowie's first concert at Carnegie Hall, where The Beatles also appeared in February 1964, but first there were two out-of-town shows, a sensible precaution with Bowie working with a new pianist.

For the opening show in Cleveland all 3,500 tickets sold out in advance, Davies and Childers having done what they were supposed to do, winding up the local press and radio station disc jockeys to ensure maximum advance promotion.

It was the same story in Memphis, where Davies and Childers were already working on the local media before Bowie's main entourage arrived in Cleveland. Defries was taking another leaf out of the circus tradition, having learned from biographies of Elvis Presley and Colonel Tom Parker that it was always the advance promotion men who went out on the road ahead of the elephants, lions and clowns. As the tour bus approached Memphis, Bowie asked the driver to take him past Graceland so that he could see Presley's home, and then it was on to the Memphis

Auditorium, also sold out in advance. 'They loved it. They screamed. They yelled. They danced on their seats and begged for more,' wrote critic John E. Dove in the *Memphis Commercial Appeal*.

News of this success was already filtering back to the radio disc jockeys and rock critics in New York. MainMan and RCA prepared Bowie's path, distributing PR leaflets, press cuttings and photographs, and making sure every rock writer living within 150 miles of New York received tickets for the shows – and not only them, but also the shakers and movers on the New York social circuit, from Andy Warhol to Lee Radziwill, sister of Jackie Kennedy, and the actors Alan Bates and Anthony Perkins. The cast of *Pork* were also doing their bit, distributing tickets to Ziggy wannabees, gays and transvestites alike, to ensure that on the night Bowie played to an audience that was geared to the occasion. They need not have worried. By the day of the concert, 28 September, tickets were selling at a black market premium, and no one at MainMan or RCA had any left to give to the clamouring socialites now desperate to be seen in the audience on the big night.

Although he had 'flu, Bowie gave them a 90-minute show to remember, again preceded by Beethoven's overture, with heavy rock guitar from Ronson, a solo acoustic treatment for *Space Oddity*, Jacques Brel's *My Death* narrated as a poem, songs from his early albums and then a change of costume for a *Ziggy Stardust* sequence, with *Rock 'n' Roll Suicide* as the finale, fingertips outstretched to the audience: 'You're not alone, give me your hands'.

Pacing around backstage, Defries was happy. Bowie had made no money, but the show was a success – because Defries pulled off another of the ancient tricks of the business, 'papering the hall' – giving away more tickets than were sold to be sure of a packed house.

On the whole, the critics were pleased. Don Heckman of the *New York Times* declared Bowie 'brings a strong sense of professionalism to every move he makes. As a performer, Bowie delivered. He understands that theatricality has more to do with presence than with gimmickry, and that beautifully co-ordinated physical movements and well-planned music can reach an audience a lot quicker than aimless prancing and high-decibel electronics ...' A week later, *Newsweek* devoted a full page to

'THE STARDUST KID' and Lilian Roxon in the *New York Daily News* mirrored Coleman of *Melody Maker*, saying 'A STAR IS BORN' and acclaiming Bowie as 'a great songwriter and lyricist ·as well as a great showman and entertainer', while the trade paper *Billboard* reported, 'Bowie set himself a number of impossible requirements for the full success of this tour, and then, being Bowie, proceeded to meet all of them with grace.'

The tour was achieving its purpose, arousing media interest in the right places (no one expects to make money on a first American tour), but it was not gaining its other main objective. *Ziggy Stardust* was not selling as well as RCA hoped. Audiences were good in Washington, Boston and Detroit, but once the Greyhound bus hit the mid-West it became clear Bowie was virtually unknown outside the big city conurbations. Less than a tenth of the seats were sold in St Louis for a hall that seated 10,000 – and MainMan staff wandered around the city unable to give them away. Bowie still went ahead with his show, gathering the audience around the stage as he had at the Hampstead Country Club, and performing directly to them. 'An embarrassing failure became a personal triumph,' says Zanetta, adding, 'By now the tour was bankrupt. The idea that David could sell 10,000 tickets in the mid-West had been a preposterous one ...' Under the terms of his own contracts, Defries was responsible for tour expenses if the tickets failed to sell and with the size of the tour party having now grown to 46 personnel, Zanetta says 'the losses were spectacular'.

In Kansas City, losses were worse, with only 250 tickets sold – and Bowie was distressed to learn HOUSE FULL notices were going up outside every venue for Cat Stevens, who was also touring the mid-West. 'The truth was clear,' says Zanetta.[3] 'David was a sensation in some cities and almost totally unknown in others. It was a truth he didn't like. It was Tony's fault for booking him in cities in which he was playing to empty seats. Empty seats destroyed the illusion of stardom. But he could not give himself permission to get angry at Tony; instead he went on stage drunk. He was so upset he got very drunk, and during the show he fell off the stage into the house. But he didn't miss a note. It was a *graceful* fall. Even in his despair, he seemed to be always watching himself.'

Defries responded to this near-crisis by encouraging Bowie and his immediate entourage to continue living like stars. 'We were encouraged to drink champagne and eat huge dinners and sign

everything,' says Leee Black Childers.[4] So MainMan's debts
started to mount across America, although Defries still managed to
keep some kind of running float by picking up the cash taken at
the box office of those concerts that were successful, and then
doling out small sums in extremis, sometimes allowing Davies and
Childers as little as a hundred dollars when they set off to prepare
Bowie's path in another city.

After Kansas, next stop Los Angeles – with four days to kill
before the first of two concerts at Santa Monica Civic Auditorium.
The New York critic Lisa Robinson told them there was only one
place to stay – The Beverly Hills Hotel. 'You're supposed to be
promoting a big star,' she told Childers. 'David and Tony must
each have his own private bungalow. The others can stay in suites.
Make sure to reserve poolside cabanas. That means you're really
important. When you're poolside you have yourself paged
continually. That's the Hollywood way.'

As the advance man, Childers told the RCA Promotion
Department in Los Angeles that this was what Mr Bowie wanted –
and all 46 members of the party, including Garson's wife and two
children, Iggy Pop, and various groupies, were booked into this
famous hotel, with Perry Como on one side of Garson's bungalow
and Elton John on the other. By now, the cash had all been spent –
and so every minor need, food, drink, cigarettes, or whatever, was
charged down to account. As no one had any money at all for
taxis, they all travelled wherever they wanted to go by hired
limousine because these could also be signed down to the RCA
account.

The tour was originally due to end with the shows at Santa
Monica but, having left Bowie's diary for the autumn clear in case
*Ziggy Stardust* became an American hit, Defries was now busily
trying to squeeze in extra concerts in the hope MainMan could
recoup its losses. This was how the whole of this entourage came
to spend a fortnight at The Beverly Hills Hotel, still signing every
bill put in front of them with the magic words 'RCA Records and
Tapes'. The bill for that fortnight came to $100,000, including
$20,000 for room service – and none of that yet earned. 'We lived
in total, total luxury,' says Garson.

Meanwhile, Angie – who had endured the spectacle of her
husband disappearing into bedrooms with any pretty woman who
came into view – was transforming herself into Mrs Superstar. She
bleached her hair platinum to look like Marilyn Monroe, shaved

her eyebrows, painted her lips a violent red and dressed in the best
finery she could buy, joining the party in Chicago with Cyrinda
Foxe, another Monroe look-alike, whom Bowie seemed to prefer
to his wife.

Cyrinda, who turned down a job with MainMan rather than
shave her head Ziggy-fashion, became part of the travelling circus
in New York, where she soon realized that part of the bodyguards'
main function was to sort through the groupies, make sure none of
them had any venereal diseases, and often pass them on to Bowie
having fucked them first.

'We'd spy through those old Plaza Hotel keyholes, and we'd
watch the bodyguards giving it to some groupie,' said Cyrinda.[5]
'After they were through, David would occasionally take over, and
I would sit in a chair and talk to him while he was having sex. I'd
watch television and sit in a chair, because he wanted somebody to
talk to, so I was good for that ...'

While Bowie was sharing his bed with whatever women were
available, Angie was enjoying a 'happy dalliance' with Anton
Jones, a tall, black Jamaican 'built like an ox'[6] whose presence
was for her 'far and away the high point of the tour'. Late one
night – she cannot remember whether it was Memphis or Louis-
ville or somewhere else – there was a fracas in a motel swimming
pool, with the management objecting to her swimming naked with
this huge Jamaican – 'who knows who had what in whose mouth?'
she says – and Bowie himself, usually reluctant to face unpleasant-
ness head-on, came down to the lobby to pacify the management.
'He got rid of me as quickly as he could,' says Angie. 'I was on
my way to New York the next day, and back to London very soon
after that. The effect was lasting. From that moment on I was
never invited along on tour. I'd go on the road for brief periods
now and then ... but usually those times would end just the way
my first tour ended.'

It was only two-and-a-half years since their wedding, but
already the marriage was an embarrassment. Bowie moved
Cyrinda Foxe in to his cabana at The Beverly Hills Hotel, and she
was followed by dozens if not hundreds of other women, many of
them black, in towns and cities in America and across the world.
Their names rarely mattered, for Bowie had sex like other men
pass urine. He was, I suspect, a deeply lonely man, trapped in a
miserable marriage, and yet with a son whom he adored, and a

relationship with Defries that was bound to end in tears. But none of this was brought to a head. The situation was allowed to drift.

\* \* \* \* \*

As they criss-crossed America in late 1972, Bowie increasingly withdrew within himself, and yet remained totally in charge musically, writing his next single *The Jean Genie* early on in the tour during an overnight stop in Nashville, then recording it in the RCA studios. With Bowie still revelling in his gay/bisexual image, the title was probably a pun on the name of the homosexual French writer Jean Genet\* with an ambiguity in the lyric, describing how 'small Jean Genie' 'lives on his back' and 'sits like a man/but smiles like a reptile'.

Also during the tour Bowie wrote the songs for the next album, *Aladdin Sane*, basing this title track on an idea taken from Evelyn Waugh's novel *Vile Bodies*, describing the young partying through the night as the threat of war is looming: 'battle cries and champagne, just in time for sunrise'. Some critics suggested the title was another Bowie play on words, describing his half-brother still in the Cane Hill institution, but Bowie himself insisted Aladdin was Ziggy Stardust in America – becoming 'a lad insane'.

Another song, *Drive-In Saturday*, was written on the road between Seattle and Phoenix, when Bowie says he saw the moon reflected on 17 or 18 domes: 'I couldn't find out from anyone what they were, but they gave me a vision of America, Britain and China after a nuclear catastrophe. The radiation has affected people's minds and reproductive organs, and they don't have a sex life. The only way they can learn to make love again is by watching films of how it used to be done.'

*Panic In Detroit* was written in Los Angeles after a night with Iggy Pop, reminiscing about his home city, with Bowie temporarily viewing Iggy as a political radical because of his stories about street violence in Detroit, while *Cracked Actor*, also written at The Beverly Hills Hotel, reflected the people he saw while being driven down Hollywood Boulevard, where Bowie thought it was

---

\* Throughout the tour, there was a strange dichotomy between press stories suggesting Bowie was gay and the private reality which saw him bedding one woman after another. No doubt Bowie enjoyed the air of sexual mystique, but when the songwriter Kim Fowley asked him if he was gay at a Hollywood party, Bowie replied: 'Don't believe all the publicity.'

impossible to tell the stars and starlets from the crooks, prostitutes and runaway children.

*     *     *     *     *

All tickets were sold for both shows at the Santa Monica Civic Auditorium, and the circus then moved on to San Francisco and Seattle, with Leee Black Childers left behind in Los Angeles by Defries to rent a house, provide a home for Iggy Pop, and establish MainMan West, while Angie, tiring of life on her own in London, gathered together Iggy's Stooges and flew with them back to Los Angeles, charging the air fares down to Defries's account, without telling him first. Everyone in Bowie's 'family' was now learning the trick of charging their expenses down to somebody else; and if not RCA, why not MainMan? Defries was furious but held back from a confrontation because he knew that although Bowie avoided his wife wherever possible, he was reluctant to actually ditch her, believing (in my view wrongly) that her judgement on career issues was often good.

With the tour now progressing across America again as 1972 waned, with dates set in Dallas, Houston, New Orleans, Nashville, Pittsburgh and Philadelphia, Angie took to materializing unexpectedly, with a new boyfriend, Scott Richardson – and in Philadelphia with another boy dressed all in green, with green lipstick, green eyeshadow and green nail polish. 'This is for you,' she said in her squeaky-shrill voice, clasping her husband's hand, and steering The Jean Genie towards the Green Genie. Bowie visibly flinched.

Bowie's life was becoming madder by the day, with drugs freely available backstage, and a steady supply of fresh (and not-so-fresh) women, but only the good news was filtered through to Britain, with MainMan staff at Gunter Grove making sure the London music papers were kept fully supplied with photographs, press cuttings and gossip column stories that kept up the mythical momentum, Ziggy Conquers America. 'The amount of publicity generated by the tour was astounding,' says Zanetta, totting up the receipts with Defries, who was back in New York ahead of the tour party, marching in and out of RCA Records with new ideas. This was the moment that he chose to tell RCA they could lease Bowie's two Mercury LPs, against an advance for the two of $75,000, which would enable them to double up on their available product and use the same promotional budget to sell four LPs instead of two. 'It won't cost you another dollar in advertising,' he told the RCA executives, telling them they could also rerelease *Space Oddity* (in fact, the first of the Mercury LPs, initially titled *David Bowie*, later reissued as *Man Of Words, Man Of Music*, now became *Space Oddity*).

Together with his bus-load of musicians, bodyguards, road crew, hairdresser, photographer and hangers-on, Bowie spent 71 days in the United States on this first tour, playing only 21 concerts in 16 cities. According to Zanetta, the box office receipts totalled $114,000, the net cost to RCA $400,000. 'RCA lost about 20,000 dollars each time David stepped on stage,' he says.

None of this distressed Defries, who was already busily making plans for Bowie to return to the United States within ten weeks for another tour. 'This first tour was merely a rehearsal,' Defries told RCA. 'We must keep going now. We mustn't lose faith. David is going to be a huge international star.' He was comforted in this belief by an offer from Japan for Bowie to appear there with a guarantee of $6,000 per show. 'It won't just be an American tour, it will be a world tour,' he insisted, immediately starting to make plans for Bowie to tour Britain as well.

This time, however, there would be one vital difference. An RCA accountant would travel with MainMan's accountant, with the touring company staying at medium-priced hotels – and only David Bowie himself allowed room service and free use of a limousine.

16

# The Spiders find God
# and Ziggy bows out

In December 1972 David Bowie returned home to London a genuine superstar. Shrewd manipulation of the press while he was away kept his name constantly in the music papers. Everyone knew of his triumphs at Carnegie Hall, Santa Monica and the Tower Theatre in Philadelphia, and Bowie came back to find RCA promoting his four albums, with a fifth, *Aladdin Sane*, due for release in April, and *The Jean Genie* his best-selling single yet. It was a media blitz, for the Iggy Pop, Lou Reed and Mott The Hoople albums were in the shops as well, and Bowie was now being projected as the supreme artist, a man of many talents.

As a performer, producer, writer and recording artist, Bowie looked like a man whose time had come, and Defries rounded off the year by arranging two more concerts at the Rainbow Theatre on 23 and 24 December (the audiences were asked to bring children's toys to be distributed among Dr Barnardo's homes, the charity for which Bowie's father had worked), and another at the Manchester Hard Rock (28th). After only a week's break over the New Year, 1973 began with concerts in Glasgow, Edinburgh, Newcastle and Preston; then Bowie was back in the recording studios.

Between all this, and choosing costumes for his next American tour, Bowie made one TV appearance, on the *Russell Harty Plus* chat show, in mid-January 1973. Harty asked if he believed in God.

'I believe in an energy force, but I wouldn't like to put a name to it,' replied Bowie.

'Do you indulge in any form of worship?' continued Harty.

'Eeeer ... um ... life. I love life very much indeed,' said a smiling Bowie, knowing (as Harty did not) that religion was tearing a hole in his band. It was a fairly well kept secret, but The

Spiders from Mars had found God, in a combination of
Scientology and the Jehovah's Witnesses.

Garson, who was flown over from New York to join Bowie and
The Spiders at Trident Studios where they were finishing off the
*Aladdin Sane* LP, was a committed Scientologist, a practising
Minister of Dianetics. Originally a form of psychotherapy defined
in L. Ron Hubbard's book *Dianetics: The Modern Science Of
Mental Health* (1950), this developed into a religious philosophy
through which its followers are supposed to gain self-knowledge, a
higher IQ and increased powers of creativity. Much emphasis is
placed on counselling, or as they call it 'auditing', an intensive
form of personal enquiry through which followers are expected to
know themselves better and become more self-reliant.

Travelling on the Greyhound bus across America, Garson found
ready listeners in Bolder and Woodmansey, easy-going, North
Country boys who were none too enthused by the decadence,
surrounding the tour. Like Ronson, they hated having to continually tell their parents and friends back home in Hull: 'We're not
gay! You mustn't believe what you read in the papers.' They also
resisted the more extreme attempts by Bowie and Defries to
persuade them to cut and bleach their hair and dress bizarrely.

While booze and drugs flowed at The Beverly Hills Hotel, and a
queue of women passed through its cabanas, Bolder and Woodmansey quietly dined with the Garsons, shared the odd bottle of
wine, and debated Scientology. When he realized how long they
would all have to stay there, Garson took them to a week-long
course at the Los Angeles Scientology Celebrity Center, a unit
especially established to gain recruits in the entertainment
industry, together with one of Bowie's bodyguards, Tony Frost.
After that, they were all changed men.

Kenneth Pitt even managed to learn about this, although nothing
appeared in the press. 'I hear there are ructions back stage,' he told
me one day. 'The band have found God.'

Garson's attempts to discuss his religion with Bowie fell on
stonier ground. Bowie was now reaching a higher plane of total
self-absorption. Already thin as a wraith, his skin stretched tight
over his rib cage, Bowie would lose 2lbs in weight during every
concert, replenish his strength through alcohol, cocaine and
smidgins of food, and take whatever the night had to offer. He was
in a world of his own and only came down to earth when he found
a good book, or when the work in hand captured his concentration.

On the road, Defries's travelling arrangements cocooned Bowie from the outside world. He might occasionally be matey with the road crew or with Ronson, but more often than not he would be sitting alone, lost in his own thoughts.

At the first mention of Scientology Bowie recoiled, but he warmed to Garson in the recording studio, sharing his enthusiasm for modern jazz and willing to learn whatever anyone had to tell him about classical music. On the *Aladdin Sane* sessions, Garson came into his own, playing with a touch of Chopin or Liszt or easily sliding into contemporary jazz piano, especially on the title track, and then firmly taking control of the rhythm on *Watch That Man*. Bowie now knew that he had, more or less by accident, found himself a pianist who could accompany anyone, from Herbie Hancock to Mel Torme. Garson was indispensable; the others were not.

\* \* \* \* \*

With *Aladdin Sane* in the can (and due to attract advance orders of over 100,000 before being released in Britain in April), Bowie left for the United States on 25 January 1973, again taking the *Queen Elizabeth 2* from Southampton while his entourage travelled by plane. Bowie did not know it, but the band were unhappy and Ronson had been deputed by the others to make contact with Dennis Katz, who had left RCA to resume his career as a showbusiness lawyer.

Woodmansey, who was closer to Garson than the others, asked how much he was being paid. When he replied 'Eight hundred dollars a week,' Woodmansey revealed that he and Bolder were still working for only £30 a week, cash in hand, with all expenses paid, while Ronson, the more experienced of the three, was on £50 a week. 'David must be making a fortune,' said Woodmansey, neither of them suspecting for a moment that Bowie was virtually penniless, that the US tour lost money, or that MainMan was spending money it did not have. After months of charging anything down to the RCA account, The Rats from Hull became convinced they were being exploited. Ronson also thought he was not being given credit for his own achievements in arranging much of Bowie's music, and they were all outraged to hear Bowie was planning to hire more musicians for this next tour. This did not impress the existing Spiders, who argued that if The Who or

The Rolling Stones could go out on the road as a four-piece or five-piece band, why couldn't they? Why wasn't the extra money being given to them? Wasn't Bowie getting too big for his boots? And weren't they being exploited? While Bowie sailed majestically across the Atlantic in his first-class suite, Ronson was telling Katz: 'We'll go ahead with this tour, but then we're quitting ... we'll form our own band. We can't go on like this. We're not making enough money. Do you think you could help us find a record deal?'

\*   \*   \*   \*   \*

Bowie arrived in New York every inch the Rock Star Arriviste, booked, it was true, into a cheaper hotel (The Gramercy Park) but still with a limousine at his disposal 24 hours a day to take him around the city: for private dinners, to visit Max's Kansas City, to catch Charlie Mingus, Thelonius Monk or The New York Dolls. He was hanging out with such friends as Alice Cooper or Todd Rundgren, and yet did not hesitate to take Rundgren's girlfriend Bebe Buell back to his bed when the opportunity arose.

Few were immune to his charm. When Bowie fainted on stage during the tour's opening show at Radio City Music Hall, Bette Midler dashed backstage to see if there was anything she could do to help. 'It's alright. I haven't been eating enough,' he explained, while Salvador Dali, Andy Warhol, Allen Ginsberg and Johnny Winter waited in the stalls to see if there would be an encore.

Two accountants were watching the money and Defries kept the tour in profit as the bus swept down to Philadelphia for five nights at the Tower Theatre, and then on to Nashville, Memphis, Detroit, Chicago and Los Angeles, where Bowie performed twice at the Long Beach Auditorium, hosting a private dinner party for Ringo Starr and Klaus Voorman, and watching Bette Midler's show at the Auditorium the following night. He was now happily mixing with established stars as an equal, leaving The Spiders from Mars far behind. When Defries heard of their plotting, Bolder and Woodmansey were bought off with a pay rise, and Ronson was told that when the tour ended Defries would make him a solo star, too – just like Bowie – and launch him upon the world stage with his own recording contract, publishing deal, backing musicians, and so on.

'Ronno looked into Defries's eyes and saw the reflection of his

own fame and glory,' says Zanetta.[1] 'The naïve guitarist accepted Defries's offer and shifted his loyalties from The Spiders to Tony. Without a spokesman, the even more naïve Spiders ... had no option but to do as they were told.'

\*  \*  \*  \*  \*

With Bowie now almost totally detached from his musicians, Defries told him it was time he started thinking about his long-term career, to become a movie star. 'I want you to tell all the writers you're going to be starring in *Stranger In A Strange Land*,' said Defries,[2] convinced he could talk Bowie up in Hollywood in much the same way that he did with RCA.

'Robert Heinlein's book?' asked Bowie, who was widely read in science fiction and still occasionally claimed to see UFOs. 'I didn't know they were going to make it into a film.'

'Doesn't matter,' said Defries, playing another of his ploys. 'We're going to tell people you're going to be the star. Doesn't matter if it's true or not. People will believe it. Word will get out. It will be in the press and the first thing you know the scripts will come piling in and you'll be a movie star. I guarantee it, mate.' And Defries was right. They did – though Bowie never made *Stranger In A Strange Land*.

\*  \*  \*  \*  \*

In April 1973, shortly after the concerts at the Long Beach Auditorium, Bowie boarded a boat for Japan, with his musicians and entourage again travelling separately by plane, breaking the journey in London with time to see their families. Besides The Spiders and Garson, the company now included Aynsley Dunbar (drums), Ken Fordham (saxophone) and Hutchinson on both rhythm and 12-string guitar, together with three back-up vocalists, a stage manager, a three-man light crew, a four-man road crew, a wardrobe mistress, a hair stylist, and just one bodyguard. Their wages had to be met before Bowie saw any money, but that was no problem on this leg of the tour. Under the terms of his deal with the Japanese, Defries was guaranteed a minimum of $6,000 for each of eight shows – which was just as well, for the shows in Hiroshima, Nagoya, Kobe and Osaka all lost money, with fewer than a thousand tickets sold for halls seating between three and

five thousand people. Again, only the good news travelled back to
London, with the MainMan staff at Gunter Grove relaying details
of Bowie's latest 'triumph' to the ever-gullible music press. Then,
ignoring every suggestion that it might be better if she stayed at
home at Haddon Hall and looked after their son, Angie arrived in
Tokyo a day after Bowie, together with Zowie. Bowie's Japanese
audiences were 'incredible', she says,[3] 'almost childlike in their
exuberance ...' They travelled on the Japanese railways with
Zowie, bought outfits from the designer Kansai Yamamoto,
studied the traditions of the Noh and Kabuki theatres, with Bowie
learning the art of make-up, Kabuki-style, from one of its stars,
Tomasu Boru.

   'Faced with an audience that we presume didn't understand a
word of what I was saying, I was more physical than on any other
tour,' said Bowie, who appeared half-naked on stage, wearing only
a Japanese-style tunic around his waist and beneath his crotch,
rather like a floppy jock strap, that made him look painfully thin,
for he now weighed no more than 120lbs. 'I activated the whole
thing with my hands and my body,' he told Charles Shaar Murray.[4]
'I needn't have sung half the time ... they're so into their own
country and their own culture. I think that a little more nationalism
would be very useful to the world. In Japan, the right wing
associates itself with the States and the left wing is very culture
conscious, in the Samurai tradition, into Kabuki theatre, wanting
to be Japanese and free.'

   Angie felt their experience in Japan brought them closer
together again,[5] saying 'we felt like a family' and 'David and I
hadn't made love together in months, but we did in Japan, several
times.' But that may have been because they were in a strange
country, with unfamiliar customs, and no other women readily
available. There were plenty of other women in New York and one
of them, the blonde-headed black singer Ava Cherry, was already
on her way to Europe.

   The Bowies had little time to say their farewells. At his last
concert at Shibuya Kokaido in Tokyo, fans rushed the stage and
police moved in to break up what they thought was a disturbance.
In the crush, some of the seating collapsed and Angie was seen
waving a chair over her head. She said she was trying to save fans
from further injury, but the police accused her of causing a riot
and, believing warrants had been issued for their arrest, she and
Zanetta quickly left the country, flying to London via Honolulu.

The rest of the party travelled back to Britain the following day, except for Bowie, Childers and Bowie's childhood friend Geoffrey MacCormack, who had been one of the back-up singers.

The schedule had been arranged so that Bowie could travel across Europe on the Trans-Siberian Express, and on 21 April the three of them boarded a boat for the mainland, picking up the Express in Vladivostock, and then travelling 6,000 miles over the next eight days to Moscow, and from there down through Russia, Poland and Germany into France and to Paris, where Angie said she would meet him.

On his return, Bowie said: 'Russia is an impossible country to talk about. It's so vast.' Apparently, he travelled 'soft class' (i.e. in a compartment with a comfortable bunk), taking his meals in the dining car, instead of 'hard class' which would have meant squeezing in with hundreds of Russian peasants, packed tight on hard seating. At some stops, he would join them all on the station platforms, buying local food, especially yoghourt.

Travelling in the next compartment was Bob Musel, a veteran American war correspondent now working for the UPI news agency, but also a songwriter with the 50s hit *Poppa Picolino* among his credits. They talked for hours, discussing world politics, literature, philosophy and the entertainment business, with Musel admitting afterwards this wasn't what he expected of a rock musician. There was something else he didn't expect, either. Night after night, Bowie would sit in his compartment, playing guitar, singing songs and readily entertaining other passengers, especially if they were young and female. 'He fucked everything that moved and quite a lot that didn't,' said Musel.

They arrived in Moscow just in time for The May Day Parade, with Bowie, Childers and MacCormack joining the crowds in Red Square, watching Kosygin, Brezhnev and other Russian leaders taking the salute near Lenin's Tomb as the pride of the Russian Army, Navy and Air Force paraded through the square with their missiles, tanks and hardware, carrying banners and portraits of Lenin.

In those Soviet days, there were few souvenirs to be found. Bowie went to the GUM department store, and all he could find was soap and underwear, and when he ate in its restaurant, to try local food, he found the meatballs and potatoes almost indigestible. 'Let me take you for a meal,' said Musel when they met again. 'I know this town ...' and they dined at the overseas visitors' hotel, The National, where the menu included caviar, sturgeon, smoked salmon and a good choice of wines.

\*   \*   \*   \*   \*

Bowie had now been away from Britain for four months, but MainMan's PR department had kept the press and disc jockeys aware of his progress, with RCA busily promoting all five albums, together with a new single – *Drive-In Saturday* coupled with a version of Chuck Berry's *Round And Round*. Many other musicians have toured the United States and Japan, but the fact that Bowie chose to travel by boat and train caught the media's imagination, and Bowie arrived at The George Cinq Hotel for two nights in Paris and a quiet supper with Jacques Brel to find that even the French press wanted him to hold an immediate press conference, while *Melody Maker* sent Ray Hollingworth over to accompany Bowie on the last stage of his journey home. In London, disc jockeys were telling their listeners what time he would leave the Gare du Nord on 4 May and when his train was due at Charing Cross station.

There hadn't been a rock 'n' roll homecoming like this since the early 60s when members of The Beatles Fan Club used to be told well in advance which flight John, Paul, George and Ringo would be travelling on, and at what time their plane would land at Heathrow Airport. Several hundred fans were waiting for Bowie at Charing Cross, but the man they saw stepping off the train was very different to the other, more private Bowie who travelled back with Hollingworth, talking freely: 'I'm sick of being Gulliver.... After America, Moscow, Siberia, Japan ... I just want to bloody well go home to Beckenham and watch the telly.' The Bowies managed to miss the train from Paris, but quickly caught another to Boulogne and then the hovercraft to Dover to make sure they would still be on the same train at Charing Cross. At Dover, Hollingworth watched an elderly lady approach Bowie for his autograph and looked over his shoulder as he signed 'Edmund Gosse'.\*

As they continued the journey home, Bowie agreed: 'It was that piece in *Melody Maker* that made me', and then went on to mourn

---

\* Hollingworth missed the schizophrenic joke. Gosse wrote the autobiographical *Father And Son*, describing it as 'the record of a struggle between two temperaments, two consciences and almost two epochs'.

the abnormality of his new life, the mystique developing around him, the phoney sophistication, and the emergent musicologists who were already casting their grim hand across rock 'n' roll. 'You know,' he said, 'the rock revolution did happen. It really did – the trouble was nobody realized when it happened ... this decadence thing is just a bloody joke. I'm very normal ... I am me, and I have to carry on with what I've started.... I never believed a hype could be made of an artist before the artist had got anywhere. That's what happened, you see. But when I saw our albums were really selling, I knew that one period was over. The hype was over. Well, it wasn't – but at least we'd done something to be hyped about ... I never thought Ziggy would become the most talked about man in the world. I never thought it would become that unreal.... I felt somewhat like a Dr Frankenstein ... you know we're all very normal, and it's about time we told people so.'

The albums were really selling now. *Aladdin Sane* was No.1 in the LP chart and *Drive-In Saturday* No. 3 in the singles chart – and as Bowie stepped off the train, 300 girls rushed forward, screaming, tearing at his clothes, bursting into tears just to touch him, while police bundled Bowie into his waiting car – a hired limousine, of course.

Next day, the Bowies invited their immediate friends – Scott and Visconti, Mick Ronson, the Underwoods, Freddi Burretti, Antonello and Daniella, MacCormack, Suzy Fussey, with all their wives, girlfriends and boyfriends – to their own homecoming party at Haddon Hall. And then it was back on the road *again*, this time with 27 British concerts, opening at Earls Court on 12 May.

Despite touring the States and Japan, Bowie still insisted on rehearsals before the British dates, hiring Led Zeppelin's central London studio, a former cinema, where Paul and Linda McCartney dropped in, just to watch and see how they worked. And then on 10 May, without prior warning, the Bowies arrived on Pitt's doorstep in Manchester Street, knocked on the door and grinned as he opened it. 'They both looked marvellous,' says Pitt.[6] 'We leapt into each other's arms and hugged and kissed and made such a commotion that the German nurse of the doctor on the ground floor looked out to see what was going on.... He seemed to be a relaxed, more assured version of the old David. He asked about old friends and places he remembered and suggested we had dinner together one night.' Angie asked if he would like tickets for the Earls Court show. 'Yes,' said Bowie. 'Come and see what your boy is doing.'

Bowie was booked for two concerts at Earls Court and it was just as well that Pitt chose to attend the first, for Bowie peremptorily cancelled the second after a disastrous show. The vast indoor arena had not previously been used for rock concerts. Its attraction to promoters was its seating capacity of 18,000 – and the tickets, at £2 each, sold out in two days, making this the largest audience ever to attend an indoor London rock concert. A sense of expectation gripped London during the preceding week, with RCA and MainMan telling the press Bowie would be performing in Japanese costumes for the first time, presenting a new selection of songs. By the day of the concert the *Evening Standard* reported that black market scalpers were asking £25 a ticket. With a build-up like that, the show should have had that extra buzz which turns a good concert into a great one, but the acoustics were horribly wrong, with an echo bouncing off the walls. Hundreds of people could not hear properly, while others could not see the stage. Faced with an unruly audience, with some youths stripping naked to dance and others openly pissing in the aisles, Bowie stopped the show at one stage and told them all to 'stop being silly', but the atmosphere did not improve and sections of the audience started walking out. Afterwards, Bowie screamed with rage at those whom he thought responsible and snapped at Defries: 'Cancel the next fucking show!' No one had ever heard him act so decisively, and Defries should have taken this as a warning.

The *New Musical Express* headlined its review 'ALADDIN DISTRESS' and said the show was 'one of the worst examples of a bad deal ever perpetrated on English rock audiences ... one doubts whether more than half were able to see what was going on down on stage, while the sound system veered from adequate to diabolical to totally inaudible'.

Whether Bowie blamed any part of this débâcle on his musicians was never said, and neither did anyone outside his immediate, closest circle of family and friends know that he had been seething with rage since The Spiders confronted Defries with their demand for a pay rise. 'David was furious, just furious,' Angie now reveals.[7] '"That's it," he told me. "They can't hold me up like that.... I simply won't have that kind of disloyalty." ... the lads' days were numbered. What is freaky – chilling – is the fact that he kept them on through the Japanese tour, then through the British tour, without even hinting at his decision.'

Three days later, on 15 May, Bowie boarded the train from King's Cross to Aberdeen to begin the biggest concert tour ever staged in Britain, with all 150,000 tickets sold out weeks in advance – apart from Leeds where students organised a boycott of the concert due to be held at their university (that had no effect; the concert was rearranged at the Rolarena, instead). Extra shows were arranged across Britain to meet the demand for tickets.

Bowie played the role of Star whenever he appeared in public, with a limousine waiting at Aberdeen railway station to take him to his hotel even though it was only a minute's walk away. That night, talking to Roy Fox-Cumming from *Disc And Music Echo*, Bowie said the title for his current album had originally been *Love Aladdin Vein*, but he changed his mind: 'The album is about the States in some kind of small concept. Originally, I felt *Love Aladdin Vein* was right, then I thought, "Maybe I shouldn't write them off so easily" – so I changed it. Also "Vein" – there was the drugs thing, but it's not that universal.'

Asked about his image of decadence, Bowie groaned and said: 'Yes, I did something very decadent the other day. I went to Yves St Laurent to buy some clothes, and didn't see anything I liked so I came out with just a pair of grey socks – that's all ... and I went in a Rolls Royce to collect them. Apart from that I don't think I've done anything decadent in the last six months.' When Fox-Cumming asked about rumours that he might give up touring, Bowie said: 'I want to play everywhere once ... but after that ... well, it just becomes like a factory, churning things out. I don't want to do that, but I won't give up completely.'

Fox-Cumming was referring to Defries's plans for a third tour of the United States. Bowie was not happy about this and neither were RCA. In his first two tours, Bowie established a following in some cities, returning where he did well a second time, but in all gave only a total of 32 concerts in 16 cities. Ticket sales were poor in six of those cities. Defries now wanted him to tour 80 bigger venues, but RCA knew Bowie was not yet ready for that scale of tour. He was making bigger waves in Britain than in the United States, and if he did badly on a grand scale, the effect upon his reputation could have been disastrous.

Zanetta, privy to these discussions, says none of Bowie's five US albums had qualified for a Gold Disc (sales of 400,000 and gross receipts in sales of $1,000,000) and adds: 'In America, David was a media celebrity perceived as a superstar even though he didn't do superstar-sized business either in record stores or at the box office.... RCA remained adamant. Defries was not distressed; nothing ever ruffled his feathers. If there was to be no arena tour the only logical thing to do was have no tour at all.... Defries told David to "retire" because he was exhausted.' That would enable Defries to begin renegotiating Bowie's publishing and record contracts on a new basis, and also resolve the problem of the two disgruntled Spiders.

Mick Ronson was told of these intentions a fortnight before the tour returned to London for the final concert at Hammersmith Odeon, which was filmed by D. A. Pennebaker, the American documentary director who made the Bob Dylan film *Don't Look Back* (1967), the rock movie classic *Monterey Pop* (also 1967) and *Keep On Rockin'* with Jerry Lee Lewis and Little Richard (1969). Bowie was planning to preserve this concert on film, using Pennebaker's cinema-verité techniques, and Ronson was under instructions not to tell his fellow Rats they were being prepared for public execution. In any case, Ronson now knew he was next for the Big Star Defries treatment, with plans for solo albums and American tours.

\*   \*   \*   \*   \*

It was an innocent audience that gathered at the Hammersmith Odeon on 3 July 1973, with Pennebaker filming the kids outside on the street and in their seats, capturing their excitement as they waited for Ziggy, eyes shining, some made up like The Spiders, with glitter on their cheeks and tinsel in their hair.

Angie arrived and walked through the crowd, signing autographs, and yet looked sadly out of it all, badly dressed, a rock 'n' roll misfit being left behind. She was not aware of this then, but Pennebaker captured an awful moment when she blundered through Bowie's dressing room door and tried to act the loving wife. In the film, she says, 'you can see what I didn't want to see: David's smiling face when it's turned toward me is a mask. The fire rekindled in Japan had gone out.' The marriage was to limp along for another four years but it was, to all intents and purposes, dead.

On stage, Bowie ran through the catalogue of songs he had now performed across America, Japan and Britain: his Jacques Brel monologue; some by Lou Reed; but mostly his own, written over the past four years and now being sold by Ziggy, his alter ego marketing man. An old hero, Jeff Beck, joined him on stage, dressed in scruffy jeans, to augment Ronson on *The Jean Genie*, but mostly it was the now-familiar Ziggy routine, with every eye focused on the skeletal star holding their attention with a smile, a raised eyebrow, a twitch of the thigh or his outstretched palms. As the show neared its end, he gripped the microphone and said: 'This show will stay the longest in our memories, not just because it is the end of the tour but because it's the last show we'll ever do ...' and then, ever the showman, Bowie started to sing the opening line of *Rock 'n' Roll Suicide* as the confused and bewildered audience looked at each other, some crying, others bemused, wondering whether they had heard him right and if he really meant it. On stage, Bolder and Woodmansey were equally perplexed. This was the first they had heard of it. As they came off, Suzy Fussey asked: 'What are you going to do now?'

Apparently unable to believe what he had just heard, Woodmansey replied: 'What do you mean, what am I going to do? We're going to America. There's another tour ...'

As she stood there, asking whether or not they had heard what Bowie said on stage, Bolder was the first to grasp it. 'He's fucking sacked us,' he said. And he had.

\*     \*     \*     \*     \*

Next day, MainMan phoned around the London homes of all the top rock stars not currently out on tour, filming or making records: 'Sorry about the short notice. David's throwing a party. Tonight. At the Café Royal. Can you come?' Of course, they could. The shock retirement of Ziggy Stardust – or was it David Bowie? – made every TV and and radio news bulletin. Every newspaper ran stories, swallowing hook, line and sinker the latest MainMan press release, timed to coincide with Bowie's on-stage announcement, headed:   'DAVID BOWIE – US TOUR THREE HAS BEEN CANCELLED'. It went on: 'The massive arenas of 80 US and Canadian cities will not now, or perhaps ever again, hold within the walls the magic essence of a live Aladdin Sane.'

As far as the press were concerned, this was proof that David Bowie was now a massively successful international star who could afford to turn down a multi-million-dollar US tour, for he now had all five albums in the British charts, and so, they thought (not knowing the finances of the music business), must be worth a fortune. Had any newspaper said Bowie was still living in a rented flat costing £8 a week, was behind with his rent and had not paid his property taxes, and had just sacked two of his musicians for asking to be paid more than £30 a week, no one would have believed it. Instead, the newspaper coverage was astonishing. 'TEARS AS BOWIE BOWS OUT', reported the *Evening Standard*, with the only hint of normality creeping through the pages of the music papers, who were now beginning to rumble Defries's strategies: 'DON'T WORRY KIDS: IT'S JUST TACTICS' reported *Melody Maker*, with Roy Hollingworth asking:

> Is Bowie really being truthful when he says he's quitting? I really hope he is, but if somebody offered his manager Tony Defries £1m to play America, would he refuse? Bowie has his head well screwed on, and so does Defries. Would it not be a very super move to 'quit' in public even before he'd reached his peak? To be very famous one has to pull many tricks these days. And however lovely Bowie is in your eyes, don't ever think he won't pull tricks. To survive, he has to…. It's simply good business.

Later, Bowie told Charles Shaar Murray that it was he who had insisted on the cancellation of the forthcoming US tour – the tour that had never been arranged in the first place! 'Those were the final gigs. That's it. Period. I don't want to do any more gigs … from now on I'll be concentrating on various activities that have little to do with rock and pop.' And to the national press, Bowie said: 'I must have a rest. I'm exhausted. I have a lot more to fulfil and to give my fans, rather than just touring for the sake of promoting albums.' They weren't to know that tickets were already booked for a train to Paris four days later, with Bowie already planning his next album.

\* \* \* \* \*

It was a good party. Nearly everyone was there, walking the deep red carpets at the Café Royal, sitting on gilt chairs, sipping champagne by candle-light in an ornate setting, with mahogany doors and surrounds and gilded plasterwork: Paul and Linda McCartney, Cat Stevens, Mick and Bianca Jagger, Barbra Streisand (in London to film a TV show), Sonny Bono, Tony Curtis, Keith Moon, Ringo and Maureen Starr, Elliott Gould, Britt Ekland, Rod Stewart, Jeff Beck, Lulu, The Goodies, Lou Reed, Ryan O'Neal, Peter Cook and Dudley Moore, with Dr John and his band providing the music.

Jagger and Reed sat at Bowie's table, while Angie danced with Bianca and photographers circled the room. 'Are you sure about quitting?' asked Reed.

'I had to do it. I was getting stifled, and it's time for me to try something else. We've got four film scripts already,' said Bowie.

'But you're a musician,' said Jagger.

'No, I'm not,' answered Bowie. 'I'm a writer and if I'd carried on the way we were I'd soon have been thought of as a rock 'n' roll singer and nothing else. That's just part of what I do. I have never wanted rock 'n' roll to be my whole life.'

17

# The MainMan emperor
# and his illusions

By the autumn of 1973 Tony Defries came to believe that it was *he* who had made David Bowie a superstar and was sure he could do it again, for those willing to heed his advice.

Now the established star, Bowie was largely left to his own devices. At last, money was rolling into MainMan and credit flowed on tap. If Bowie wanted to go off to Paris to make an album: fine, the staff would book his train tickets, find accommodation, hire the musicians and arrange studio time; and then if Bowie wished to go on to Rome for a short holiday: fine, no problem. 'Leave everything to me,' was what Defries always said, and all Bowie had to do was charge expenditure down to his account at MainMan. Days, even weeks would pass without a meeting between Bowie and his manager, for Defries was concentrating on MainMan America, knowing that the United States comprised nearly 60 per cent of the world record market.

The staff at MainMan in New York were moved into a luxurious suite of 14 offices on Park Avenue and East Fifty-Fourth Street, equipped with state-of-the-art office machinery. Soon, there were 26 members of staff working there – and that did not include the domestic staff and drivers also on the MainMan payroll. The senior executives, the boys from *Pork*, each had a room of their own with little stacks of MainMan artefacts to give away to callers: MainMan pens and pencils, boxes of matches, diaries and notepads, each bearing the company motif of a mini-MainMan, a Superman-style figure designed by George Underwood, who was also put on the payroll as a sort of wandering artist-in-residence. At the heart of this crazy empire sat Defries, more over-dressed than ever and always sporting a vast cigar as he sat back in his leather armchair; stretched out on his leather couch, or sat at his leather-inlaid desk, with its solid gold and silver

executive accessories all neatly arranged, for Defries was essentially a tidy man, who liked this private world well-ordered. He
would sit there for hours, doing deals and planning people's
futures while his uniformed chauffeur Charles waited down below
at the wheel of the MainMan limousine. This was a brown custom-
built Cadillac with electronically controlled matching brown
windows, air conditioning and a spotless, cream-coloured leather
interior. There was also a MainMan estate near Greenwich,
Connecticut, complete with a 20-room mansion; a MainMan
apartment at the Sherry Netherlands Hotel; a MainMan penthouse
on Upper East Side; the MainMan duplex on East Fifty-Eighth
Street, where Defries first set up his New York operation little
more than 12 months earlier, and four MainMan apartments, not to
mention the MainMan operation at Gunter Grove in West London;
MainMan Japan in Tokyo, and MainMan West, a house rented just
off Mulholland Drive in Hollywood.

Money was no impediment to anyone's plans. When Cherry
Vanilla was put in charge of 'The MainMan Film Department' she
immediately had her room painted cherry-red, with cherry-red
carpets, curtains and furniture. No one minded: this was MainMan.
'Defries encouraged everyone to spend recklessly to create the
illusion that MainMan was a company of great wealth,' says
Zanetta. One secretary had an operation to lift her breasts and
charged this down to expenses; others had their teeth capped.
Expense accounts were also arranged at the Four Seasons
restaurant and Max's Kansas City. Zanetta says: 'The company
ran up staggering flower and limousine bills ... all the members of
"the MainMan family" considered Tony Defries – not David
Bowie – to be the real star. He had *manufactured* David Bowie,
who existed to generate the funds necessary to enable the
MainMan machine to thrive. To be a star, one had to act like one,
and to be a star-making machine a company had to act
accordingly ...' That this was no more than a house of cards, built
upon the earning capacity of just one performer, was known
throughout the music business – but no one puffed, or sought to
blow it down.

Periodically, Defries would talk of one day buying out RCA
Records or Sony of Japan and he undoubtedly believed that
MainMan would eventually occupy a block of offices as
prestigious as the Pan Am Building – and this might have
happened had he discovered another dozen stars with David

Bowie's income potential. But Defries still talked about marketing, distribution and packaging the product, apparently oblivious
to the one fact that all he had was a one-product company.

The poor man tried to change that, giving Mick Ronson the full
star treatment with full-page advertisements in the music papers
and a huge billboard on Times Square itself to promote Ronson's
solo album *Slaughter On Tenth Avenue* (RCA), and the single
*Love Me Tender/Slaughter On Tenth Avenue* (RCA), and then his
first solo tour. Even though Bowie wrote three of the songs, the
album failed and so did the tour. Nothing could disguise the fact
that Ronson, a brilliant guitarist and a perfect foil to a frontman
like Bowie, lacked star quality. On stage alone, focused by a
spotlight, Ronson had the charisma of a half-drowned sheep.

And then there was Dana Gillespie, Bowie's huge-breasted
former lover, whom he also recommended for a solo career, co-
producing her album *Weren't Born A Man* (RCA), which included
two of his songs, *Andy Warhol* and *Backed A Loser*. That was
another disaster, and so was the career of another Bowie protégé,
the extraordinarily ugly transvestite Wayne County, and that of the
singing group The Astronettes, who included Bowie's black lover
Ava Cherry, *and* that of the cocaine-pooped band Iggy Pop and
The Stooges, whose contract Defries personally terminated when
Iggy took his clothes off in a studio and told radio listeners he was
masturbating.

'I think in a way we were all Ziggy Stardust,' says Zanetta, who
was appointed President of MainMan America (it was another
MainMan principle that every member of staff had to have an
impressive-sounding title, and his job was looking after artistes).
'An incredible arrogance and corruption and decadence set in....
MainMan kind of mushroomed into this enormous spending
machine that really got out of control and was, I think, a very
destructive influence on everyone who was involved.'

Like the Golden Goose, the staff and the 'stars' believed in
MainMan while it still kept laying their golden eggs. Dana
Gillespie was supplied with a secretary, a magnificent car (which
she thought was hers until it was repossessed), hired limousines
when she travelled further afield, and a charge account at
Bloomingdales. 'MainMan really looked after their artistes
extremely well,' she says.¹ 'Defries gave me a fur coat. He said,
"If you're a singer, you've got to keep yourself warm." ... I
remember we were all in The Beverly Hills Wilshire. Defries was

in the Christian Dior Suite, Marc Bolan was in the Marc Bolan Suite, David was in the next one, Jagger was there and all the Stones, and every night was party night ... You only had to say MainMan or Bowie and all the doors opened.'

However, as one MainMan disaster followed another during the latter months of 1973 and early months of 1974, it was clear that David Bowie was still the only 'artiste' generating substantial income.

As soon as his British tour ended at the Hammersmith Odeon, and after his 'farewell party' (which became known in the business as 'The Last Supper') and just four days' rest, Bowie caught the boat train to Paris, having been told by Elton John that 'the sound is good' at the Château d'Herouville. The idea of working there appealed to Bowie. Formerly Chopin's home, the Château had been converted into a modern recording studio with full 16-track facilities, rooms in which to sleep and relax, and in-house catering so that musicians could take a break, have a meal and start working again, all within one ambience.

Bowie went to the Château with a mission. He wanted to rerecord the music of his teens. His original idea was to bring in the 60s bass player Jack Bruce, who had been in Cream with Eric Clapton, but Bruce declined – and so Trevor Bolder was invited to join them in Paris after all.* Another 60s musician, Aynsley Dunbar, who accompanied Bowie on the second tour of the US and then Japan, agreed to go to Paris – and so Woodmansey received a phone call from MainMan to say his services were no longer required. Woodmansey and his girlfriend were sharing a house in London with Garson and his wife, and it was Garson who took the phone call. He decided not to tell Woodmansey immediately because he was due to officiate at Woodmansey's wedding that very afternoon. 'I told him afterwards and he was devastated,' says Garson, who nevertheless joined Bowie in Paris. With such undercurrents, and Bolder also sensing his future was in doubt, the Paris sessions were not happy ones, for Ronson also ended his working relationship with Bowie as they finished the album. This may be why the *Pin-Ups* LP was such a disappointment, although commercially it was the only good thing going for

---

* This was purely a temporary reprieve, arranged solely for Bowie's convenience. Bolder was dispensed with as soon as the album was finished, and returned home to Hull.

MainMan, with advance orders totalling 150,000 when it was released in October 1973.

Trying to recall the music that turned one's thoughts to rock 'n' roll and interpreting each song personally, showing just what it was that caught one's ear, is difficult. I feel, having listened to *Pin-Ups* several times while preparing this chapter, that Bowie failed. Partly, it was the content. Generally, the lyrics are poor by Bowie's standards. Furthermore, no performer should interpret another's work unless he can improve upon it. Bowie's *Here Comes The Night*, originally recorded by Van Morrison with Them, sounds weak by comparison with the original, and there is little point anyone trying to recreate the sound of The Pretty Things when they achieved so little themselves in the first place. However, Bowie does come into his own with *Sorrow*, improving on the original version by The Merseys, with gentle saxophones and a swinging rhythm, while Garson brings an unexpected modern jazz piano run to Pink Floyd's *See Emily Play* that totally reinterprets Syd Barrett's song. Likewise, on The Mojos number *Everything's Alright* it's a persistent drum solo from Dunbar that lifts Bowie's interpretation beyond the original, while The Who's *Anyway Anyhow Anywhere* has a cohesive strength that was missing in their own version.

Having completed the album, Bowie went to Rome where he began working on a stage musical adaptation of George Orwell's novel *1984*. At the time, MainMan told me Bowie was hoping to have his musical staged in London and then New York, recording his own *1984* album along the way, and eventually filming it. I duly included news of this in my syndicated overseas column, and noticed that Bowie also discussed the project in considerable detail with the London music papers. This was unfortunate, for he did so without securing copyright clearance from the Trustees of the George Orwell Estate. And when their agents, who also happen to be mine, said they would require a royalty, Bowie's project fell apart – possibly because Defries was inexperienced in this aspect of the entertainment business. Bowie was planning an avant-garde musical, with Big Brother ruling an urban jungle, three years before Andrew Lloyd-Webber and Tim Rice moved on from *Jesus Christ Superstar* to *Evita* and Lloyd-Webber transformed T. S. Eliot's *Old Possum's Book Of Practical Cats* into the far more profitable *Cats*. Had MainMan known what they were doing and the Orwell Estate been a little more accommodating to rock 'n' roll, Bowie's musical would have been up and running, setting a far more challenging tone to West End theatre ... and it nearly happened. Tony Ingrassia, now Creative Consultant to MainMan in New York, was sent to London by Defries to prepare the musical for the stage, and when Bowie returned home from Rome in August they immediately got down to work with Bowie writing late into the night through August and September. His concentration was disturbed only by the need to move home (a small army of fans now camped on the doorstep at Haddon Hall, and someone broke into the house and stole money), and to spend several days working on a television show for the American channel NBC.

The Bowies moved first, in October 1973, to a rented flat in Maida Vale, while he continued to plan the musical and the TV show, finding himself on the radio every day in September when Decca rereleased *The Laughing Gnome*, which sold over 250,000 copies and reached No. 4 in the charts without any personal promotion. His next single, *Sorrow/Amsterdam*, was marginally more successful, reaching No. 3 the following month.

Meanwhile, Bowie, who was still making no personal appearances, broke away from his writing schedule to film *The 1980 Floor Show*, a programme that he devised to fill the entire one-hour slot for the NBC late-night rock show *The Midnight Special*. It was his most ambitious film production yet, arranged through the Main-Man office in New York and Michael Lippman at CMA, the agency now handling Bowie's American bookings. With Burt Sugarman at NBC persuaded that Bowie had a sufficiently strong following to justify a full one-hour show, his old stomping ground The Marquee was booked for three days between 18 and 20 October and Bowie began creating another new vehicle for himself, with costumes designed by Natasha Korniloff and Freddi Burretti, graphics by George Underwood and his new singing group The Astronettes providing backing vocals. It was intended to be much more than a one-man show promoting *Pin-Ups*, with spots by The Troggs and another group called Carmen, and Bowie performing the Sonny and Cher *I Got You Babe* duet with Marianne Faithfull, dressed as a nun – but a nun with a backless dress.

Yet again, there were tensions backstage, not only between The Spiders from Mars (back together for this one final show) but also between Bowie and Angie, who knew that Ava Cherry was his latest mistress. According to Angie, Ava weighed 200lbs and she was certainly a very big girl, a black woman with a round, smiling, friendly face and bleached-white curly hair. Bowie met her in New York when she was a waitress at the Genesis Club, invited her to join him in Paris while making *Pin-Ups*, and then installed her in a London flat. Later, she was moved to a MainMan flat in New York and given a weekly allowance of $175 as a member of The Astronettes, with Bowie promising her, 'You could be the next Josephine Baker. You could be a star.' None of this amused Angie, who thought it was *her* turn to become a star.

Angie was far less concerned that Bowie was also fucking Marianne Faithfull, for this she understood. Marianne once lived with Mick Jagger so Bowie had to have her, as well. It was the oldest form of oneupmanship.

\*    \*    \*    \*    \*

When the Bowies moved to Maida Vale in October, they took with them Scott Richardson – a young, clean-cut American who arrived at Haddon Hall as Angie's latest boyfriend and now spent much of his time talking rock 'n' roll and snorting coke with Bowie. As always, it was a travelling house party, with Marianne Faithfull and Ava Cherry passing through while Burretti's girlfriend Daniella looked after Zowie. Who might be sleeping with whom was a source of some speculation in the late-night London clubs, for the Bowies would come and go, clearly not together as man and wife, yet loyal to each other in an odd kind of way, with Angie frenetically doing whatever she thought had to be done to advance Bowie's career.

This meant she was always close to Bowie, and often travelled around with him, and each tolerated the other's lovers – until Angie felt threatened. Marianne Faithfull was no threat, just another notch on the headboard; but Zanetta says Angie was 'enraged' when she heard Bowie was also fucking Amanda Lear, who had a small part in *The Midnight Special*. Stunningly beautiful with Eurasian features, Amanda was articulate and intelligent, introducing Bowie to her friend Salvador Dali, the work of the designer Erté and the films of Fritz Lang. She was also mysteriously sexual, for a London newspaper published a front-page story that 'she' had been born a man, a revelation that Amanda handled like a true professional, neither confirming it nor denying it.

\* \* \* \* \*

The Maida Vale flat was meant to be a temporary refuge while the Bowies found themselves a home. It was a tiny, cramped apartment and fans were soon camping on the doorstep, and managing to discover the telephone number no matter how many times Bowie changed it. There was one house in Kensington he coveted, but Jimmy Page of Led Zeppelin beat him to it when film star Richard Harris put the house on the market. Angie then decided to go house-hunting in Chelsea, and found a townhouse between the King's Road and Cheyne Walk. When she asked Defries to arrange the finance, he said it was too soon for them to be buying a house like this, adding, 'Maybe you can live like royalty when David's record sales have earned back his advances from RCA, but until then you have to be reasonable.'[2]

'He's got a point,' said Bowie when Angie told him this. 'I think you should find something cheaper ...' and this was how they came to move to a rented three-storey house in Oakley Street, Chelsea, in November 1973, owned by Diana Rigg. The rent, £600 a month (enough to fund a substantial mortgage had they bought a property), was paid through Bowie's account at MainMan.

The Bowies moved their possessions up from Haddon Hall, with a large oil painting by Lindsay Kemp, *Faces*, on one living room wall and a portrait of Bowie by Underwood on another, and all the usual apparatus of a contemporary musician's home – two pianos, guitars, saxophones, synthesizers, amplifiers, three televisions, record and cassette decks, hundreds of LPs and cassettes and enough books to line the shelves of a suburban branch library. It was very definitely not their home, with its fitted Wilton carpets and Diana Rigg's bijou choice of lounge and dining room suites, but it was a base, somewhere to keep their gear, with two bedrooms, one for Zowie and another with a vast 6-foot bed for the Bowies, who initially shared it with Ava Cherry and 'a real jive black chick from Trinidad'.

The House On Oakley Street, as it came to be known, was just around the corner from Mick Jagger's home, and their friendship deepened. It seemed an odd friendship in some ways, for Jagger was already an established star while Bowie was very much Rock Nouveau (and there does tend to be a caste system among the rock 'n' roll gentry). Angie has claimed several times that Bowie and Jagger were lovers, but they deny it. Jagger was the older hand at dealing with managers, accountants, lawyers and international banks. The Stones now had homes in New York, Los Angeles, Jamaica and the South of France, and Bowie could see that they were rich and he was not.

'Everywhere David and Angela turned there were unpaid bills and overdrawn bank accounts,' says Zanetta.[3] MainMan's cheques began bouncing, and word whistled around the music business that Defries was in trouble. 'It looks as though the bubble's burst,' said Pitt, telling me Bowie was trapped inside The House On Oakley Street with his bills going through to MainMan and hardly any cash in his pocket. Angie's phone calls to MainMan for a cheque would provoke just evasion, and eventually she would go to the office to get it, she would find it had not been signed – and by the time it was, the banks would have shut for the day or she would be told by a bank clerk there were insufficient funds in MainMan's account to meet it.[4] These daily dramas continued through the bleak winter of 1973/4, and it was no secret in London clubs that Bowie did not have enough money in his pocket to buy his own cigarettes ... yet he was able to cadge and borrow, get enough cocaine from somewhere to keep him going through the night and carry on working.

But it hurt when he compared his condition to Jagger's, and Bowie became extremely angry when he heard about each new MainMan venture in New York. 'Everything I've got is leased or borrowed, or MainMan owns it, and I've never got any cash,' he'd complain bitterly to Angie. 'It seems to me that I'm making it. What's happening? Were all those people getting into my concerts for nothing? I can't fucking stand it! Where's my money?' Unintentionally adding salt to the wounds, RCA announced as the year ended that Bowie's total British sales were now 1,056,400 LPs and 1,024,068 singles.

Under these pressures, Bowie spent hardly any time at Oakley Street and, like Bolan who also had a serious cocaine problem, started floating with the coke-heads, with only one toe in the real world. 'I saw less and less of him, and I just hated that,' says Angie.[5] 'David's whole way of life changed, then, everything from his daily schedule to his choice of companions. He started living largely in the dark, in the company of other coke freaks.'

It is one thing to take cocaine, quite another to let cocaine take over one's life – and Bowie was in the first phase, experimenting, stimulated, enjoying the lift, mentally looser, thinking faster, rarely bothering to eat or drink, needing little sleep, and sometimes fucking for five or six hours at a time. He thought he was in control, and perhaps he was, for the proof is in *Diamond Dogs*, a rock 'n' roll masterwork which he arranged and produced himself, writing every track except *Bewitched, Bothered And Bewildered*, playing saxophone, harmonizing Moog and Mellotron in ways he had not tried since Ralph Mace showed him the potential of synthesizers on *The Man Who Sold The World*. Bowie also laid down nearly all the guitar tracks, apart from Alan Parker's on *1984*, so there was no work for Ronson. Drummers Tony Newman and Aynsley Dunbar were brought in to replace Woodmansey, joining Herbie Flowers on bass and erasing all trace of The Spiders from Mars. Mick Jagger joined Bowie in the studio many nights, but no one ever said whether or not he contributed to any tracks.

Cocaine heightens mental sensations, be they verging on paranoia or schizophrenia, and so all Bowie's nervous preoccupations with isolation and self-diagnosis are in there, too, for *Diamond Dogs* was conceived, written and recorded when Bowie was at his most vulnerable, with constant money troubles and both his marriage and his relationship with Defries under stress. It is a dark album with Bowie, always obsessed by 'control', fantasizing on some alternate plane about disasters as yet unknown.

*Ziggy Stardust* portrayed a society with five years yet to live in which a rock star loses his soul, and now in *Diamond Dogs* Bowie describes an urban wasteland with the dogs bellowing through empty streets while the survivors of a holocaust battle for survival in their rags, searching for love and desperately afraid. Bowie takes command of the music, using rock 'n' roll in much the same way that Samuel Beckett or Bertolt Brecht worked through the rhythm of words – a concept totally lost on the London music papers who did not understand what Bowie was doing at all. Roy Carr and Charles Shaar Murray recognized this seven years later in their reflective study of Bowie's work, admitting, 'Bowie has every right to feel extremely proud of *Diamond Dogs*. It is a far more powerful and coherent work than even the most perceptive of his critics realized at the time.'[6]

Bowie packaged the album as a complete work, bringing in Guy Pellaert to design a gate-fold sleeve, depicting the Diamond Dogs, Bowie and the ravaged creatures of his wasteland against an inflamed New York skyline. This was the LP sleeve as high art.

\*   \*   \*   \*   \*

He was now cut off from the media, cocooned in the studios or The House On Oakley Street, with MainMan fending off all requests for interviews. Only one journalist broke through, Craig Copetas, who arranged for Bowie to meet the Beat writer William Burroughs whose pioneer novels on drugs and homosexuality, *Junkie* (1953) and *The Naked Lunch* (1959), dealt with a similar world to Bowie's. Harvard-educated and born wealthy (his family owned the Burroughs office machinery company), Burroughs had been an addict himself, living among them in Paris and North Africa at the same time as Jean Genet.\*

Copetas prepared his ground carefully. He delivered copies of Burroughs's novels to Bowie in advance and made sure Burroughs had an opportunity to read Bowie's lyrics and listen to his music. The interview was held at Oakley Street on 17 November 1973. Copetas tape-recorded their conversation, publishing it in *Rolling Stone*[7] with the title 'BEAT GODFATHER MEETS GLITTER MAINMAN'. This was a rare glimpse of Bowie as I remembered him, intellectually in command, testing his visitor, unaffected by the trappings of fame, and still driven by the same influences. Burroughs must have found it a strange experience, seated in this comfortable setting, eating a Jamaican fish dish, with avocados stuffed with shrimp, and drinking a Beaujolais Nouveau, while Bowie talked of love, Lou Reed, Andy Warhol, Jack Kerouac, Mick Jagger and Puerto Rican music.

When Burroughs suggested that *Eight Line Poem* on the *Hunky Dory* LP reminded him of T. S. Eliot's *The Waste Land*, Bowie said sharply, 'Never read him ...' which may or may not be true, for there would be no way Bowie would acknowledge an influence like that to a stranger.

\* More recent research explains why Bowie was so drawn to Burroughs. Peter Swales, a former personal assistant to The Rolling Stones and subsequently a publisher, acquired the North American rights to Freud's papers on the use of cocaine in 1973 and then in 1992 discovered the literary estate of Paul Federn, a psychoanalyst who committed suicide in 1950. Federn prepared a case study of Burroughs, covering the period from when he left Harvard in 1936 until he met Allen Ginsberg in 1944. This reveals that Burroughs was diagnosed schizophrenic in 1939, suffered deep anguish over his homosexuality, entered a marriage of convenience in 1937 and in the early 50s thought he was possessed by demons. This was discussed by Dr Hugh Barker in the essay *Creative Madness* in the *Observer* (30 January 1994). Dr Barker also revealed that there was evidence of schizophrenia in James Joyce's family, his daughter Lucy having been diagnosed thus after developing a fixation for Samuel Beckett.

'The rock stars have assimilated all kinds of philosophies, styles, histories, writings, and they throw out what they have gleaned from that,' said Bowie in another part of the interview, before responding to Burroughs's observation that his lyrics were 'quite perceptive' and that he was surprised 'that such complicated lyrics go down with a mass audience'.

'I'm quite certain that the audience I've got for my stuff listen to the lyrics,' said Bowie, explaining that fans often wrote to him, discussing his lyrics, 'which is great for me because sometimes I don't know [where the ideas have come from] ... there have been times when I've written something and it goes out and it comes back in a letter from some kid as to what they think about it and I've taken their analysis to heart so much that I have taken up this thing. Writing what my audience is telling me to write. Lou Reed is the most important writer in modern rock, not because of the stuff that he does, but the direction he will take it. Half the new bands would not be around if it were not for Lou. The movement that Lou's stuff has created is amazing. New York City is Lou Reed. Lou writes in the street-gut level and the English tend to intellectualize more ...'

Telling Burroughs how reading Kerouac led him into Buddhism, an interest in Tibet and to come within two weeks of becoming a novice monk, Bowie described these experiences word-for-word as he told them to me four years earlier, and it was the same with his references to Warhol, with Bowie observing how Warhol was changing when he was not: 'I adore what he *was* doing. I think his importance was very heavy. It's become a big thing to like him now, but Warhol wanted to be cliché, he wanted to be available in Woolworth's, and be talked about in the glib type of manner. I hear he wants to make real films now, which is very sad because the films he was making were the films that should be happening. I left him knowing as little about him as a person as when I went in ...'

Burroughs commented: 'I don't think there is any person there. It's a very alien thing, completely and totally unemotional. He's really a science fiction character. He's got a strange green colour.'

'That's what struck me,' said Bowie. 'He's the wrong colour. This man is the wrong colour to be a human being, especially under the stark neon lighting in The Factory. Apparently it is a real experience to behold him in the daylight.' Bowie was equally wry in a comment on Mick Jagger – 'He's not a cockadoodledoo; he's

much more sexy, like a brothel-keeper or a madame ... I also find
him motherly and maternal, clutched into his bosom of ethnic
blues' – making me realize Bowie was now observing rock from
the inside, without losing his sense of detachment. Much as
Truman Capote was lionized by New York society and yet kept
that keen sense of truth that lay behind his plans for *Answered
Prayers*.

   This interview and *Diamond Dogs*, taken together, show an
enquiring artist, in command, doubting, searching for new ways of
expression. No one else in rock 'n' roll, then or now, thinks or
talks like that.

*   *   *   *   *

Less than six months had passed since Bowie's 'retirement' – and
by the turn of the year he was under pressure to go back on the
road again. Every other project MainMan touched seemed
doomed, and only Bowie could save their company – his
company, the one he and Defries had formed together. The
MainMan financial situation was more distressing than anyone
cared to admit, but in *Diamond Dogs* there was an excuse to
change direction, and in one track, *Rebel Rebel*, a thundering
number with a Rolling Stones rhythm, a certain hit single with
which to launch a tour.

   'I hear David's very upset about it,' Pitt told me, his ear as
always close to the millwheel. 'He wanted to spend more time
writing, but now Defries is telling him he ought to go back on the
road.'

   There were other factors, too. His marriage was now a shell,
with Bowie openly living with Ava Cherry and Angie engaged in
a long affair with actor and director Roy Martin that was to last
three years. There was nothing to keep him at home but his love
for his son.

*   *   *   *   *

Early in 1974, *Melody Maker* announced that Bowie had been
voted No. 1 British Male Singer in their annual readers' poll, and
also the country's leading Record Producer and Composer, with
*Jean Genie* the previous year's Best Single. In a similar poll,
readers of *Sounds* voted Bowie top Producer, leading Songwriter

and Britain's No. 2 Male Vocalist, so there could be no doubting
his appeal, even as one MainMan project after another collapsed.
There was still money coming in to MainMan, for Defries secured
a higher percentage on Bowie's songwriting royalties from
Chrysalis, and RCA agreed to increase their advance per Bowie
album to $100,000, but it was never enough to match the
outgoings – and Bowie agreed to another US concert tour. Just
before the 1973/4 tax year ended, he slipped away to France to
discuss ways of presenting *Diamond Dogs* on stage with John
Dexter, Director of the National Theatre in London and the
Metropolitan Opera House in New York, and then boarded the SS
*France*, bound for New York, with his fourth North American tour
due to open in Montreal on 14 June.

18

## *Diamond Dogs* and living
## 'only in theory'

David Bowie arrived in New York on 11 April 1974, determined to make *Diamond Dogs* the most sensational touring stage show in the history of rock 'n' roll. Bowie had total faith in the album and now wanted a theatrical production to match its quality, one bigger and better than *Ziggy Stardust*, with striking stage sets, backcloths and props, choreographed dance routines and a tightly coordinated musical accompaniment that would work under its own director, leaving him free to front the show, presenting his songs.

No other rock musician had ever attempted anything quite like this, such a supreme test of their own self-confidence, and MainMan went into overdrive to ensure he succeeded, launching a marketing operation as remarkable as his plans for the show.

Driven by Defries's belief that success depended upon marketing and distribution, MainMan had a press department and mailing room, equipped with state-of-the-art copying, addressing, sealing and franking machines that could channel a mailing shot to all parts of the world. Its mailing list had five thousand addressees, which was five times more than any other known operation in this field, and included TV and radio producers, disc jockeys, music papers and columnists on even the tiniest publications.

The first shot in what became a promotional barrage was fired on 1 April 1974, with every addressee receiving a statement from MainMan:

### BOWIE RETURNS TO AMERICA

Currently in France conferring with John Dexter (the director of the National Theatre in London and the Metropolitan Opera House in New York), Bowie is scheduled to arrive in New York on the SS *France* April 11.

He will then prepare for an extensive series of theatrical presentations. These have been designed and staged by Bowie in collaboration with Jules Fisher (Tony Award winning lighting designer, whose vast credits include *Pippin*, *Lenny*, *Seesaw* and *Hair*) and will have their first presentation in Montreal on June 14. Subsequent performance will continue throughout the months of June and July in selected cities in Canada and the East Coast of the United States.

Much of the content of these shows is taken from Bowie's new RCA album *Diamond Dogs* (release date May). 'In simplest terms, *Diamond Dogs* is about the breakdown of an overmechanized society. Bowie conceptualizes this vision of a future world with images of urban decadence and collapse. This theme will be extended into a visual form for the stage.'

Something was missing in this press release: the word 'David'. The MainMan star was now 'Bowie', with Defries instructing his staff to refer to him thus at all times, so that newspapers and magazines would pick up the tag, making him one of those stars who was described by a single word, like ELVIS, GARBO, or SINATRA. BOWIE was good, BOWIE was strong – five letters that would fit any newspaper headline and always stand out on theatrical posters, and this was to be his year, Defries told the MainMan staff, instructing them to say on all occasions when speaking to outsiders that this was 'THE YEAR OF THE DIAMOND DOGS'.

This was Tony Defries at his best. One might criticize him for spending money he did not have, for wasting MainMan money on other 'artistes' who never stood a chance, for proving by that wastage that he did not know good from bad, or for planning this tour on the 'never-never' (which he called amortizing), but no one but Defries – not even Brian Epstein or Colonel Tom Parker – would have thrown such resources behind one album, whatever the quality of 'the product'.

Twelve days after the first mailing shot came the second, announcing the first concerts in Bowie's tour and enclosing a monochrome copy of the Pellaert artwork for *Diamond Dogs*. By promoting it as art and not commercial packaging Defries cleverly secured its reproduction in newspapers and magazines throughout the world, without having to pay a penny for advertising.

Over the next six weeks, there were another three mailing shots, each one sent to all five thousand addressees, enclosing in all seven different photographs of Bowie – shots of him on stage at the Hammersmith 'farewell concert', sitting with Lou Reed and Mick Jagger at the Café Royal party, and at work in Olympic Studios, London, recording *Diamond Dogs*. It would be rare for any new album to be publicized with a tenth of this promotion. MainMan was giving the largest mailing list in the business the most unrelenting series of mailings in the history of pop music promotion. Anyone who had any influence on the record-buying public was browbeaten into perceiving Bowie's return as the second coming. The message was firmly implanted upon their minds that Bowie worked creatively on a grand scale, associating with major figures in the theatre – and the response was extraordinary. Sackloads of press clippings were delivered to MainMan, showing that the stories and photographs were being printed in every territory.

MainMan's next manoeuvre was to contact key writers and magazine editors to see whether they needed any extra photographs, in colour or black and white, to personalize their coverage of Bowie's new venture. The MainMan office in New York even phoned me in London to see whether there was anything I wanted. This struck me as odd, for I knew the London office had no cash to pay day-to-day creditors, and there was some fear that the electricity and telephones would be cut off. Still, it was a clever ploy, with American magazines *Creem, Circus, Rock Scene* and *Hit Parade* all agreeing to print cover stories of Bowie, and similar coverage in Britain in the *New Musical Express, Sounds, Disc and Music Echo* and *Record Mirror*. This was free publicity of the most telling kind; cover stories sell records as much as they sell publications.

Although unwilling to finance the *Diamond Dogs* tour, after losing so much money backing Bowie's previous tours, RCA agreed to allocate $150,000 to advertising, and so MainMan's success in achieving free news coverage for Bowie was counter-weighted by full-page colour advertisements in the main trade publications *Billboard, Cash Box, Record World, Phonograph Record Magazine* and *The Hollywood Reporter*; more in consumer magazines *Rolling Stone, After Dark, Creem, Circus, Rock Scene*, Andy Warhol's *Interview, Village Voice* and *National Lampoon*; parallel advertising in British magazines; billboard advertising on Times Square in New York, Sunset Boulevard in Los Angeles and Piccadilly Circus, London; and display models distributed to every major record shop.

Making sure no potential market was overlooked, Defries arranged for Bowie to produce TV and radio commercials so that local advertising could also be lined up as part of the advance promotion in every major city, with radio commercials running before each concert and TV spots slotted in between regional showings of programmes that drew a strong teenage audience, such as *Mission Impossible*, *The Partridge Family, Star Trek* and *Don Kirschner's Rock 'n' Roll Concert*. 'The blitz produced so much publicity RCA felt compelled to spend even more to promote David,' says Zanetta[1] and Defries felt able to demand higher fees from promoters for Bowie's concerts.

As part of MainMan's overall promotional strategy, Bowie himself was still cocooned, with no disc jockeys or journalists allowed anywhere near him. He was being cast as the elusive superstar, the Greta Garbo or Marlene Dietrich of rock 'n' roll – and was perfectly willing to live up to that image.

Bowie travelled from France with the tiniest of retinues. Corinne or 'Coco' Schwab, a former secretary in MainMan's London office, became his personal assistant,* and Bowie was also accompanied by bodyguard Stuey George, driver Jim James and old friend Geoffrey MacCormack, who doubled up as backing singer Warren Peace on stage and friend to lean on in the wee small hours of the night when Bowie needed a man to talk to.

Ava Cherry, with whom he had been living for the past six months, had flown ahead and moved into Bowie's suite at The Sherry Netherland Hotel, where Bowie arrived to find his world had changed. Contact with Defries over the past nine months had mostly been by telephone, but now he expected to see Defries personally, just as he had always done. This was no longer the way Defries operated. MainMan 'artistes' were expected to make appointments before calling at the office, and Defries let it be known that he did not want Bowie dropping in without prior arrangement, and also expressed strong disapproval of his drug-taking.

'It was obvious to David that MainMan was no longer his

* Schwab is still with him today, 20 years later, travelling the world at his side, totally loyal and shielding him from all outside intrusion. Like Bowie, she speaks several languages. Her father was an American photographer while her mother became a psychiatrist, living in Switzerland. Coco was born in a stockroom at the New York department store Bloomingdales, her mother having gone into labour in the linen department. Coco made her name within MainMan by keeping the London office running when its creditors were constantly hammering at the door.

family but Defries's, and a feeling of abandonment surged through him,' says Zanetta.[2] Ignoring Defries's wishes, Bowie started calling in at MainMan on his own, talking to the staff, discussing their ideas and even inviting them to join him at night touring clubs, discos and the Apollo Theater, listening to new bands and soul musicians from Marvin Gaye and The Temptations to Roxy Music, Todd Rundgren and Television. 'Defries was not pleased by their affection for his errant son,' continued Zanetta. 'At a meeting with the MainMan publicity staff, David found himself continually referred to as "Bowie" by his old friends. It was clear that in the eyes of the original members of Defries's staff, David the man did not exist. To his face he was treated as a commodity, the object MainMan was in business to sell. He felt deeply hurt.'

Bowie was better at swallowing his pride than people realized, and went straight into two months of rehearsals for the *Diamond Dogs* tour. He had to familiarize himself with a huge, six-ton stage set, Hunger City, portraying the decaying landscape of the Diamond Dogs, with no fewer than 20,000 moving parts. The ideas were his, with designer Mark Ravitz helping to construct a bridge that could be raised or lowered by remote control; a four-ton 35-foot 'Catapult' that could hover over the audience with Bowie within it, and a 'Diamond' that would open out like a flower with Bowie inside it. Nothing like this had been tried in rock 'n' roll, and Bowie was hoping that their imagery would have the same impact as the podiums designed by Albert Speer for Hitler's speeches, or the sets designed by Fritz Lang for the film *Metropolis*. Economically, the concept was crazy because the set had to be put together, used, dismantled, transported to the next city and then reassembled, with several hours of travelling in between. This had to be done on a daily basis to keep costs down. The budget was too tight to allow the road crew time to rest.

The show was due to open at the Montreal Forum on 14 June, moving on to Ottawa Civic Center (15th) and Toronto O'Keefe Auditorium (16th), then crossing into the United States for 12 dates before the end of the month. It continued for three more weeks, including a week at the Philadelphia Tower, where Bowie always drew packed houses (8–15 July), and ended up with two shows at Madison Square Gardens, New York (19 and 20 July).

It wasn't only the stage sets that had to be right. Jules Fisher was co-ordinating the lighting, and Bowie brought in Toni Basil to choreograph the movements of two dancers, Gui Andrisano and

MacCormack, who was now being trained to dance. For the first time, Bowie chose a musical director, Michael Kamen, to lead his accompaniment. Kamen, a classically trained pianist, worked with The New York Rock Ensemble, and has also written scores for ballet and Hollywood movies. The other musicians were Mike Garson, Herbie Flowers and Tony Newman, augmented by two of Kamen's friends, Earl Slick (lead guitar) and Dave Sanborn (alto sax and flute), with Richard Grando on baritone sax and flute. The rehearsals were held at the Capital Theatre at Rye, upstate New York, and Defries and Zanetta were not invited to see the show until the dress rehearsals, by which time pre-production costs exceeded $400,000. 'Defries strolled into the theatre, and looked around grandly as if he owned the building – if not the world,' wrote Zanetta.[3] 'He took a puff on his Cuban cigar as his eyes roamed over the pandemonium. His first response was a look of amusement. His next response was curiosity. Finally, after eight weeks, he was seeing for himself where all the money, *his* money, was being spent. He glanced at the gigantic stage set. Hunger City was not only immense but also haunting and beautiful…. Defries walked slowly to the apron of the stage, and looked up at David. Sweat poured down David's face. He looked impatiently at Defries, but his impatience had no effect. Defries stared at David, one of those long, awkward stares he used to make people uncomfortable …'

In that vignette, Zanetta reveals how far the relationship had deteriorated. Bowie was preparing to work like a Diamond Dog to rescue MainMan, yet there was virtually no communication between them. Worse still, when Schwab led Defries to his seat, everything seemed to go wrong. The bridge mechanism locked and the bridge would not descend, leaving Bowie suspended in air. As he began singing *Space Oddity*, another mechanism locked, leaving him suspended over the audience, and the sound system was clearly out of balance. 'Defries smelled disaster,' says Zanetta. 'He believed David's concept had been taken far too literally, and that the show was out of control. He didn't know why David needed dancers, singers, dogs and diamonds … all he really needed was a stool, his guitar and a spotlight…. Defries's tone indicated that David had failed him. No matter how hard David worked he knew he was perceived as a failure. That was what really hurt.'

A more experienced manager would not have allowed the

situation to come to this. He would have been at the theatre every
day, keeping costs under control, and Bowie's feet on the ground,
but Defries was now allowing abstract principles of business
management to overwhelm his common sense, delegating important matters to an office that had grown far too quickly and was
still largely staffed by the cast of *Pork*.

*     *     *     *     *

The show opened in Montreal as planned, although the stage
hands found it took 36 hours to erect the scenery and during the
show itself the bridge crashed with Bowie on it. This did not
bother the audience. How were they to know this was not part of
the show? The sound system also malfunctioned, producing a
distortion and nearly melting the wires through electrical over-
loading – but that did not worry the audience, either.

Bowie remained aloof, sustaining his own image of stardom by
making every entrance on key – and every exit. 'Thank you.
Thank you for your help,' he told the stage crew before
disappearing into his cocoon with Ava Cherry and a supply of
cocaine, protected against all intrusion by Coco Schwab, his driver
and bodyguard, dresser, hairdresser, make-up artist and wardrobe
mistress, the only people to see him before and after each show.
On this tour, Bowie did not even talk to his musicians.

MainMan sensibly waited two days before arranging press
coverage, giving the company a chance to sort out their first-night
problems – and by Toronto, the stage machinery and the sound
system were working well, enabling Bowie to present a near-
perfect performance. MainMan flew in critics from the key
English music papers, together with those from the main US
newspapers and magazines. They could see this was a personal
*tour de force*, with Bowie employing advanced theatrics to sell his
songs, slipping into a mimed boxing routine, wearing shorts and
gloves inside a ring to sing *Panic In Detroit*, performing *Cracked
Actor* as if at a press conference confronted by cameramen, and in
his final numbers *The Jean Genie* and *Rock 'n' Roll Suicide* using
the whole box of tricks – dancers, back-up singers and musicians,
against the Pellaert backcloth. As the show ended, the stage
cleared – and the audience applauded for nearly 20 minutes,
calling for encores, before a voice announced from a loud-speaker,
'David Bowie has already left the building ...'

For the most part, press coverage was ecstatic. Chris Charles-worth of *Melody Maker* called this 'a completely new concept in rock theatre – the most original spectacle in rock I have ever seen,' which, indeed, it was. The problem was that its costs were greater than the show could take at the box office, but the significance of this fundamental flaw seems to have been lost upon MainMan. Zanetta says, 'MainMan were thrilled. Against all odds it seemed to them that Defries had done it again.'[4] Next day, Defries flew back to New York, another error of judgement. On a major ground-breaking tour like this, and even more so when the finances are risky, a good manager stays right in there, taking care of business.

More problems arose in Philadelphia. Tony Visconti was called over from London to oversee a live recording at the Tower Theatre. The idea was to record both shows on 14 and 15 July, taping enough material for a double-LP. The RCA advance would offset the losses on the touring show. Somehow, news of this reached the musicians who had no idea the tour was losing money or that MainMan were in debt. 'How much are we getting for this?' asked Herbie Flowers, and when he heard MainMan were only planning to pay them the standard Musicians Union rate of $150 per man for the recording, there were ructions. The musicians decided to ask for $5,000 a head – and Defries was outraged.

'Defries believed they should be paid nothing,' says Zanetta.[5] 'He wouldn't think of going to Philadelphia to negotiate with the musicians. He now lived in the clouds, and had no desire to ever operate at sea level again.... Then the best sound equipment began to arrive in Philadelphia. From the beginning they had complained that the sound was inferior. The fact that the band could have whatever it wanted when a recording was to be made infuriated them ... they began to perceive the company as an invisible enemy. MainMan had scrimped on the sound equipment. Secret meetings were held to plot strategy. One of the things that concerned them was David. Was he for Defries or for them? They liked him very much, but they didn't know where he stood ...'

There was no easy way of finding out, for Bowie would arrive before each show for a sound-check, disappear into his dressing room, and vanish after the performance – and so the musicians waited sullenly to see what would happen next. On 14 July, sound technicians began wiring up equipment for Visconti. Half an hour before the show was due to begin, Flowers announced: 'I'm not playing a note until all that recording equipment has been unplugged.'

In the past, backstage problems were dealt with by MainMan. This time, Flowers was called to Bowie's dressing room and asked to explain what was wrong. What happened next is a mystery. It has been said Bowie burst into tears. Other reports suggest he threw a chair at Flowers, but after 20 minutes Flowers came out with a smile. 'He's guaranteed us $5,000 each, even if he has to pay us out of his own pocket,' said Flowers. 'And we'll all have written contracts by the time we get to Madison Square Garden.'

Cheered and feeling justified, the nine musicians settled down to prepare for the show. Zanetta says the $45,000 Bowie promised them 'had no real meaning to him. He didn't care about the cost of anything' – but he disliked having to resolve the dispute himself. MainMan had made another error of judgement, and Bowie blamed Defries.

\*　　\*　　\*　　\*　　\*

By recording the double-LP early in the tour, Bowie was able to secure release of *David Live* by 29 October, in time for the peak pre-Christmas trade. This was his first live album; although RCA recorded his 1972 concerts at Carnegie Hall and Santa Monica Civic Auditorium, and also the 'farewell concert' at Hammersmith Odeon, nothing was released, largely because sound quality was poor.

Even with the best equipment, Bowie's voice sounded tired and strained. The project was a nightmare for Visconti. Bowie was singing through eight different microphones. Visconti had to balance them against the music, which suffered from similar distortion. The songs were taken from *Ziggy Stardust, Aladdin Sane* and *The Man Who Sold The World*, as well as *Diamond Dogs*, together with Bowie's first recorded version of *All The Young Dudes*, and his interpretation of the Eddie Floyd/Steve Cropper soul number, *Knock On Wood*, which reached No. 10 in the British charts as a single. This was Bowie's first excursion into soul, the start of another change of direction.

Just how dissatisfied Bowie was with this recording became apparent in a later interview when he said: '*David Live* was the final death of Ziggy. God, that album…. I've never played it. The tension it must contain must be like a vampire's teeth coming down on you. And that photo on the cover! My God, it looks as if I've just stepped out of the grave. That's actually how I felt. That record should have been called *David Bowie Is Alive And Living Only In Theory*.'

After the last Philadelphia show on 15 July, the tour moved on to Boston and Hartford, arriving in New York with an extra day to prepare for Bowie's first concert at Madison Square Gardens, where the huge trucks shifting stage equipment blocked the local one-way traffic system for a whole day. Over at MainMan there was chaos of a different kind. Angie was back in town, convinced as ever that she was providing momentum for Bowie's career. Defries agreed to meet her in the MainMan penthouse, a pied-à-terre well away from the main offices decorated like the set for an Arthurian movie. This was where the MainMan MainMan used to fire his employees, and it was known within the company as 'The Executioner's Suite'.

After Bowie left London, Angie repainted The House On Oakley Street and renamed it The MainMan Studio, and there she sat most days planning career moves for her husband (mostly without his knowledge), still believing that MainMan was 50 per cent owned by Bowie. Now she arrived to outline her future plans, which included publicity campaigns for Bowie, a TV and radio tour for Dana Gillespie, taking British journalists to New York at MainMan's expense, the establishment of a chain of MainMan shops selling clothes designed by Freddi Burretti and plans for a MainMan-financed TV spectacular based upon the legend of the water spirit Ondine, in which Angie intended to star herself.

Even before she arrived, dressed in a Chanel-style suit with her hair swept back so that she looked, in her own eyes, like a busy young executive, Defries told Zanetta her spending had to be stopped; that she was a nuisance, a meddler with no real function; and that all her silly plans should be brought to an end.

The scene was set for a confrontation. As Angie ran through her eight-page list of proposals, Defries knocked them down one by one, telling Angie it was he who managed Dana Gillespie, not her; that MainMan and RCA both had press departments, and so they did not need her services in planning Bowie's campaigns; and that it was his money she was spending AND THIS MUST STOP – adding as an afterthought that he 'didn't want his English house used as a place where she entertained her boyfriends ...' And that was just for starters. Defries went on to say MainMan's accounts office had checked through her bills for airline tickets, hotel accommodation and car hire, discovering she had spent over $100,000 that year on travel. After waiting for this to sink in, Defries 'told her she ought to stop fooling around. She didn't have a real marriage, and she was getting in the way.'[6]

Zanetta, the only other person in the room, says: 'Angela stared at him in disbelief. She looked like a prize fighter who had just taken a powerful blow to the solar plexus ...' Faced with her distress, Defries backed off, saying he would still support her as a MainMan artiste but her personal projects would have to wait until after Bowie's tour. But he was too late. The damage was done.

\*     \*     \*     \*     \*

All the risks were becoming justified. The promotional blitz made Bowie's name across North America. *Diamond Dogs* and *Ziggy Stardust* qualified for Gold Discs on US sales alone and Bowie arrived in New York a confirmed star, able to fill the Madison Square Garden two nights running, despite an overwhelming smell of elephant shit left by the circus that had just vacated the complex. As in other cities, the audience were overwhelmed by Bowie's vision of Hunger City, with sets so like their own familiar landscape and the sound of barking, yelping dogs coming through the speaker system as they took their seats, and he made his entrance on The Catapult, high above the front part of the arena, bathed in a changing light as if travelling through space.

Afterwards, a party was held at The Plaza Hotel with Bette Midler, Mick Jagger and Rudolf Nureyev joining the MainMan staff and other guests. By now, after a month on the road, Bowie was thinner than ever, down to around 112lbs, and looking gaunt and haggard, for he was living on cocaine rather than food, often driving himself through the night without sleep. This was one of those rock tours where nearly everyone took cocaine, except Garson who never touched drugs of any kind. Bowie was not so far gone that he didn't notice things like that. 'I love Mike – because he never touches the stuff,' he would say, while Garson openly expressed the view that he was living in 'some X-rated movie ... I think the whole thing was pretty sick, to tell you the truth.' Michael Kamen thought he was 'working with someone who under any other circumstances would be under lock and key'.[7]

At The Plaza, Midler, Jagger and Nureyev stood silently waiting for The Star to arrive, led by his bodyguard with Ava Cherry on his arm. Angie was friendly to them both. Bowie picked up a glass of champagne, and began to move around the room, exchanging small talk with his guests. Zanetta saw what happened next: 'Off the bedroom was a large walk-in closet. The only people at the party who really interested David were Bette Midler and Mick Jagger. The trio stepped into the closet and closed the door.... Every pair of eyes in the room was riveted to the closet door. The stars emerged from the closet an hour later. David was ready to leave the party ...' and off he went to his suite at The Sherry Netherland, taking with him 'the beautiful daughter of a very famous actor'. Ava Cherry was sent back to her MainMan apartment in Greenwich Village. Angie returned to her own room at The Sherry Netherland. Bowie may have been exhausted by travelling, performing, cocaine and sexual excess, but he was still in control.

Next day, Sunday 21 July, Zanetta received a phone call from Angie, and soon realized the Bowies were now back together in his suite. 'Why don't you come over at the end of the afternoon?' she said, adding, 'David would also like to see you ...' Zanetta arrived to find Angie had gone for a walk with Zowie in Central Park. Coco was sitting by the telephone handling incoming calls, and Bowie was still in bed, fast asleep. Notebooks, drawing pads and pencils were scattered around the room, and Zanetta could see Bowie had been working, leaving magazines open at pages that made an impression.

'I can't deal with the attitude of the office,' said Coco, who was also looking exhausted, with dark circles beneath her eyes, after a month travelling across America, working more than 16 hours a day. She said Bowie had given her a list of Latino albums he wanted to listen to before making his next album, and even though she sent this through to MainMan the albums had not been sent to him. It was a small matter, costing only $30, but 'they seem so busy having a wonderful time, they don't have any time to do any work. Whenever I ask for a cheque for anything, they make me feel like a criminal ...'

Zanetta thought it absurd that neither Bowie nor his assistant had $30 to buy records, especially as it was MainMan office practice that most costs should be charged down to account. During one week at The Sherry Netherlands, he maintains Bowie ran up a bill of $17,000 for room service 'after allowing everyone who visited him to order whatever they wanted all night long'. Coco had her own weekly allowance of $200 for out-of-pocket expenses and Zanetta says Bowie also received $500 a week. Having told him these allowances barely covered their cigarettes and taxis, Coco continued: 'I'm worried about David. He never eats any more, and I'm afraid he's going to get sick.... I'm so worried about the cocaine. He's using more and more of it. It's the only thing that keeps him going. It scares me. I'm in this all by myself, and there are days when I don't know what to do.'

Sensing that Bowie was waking, Coco took him orange juice, coffee and cigarettes together with the morning paper, the *New York Times*, which was a routine Bowie enjoyed, no matter where he happened to be or who he was with; Angie used to ensure his days started like this at Haddon Hall. Later, dressed in a kimono with Angie cuddling up to him on a couch, Bowie snorted his first line of cocaine of the day, using a $100 bill. Zanetta realized Bowie was preparing to say what was on his mind.

'Every day I wake up to face a nightmare,' said Bowie, 'a nightmare I don't understand ...' as he went on to say that at the beginning of his relationship with Defries, they shared a dream, a dream of success in which their roles were defined, artiste and manager, each with separate functions to fulfil. 'I've done my part, haven't I?' he said. 'I've upheld my part of the bargain. I don't understand why he has done this ...'

Bowie then went on to complain about the way Defries treated Angie at their meeting, saying this was 'meddling in my personal life ... he's crossed my boundaries with that one. He's in charge of my business, not my personal life or my work. All I know is I don't have the money to give Angie to spend while he has all the money in the world to give to Melanie.'* At this, Angie interrupted to say: 'I was never so insulted in my life. He really hurt me ...' At that moment, according to Zanetta, they looked 'so childlike and wounded they could have been posing for an orphanage poster'.

Telling Zanetta that he did not have a cent in his pocket, and

* Melanie McDonald, Defries's girlfriend, who lived with him for ten years. They have a daughter, Fleur.

could never get Defries on the phone, Bowie continued: 'I feel very alone. I feel totally defenceless ... You're the only one in that office I can trust, whom I can expect to give me answers about what's going on. I'm financially dependent on Tony.... I don't know what I'm worth. I don't know who's paying for everything. Where's the money coming from for all the projects? Who's paying for the Wayne County film? Who's paying for the Broadway production of *Fame*? Who's paying for Mick Ronson's campaign? Who's paying for Dana's campaign? Who's paying for the billboards?* Half this company is mine, but I have no say in anything ...'

Zanetta does not say how he reacted to this cry of distress, but what follows next is the key sentence in his book, for he confirms something that Pitt already knew, and which Pitt had told me, but which apparently came as a bombshell to Bowie: 'David, your deal is no secret. You are to receive 50 per cent of the profits – after your expenses are deducted – of the monies generated by you and you alone. You own no portion of MainMan. MainMan belongs exclusively to Tony.' For a moment, the import of what Zanetta said did not get through. Three years of self-delusion were being challenged. Zanetta says Bowie began to look determined, with his jaw jutting out. 'I don't understand,' he said. 'Tony and I are partners, our agreement has always been 50:50.'

Zanetta countered: 'You own 50 per cent of your income after all expenses are deducted. Tony is under no obligation to pay you anything other than your salary and to support you, your family and your staff. The money you generate is MainMan income, not Bowie income. It remains MainMan income until Tony decides to distribute it. You have given him permission to use this money to develop other acts and to build MainMan. All your money goes to him, and he has total control over it. You have never had any control over your money.'

'I *know* I own 50 per cent of MainMan,' Bowie continued, unable to accept what Zanetta was saying.

'Surely you always knew what your deal with Tony was?' said Zanetta.

After some hesitation, Bowie admitted that he had never really understood the various agreements he'd signed, but continued to

---

* The Wayne County film was never made; *Fame* was a MainMan stage play based on the life of Marilyn Monroe that collapsed after one night on Broadway with a loss of $250,000; the attempts to launch Mick Ronson and Dana Gillespie both failed disastrously.

maintain: 'I *know* I own 50 per cent of MainMan ...' They
continued to talk around and around this one central point, with
Bowie refusing to believe he did not own half the company, and
Zanetta telling him that if he had any suspicions he should hire his
own independent lawyer and accountant to see where the money
was going and if the expenses were legitimate; but his sound
advice was falling on deaf ears. Bowie had to believe what he
wanted to believe, and as they sat together through the night, with
Bowie now charged up with more cocaine, the sun started to rise
above the Manhattan skyline. Bowie's mood became more
sombre, for despite the cocaine he was still in command of his
faculties. 'How did it come to this?' he asked Zanetta quietly.
'Why did it come to this? You know it shouldn't have. I don't
understand any of it.'

    The die was now cast, but neither Defries nor Zanetta knew
their man. Both must have known Bowie would react, but how and
when? As in so many situations in his life, he kept them guessing,
for whatever happened around him, however dire his crises, there
was always another side of his personality that remained remote
and beyond their contact. Mistakes may have been made, the
wrong contracts signed, but essentially the achievements were all
his. *He* was the creative artiste whose music would last; *they* were
... disposable.

                          *   *   *   *   *

Bowie threw himself back into work, hiding behind a mask, but
knowing instinctively what to do next. It was now 22 July. There
was a six-week gap in the tour schedule, before he was due to
open in Los Angeles on 2 September, appearing for seven nights at
the Universal Ampitheater, and then resuming the tour itself,
visiting 25 more cities between 11 September and the final concert
at Tuscaloosa, Alabama, on 2 December.

    Most days, Bowie stayed in bed until late afternoon at The
Sherry Netherland Hotel, and then – with his driver, bodyguard
and Coco Schwab by his side – he would travel down to the
Electric Ladyland Studio in Greenwich Village, mixing the tapes
for *David Live*. One night, Bette Midler dropped in to see him and
they talked for hours about soul music and rhythm 'n' blues, and
how good the sound was at Sigma Sound Studios in Philadelphia,
where he had sat in the control room, listening to Ava Cherry

recording songs for an album. 'That's where I'm going next,' he said, mentioning Kenny Gamble and Leon Huff, who owned the studios and whose company Philadelphia International Records was the most successful black music label in the States after Motown.

Bowie made little attempt to keep together the musicians who had worked with him on the first part of the *Diamond Dogs* tour. Herbie Flowers and Tony Newman returned home to Britain on the SS *France*, and instead, partly on the recommendation of Garson and partly that of Alomar, Bowie brought in the black bass player Willie Weeks to replace Flowers, and the drummers Dennis Davis and Andy Newmark instead of Newman. As backing singers, he recruited Alomar's wife Robin Clark, Jean Millington (who later married guitarist Earl Slick, who also worked on these sessions), Jean Fineberg, and a hugely built and previously unknown black soul singer, Luther Vandross. During August, they all moved down to Philadelphia, together with another bass player Emir Kasan, percussionists Larry Washington, Pablo Rosario and Ralph McDonald, and alto saxophone player Dave Sanborn. In his hour of trouble, Bowie was changing direction, developing a new sound, creating what he latter dubbed 'plastic soul'. As soon as he heard Willie Weeks was there, Visconti agreed to catch the next plane from London.

Many of the songs for what became the *Young Americans* album were written in the studio, with Bowie, who was still snorting cocaine, sometimes finishing a lyric in ten or fifteen minutes, and immediately going on to record it, composing the music more or less spontaneously. One track, an electrifying version of one of Bowie's earlier songs, *John I'm Only Dancing*, was a six-minute segment from a two-hour jam, while he reworked the Luther Vandross number *Funky Music (Is A Part Of Me)*, again spontaneously, retitling it *Fascination*, and sharing credits with Vandross. Another track, which gave the album its title and became a huge hit, *Young Americans*, was recorded straight-off in one evening, blending Sanborn's jazz saxophone and Vandross singing a backing vocal that was neither soul nor rhythm 'n' blues but somewhere in between, with a Latino percussion by Pablo Rosario.

All the songs were recorded in only eight days, with Bowie arriving at Sigma each night some time after nine o'clock, always stoned, and working through until the following afternoon. By the time they finished, several tracks were left over, including three written by a new young musician called Bruce Springsteen, whom Bowie spotted playing at Max's Kansas City. Springsteen came down to Sigma and slept on a couch, waiting to hear them record his songs. (Bowie later hired Springsteen's pianist Roy Bittan for the *Station To Station* LP which he recorded the following year.)

While Bowie worked at Sigma, there was minimal contact between him and MainMan – although Angie came down unexpectedly (and left in a hurry when she realized Bowie and Ava Cherry were still together), and Defries turned up, uninvited, to see how MainMan's money was being spent. According to Jerry Hopkins, there was an immediate 'loud, unpleasant confrontation. Defries didn't like David's new music and he was openly worried about his habitual use of drugs. David was going to throw away his career, Tony said, and more immediately, David was going to be unable to go back on the road in September. David told Tony to mind his own business. Defries said that that was what he was doing – minding the business ... and it was about time David started doing the same. David told Defries to go screw himself.'

Whatever Defries might think, and however haggard he appeared, Bowie still held the firmest of grips upon his career and told Defries bluntly that he would be dropping the stage sets and more extravagant parts of the lighting system for the next leg of the tour. 'They're too expensive,' he said, which was true.[8]

'Wait until after Los Angeles,' Defries counselled, arguing sensibly that after so much advance publicity it would be a mistake not to let the show be seen by the TV, movies and media communities on the West Coast. Bowie agreed, and on 24 August boarded a train in New York for the three-day journey to Los Angeles. There, Bowie told Zanetta that he was going to abandon the complex stage sets and wanted the focus of the tour 'to be on music and not on theatre .... I want a clean, elegant image; a simple white background, a couple of levels. We can use slides and projections against that background to give the show some colour.'

Seven shows had been cancelled, because a promoter refused to accept Defries's financial demands, and Zanetta said there would now be a gap in the schedule between 16 September and 5 October. 'That would be the ideal time to change over to the new sets,' said Bowie, giving Zanetta some sketches he had drawn on the train, showing how he wanted the backcloths to hang, and where they should be positioned.

Bowie spent nearly a month in Los Angeles, using that as his base when the tour resumed, with Marc Bolan and his new girlfriend, black singer Gloria Jones, also staying at The Beverly Hills Wilshire Hotel. Bowie was now the ascendant star whereas Bolan, a millionaire through his record and publishing deals, was already in decline, sadly misshapen, bloated and puffy around the eyes through brandy and cocaine abuse and excessive eating of fatty foods.

Sometimes their rivalry was silly, with Bolan answering the success of *Ziggy Stardust* with the all-too-obvious *Zinc Alloy And The Hidden Riders Of Tomorrow* (which was also produced by Visconti, making comparisons even more painful) – and now here they were together again, with Bowie appearing seven nights at the Universal Theater, and BBC TV producer Alan Yentob on hand to study Bowie's ability to explore alter egos and fuse other art forms with rock 'n' roll in his documentary film *Cracked Actor*. All Bolan could do was watch. Bowie felt sorry for Bolan who had been arrogant in success, and was now down again, dropped by Warner Records. 'When people were in trouble, David slipped into the role of wise father,' observed Zanetta. 'The way he had been counselled by his father, Ken Pitt and Tony Defries was the way he dealt with the lost children around him.' Bowie told Bolan how American audiences needed an American, Hollywood-style image to which they could relate, and suggested he try a more American sound.

Angie turned up, too, booking into the suite below Bowie with Zowie and the nanny, restyling her appearance to look like a 'raving dyke' and, as Zanetta describes it, roaming Rodeo Drive with a vengeance, 'leaving no 300 dollar pair of underpants unpurchased'. Bowie made no attempt to contact her, preferring the company of Iggy Pop and Ava Cherry.

The concerts were 'an amazing series of triumphs', with Diana Ross, Bette Midler, Michael Jackson and Raquel Welch and many film directors and producers, but already Bowie's mind was turning to new ways of presenting what he was later to call 'plastic soul'. By the fourth night he was introducing new songs from his next album, preparing to make the transition. The *Diamond Dogs* sets were kept for just four more shows, in San Diego, Phoenix and Tucson, and then the final performance at Anaheim, attended by Elton John, Elizabeth Taylor, Desi Arnez and Sally Kellerman.

Bowie gave the sets away to a school, rather than pay storage costs, and began two weeks of rehearsals, many of them attended by Elizabeth Taylor, who sat quietly at the edge of the studio, watching him take control, deciding where to position lights and microphones, and how to perform each song against a simple backcloth. Between numbers, Bowie would walk across, engage in small talk or give her a kiss, while she discussed them making a film in Russia, based on *The Bluebird*, a short story by Maurice Maeterlinck. This was the last thing Bowie wanted to do, but it pleased him to have the famous Hollywood star making such a suggestion when Defries had failed to find him a suitable movie project, and he was far too polite to turn her down abruptly.

One night she invited him to a party at her home in Beverly Hills, along with Elton John and John Lennon, who was then living with May Pang. Lennon always enjoyed meeting famous people, even when he was better known than they were, and kept asking, 'Where's Elizabeth? I want to meet Elizabeth.' When she arrived, wearing an enormous diamond surrounded by emeralds and a pink-panelled paisley dress, Elizabeth Taylor seized Bowie[9] by the arm and took him over to meet the other two rock stars.

'David, do you know John?' she said.

'No – but I've always wanted to meet him,' said Bowie, with an open smile and, so May Pang says, 'a look of genuine admiration in his eyes'. She adds that Lennon 'found Bowie's music fascinating, and was very cordial. David had great charm and was also very funny. The dialogue began to flow even more quickly. The group finally broke up, and David announced, "I've got to go. I've got to go." He turned to leave. Later in the evening we found him in deep conversation with Elizabeth Taylor on a couch in a deserted room at the back of the house. John and I stared at them. The screen goddess and the porcelain-faced, orange-haired rock star made a startling-looking couple. Yet, sitting there, gazing into each other's eyes, they seemed to be long-lost friends, sharing the most intimate secrets.'

On their way home, Lennon and Pang talked about the evening, meeting Bowie and their impressions of Elizabeth Taylor. 'She's not rock 'n' roll,' said Lennon. 'She's not like us. She comes from another school. We get crazy as we get older. She's been trained to deal with things.'

Agreeing to meet Lennon again in New York, Bowie continued his rehearsals, augmenting his backing group to produce a deeper soul sound, retaining Geoffrey MacCormack and Ava Cherry but bringing in four black singers: Luther Vandross, Anthony Hinton, Dianne Summler and Robin Clark. Bowie was now calling his musicians The Garson Band, and also planned to change his appearance. By the time he presented the first show at St Paul on 3 October he would look what he was, a solo singer presenting his own songs with musical accompaniment. Out went the costumes designed for *Diamond Dogs*, and anything that looked in any way homosexual. In came baggy trousers, a jacket cut tight at the waist, a shirt and necktie, in co-ordinated colours of brown and blue, with Bowie's hair dyed yellow and flatter across his head, more like a movie star than a harbinger of death and inner-city destruction. When he walked out on stage for the first time in this new outfit, he would be carrying a walking stick like the Hollywood dancers of old. A spotlight mounted at the front of the stage would magnify his silhouette against the backcloth. It was both a new image and a new direction. He was no longer appealing to gays and bisexuals. Everything MainMan and *Pork* represented was being put behind him.

David Bowie was now searching for the mainstream rock audience. He was going straight.

## 19

# John Lennon, *Fame* and
# the sci-fi alien

David Bowie returned to New York a happier man. The tour was going well. Even those fans who turned up dressed like Ziggy Stardust or Aladdin Sane were still rushing down to the edge of the stage to touch his fingertips as he reached out to the audience. The bond between them was unbroken, the tour now less expensive, and musically he was moving on. After less than six months, everyone had forgotten that this was supposed to be The Year of the Diamond Dogs.

All Bowie's previous albums were selling well, and when the *David Live* double-LP was released on 29 October 1974 it immediately qualified for a Gold Disc. There could be no doubting his status now.

All tickets were quickly sold for his appearances at Radio City Music Hall on 1, 2 and 3 November – and Defries therefore booked him in for two extras shows on 30 and 31 October. Unfortunately, this was another error of judgement, for these additional tickets did not sell and Bowie was faced with the prospect of an opening night in a half-empty theatre. Yet again, Bowie felt let down by MainMan while Defries's attitude 'implied that David's inability to sell out the five shows was a reflection of his failure as an artist, an attitude that was picked up by the MainMan staff'.[1] Such tensions should never have arisen – most performers would have been pleased to sell out Radio City Music Hall three nights running – and Bowie felt Defries's greed had caused this embarrassment, fuelling his sense of grievance.

On the first night, the sound system was out of balance, Bowie's voice was hoarse, the hall was half-empty – and the critics were merciless, reporting that a heckler shouted, 'Get off', 'We want Ziggy Stardust' and 'Give us our money back'. Returning afterwards to the Pierre Hotel, Bowie complained that it was humiliating to perform to such an audience in front of the press. 'It looked like I couldn't sell New York,' he said – and blamed MainMan. Next day, the *New York Times* described the show as 'disappointing' and said Bowie looked 'self-consciously uncomfortable without routines to act out'; another critic called the show 'shoddy'.

Whatever he may have felt, Bowie kept his opinions largely to himself, seeing John Lennon occasionally, avoiding all contact with Defries and taking the show off to various East Coast and southern venues, reaching Atlanta on 1 December. Shows at Norfolk and Tuscaloosa were cancelled when ticket sales were too low. Defries kept well away but was 'thoroughly involved in the business end of things',[2] checking hall receipts and insisting on ticket prices that maximized MainMan's return.

Once the tour was over, Bowie returned to New York and a suite at the Pierre Hotel, provided by MainMan. He discussed his problems with Bette Midler, John Lennon and Mick Jagger, but told no one what they said. The cards were kept close to his chest, although he realized he was on his own and would end up having to pay for whatever MainMan did for him. Once again, he sent for Zanetta and complained, 'Tony has apartments and houses and cars ... all I've got is a hotel bill of $20,000 a month that I'm personally paying. Every time I order a cup of coffee, it costs me five dollars. I'm being ripped off. I've got to get out of here.' Zanetta's assistant Jaime Andrews, Vice President of MainMan, was given the job of finding Bowie somewhere cheaper to live, and came up with a three-storey house in Chelsea, New York. It became known as The House on Twentieth Street to distinguish it from The House on Oakley Street, which was still Bowie's London home, even though he had not been there since March.

*     *     *     *     *

It was many months now since Bowie had spoken to the press, and on 4 December he agreed to be interviewed on Dick Cavett's NBC TV show *The Wide World Of Entertainment*. Bowie looked ill at ease, carrying the cane he used on stage as a prop, poking the carpet with it, and continually sniffing, a sure sign he was still heavily using cocaine. Asked to describe himself, Bowie said disingenuously: 'I'm a person of diverse interest. I'm not very academic.'

'What does your mother think of you?' asked Cavett.

'She pretends I'm not hers,' said Bowie, which was far from the truth. 'We've never been that close, but we have an understanding.'

What Cavett could not know was that Bowie thought himself penniless, had lost all confidence in his management and was about to take charge of his own affairs – but as always, whenever one part of Bowie's personality seemed to find all options hopeless another seemed to find some inner strength to fall back on.

A week before Christmas, Bowie started making his moves, first calling Geoff Hannington, managing director of RCA Records in London, to tell him how unhappy he felt. Hannington, who was a staunch friend, dropped everything and flew straight to New York. Together, they went to see Ken Glancey, who had transferred from London to New York as the new President of RCA Records. This was a repeat performance of Bowie's break with Ken Pitt less than four years before, only this time when asking for help in breaking away from his management Bowie was in a greater position of strength, a top-selling artist with an established international audience.

Bowie showed them his management contract with MainMan, and in return they opened the RCA books, letting him know for the first time how fully RCA had demonstrated their confidence in him, funding his early tours and increasing their advances as his record sales increased. According to Zanetta,[3] 'RCA couldn't wait to turn the tables on Defries by showing David the books.... Bowie learned that the company had advanced him anywhere between $3m and $7m.'*

When Bowie asked whether his future royalties could be paid directly to him, and in particular the advances that would become due when he delivered the master tapes of his next LP, *Young Americans*, Glancey explained this could not be done under the terms of the agreement between RCA and MainMan – but said they were willing to freeze the account with MainMan, and pay all monies due into an escrow account, where neither party could touch them until his dispute with Defries was settled. Bowie knew Defries had gone to Mustique for Christmas with Melanie and Dana Gillespie, a personal friend of the island's owner Colin

* Zanetta's account of this period is suspect, for he was President of Mainman when the company was being sued by Bowie. Inevitably, he only heard one side of the dispute. This account strikes a balance between his viewpoint and the other parties.

Tennant – and sent Defries a telegram saying his services were no longer required.

'He didn't talk about it except to say that he couldn't handle David any more,' says Gillespie.[4] 'I flew back to London, leaving everything in New York and never saw any of it again.... I was sort of put-out-to-grass, kept at bay in London. Everyone went into a kind of shock.... David was only speaking to Defries through lawyers ... it left me very emotionally crushed ...'

This was all known to Pitt in London, whom I phoned several times, surprised that he should still be so informed about Bowie's affairs. 'They tell me Defries couldn't believe it when he received the telegram,' said Pitt. 'I gather it ruined his holiday ...' (Some time later I learned that Bowie phoned him several times for advice.)

\* \* \* \* \*

Bowie moved into The House On Twentieth Street at the end of December 1974 with Geoffrey MacCormack to keep him company, Coco Schwab to fend of all callers, and Ava Cherry to share his bed. Defries terminated Ava's management contract and stopped paying her rent. Angie was living five blocks away in another MainMan apartment.

'David remained aloof,' says Zanetta.[5] 'He knew that if he ignored her long enough she would eventually flee' – as, indeed, she did as soon as Defries said he would stop paying *her* rent as well. Angie flew back to London, taking Zowie and the nanny, and resuming her round of the city's clubs, restaurants and boutiques, knowing that once she moved back into The House On Oakley Street she was in Bowie's house as Bowie's wife and mother of Bowie's child.

Meanwhile, some final work still had to be done on the new album. Bowie was booked to spend three nights in early January 1975 at Record Plant Studios, working on a 24-track mix, with the LP due for completion on 12 January. Even at this late stage, Bowie was still wondering whether to include another track and asked John Lennon if he would like to hear him recording his interpretation of the little-known Beatles number *Across The Universe*, originally given to the World Wildlife Fund in 1969 for the LP *No-one's Gonna Change Our World* and later included in the *Let It Be* album with an overpowering arrangement by Phil

Spector. Lennon was proud of the song, having written its politically idealistic lyric. When asked if he would like to go down to the studios, Lennon not only agreed at once; he also took his guitar.

By then, Bowie and Lennon were getting to know each other better, although there was never a real intimacy between them. May Pang tells the story[6] of Paul and Linda McCartney being at Lennon's New York apartment while he was remastering his *Rock 'n' Roll* album. McCartney said, 'Let's call David', who promptly invited them all over to his suite at the Pierre Hotel, where he insisted on playing them the *Young Americans* tape even though he had already played it 'many times before' to Lennon.

'When it was over, he played it again. I could see Paul was getting restless. "Can we hear a different album?" he asked. David ignored him, and when he began to play it a third time, John said, "It's great. Do you have any other albums that might be of interest?" For a moment Bowie seemed startled by John's request, then he smiled and told me to pick another record. I selected an Aretha Franklin album and put it on the turntable. Then David said, "Excuse me for a second." He marched out of the room.'

'I think you hurt Bowie's feelings,' Pang told Lennon.

'Paul's been asking him all night to change the record,' said Lennon, but later that night, he phoned Bowie and afterwards told Pang, 'David really did feel hurt.... He was very upset. I kept telling him I didn't mean it like that.'

Several years later,[7] recalling his relationship with Bowie, Lennon said, 'Amazing guy, isn't he?... I admire him for the vast repertoire of talent the guy has, you know. I was never around when the Ziggy Stardust thing came, because I'd already left England while all that was going on, so I never really knew what he was. And meeting him doesn't give you much of a clue, you know.... Because you don't know which one you're talking to.'

It was just a few days after this incident that Bowie invited Lennon down to the Record Plant Studios. When Lennon arrived, Bowie was in another room supervising some overdubbing. Carlos Alomar was sitting in the studio as Lennon picked up his guitar and started to play the riff from *Shame, Shame, Shame*, then a hit single for Shirley and Company. Alomar followed him, picking up the riff, and as Bowie walked back into the studio he asked, 'What's that you're playing?'

'*Shame, Shame, Shame*,' said Lennon.

This is the moment Lennon is believed to have told Bowie with characteristic bluntness that it was easy making hit records, 'Look, it's very simple. Say what you mean, make it rhyme and put a backbeat to it.'[8] Bowie left the studio and returned minutes later (he has a reputation for writing extraordinarily fast) with a scrap of paper – the lyric for *Fame.* Alomar says Bowie 'took out the lyrics and ended up with the music and put it on a master so that he would have a classic rhythm 'n' blues form. He's a perfectionist and experiments with the original tape, running it backwards, cutting it up, doing things on the master as opposed to recording them live. *Fame* was totally cut up.'[9]

As Zanetta says, *Fame* was 'a classic Bowie synthesis' with a vocal track by Lennon added to the *Shame, Shame, Shame* riff, ideas taken from other rhythm 'n' blues records, Alomar's chord changes and then Bowie's own vocal track, all inter-woven, adapting the cut-and-paste technique Bowie picked up from William Burroughs, who had in turn adapted it from Brion Gysin (a minor literary figure of the 50s), and using all of this to express his anger at the way Defries was handling his affairs. In his words, when you find *Fame,* 'What you get is no tomorrow'; and 'What you need you have to borrow'.

These judgements sound all the sharper, spat to this tight, disciplined, basically rhythm 'n' blues beat – although it becomes far more than that in Bowie's hands. Bowie has acknowledged Lennon's contribution. 'It was more the influence of having him in the studio that helped,' said Bowie. 'There's always a lot of adrenalin flowing when John is around, but his chief addition to the song was his high-pitched singing. The riff came from Carlos, and the melody and most of the lyrics from me, but it wouldn't have happened if John hadn't been there. He was the energy, and that's why he got a writing credit for writing it; he was the inspiration.'[10]

The timing of *Fame* could not have been better. RCA were already convinced *Young Americans* would be a top-selling album, and were so sure of the title track that they ordered an advance pressing of 250,000 singles, backed up by an advertising campaign costing $200,000 – and now they had an even stronger number in *Fame,* which was to give Bowie his first No. 1 hit single.

Legally, the mastertapes belonged to MainMan, but Bowie did what any sensible person would have done: he put them in a bank vault and continued to deal directly over the heads of MainMan

with Glancey and Harrington. The RCA contract may have been
with MainMan, but in disputes like these record companies
invariably stand by their artistes – and RCA did so with cash,
advancing Bowie money to pay his staff, meet personal expenses,
pay for his car (which Bowie thought Defries might attempt to
repossess), and hire a suite at The Algonquin Hotel to use as
offices until the dispute was resolved. Bowie installed Coco
Schwab and Pat Gibbons, whom he poached from MainMan,
having been impressed by the way Gibbons handled arrangements
for the *Diamond Dogs* tour. The third member of the team, and
perhaps the most crucial, was the lawyer Michael Lippman, who
left the agency handling Bowie's bookings to return to his legal
practice in Hollywood. For the next three months Lippman flew
the 'red eye shuttle' between Los Angeles and New York,
advising Bowie and representing him in negotiations with RCA
and Defries.

Such rock 'n' roll disputes follow a pattern. Writs are issued,
defences filed, counter-claims made – with both parties knowing
that if they cannot bear the thought of working together again, a
settlement will have to be agreed. Bowie wanted his freedom, and
knowing how strongly he felt, Defries demanded a high price –
and got it. The comings and goings in between, an attempt by
Defries to block the release of *Young Americans*, the accusations
made against each other, are merely the games lawyers play – and
once Bowie agreed to the main part of Defries's demands the
game was over.

It has been claimed that Defries came out of these negotiations
with the better deal, but Bowie has never discussed the terms they
agreed. Other published accounts overlook two crucial factors –
firstly, that Bowie's record sales had already recouped the RCA
advances to MainMan, and secondly, that although Bowie may
have signed away half his current income he nevertheless ensured
that half would be all his and not spent by MainMan.

The agreement dated from 1 March 1975, and provided that
thereafter MainMan and Bowie would jointly own the two LPs
acquired from Mercury and the six recorded for RCA (*Hunky
Dory, Ziggy Stardust, Aladdin Sane, Pin-Ups, Diamond Dogs* and
*David Live*) with royalties divided equally between them. This
was a significant achievement for Bowie; he was getting back
rights foolishly signed away – and would now receive 50 per cent
of the royalties instead of 50 per cent of the profits after all

MainMan expenses had been deducted. In addition, he agreed MainMan would receive 16.66 per cent of royalties from *Young Americans* and from all other material recorded by Bowie between 1 March 1975 and the expiry of his contracts with RCA and MainMan at the end of 1982. MainMan would also receive 25 per cent of Bowie's publishing income and 5 per cent of his income from live appearances. Most importantly of all for Bowie as a creative artiste with a genuine pride in his work, he gained both financial and artistic control and became his own man.* RCA agreed to make a payment of $325,000 to MainMan so that Bowie could be paid money that was owing to him. RCA also agreed to pay MainMan's unpaid bills, which by March 1975 amounted to $530,071 in the United States and $57,845 in Britain. In effect, the slate was being wiped clean.

\*   \*   \*   \*   \*

On 26 January 1975, early in Bowie's dispute with Defries, Alan Yentob's *Cracked Actor* documentary was shown on BBC Television. Watching it at his home, the English film director Nicholas Roeg, who also made Mick Jagger's first movie *Performance*, was immediately convinced that Bowie was the person to star in his next film, *The Man Who Fell To Earth.* Roeg never chooses actors for a film until his shooting script is ready, and then, 'I sit back and ask myself, "Who are these people?" I never have the characters described. I prefer to let the scenes and interaction form the character rather than neat description.' He believes in 'odd omens' and was so excited by *Cracked Actor* that he phoned his scriptwriter Paul Mayersberg while the documentary was still on the air, and said, 'Look at this' – and immediately acquired a tape of *Cracked Actor* to study again. 'It was his approach to life that appealed to me,' says Roeg of Bowie.[11] 'He was giving and secretive in the best possible way. He wasn't secretive for the reason of hiding something but secretive because that part of him hadn't been fully understood by himself.' This was also how I viewed *Cracked Actor.* Bowie was clearly in

* These figures are disclosed by Zanetta. As he was President of MainMan and therefore privy to the legal action, the figures are presumably correct. (*See Stardust,* p. 340.) Slightly different figures are given in *Alias David Bowie* (pp. 498–509), but the Gillmans do not appear to have understood the significance of the dispute. They quote various sources that were ill-informed.

command, communicating on one level, chuckling on another –
holding the film crew at a distance so that they remained
spectators, and nothing more.

Readers familiar with other Bowie biographies will know that
this period in his life – from the beginning of *Diamond Dogs*
through the making of *Young Americans* and his dispute with
Defries to the filming of *The Man Who Fell To Earth* – is treated
oddly. There are stories that Bowie drew Black Magic symbols,
saw disembodied beings, thought he was the new Messiah, kept
bottles of his own urine in a fridge to use in occult rituals (this
comes from Jerry Hopkins's book), thought a scriptwriter working
on an aborted *Diamond Dogs* movie was a CIA agent, suspected
The Rolling Stones of talking to him through their record sleeves
(Zanetta is the source of this one), saw UFOs coming over every
night at 6.15 p.m. (*Creem*), fought 'a furious struggle for unspoken
power' with Jimmy Page of Led Zeppelin, thought he might
become both British Prime Minister and President of the United
States (the Gillmans) … and many, many more stories in similar
vein. I hope it's not a disappointment, but there is none of that in
this book.

The trouble with all these stories is that they are written second-
hand, based on the writings of 17-year-old Cameron Crowe who
managed to break through the Bowie security cordon with a tape
recorder and followed him around for several days. Crowe then
sold separate narratives to *Rolling Stone* and *Playboy*. Other
writers have lifted this material without knowing what was true
and what was not. Bowie frequently played with interviewers, and
I suspect something like that happened to Crowe. In paragraph
after paragraph, one can see Bowie leading him on, inventing
anecdotes, playing fey, being ironic – but anyone who knew the
ropes would see, as Nicholas Roeg saw when he watched *Cracked
Actor*, that Bowie was being 'giving and secretive in the best
possible way'.

Cocaine kept Bowie supercharged, pulling something extra
from within, able to keep on working when others flagged. Bowie
would veer emotionally, from tears to screams and howls of rage if
he thought anyone might have let him down or taken him less
seriously than he sometimes takes himself (although he is equally
capable of self-mockery). Weighing little more than eight stone, or
112lbs, with muscles like whipcord, carrying no surplus body fat
or excess fluid, he drove himself on, snapping emotionally on one

level, keeping control on another. 'My chemistry must have been superhuman,' he said years later.[12] 'I'd stay up seven or eight days on the trot. The Stones would be absolutely floored by me. They'd see me days later and find out that I hadn't been to bed.... Of course, every day you stayed up longer – and there's things you have to do to stay up that long – the impending tiredness and fatigue produces that hallucinogenic state naturally. Well, half-naturally. By the end of the week my whole life would be transformed into this bizarre, nihilistic, fantasy world.' Crowe caught him like this, without realizing Bowie was still in control, not necessarily of every faculty, but still watching himself carefully.

Roeg's intended film was based upon the novel *The Man Who Fell To Earth* by Walter Tevis. Its main character is T. J. Newton, an alien from another planet who hopes to raise half a billion dollars to build a spaceship so that he can make his own way home. When people try to understand his mind and steal his secrets, Newton turns to drink. Roeg sent a script through to Bowie's film agent at International Creative Management, Maggie Abbott, who went to discuss it with Bowie at The House On Twentieth Street. 'Abbott felt that he was living unnaturally; the feeling in the house reeked of isolation and temporariness,' says Zanetta,[13] suggesting Defries would never have allowed such a meeting or Bowie to have made less than a 'major' film. In these remarks, Zanetta reveals how little MainMan knew their man. As soon as he heard the film was in the offing, Bowie obtained copies of Roeg's previous films, *Performance*, *Walkabout* and *Don't Look Now*, checked Roeg out with Mick Jagger, and carefully studied the script of *The Man Who Fell To Earth*. He then told Abbott that he would like to meet the director – and Roeg flew to New York to see him.

On the day Roeg arrived at The House On Twentieth Street, Bowie was still at Record Plant remixing *Young Americans*. Coco Schwab sat Roeg down in the house – and there he sat for the next eight hours, with Bowie phoning in to apologize every hour. This was never the way MainMan worked, but this was Bowie, the real Bowie, talking ideas through, satisfying himself that the project was sound in every artistic way and far more bothered about the film's purpose than its funding. After all that waiting, his meeting with Roeg lasted only 15 minutes. 'Don't worry,' said Bowie, 'I'm going to do this.'

'I proceeded along those lines,' says Roeg. 'Nothing was signed, he was under no contractual obligation but I had a sense of trust from him. I phoned him only twice afterwards, and everyone was saying, "What if he suddenly decides against doing the movie?" But he said, "I'm going to do this" with such sincerity that I totally believed in him.'

When the filming schedule had to be delayed three months, Bowie accepted that, too, and spent that time fooling around in Hollywood, staying with different friends (including Michael Lippman and Glen Hughes of Deep Purple), while Roeg sorted out the finance and production details. This was the period when Bowie took more cocaine than any other, between late March 1975 when he left for Hollywood and his late June departure for New Mexico to begin work on the film. Initially, he was moving from friend to friend, without cash, still waiting for the Defries settlement money to come through.

One night, well the worse for cocaine, Bowie phoned Angie at The House On Oakley Street, and she found him 'a friend-abusing, sense-mangling, money-bleeding, full-fledged Vampire of Velocity … his mind spinning in tight circles even when standing perfectly still'.[14] Bowie said he was somewhere in Los Angeles, with a warlock and two witches who were trying to capture his semen for use in a Black Magic ritual on Walpurgis Night, 30 April. 'He wanted to get away, he said, but he didn't have any money, and he didn't know where he was and, anyway, the witches wouldn't let him leave. He was talking in slurred, hushed tones, and hardly making any sense and he was crazed with fear …'

Sensing this was a form of drug-induced paranoia, Angie phoned Lippman who contacted Bowie immediately at the phone number he had given her, told him to leave whatever house he was in and catch a taxi. Meanwhile, Angie dropped everything and flew to his side, finding a house on Doheny Drive, moving in with him, and getting him back to eating food. Even in this condition, Bowie was still working – recording an album at the RCA studios in Los Angeles with Nina Simone. The marriage was like this, a strange dependence rather than a union of body and mind. However much he hurt her (and she was equally capable of hurting him), Angie would still come running whenever he called. Sadly for her, Bowie never needed her for long.

In June, Bowie caught the train to Santa Fe, accompanied by

MacCormack, Coco Schwab and his new bodyguard, Tony Mascia, a huge 350lb black man with the build of an all-in wrestler, arriving two days early with a small library of over 300 books. When he walked on the set, having still not signed a contract, Bowie walked up to Roeg and said with a broad grin, 'I told you I'd be here, didn't I?'

Roeg says Bowie committed himself totally to the film, having 'the wit and the intelligence to concentrate on his role', with his free days spent visiting Taos, where D. H. Lawrence painted and wrote short stories, He only phoned Angie once and that was to say he was unhappy with the catering arrangements – and she at once flew down to take over as cook. At the end of each day, he would walk off the set and disappear. In an interview with the BBC TV programme *Arena,*[15] Roeg said, 'What I found difficult was that he was hard to reach – not emotionally, just on a purely physical level. There are barriers, a filter system, around every star ... but they seemed particularly strong around Bowie.'

Three months later, Bowie returned to Doheny Drive, where he began planning his next world tour, timed to coincide with the release of *The Man Who Fell To Earth* and the soundtrack LP. Some days, he also worked down at the Cherokee Studios in Los Angeles, recording the songs that were later included in the *Station To Station* LP, and breaking off for the occasional television appearance.

Michael Lippman was now his manager, but the arrangement was not working well. Bowie had understood his music was going to be used on the soundtrack and was mortified to learn another soundtrack was being recorded by John Phillips of The Mamas and The Papas. Bowie blamed Lippman and sacked him, having taken advice from the Los Angeles lawyer Stanley Diamond on Lippman's proposed management agreement. Bowie filed a law suit, claiming Lippman had taken 15 per cent of his earnings instead of 10 per cent, and alleging Lippman withheld $475,000 after being dismissed. This happened in the last weeks of 1975, when the tour dates were being finalized, with the first concert set for Vancouver on 2 February and Bowie planning to spend Christmas in Jamaica, staying at Keith Richard's house at Ochios Point, and rehearsing with the musicians chosen for the tour.

Diamond, who advised Bowie not to sign the Lippman contract shortly before the dispute arose, also warned him he might have to pay $300,000 taxes unless he left California swiftly. Tax debts had accumulated and Angie says the money had gone 'into various murky areas, David's nasal cavities being only the most apparent'.[16] Over dinner at Doheny Drive, Diamond told her the solution was for Bowie to go into tax exile. 'We've tried Switzerland, which is by far the best option,' said Diamond. 'But no go. We can't get residency there.'

Unfortunately for her, as events turned out, Angie told them she had been educated in Switzerland and knew her way around the Alps. 'If you want it, I'll get it done,' she said, not thinking for a moment that if Bowie became a Swiss resident he would be able to divorce her under Swiss law, retain custody of their son, and send her packing with a reduced settlement.

20

# Flight into tax exile

After years of pleading poverty, complaining he had no money in his pocket to buy everyday necessities, which in his case meant at least and usually four packets of Gitanes each day, David Bowie now became extremely rich – and it happened very quickly. As part of his settlement with MainMan, Bowie received $325,000 in a lump sum, and he probably increased that ten-fold within a year. At the same time he cut costs in all directions, continued to live frugally (although Angie did not) – and after gaining control of his life, his work and his money, Bowie's health began to improve. His daily intake of cocaine dropped dramatically.

While he was rehearsing in Jamaica over Christmas and the New Year, Angie flew to Switzerland, where staff at her old school near Montreux gave her the names and addresses of three different attorneys. She went to see all three, and sorted out which decisions Bowie would have to take, and which documents he would need to sign before he could qualify for residential status. Angie says the Swiss are 'incredibly particular about who gets in, and where and how they can live once they're there' but that 'after much exquisite and very enjoyable negotiation, I got what we wanted, and better'. She found them 'a commodious cuckoo-clock of a house' with seven or eight bedrooms and even more bathrooms, a caretaker's lodge and six acres of 'prime real estate'. Known as Clos de Mesanges, the house is situated at Blonay, a French-speaking village in the canton of Vaud, in snow-capped mountains above Lake Geneva, near Montreux – not far from Fribourg, where Defries established his Swiss company, MainMan SA.

I have not seen the 53-page document detailing the settlement between Bowie and MainMan, but the general practice within the music industry when a separation occurs like this is for all royalties due to be divided as agreed between the parties by the record company, and also by the publishing company. Separate cheques are then sent to artiste and manager at each accounting date. This makes life simple. Everyone gets their share. Bowie could now look forward to a regular flow of quarterly and half-yearly royalty cheques. Likewise, having long since recouped his advances from Essex Music and Chrysalis, who also have a Swiss operation, he could expect regular cheques from them, as well.

Substantial though this would be (and over the 20 years since Bowie settled in Switzerland this would amount to many millions of dollars, for he receives a royalty whenever one of his songs is played on radio or television anywhere in the world), it was peanuts compared with what followed thereafter, for Bowie set up his own song-publishing companies Jones Music SA, Bewlay Brothers SA and Tintoretto Music SA, another company, Stenton SA (named after his father), to handle film projects and video distribution deals, and Isolar to promote his world tours. Most artistes of his stature also have other companies on both the East and West Coasts of the United States, and holding companies in the Bahamas, Virgin or Channel Islands, or positioned within the Common Market, usually in Holland where there are tax advantages. One of the favourite tricks – and I don't know whether Bowie has tried this one – is to give the companies the same name in each territory, and then money just disappears, with the tax authorities never knowing which hole it has gone through. The significance of this in Bowie's case is that he began establishing this financial structure in 1976, once he was legally divorced from MainMan; and after firing Lippman there were to be no more managers, no more percentages for anyone but Bowie. Anyone who worked with him was paid a wage, other than in rare situations (as with the writing of *Fame*) when he shared royalties with co-writers of songs.

*     *     *     *     *

Once he was in control of his own finances, the tight-fisted Yorkshireman in Bowie began to emerge. He began reducing his outgoings wherever he could. Finding that his soundtrack for *The Man Who Fell To Earth* was not going to be used, he brought the musicians back together again, went into the studios and finished his next LP, *Station To Station*, in little more than a week, then went ahead with his concert schedule as planned, but calling it The

Station To Station World Tour, and still opened on time in Vancouver on 2 February 1976.

Faced with his biggest schedule yet, and performing in larger arenas, Bowie maximized profits by keeping down his costs, using only five backing musicians as he did on the album. These were Carlos Alomar (guitar), George Murray (bass) and Dennis Davis (drums), on the LP, former Yes pianist Tony Kaye (replacing Roy Bittan, who had other commitments) and Stacey Heydon instead of Earl Slick (who dropped out because Lippman was his manager). Bowie dispensed with backing singers Ava Cherry and Claudia Lennear after living with Ava Cherry for over two years. (During his phase of cocaine-induced paranoia, Bowie managed to convince himself she was having an affair with someone else – she wasn't, but she went.) So there were just the five musicians, plus Coco Schwab, bodyguard Tony Mascia, tour manager Pat Gibbons, and Barbara de Witt handling publicity, with a minimal lighting and road crew. Despite the cost-cutting, the show was stunning – for Bowie used simple black and white backcloths with images projected from *Un Chien Andalou* (1922), the classic surrealist movie by Salvador Dali and Louis Buñuel, and also the stark monochrome photographs made famous in the 20s and 30s by the French fashion photographer Man Ray. Bowie's costumes were in similar vein – black pants and waistcoat, a plain white shirt, black shoes. He was reducing his show to its elements, as the French singers of the 40s and 50s had done, using only minimum props, his guitar, saxophone and a packet of Gitanes.

From its 2 February 1976 start in Vancouver, the tour went on to numerous major venues, including Los Angeles (8th–11th). In Detroit (29 February and 1 March), he was interviewed by Chris Charlesworth, one of the better London music writers who was then based in the States as US editor for *Melody Maker*, before joining RCA as Press Officer.

'This is the most efficient tour I've ever seen,' Bowie told Charlesworth,[1] revealing that his personal staff were only the handful already mentioned and that his total entourage, including the five musicians, his road crew engineers and drivers, came to 26 – less than a third of the usual strength for such a tour. 'It wasn't until John Lennon pointed it out to me that I realized maybe an artist is as good at managing as anybody else. It was John who sorted me out all down the line. He took me on one side and told me what it was all about and I realized I was very naïve. I still thought you had to have somebody else who dealt with these things called contracts, but now I have a better understanding of the showbusiness business.'

Bowie was clearly recovering fast, now that he had total control, and was anxious to put Los Angeles well behind him, describing it as 'the most repulsive wart on the backside of humanity' and saying that since arriving in the United States two years earlier, 'I've been here but I haven't lived.... My affairs have been so badly messed up that I haven't had time to go back to England recently. I was told I couldn't go back to England because I had tax problems there and didn't have the money to pay for them, but now I do so I'm going back.... I never saw any money from the *Diamond Dogs* tour. I'm only making money now. That's why I wanted to simplify things this time round, to make money. I'm managing myself now simply because I've got fed up with the managers I've known.... I haven't kept a band together since The Spiders and I don't want the responsibility of keeping one. It's too much money, anyway, to keep a band together – a lot of problems that I don't need.... I'm just doing this tour for the money. I never earned any money before, but this time I'm going to make some. I think I deserve it, don't you?'

In another part of the interview, Bowie was engagingly frank – confirming what I had suspected all along, that his original confession to *Melody Maker* about his sexuality was no more than a stunt. 'Bisexual?' he asked. 'Oh Lord, no! Positively not! That was just a lie. They gave me that image so I stuck to it pretty well for a few years. I never adopted that stance. It was given to me. I've never done a bisexual action in my life, on stage, on record or anywhere else. I don't think I even had much of a gay following.'

Bowie now had a travelling companion, Iggy Pop, who was also weaning himself off drugs. Nine months earlier, a few days before his departure for New Mexico, Bowie found Iggy, abandoned and destitute, in the Neuropsychiatric Institute at the University of California, Los Angeles. Iggy, a voluntary patient, was being treated for heroin addiction. Bowie visited him every day, forging the closest of all intangible bonds, for Iggy has that same high-tensile manic quality that sometimes comes with extreme intelligence. 'I don't like hardly anybody,' Iggy said subsequently, 'but I do like him very much. I have a place in my heart for him.' Iggy turned up backstage when the tour reached Los Angeles, and Bowie invited him to join the party, with them visiting Iggy's home in Detroit and from there travelling on to other tour venues, starting with Chicago on 3 March. At Rochester, New York (20th), they were both arrested in the early hours of the morning and accused of possessing eight ounces of marijuana, together with a friend, Dwain A. Vaughn, and a female companion, Chivah Soo. They were each allowed $2,000 bail, with Bowie putting up the money for all of them – and a year later the case was dropped.

After the New York date at Madison Square Garden (26 March), Bowie and Iggy took a boat to Cannes where a huge Mercedes limousine, formerly belonging to the President of Sierra Leone, was waiting at the quayside to take them through Europe, with Tony Mascia driving. After concerts in Munich and Dusseldorf, they drove to Berlin, passing through Checkpoint Charlie so that Bowie could visit the bunker where Hitler committed suicide, with a concert that night in Berlin (10 April). Others followed in Hamburg, Frankfurt and Zurich, when Bowie was taken to see the house Angie had chosen at Blonay for the first time.

Meanwhile, unbeknown to all but his closest friends, Bowie's possessions were collected from his rented home in Los Angeles – all the books and LPs he bought in America, his furniture and antiques, clothes, musical instruments and recording equipment, together with all the stage costumes, props and other personal memorabilia Bowie kept in storage in New York after his previous US tours. They were all transported to Switzerland. Bowie told no one that he was now a tax exile, and evaded the question whenever it was asked, hiding sometimes behind the smokescreen of a rented flat in Berlin. Quietly, he established Swiss residential status and thereby domiciliary status for his companies which enabled them to benefit under Swiss tax law.

Angie was at Clos de Mesanges when he arrived, but they could barely stand each other's company for more than a few hours before rows and accusations began, and after two days he was off, performing again in Frankfurt (15 April) and then Berne, preferring to spend the next week with Iggy Pop travelling through Europe and up to Scandinavia. On the borders of Russia and Poland, they were stopped and searched by the KGB, before driving on to Moscow to visit Red Square, St Basil's Cathedral, the art galleries and the GUM department store, spending several nights at the Metropole Hotel.

Reports of these strangely dressed young men travelling with their equipment and a huge black bodyguard were evidently phoned through to the guards on the Russian-Finnish border, for there Bowie and Iggy were ordered to strip and were body searched. When the guards looked through Bowie's baggage, they found books on Goebbels and other Nazi leaders. These were confiscated, despite Bowie's insistence that he was using them for research purposes and intended to write a stage musical based on the life of Goebbels (which may have been an extension of the original idea behind *Diamond Dogs*). The interrogation and the seizure of Bowie's books was witnessed by a journalist, and, whatever his true motivations, Bowie became Bowie the putative Nazi as he continued his journey, dogged thereafter with questions about his Nazi books as he prepared for his concerts in Helsinki and Stockholm. There he allegedly answered a question from another journalist by saying, 'I think Britain could benefit from a Fascist leader. I mean, Fascist in its true sense – not Nazi. After all, Fascism is really nationalism. In a sense, it is a very pure form of communism.' These comments, which Bowie furiously denied making, were wired through by the international press agencies. By the time the Scandinavian segment of the tour ended with concerts in Copenhagen (29 and 30 April), with Bowie preparing to travel back down through Europe to catch the boat train to London, Britain's national newspapers were front-paging his return.

As luck would have it Bowie turned to wave to his waiting fans as his train drew into Victoria Station and his outstretched arm looked just like a Nazi salute. Photographs of that moment appeared in nearly every newspaper the following day, and abuse rained down upon his head. One person was particularly outraged – his mother, Mrs Peggy Jones, who phoned the *New Musical Express* to let them know what she thought of her son. 'He's a terrible hypocrite,' she told Charles Shaar Murray, and went on to discuss the strife within the family, complaining how little she saw him, although Bowie had once sent her a mink coat for Christmas. She was 'chuffed' by that – but where could an old age pensioner wear a mink coat? she asked.

Bowie was beside himself with rage when he read her interview. He had never been that close to his mother, but it was quite another matter to have her phoning his own trade papers to criticize him. He phoned her angrily and told her never, never, never give another interview; but also, in the calmer light of day, he began looking after her better than he had in the past, finding her a new home, providing her with a regular financial allowance, and ensuring she faced her old age in comfort. This has continued ever since, with Mrs Jones, now in her early 80s, frequently staying at Bowie's home in Switzerland, holidaying with him in New York, attending his more important concerts and his second wedding, and thus being genuinely and lovingly brought within his family, as Granny to Zowie, and as Mum. This was all part of the process of escaping cocaine, fighting off witches and demons, and coming back to earth.

\*   \*   \*   \*   \*

By the time Bowie returned to Europe, *Station To Station* was another success, reaching No. 5 in the British LP charts, and *Golden Years* and *TVC 15* reaching No. 8 and No. 33 in the singles charts. *Golden Years* was apparently written for Angie in one of those optimistic moments when he still thought the marriage might survive. After composing it, Bowie played it over the phone to her and now it was a little bit of everything, rock intro, disco-funk rhythm, even maracas and a whistle and a flowing lyric line that told her 'Don't let me hear you. say/life's taking you nowhere'; that he loved her for the way she opened doors and pulled strings, and 'I'll stick to you, baby, for a thousand years./Nothing's gonna touch you in these golden years'. It was a strange message to send to a wife when their marriage was in terminal decline. Perhaps he believed it, or one part of him did, still loving what he longed for in one part of his mind, while slowly accepting reality in another.

This was his last album to be recorded in America for four years, and, in a sense, acts as a bridge between that American period in his life and the sequence of albums that were to become known as his 'Berlin triptych' – and there are a few clues to what was to follow. *TVC 15* was another attempt to write a song using the William Burroughs technique of cutting up dozens of words from a printed page – a book, a newspaper or a poem – and then haphazardly rearranging them. *Station To Station* was marketed cold, as a new LP from David Bowie and no more, but Bowie – who was careful not to explain the album – may have conceived it as a transitional work, for this is how it comes across. The fact that he was using its songs as the crux of his tour, playing the role of 'The Thin White Duke' on stage, enclosed in black and white with 'curtains of light', tends to strengthen that explanation. It was written at a time when he was studying religion, with a wide range of theological works in his travelling library (on this world tour as on location in Mexico, Bowie travelled with a personal reference library to hand so that when he wasn't rehearsing a sound check or looking up the local art galleries – always a favourite pursuit on every tour – he could while away the hours when travelling or in a hotel room, especially when concerts were sometimes spaced two or three days apart). The library also included studies of Arthurian myths, Buddhism, research into Fascism as a philosophy with ancient roots, art, architecture, and the histories of the Grecian and Roman empires.

I have often wondered whether in Bowie's mind 'The Thin White Duke' was meant to be a character striding across the surface of the earth, between New World and Old, from America back to Europe and the Mediterranean 'cradle of civilization', following a path similar in thought to the Stations of the Cross, which were a favourite theme of art, music and religious thought through many centuries.* After all, apotheosis was also an undercurrent to *The Rise And Fall Of Ziggy Stardust And The Spiders From Mars* – but if that was what he was thinking, Bowie was far too smart to say. Like all the better poets and novelists, he was leaving the audience to discover his meaning.

*    *    *    *    *

Taking cocaine while filming *The Man Who Fell To Earth*, which is as much a study of the workings of the human psyche as it is a sci-fi story, clearly unnerved Bowie. 'There were days of such psychological terror ... that I nearly started to approach my

---

* Periodically, Bowie has been ridiculed for such interests as these, especially after the controversy over his alleged Nazi salute and suggestions he was now anti-homosexual, anti-socialist and racist, all of which he denies. These criticisms in the music press coincided with a swing to the left in the British Labour Party, the rise of the Socialist Workers' Party and Rock Against Racism, and the emergence of Militant as a political force, all of which was reflected in the British music papers. Its writers became self-consciously trendy, identifying this movement with Punk Rock. I would argue that each train of thought should be viewed separately. Bowie's library represented genuine interests on his part. Fascism does have ancient roots. It takes its name from the symbols of power, the fasces (bundles of rods held by magistrates) in ancient Rome, and there is an interesting parallel between the architectural devices used in Nazi Germany to project the speeches of Nazi leaders and the way musicians use lighting, staging and amplification to project themselves to vast audiences in modern rock arenas.

reborn, born again thing,' he revealed in a much later interview with Angus McKinnon of the *New Musical Express.*[2] 'It was the first time I really seriously thought about Christ and God in any depth and *Word On A Wing* was a protection,' he said, revealing that this was when he started wearing a silver crucifix around his neck, usually hidden by a shirt. 'I really needed this,' he added, fingering the crucifix. 'We're getting into heavy waters ... but yes, the song was something I needed to produce from within myself to safeguard myself against some of the situations that I felt were happening on the film set.'

One could also draw parallels between *Station To Station* and *The Man Who Fell To Earth*, for Bowie always tends to draw on other sources, and both are transitional. Bowie often concerns himself with visions that can be seen on different planes, like a novelist using one story to tell another. Although not unusual in literature, this was innovatory in rock 'n' roll.

*Station To Station* comprised only six pieces. The title track advanced the notion that his influences were 'not the side effects of cocaine' but 'I'm thinking it must be love'. Bowie, careful not to define what he meant by love in any one situation, went straight into *Golden Years*, an avowal of enduring love, and *Word On A Wing*, with its first clue that there might be a religious undercurrent: 'Just because I believe/don't mean I don't think as well'. He continues the idea through the confusion of *TVC 15* and the romantic ballad *Stay*. This could also have been written for Angie, with Bowie asking her to stay with him and saying 'You can never really tell when somebody/really loves you'. The finale is *Wild Is The Wind*, which really has to be seen and heard in his later monochromatic video, portraying Bowie in shades of grey rather than black and white, singing the song written by Dmitri Tiomkin and recorded by Johnny Mathis as the theme music for the film *Wild Is The Wind* (1957), an earthily romantic love story made when Bowie was ten years old; his voice wails like the wind with poignant force as he tears out its meaning: 'Don't you know you are life itself?' This was both the message of the film, and also, perhaps, the question he was answering himself as he left The City of The Angels.

\* \* \* \* \*

Still travelling by sea and land, Bowie arrived in London on 2

May 1976 with another album to promote. Long before it became a fashion, he packaged a 'greatest hits' album, selecting its title and their sequence himself, giving it the symbolic name *CHANGESONEBOWIE* (which freed him to subsequently issue another with the title *CHANGESTWOBOWIE*). Everything about it was well chosen, with a new, moody, Hollywood-style photo on the cover capturing Bowie as if lost in thought. This was taken by Tom Kelley, creator of the famous nude calendar photographs of Marilyn Monroe. Once again, the effect was subliminal: it was as if Bowie had packaged his best work to date, like a poet preparing a volume of 'Collected Works' before moving on to something new. *CHANGESONEBOWIE* was also another good business move, showing that when it came to making commercial judgements Bowie's instincts were often better than those of most marketing managers. Most of the tracks, such as *Fame*, *Ziggy Stardust* and *Golden Years*, were available on other LPs in every record shop, but not gathered together in this way and with the direct force that his best songs have when heard one after another – and so he was, in effect, asking his fans to buy these songs again, having already recouped his RCA advances for the originals. And they did. No one had thought of doing that before, but other artistes on other labels soon followed suit.

CHANGESONEBOWIE* sold over 1.5m copies, three times as many as *Station To Station* – and more than any other Bowie LP except *Ziggy Stardust*.

Bowie stayed in Britain for only one week, performing to packed houses six nights running at the Wembley Empire Pool – introducing himself to the audience as David 'Winston' Bowie. This was another of those obtuse jokes that he would crack without explanation. Was it 'Winston' as in John Winston Lennon? Or 'Winston' as in Churchill, to show them all he wasn't really a Fascist after all? Or 'Winston' as in George Orwell's *Nineteen Eighty-Four*? The press were keen to find out what the joke meant, to enquire if he truly was a Fascist, to discuss *The Man Who Fell To Earth* (then showing in London after mixed reviews: 'a parable' (*The Times*); 'enough ideas for six films' (*Financial Times*). The *Evening Standard* proclaimed it a modern version of Icarus), not to mention all his other plans. But Bowie only agreed to meet one journalist – Jean Rook of the *Daily Express*. If any Fleet Street writer could slice through pretension, she could; but Jean Rook realized she was witnessing something very strange.

Denying all the interpretations she had read, Bowie said: 'I've a terrible feeling I did say something like it to a Stockholm journalist, who kept asking me political questions – I'm astounded anyone could believe it. I have to keep reading it to believe it myself. I'm not sinister.... I don't stand up in cars waving to people because I think I'm Hitler. I stand up in cars waving to my fans.' When she asked whether this mattered, as it was all publicity, Bowie said: 'Yes it does. It upsets me. Strong I may be. Arrogant I may be. Sinister I'm not.'

And when she went on to develop the argument, taking up his challenge to make a comparison, and suggesting that perhaps he could be compared with Dracula, Berenice, a zombie or an emaciated Marlon Brando playing a Hitler youth, Bowie came back: 'No, no, no ... I'm Pierrot, I'm Everyman. What I'm doing is Theatre, and only Theatre ... what you see on stage isn't sinister. It's pure clown. I'm using my face as a canvas and trying to paint the truth of our time on it. The white face, the baggy pants – they're Pierrot, the eternal clown putting over the great sadness of 1976 ...' Bowie then asked whether she remembered him as Ziggy Stardust, and continued, 'Ziggy was putting over the bizarre of our time. Now Bowie's putting over the sadness.'

The interview turned around and around, like those we used to have, and she concluded:

If you hadn't seen – and heard – Bowie perform, you'd accuse him of swotting up the lyrical phrases for the interview. In fact Bowie is a poet, possibly a modern day genius. What W. B. Yeats – referring to an Irish dustman – called 'living poetry' flows from his death-pale lips (pancake make-up, and not, thank God, leukaemia). He describes his one ear-ring Ziggy Stardust period as 'looking like a cross between Nijinsky and Woolworth's' without self-consciousness of his own cleverness. The words his mother wouldn't understand pour naturally out of him. Like Dylan Thomasian chat.

and that

I'm surprised – and even game to tell his mother – that I've found David Bowie one of the most mystical, exquisite, thoroughly odd and totally nice people I've ever met.

With his presence reverberating around the country, *The Man Who Fell To Earth* about to go out on general release, *Cracked Actor* being repeated on BBC TV, *The David Bowie Story* serialized on radio, the press clamouring for interviews and both *Station To Station* and *CHANGESONEBOWIE* out in the shops, Bowie and Iggy were off again – this time to Holland and a concert in Rotterdam (13 May), then two shows in Paris and straight back to the Château d'Herouville where he recorded *Pin-Ups* three years before. No one knew where he had gone, but the next stage of Bowie's career was now taking shape.

When Chris Charlesworth interviewed him at the Pontchartrain Hotel in Detroit on 1 March, earlier in this tour, Bowie said something that indicated the way he was thinking. He said he would be making some more commercial albums, 'and I'll make some that possibly aren't as commercial. I'll probably keep alternating, providing myself with a hit album to make the money to do the next album, which probably won't sell as well ...'

Actors think like that, accepting highly paid jobs in films or television so they can afford to take a cut in income and appear in a stage play, either with the National Theatre or the Royal Shakespeare Company – but it's not the way musicians usually express themselves, and especially not in rock where record companies then, and even more so now, tend to drop an artiste from their books if his record sales fail to reach a pre-ordained target. Bowie was not only making more money (in my view he cleared at least $3–4m that year) but was also consciously treating rock as art, creating songs and videos, or 'Sound and Vision', that were each in themselves a perfect form of expression, like a sonnet, a triolet, a sculpture or portrait in oils.

21

# Wealth, Berlin and divorce

Bowie was now as free as a bird. His diary was empty, his commitments few and he was able to travel wherever he wished and do whatever he willed. All musicians hope for a moment like this, when they can go into a studio and work at their own pace, for as long as they want to. Bowie was carrying this principle one stage further, managing his own affairs with a staff of only three, keeping his overheads down to a minimum, and living on the hoof – which you can do when your money is tucked away in a Swiss bank, there are few tax liabilities, and your personal assistant travels wherever you go, dealing with every eventuality. Laundry, meals and hiring studio time were his only worries – and these were solved by making Château d'Herouville his temporary home, paying £20,000 to ensure he had the place to himself during July and September (the studio was already booked for August).

Bowie's sudden wealth made his changed lifestyle feasible. This transformation began with the $325,000 received from MainMan at the time of his settlement with Defries. He would have received a substantial payment from RCA on the delivery of *Station To Station* (his advances per album went up from $150,000 to $200,000 in 1976), and a big royalty cheque for *CHANGES-ONEBOWIE*. And then there was his songwriting income, from all the fees paid whenever one of his songs was played anywhere in the world – on radio or television, or performed by another artiste – and the cash earned on the road from his 39 US concerts, 6 at the Wembley Empire Pool and the 17 in Germany, Switzerland, Scandinavia, Holland and France. Zanetta reveals in *Stardust* that even before Bowie started cutting costs, the second leg of the 1974 *Diamond Dogs* tour was expected to gross around $3.7m with a net profit for MainMan of approximately $537,000, so it is not unreasonable to suppose that Bowie made three or four times that this time round, playing twice as many venues, slashing his

expenses and only paying five per cent to MainMan. My figure of
$3–4m veers on the safe side; it was possibly twice that.

Ever the loving father (and whatever her bitterness, Angie says
he was always that), Bowie made sure he was back at Clos de
Mesanges in time for Zowie's fifth birthday on 28 May 1976. This
year, with a new home in a new country and Daddy now a wealthy
man, it was a birthday to remember, with Bowie hiring the Casino
in Montreux, moving in his musical instruments and encouraging
Zowie and his new-found friends to put on their own impromptu
production of *Jack And The Beanstalk*, with Bowie as narrator.
Angie says, 'He loves that street theatre and improvisation with
kids, [and he made] a wonderful video.'

She and Bowie could barely stand each other's company. Her
presence made him feel he was on the verge of a nervous
breakdown. He went to see a psychiatrist in Zurich. Clearly the
marriage was in a terrible state, but Bowie was still reluctant to
end it, partly through a sense of propriety and also a feeling of
responsibility towards their son, and yet in any argument that
involved Coco, Bowie would invariably back her against Angie,
which made the tensions worse. There had been an incident a few
months earlier as he was preparing to leave for Jamaica. Coco and
Angie argued over the baggage needed for the trip, and as Angie
snapped, 'Don't you *dare* talk to me like that!' Bowie 'hurtled
across the room, grabbed my throat in both hands and started to
throttle me … [Coco] pulled him off and saved me. So it's
possible, irony of ironies, that I owe her my life.'[1] Within days of
this drama, Angie had flown to Switzerland searching for their
new home. Between then and his arrival in London, they barely
saw each other – yet she was there at his London hotel when Jean
Rook went to interview him on 4 May. Asked whether they
expected to be married in ten years' time, Angie said, 'Yes' and
Bowie replied, 'How could I ever let go of this divine being?'

Only days later in Paris, there was another violent row between
Angie and Coco which ended with Bowie ordering his wife out of
the room and Angie clutching at her throat, unable to swallow, her
eyes swelling and prickly with salt.[2] Although they were together
for Zowie's birthday, Bowie would not sleep in the house while
she was there, preferring to stay at a hotel until he was due to meet
the lawyers handling his dispute with Lippman – when he would
turn up promptly, right to the minute, still insisting Lippman had

taken too much commission and had borrowed money without his consent.*

* * * * *

There were many times during the months that followed when Bowie was distraught, breaking down into tears, drinking too much, taking drugs again – or going to the other extreme, fits of laughter – but he continued to spend nearly every day in the studios. Initially, he was producing *The Idiot* for Iggy Pop, writing the lyrics while Iggy wrote the music. The tracks included *China Girl*, which Bowie rerecorded himself six years later for his own LP *Let's Dance*, and another song which he and Iggy wrote with Carlos Alomar, *Sister Midnight*.

When *The Idiot* was released by RCA the following March, Bowie was credited as producer, arranger and joint-writer – but there were no acknowledgements for the musicians, who probably included Alomar, George Murray and Dennis Davis, who stayed on with Bowie after the tour, and Ricky Gardiner (guitar) who joined them at the Château to begin work on Bowie's own album, *Low*. While the musicians went on holiday with their families during August, Bowie and Iggy moved to Munich to continue mixing *The Idiot* at Musicland Studios, completing the final cut at the Hansa by the Wall Studios in Berlin and returning to the Château on 1 September to resume work on *Low*.

This was one of those albums Bowie was determined to make whether it made money or not, for he had long been fascinated by synthesizers, using them first on *The Man Who Sold The World*, a year before Brian Eno recorded the first of his two LPs with Roxy Music. Eno, the strikingly bald keyboards player, who had been President of the Students' Union at Winchester School of Art, seemed the group's intellectual, trying to harness new technology and make the band more avant-garde. It was no surprise when Eno left Roxy music to work with more innovative musicians such as Robert Fripp, John Cale, Nico and Robert Wyatt, experimenting with ambient music, using synthesized sounds rather than melody

* This dispute continued for over a year, with writs filed on both sides. Details of the settlement were not revealed, but Angie says in *Backstage Passes* (p. 247) that Lippman borrowed money from Bowie's account for the down-payment on a house. She says this had been agreed in advance and was 'all perfectly above board' but that Bowie was so 'cocaine-paranoid' that when the matter was brought to his attention again, 'he lost control'.

lines to create a musical atmosphere. He responded immediately when Bowie suggested he might like to join him at the Château. Visconti also received a phone call from Bowie, saying, 'Look, I'd like to make an experimental album. I'm really tired of doing what's right, what's commercial and being one step ahead.'

At the Château, Bowie refused to sleep in the master bedroom, which was said to be haunted by Chopin and his lover, the novelist George Sand. Visconti slept there instead, and found it 'very spooky' with one dark corner 'that seemed to suck light into it'.[3] 'I'd been there with Marc Bolan, but we never had anything like this and I think it may be because David is a psychically charged person ... and he was absolutely morbid.'

Bowie also became distrustful of those around him, except Coco Schwab, who devotedly carried out every instruction. Nearly everyone else was treated with suspicion. Bowie was convinced 'people' were trying to rip him off, and had a fight with Angie's current boyfriend. 'They had a punch-up in the dining room and started throwing bottles around and I remember going in there and tearing them apart,' says Visconti.[4]

*Low* is how Bowie felt at the time, but in no sense does it mark a low point in his career; this was the real man breaking free, using his new-found freedom to explore synthesized sound, creating tone poems in which emotions like sorrow, wonder, fear and bewilderment are expressed through tonal layers rather than words. Bowie saw it as 'a reaction to having gone through ... that dull greeny-grey limelight of American rock 'n' roll and its repercussions: pulling myself out of it and getting to Europe and saying for God's sake re-evaluate why you wanted to get into this in the first place'.[5]

At the Château, food was a major problem. The studio's domestic staff were on holiday during September and although Bowie knew this when he booked the studio, none of them realized how little they would have to eat. The last straw was when they started going down with sickness and diarrhoea, and they immediately moved to Berlin, with Bowie occupying a suite at the Hotel Gehrus, a former castle close to the Grunewald Forest, and then into a nineteenth-century mansion-block at 155 Haupt-strasse in the Schöneberg district of the city, not expecting for a moment that this would later be seen as a decision of crucial significance in his career.

Bowie did this to save money. It was far cheaper to take a five-year lease on an apartment than book into an expensive suite at a luxury hotel. Bowie intended to work in Berlin, but he had also been fascinated by its history, by the German arts movement, its traditions of transvestite theatre, the work of Bertolt Brecht and Kurt Weill and of Weill's one-time wife, the singer Lotte Lenya, who had the kind of disturbed background that always intrigued Bowie, graduating from prostitution to a succession of homosexual husbands. Bowie saw Berlin as 'the artistic and cultural gateway to Europe in the 20s', saying, 'virtually anything important that happened in the arts happened there'.

The Berlin newspapers *Berliner Morgenpost* and *Bild* found out where Bowie was living early in October, but the news did not travel to London. When he began giving interviews again two years later, Bowie played down his address, saying that 155 Hauptstrasse was 'in one of the poorest areas of Berlin', 'in the Turkish quarter' and 'just a simple flat above a shop selling car spares'. In fact, the apartment, approached through a wrought-iron doorway from the street, was spacious and comfortable, and had seven rooms, all with panelled doors, high ceilings and decorative cornices. It was a sparsely furnished crash-pad, somewhere to live while working in Berlin, with rooms for Iggy and Coco, an office, a room for Zowie and his nanny when they came down from Montreux, and a room Bowie set aside as a studio to develop his interests in painting, drawing and sculpture. Bowie also claimed he could live anonymously in Berlin, moving around the city as he wished without being bothered by strangers, but this was not wholly true, either. He had to disguise himself, cutting his hair short, growing a moustache and wearing workmen's overalls before he could walk the streets unnoticed, drop in at the Turkish café for breakfast or call at the local pipe shop for Gitanes. Even so, his life was never quite as simple as he chose to make it appear, for Bowie was really dissembling, avoiding any appearance of wealth, whereas he was now undoubtedly a multi-millionaire, acquiring land on the island of Mustique, where he and Mick Jagger both had houses built for them, while continuing to be officially resident at Clos de Mesanges.

Most days Bowie would stay in bed until after noon, and only then would his new day begin with a light breakfast of coffee, juice and cigarettes, and a brisk walk to the Hansa studio, where he would pick up where he left off the previous 'day'– which might have been earlier that morning, just a few hours before. Bowie would frequently work through the night, well into the following morning – but was equally capable of deciding after just two hours that he had done enough for one day, or of taking the day off, and then, dressed like a painter and decorator, with Iggy Pop in similar garb, disappearing with Coco, riding around Berlin on bicycles, or with their bicycles tucked away in the boot of their car.

All this was totally incomprehensible to Angie, who would still turn up unexpectedly, shattering his sense of calm, partly because she now saw it as her mission to get rid of Coco, upon whom Bowie depended far more than his wife. 'I was in turmoil, not being able to speak to him face to face, and I couldn't understand why he had gone to Berlin,' she says,[6] revealing how little she knew about his day-to-day life. 'He had never asked me if I wanted to live there .... It never once occurred to David to stay at home with Zowie and me. His boredom threshold was too intense to live with. He swung from genius to the erratic without warning. ... David was commuting between Berlin and Montreux as the mood took him.'

In November 1976, little more than a month after he moved in, Angie visited Bowie at his apartment, describing this in *Free Spirit* as 'our one last chance of a possible reconciliation'. Relations between them were calm enough on the first day, but on the second Bowie developed sharp pains in the chest. Angie asked the British Army clinic to send an ambulance, thinking he might have had a heart attack. Bowie was kept in the clinic for 24 hours, given an electro-cardiogram and sent home. So far as the doctors could tell, there was nothing much the matter with him. 'I thought it was a manifestation of depression,' she says in *Free Spirit*. By the time she was interviewed for Kerry Juby's radio series six years later, her divorce long behind her, she admitted his collapse was diagnosed as 'an anxiety attack' and blamed this on the fact that Coco was unwilling to return to the apartment while she was there. 'It was very exciting in the middle of the night calling up the hospital and all that. He was alright. He was fine in the morning, once he could get away from all the things that were pecking at his brain – poor thing.'

Meanwhile, Angie tried to burn Coco's room, gathering her clothes in a heap and splashing them with vodka which she thought would burn like petrol. When it did not, she slashed them, threw them out into the street, together with Coco's bed – and caught the next flight out of Berlin.

* * * * *

When *Low* was delivered to RCA, its executives could barely believe their ears, astonished by *Low's* lack of catchy rock 'n' roll songs like *Fame, Rebel Rebel, The Jean Genie* or *Golden Years*. They felt there was nothing to promote, no obvious singles – although Bowie soon proved them wrong with *Sound And Vision*, an attractive, melodic use for electronic sound with a rock backbeat released in February 1977, which rose to No. 3 in the UK charts. Overall, the album was as depressed as Bowie felt when he made it, with the B-side containing instrumental pieces, or tone poems. These included *Warszawa*, a hauntingly poignant 6.17-minute musical essay with a wavering electronic pitch that sounded at first like orchestral strings, only with more resonance. It was inspired by the Nazi persecution of the Jews in Warsaw, and in my view will come to be recognized as one of Bowie's finer achievements, along with *Weeping Wall*, a composition with the same sense of sorrow that he created wholly on his own in the studio, playing strings, piano, vibraphones and xylophones with synthetic strings and synthesizers. It was a bold experiment,* but RCA wanted more tracks like *Fame* and even contacted Defries to see if he could persuade Bowie to make the album more commercial, if only by adding vocal tracks to the tone poems. There was no mention of Defries's intervention in the trade press, or the Bowie biographies, but Visconti told Kerry Juby: 'Tony Defries suddenly arrived and still purported to be David's manager. RCA complained that there weren't enough vocals.... David just looked at the small print of his contract which read that they had to put it out. He took a very great risk on that album and although it wasn't a big seller, I've got a gold record here somewhere, so it must have sold over a million.'

Bowie refused to promote *Low* in the conventional way: there were no radio or TV appearances, and he would not give any press

---

* Bowie refused to discuss the LP when it was released, apparently believing *Low* should speak for itself. He broke his silence many months later, travelling back to London on a train after filming the TV show *Marc* in Manchester. The journalist Tim Lott asked him about *Low* and Bowie opened out: 'It's my reaction to certain places. *Warszawa* is about Warsaw and the very bleak atmosphere I got from the city. *Art Decade* is West Berlin – a city cut off from its world, art and culture, dying with no hope of retribution. *Weeping Wall* is about the Berlin Wall, the misery of it, and *Subterraneans* is about the people who got caught in East Berlin after the separation – hence the faint jazz saxophones representing the memory of what it was.'

interviews. He packaged it well, using the same still from *The Man Who Fell To Earth* for the LP sleeve that Underwood adapted for the jacket of the book upon which the film was based – Bowie's way of letting his fans know he had now recorded the kind of music he would have written for the film.

Clearly still sore over missing that soundtrack commission, angry with Lippman and distressed by his relationship with Angie, Bowie continued to spend more time in Berlin than Montreux, maintaining his new image as a hard-worked musician living in exile, enduring poverty as the price of fame. When *Melody Maker* suggested he was now moving into management himself to handle the affairs of Iggy Pop, he promptly wrote them a personal letter to 'correct the misconception': 'Iggy looks after his own business affairs. I would appreciate a printed correction.' It was signed simply 'David Bowie, Berlin'.

Even more disconcerting for RCA, their star performer decided to promote Iggy Pop's new album rather than his own – and arrived in London at the end of February 1977 to begin a British tour with Iggy, playing keyboards in his band, standing at the back of the stage in semi-darkness, without a spotlight, so as not to draw attention away from Iggy's performance, singing songs from *The Idiot*. It was unfortunate timing for both of them. The London music papers were in the grip of punk fever, and so Iggy's tour, *The Idiot* and *Low* were all largely ignored, with the music papers preferring to write about The Sex Pistols, The Jam, Slits, Wire, Eater, The Buzzcocks, etc., whose sales very rapidly peaked and then declined. This meant that a formative part of Bowie's career was overlooked; Iggy's backing group included the brothers Hunt and Tony Sales, playing drums and bass, with whom Bowie formed Tin Machine ten years later. They played Aylesbury, Newcastle and Manchester with three shows at the Rainbow Theatre before beginning a tour of 16 North American cities – and then returning to Berlin to record Iggy's next LP, *Lust For Life*.

In London, Bowie lunched with Bolan at Toscanini's in the King's Road. They drank too much wine, and ended up wandering through the heart of Chelsea, singing like young lads on a football outing – with nobody recognizing them. A few days later, Bolan wrote a piece about Bowie titled 'MUSIC HALL HUMORIST' for *Melody Maker*, which contained some shrewd observations, for Bowie was, as I have mentioned before, very much part of the vaudeville tradition:

We were all looking for something to get into then. I wanted to be Bob Dylan, but I think David was looking into that music hall humour.

It was the wrong time to do it, but all his songs were story songs, like *London Boys*. They had a flavour, a very theatrical flavour, with very square kinda backing.

But in those days there weren't any groovy backings being laid down. I think if he played back those records now he'd smile at them, because he was an unformed talent then. He was putting together the nucleus of what he was eventually going to be.

Bolan was right; he was so often right – and none of us would have guessed that within six months he would be dead. Bolan, like Bowie, had been through the terrible cocaine abyss where all your friends seem enemies and the nights never end, and now here he was, coming out of it. Only now was he beginning to conquer that kink in his character that made him ruthless, jealous, mean and grasping when he seemed to have the world sitting neatly in his palm. Bolan conquered his demons, stopped the cocaine and brandy ritual, slimmed down, and was his old sweet, gentle self again. I saw him twice that spring. Tony Secunda told me Bolan phoned him again. After three years of bitterness, they met for a drink in a Fulham pub, started seeing each other once more, and talked of picking up the pieces, for Bolan now realized that he could not do everything himself.

\*   \*   \*   \*   \*

While Bowie was in London, Angie told the *Daily Express* they were broke. 'David's been robbed blind,' she said. No one bothered to correct her. Bowie was far from broke, and she no longer lived with him – but there was no reason why he should tell the press that.

Bowie and Iggy were back at their apartment in Berlin by the end of April 1977, accompanied by the Sales brothers and ready to begin work on *Lust For Life* – and then Bowie went straight on to his next LP, *Heroes*, which he co-produced with Visconti. This was a more calculated album. Bowie made his point with *Low*; now he made money again.

His relationship with RCA was strained. Bowie believed they

should have backed his artistic judgement and promoted both *Low* and *The Idiot* with a far more upbeat advertising campaign. He also resented their attempt to use Defries to bring pressure upon him, and was disconcerted by the way RCA kept releasing tracks from his albums as singles without consulting him first on packaging or even the choice of B-sides, which frequently seemed eccentric; album tracks that were three or four years old would sometimes be recycled as B-sides to new singles. Over the next five years, stories occasionally appeared in the trade press suggesting Bowie was unhappy with RCA and looking elsewhere (Warners and CBS were the alternatives most frequently mentioned), but he was careful not to put himself in a position that might not be legally defensible. After all, he was still bound by contract to RCA and Defries until the end of 1982 – and realized he needed the occasional hit single and strongly commercial album to maintain the momentum of his career.

*Heroes* was that kind of album, with Eno again collaborating on four tracks and his usual nucleus of musicians – Alomar, Murray and Davis – and another long-standing friend of Eno's, Robert Fripp, laying down additional lead guitar tracks at the mixing stage. Antonia Maass and Visconti's wife, Mary Hopkin, provided backing vocals. Music paper coverage of Bowie's recordings in Berlin suggested this was a period of intense concentration, with months spent in the Hansa producing each album; it was not like that.

When there were no external stresses to worry him, Bowie was intensely self-disciplined in the studio, totally in command, bouncing ideas off the musicians and usually laying down his backing tracks before writing a lyric. Often, as when writing *Fame*, he would disappear for ten or fifteen minutes, sometimes with a daily newspaper in his hand – and then return with the lyrics written on whatever piece of paper happened to be at hand, a headline or a photograph giving him an idea. On other occasions, he would go to the microphone and start singing, composing the lyrics as he sang, which never ceased to astonish Visconti and the other musicians. 'He was the only person I could work with who was like that,' says Visconti,[7] confirming that *Heroes* was 'the best, most positive album that we'd made together. We just couldn't do any wrong.... The vocals were still being written on the mike. David never stopped that – and he'd never have a clue what he'd sing about until he actually walked in front of the microphone. But by this time I was used to it and it was no longer a nightmare for me. It was fun.'

There was a similar spontaneity in Bowie's relationship with Fripp, who led King Crimson in the early 70s and later recorded two LPs with Eno, *No Pussyfooting* (1975) and *Evening Star* (1976). Bowie and Eno were having problems on a couple of tracks, which were not turning out the way they wanted them to, and Eno suggested calling Fripp, who was in New York. 'Bob, we're having a bit of trouble,' said Eno. 'Do you think you could come and give us a hand?' Fripp demurred at first, saying he had been working with synthesizers and electronic instruments of late and hadn't played guitar in three years. So Eno passed the phone to Bowie who asked, 'Well, do you think you could play some hoary rock 'n' roll?' Whenever he tried to charm someone like this, it usually worked. Fripp dropped everything, caught the next available plane and walked into the Hansa Studio the following day at 11 p.m., less than 24 hours after the phone call. 'Well, what's the problem then?' he asked. He listened to their backing tracks, took out his guitar, laid down a guitar accompaniment in the way he thought they might want it – and there was no further discussion. 'It was quite extraordinary,' said Eno. 'By the following day, he'd finished, packed up and gone home.'

The whole album was made in this kind of spirit, although I am sure Bowie would have been careful not to create the impression that it all came easily when the masters were delivered to RCA. After all, they were paying him an advance of $200,000 on each album now.

There were ten tracks on *Heroes*, with the more commercial numbers on the A-side and the B-side again largely instrumental – but it was the title song that made the impact, with a romantic lyric that told a story. He said the idea came when he saw two lovers standing by the Berlin Wall with an East German watchtower high above them, manned by armed guards. For him, they were a king and queen, lovers whose bond transcended the world around them, and when we are like them, 'We can be heroes/just for one day'. Bowie wrote the music with Eno and composed the lyric himself, and Eno says he knew the moment he heard the mix that this song was something special; it made him 'tingle', just listening to it. Although it was a fairly obtuse point that has since been largely ignored, Bowie insisted that the title should really be *'Heroes'* with the quotation marks to emphasise his sense of irony, and his point that love rises above walls and conflict.

None of the other tracks had the same immediacy, with Bowie and Visconti between them as co-producers managing to ruin *Beauty And The Beast* and *Joe The Lion* by over-dubbing, like a painter losing effect by adding extra brush-strokes, not knowing quite when to stop. (Oddly, Bowie recorded another far more effective version of *Joe The Lion*, without too much electronic clutter, but kept that back until 1991 when both versions were included on the reissued *Heroes*.) *Beauty And The Beast* also needed stripping down to its essentials, for there was a strong underlying rhythm and melody and an effectively memorable vocal track; it suffered death by synthesizer. The only other track that deserved, and received, frequent radio plays was *V-2 Schneider*, a tongue-in-cheek tribute to the German musician Florian Schneider, comparing his influence on music with a V-2 Rocket. It was Schneider who pioneered many of the techno and electronic techniques with which Bowie and Eno were now experimenting, and here they were harmonizing this with a strong sense of melody and Bowie's saxophone to make a point of their own. The other tracks, particularly those on the second side, were really tone poems. Bowie managed to convey a feeling of spatial foreboding in *Sense Of Doubt*, another piece not developed to its full potential, while *Moss Garden*, on which he plays koto (a Japanese stringed instrument), sounds more like an extract from a film score, with a rippling string effect flowing into an electronic echo.

Having finished the album, the musicians dispersed, with Alomar, Murray and Davis going back to the United States, Eno returning home to London and Visconti going off to New York to supervise the final cuts – leaving Bowie, Iggy and Coco to enjoy the intimacy of Berlin.

It is all changing now with the reunification of Germany, but Bowie was there at the time of schism, when large, black West German tanks rumbled through the streets enhancing an atmosphere of constant tension. No other rock star of his prominence had chosen to base himself there before and Bowie found himself drawn into the city's night life, meeting other musicians and inevitably, since this was always the pattern of his life, picking up women for the night.

Bowie interrupted this holiday to visit Paris, being interviewed on two French TV programmes and also attending the French premiere of *The Man Who Fell To Earth*. He had also gone to discuss a film based on the life of the erotic artist Egon Schiele, an Austrian impressionist who died in 1918, still in his 20s. His co-star would have been Sydne Rome, who accompanied him to the premiere. Although the Schiele project failed to come to fruition, they did make a film the following year, *Just A Gigolo*. Anyone who doubted the real macho Bowie should have been at the premiere when a pickpocket tried to steal Bowie's wallet. Bowie swung round sharply, punching him hard – and kept his wallet but broke his thumb. Later that month (July 1977), Bowie was also seen around the Parisian nightclubs dating Bianca Jagger, who was there making the film *Flesh Coloured*. Afterwards, they holidayed in Spain, refusing to talk to the press and avoiding photographers – she was still married to Mick Jagger.

The *Heroes* single was released early in September 1976 and, much to the surprise of RCA after his refusal to promote *Low*, Bowie suddenly became totally co-operative again, willing to do whatever they wished to make the record a success. It was another astonishing change in character, with Bowie noticeably healthier, his cheeks less hollow, more colour in his face and his weight nearly back to his normal weight of around 112lbs. He was immaculately suited and booted, and at his most charming. There was a motive, of course; there always was a motive. With another world tour planned for the spring, promotion now would sell the tickets and boost his income – with only 5 per cent going to MainMan.

In September, Bowie surprised the press again by filming a sequence for *Bing Crosby's Merrie Old Christmas* TV show and becoming the first major rock star in years to appear live on a children's TV show. He flew in from Switzerland, no longer disguising the fact that this was his home, to perform *Heroes* and sing a duet with Crosby, *Little Drummer Boy* and *Peace On Earth*. 'He sings a lovely counter-point,' said Crosby, who died shortly after the show was recorded (their duet became a Christmas hit single five years later).

The children's TV appearance was a personal favour for Bolan, who was beginning his come-back with a weekly Granada TV series, *Marc*, which was shown at tea-time just as children were coming home from school. Again, Bowie performed *Heroes* and finished the show with an impromptu jam session, creating the

song *Standing Next To You* live in the studio. Bolan was clearly
overshadowed and started drinking between the video takes. As
the jam finished, he fell off the stage, drunk – but this was never
seen. The director cut filming, rolled up the credits – and a week
later Bolan was dead.

On the way back from a night drinking in the London clubs,
Bolan was killed when his car hit a tree on Barnes Common. The
mother of his son, Gloria Jones, was driving. Bowie flew back
from Switzerland to attend the funeral at Golders Green Crematorium, and later set up a trust fund for the son, Rolan, knowing that
Bolan had died without remaking his will. I have a copy of the
will. It was made while Bolan and his wife June were still happily
married, and, quite understandably, there was no provision for
what might happen if they parted, he met someone else, fathered a
child and died before a divorce had been finalized and he was free
to remarry.

*     *     *     *     *

That last night in Manchester, Bowie dispensed with his car and
travelled back to London on the train with Eddie and The Hot
Rods and Tim Lott, a journalist with *Record Mirror*. Lott asked
Bowie about the tone poems recorded for *Low* (Bowie's answer
was given as a footnote earlier in this chapter), and then enquired
about the silver crucifix Bowie had worn since *Station To Station*.
'Yes,' said Bowie, 'it has some religious significance, but not
necessarily as a Christian symbol. Before Christianity the crucifix
had quite a different significance. The vertical line represented
Heaven, the horizontal line, Earth. The crucifix was the meeting of
the two.... I have a spirit and I believe that comes from God.'
Purely by being on that train, Lott found the answer to a question
that intrigued Bowie's fans. Yes, he did have a personal faith – but
it was a spiritual belief, rather than membership of any one
particular church.

The enthusiasm with which Bowie promoted *Heroes* was
exemplary. He recorded other versions in French and German to
encourage European sales and in some territories (notably Spain)
released a longer 6.7-minute version of the song, whereas for
Britain, with its radio tradition of three-minute singles, he trimmed
his music to suit. Bowie also produced his own videos for three
tracks taken from the album, *Blackout*, *Sense of Doubt* and

*Heroes*, beginning a pattern of marketing his own music with his own films which he continues to this day. In September and October, he travelled around Europe promoting the single with TV, radio and press interviews, arriving in London on 19 October to perform *Heroes* live on *Top Of The Pops* that same evening. No other rock musician of his reputation had appeared live on *Top Of The Pops* in several years, for fear they might not be able to reproduce their studio sound. Usually, they mimed to backing tapes – but Bowie had no such worries, even though Robert Fripp was unable to join him that night to perform the lead guitar track.

Instead, he phoned Sean Mayes, lead guitarist with the virtually unknown band Fumble who were his support act during the *Ziggy Stardust* tours of Britain and America four years earlier. 'I just got a phone call out of the blue,' said Mayes, who had not spoken to Bowie since. 'When I asked him if he'd phoned me because of the work we'd been doing since he said, "No. I just hoped you'd be the same as you were with Fumble – and you were. Exactly the same!"' Which shows how carefully Bowie learned to observe other musicians over the years, knowing precisely whom to go to when he needed help.

Next day (20 October), Bowie sat patiently in a suite at the Dorchester Hotel while his publicists worked closely with the RCA press office, wheeling in journalists from the music papers and national press for the usual 15-minute interviews. The only genuinely interesting new quote came that evening when Bowie was interviewed by Nicky Horne, live in the studio, for his Capital Radio phone-in programme *Your Mother Wouldn't Like It*. One listener, called Alan, asked Bowie a question – 'Who are, or were, the Bewlay Brothers?' – he had been refusing to answer for years. Perhaps because of the intimacy of the moment, speaking one-to-one with someone who was clearly a fan and familiar with his work, Bowie responded as openly as he did on the train back from Manchester:

The Bewlay Brothers were, I suppose, very much based on myself and my brother. My brother was one of the bigger influences in my life, in as much as he told me I didn't have to read the choice of books that I was recommended at school, and that I could go out to the library and go and choose my own, and sort of introduced me to authors that I wouldn't have read, probably. You know, the usual things like the Jack Kerouacs, the Ginsbergs, the e. e. cummings and stuff.

When Alan commented on Bowie's interest in Burroughs, the reply was:

> Burroughs was instrumental, as soon as I met him. I mean he convinced me about the marvellous things you can do with the cut-up technique, and I incorporated that in some of the stuff like *Diamond Dogs* and I've never dropped it. In fact, it reveals itself to its fullest extent, I guess, on *Heroes*, more than anything else.

After promoting *Heroes* in Europe, Bowie left for Kenya for a safari holiday, basing himself at the Treetops Hotel and travelling among the Masai with an interpreter (an experience that was to produce *African Night Flight* for his next album), and from there flew to New York to promote *Heroes* in the US, to attend his bodyguard Tony Mascia's wedding with Iggy Pop, and also narrate Prokofiev's *Peter And The Wolf* for a recording with the Philadelphia Symphony Orchestra, conducted by Eugene Ormandy. No other leading rock musician had engaged in a promotional campaign as vigorous as this for several years, for they had all tended towards remoteness, and this had its effect. Both the *Heroes* album and the single were a hit throughout Europe, with readers of *Melody Maker* voting this the Album of the Year, and readers of the *New Musical Express* voting Bowie Singer of the Year and Songwriter of the Year. Bowie had positioned himself carefully for his new world tour.

Throughout this promotional campaign, Bowie deflected intrusive questions regarding his private life. He now had a masterly ability to disarm interviewers, either by turning to another subject or saying with a charming smile, 'I don't think we want to talk about that', never losing his temper but able to dictate the course of any conversation by changing his mood from charming to icily polite. He dropped his guard only once, and that was during an interview for the Dutch TV show *Pop Shop* in Amsterdam when the interviewer Vic Dennis provoked Bowie into denying that he had based himself in Berlin for political reasons. 'That's absolutely wrong,' said Bowie, adding, 'I am apolitical and I think a real artist is apolitical ... an artist is a dreamer.' Dennis then asked him about his private life, and Bowie started to hedge, but quickly realized he was on camera and said: 'I don't like talking about that. It's not easy to live with me. I'm not blaming Angie. I've got many things to do and I have not got much time for others. I know that, but what can I do? I'm selfish by nature though I know it's a shame. The only person I really love is my son. He's six years old and he's quite often with me. I don't want reporters to see him because I think he's too young for that kind of thing ...'

Bowie had barely spoken to his wife since she left the flat in Berlin after throwing Coco's possessions out of the window into the street, but he clearly still had a lingering feeling that they ought to be together as the parents of their son, even though they rarely saw each other and openly engaged in sexual affairs, often on a merely casual, one-night-stand basis. This was not an 'open marriage', as Angie chose to describe it when speaking to the press, but a distressed marriage held together by fading memories and his genuine love for his son. That Christmas, Bowie sought to make amends by suggesting they spend the holiday together. Angie flew to Montreux, only to find that Bowie was in Berlin, planning to start work on the film *Just A Gigolo*, and wanted her to join him there with Zowie. Discovering Coco was also in Berlin (which was hardly surprising, for she travelled wherever he went as his personal assistant), Angie took umbrage and flew back to New York to rejoin her latest boyfriend, Keeth Paul, a 24-year-old sound engineer with Tom Petty and The Heartbreakers.

Angie stayed with Paul's mother over Christmas and then flew back to Switzerland with him, arriving at the Bowies' home on 2 January 1978. The house was empty, and the press heard rumours she had left her son over Christmas. Angie was now broke, and instead of going to Berlin to join her husband she phoned the *Sunday Mirror* in London and offered to sell her story, telling its reporter Tony Robinson he should come to Switzerland with the money. By the time Robinson arrived at Clos de Mesanges, she was drinking heavily. At four o'clock the following morning she locked herself in a bathroom and took an overdose of sleeping pills – and then on Bowie's birthday (8 January) Angie began trying to destroy the house, or perhaps just his possessions, just as she had attacked Coco's possessions in Berlin. She hit Keeth Paul on the knee with a rolling pin when he went to calm her, and threatened to stab herself with a carving knife. He and Robinson took her to hospital.

Angie admitted to Robinson that she had not slept with Bowie for five years, and accused him of thwarting her own career by refusing to allow her to sign a recording contract.* It was also disclosed in the *Sunday Mirror* that Bowie gave her $40,000 a year and also paid her rent and travelling expenses. She was said to have spent $25,000 in 1977 alone just in hiring taxis, even calling a taxi when she wanted to go out and buy packets of cigarettes or chewing gum.

In Berlin, Bowie issued a terse formal statement saying: 'My wife was not aware that my son was with me. A few days before Christmas she decided she would leave Switzerland and spend the holidays with friends elsewhere. From that day to her arrival back on 2 January, she didn't phone me or the boy to say where she was.'

Robinson's story in the *Sunday Mirror* was headlined 'DRAMA AT SNOW CHALET IN SWITZERLAND' and he wrote:

It was a sight I will never forget. There, crumpled at the foot of the stairs, lay Angie Bowie. Her face was covered in blood. Angie, wife of pop star David Bowie, had tried to kill herself in a fit of anxiety over her son on Bowie's birthday seven days ago.

She swallowed three handfuls of pills and tried to stab herself with a carving knife and finally threw herself downstairs.

Angie, 28, was unconscious on and off for nearly two days and when she recovered in hospital with a broken nose, two black eyes and cuts and bruises, she revealed to me that she had been expecting her lover's child. Later, her pop musician boy friend Keeth Paul, who has been living with Angie in a luxurious rented chalet in Switzerland, told me: 'If I hadn't been there to help her, she would have died.'

I had gone to see Angie at the cuckoo-clock chalet on the snow-covered slopes of Lake Geneva after she asked for the

* This was a reference to an offer she received from the music publisher Dick James. He offered her an advance of £60,000 to record an album of her own poems, set to music. James did not have a good reputation with the rock generation. He was successfully sued by Elton John, and loathed by The Beatles for selling his share in their song publishing company to Lew Grade without telling them first – which was how Lennon and McCartney came to lose control of the Northern Songs catalogue. Bowie was probably giving his wife sound advice when he advised her not to sign the contract.

*Sunday Mirror*'s help in resolving her anxieties over her six-year-old son.

We were able to establish that while she had been on a visit to America, David Bowie had invited young Zowie and the boy's young nanny to join him in Berlin where he is making a film.

Zowie was returned to Angie on the Thursday night. With him was his nanny, a bodyguard and another woman. Earlier, when I spoke to her on the plane, she was furious, almost hysterical and said that she was seeking a divorce so that she could get legal custody of Zowie.

By talking to the press like this, and more particularly going to them herself and asking for money, Angie committed an unforgivable sin. In rock 'n' roll, you may use the press to sell records, but you never, never, never give them your family secrets. Angie was finished. Bowie proceeded to write her out of his life. He filed for divorce, demanded custody of Zowie on the grounds that she was an unfit mother – and, when she resisted, produced photographs of her taken by lover Roy Martin showing Angie engaged in drugged-up lesbian sex with a female heroin dealer. It was an acrimonious divorce, and the settlement was not finalized until 1980. Bowie agreed to pay her $750,000 over ten years – less than she had been costing him as a wayward, extravagant wife. Angie also demanded a $1m cash settlement in return for not publishing a book about their marriage – and was told, in effect, Publish and Be Damned. She has published two books. And they have damned her.

22

# Marking time with
## *The Elephant Man*

Bowie was now in command of most areas of his life, but he was determined to secure that position, broaden his base as an artist, fence himself around with barriers to preserve his privacy – and achieve total control. Financially, this made sense. Artistically, it did not – for Bowie was becoming the authoritarian artist who has no one to tell him when his work is poor, surrounding himself with 'friends' who are either dependent upon him or so wary of what they perceive as his 'power' that they dare not speak out. Anyone who worked for Bowie was required to sign a legally enforceable contract of employment forbidding them to give newspaper interviews or take part in television or radio programmes about him or referring to their relationship with him.

Other leading musicians placed a similar embargo on their staff, including John Lennon, Paul McCartney, Rod Stewart and Elton John, but Bowie went about this with exceptional zeal. Friends who spoke to the press were dropped; others who might have been tempted were firmly warned off, and, just to make sure, Bowie began buying the copyright of earlier photographs wherever he could to ensure that little was published without his approval. When I began work upon this book, after Bowie politely declined to co-operate, I was told by his personal publicist, Alan Edwards, 'No one will speak to you, except a few crazy aunts. Everyone else will do whatever he tells them. David's sewn everything up' – and he looked startled when I said that I had more than enough material to write a book about David Bowie without their help if I had to, and probably knew more about Bowie than he did. 'Don't forget, I was there when it happened, before he started taking control,' I told him. This sense of Bowie taking personal charge became apparent a few weeks after his public separation from Angie. She returned to New York and made another bungled attempt to kill herself while he stayed in Berlin making *Just A Gigolo*.

The film was a disaster. Bowie admitted afterwards that he only made it because the actor and director David Hemmings went to see him in Switzerland 'and dangled Marlene Dietrich in front of me'. The legendary German star had not made a film since *Judgement At Nuremburg* (1961), and lived in seclusion in Paris. She agreed to make the film but no one was allowed to meet her in advance, not even Hemmings, who was permitted just one phone call, and when the film went into production in Berlin she refused to leave her apartment in Paris, saying she was working on her memoirs – so Hemmings shot most of the movie (which also starred Kurt Jurgens, Maria Schell and Kim Novak) in Berlin, interweaving footage from Paris.

The story was strong enough, describing the life of a Prussian officer who comes home to Berlin after the First World War to find his life has changed forever. Unable to adapt to the faster society of post-war Germany, he drifts into life as a gigolo employed by Baroness von Semering (Dietrich) and is eventually killed by a stray bullet when fighting breaks out between the Communists and early Nazis, with both sides claiming his body as one of their martyrs. In death, the gigolo becomes a symbol of something he despised: emergent Nazism.

'I only agreed to make this film because I believed in the ideas and the issues it represented,' said Bowie. 'It's a subject I'm fascinated in ... gigolos, male escorts, male hookers. I've met people like that, but I've always found them rather inscrutable and difficult to get to know, so the role was that much more of a challenge.... It also allowed me to display a more sensual, sexual side of myself that was totally lacking in *The Man Who Fell To Earth*, where I didn't even have any genitals.'

Critics slaughtered the film when it was first shown. Hemmings hurriedly withdrew and re-edited it, but the damage was done. *Just A Gigolo* received little distribution after that, and once the dust had settled Bowie admitted he had made a mistake. 'It was my 16 Elvis Presley movies rolled into one,' he said, adding on another occasion, 'Every real legitimate actor that I've ever met has told me never even to approach a film unless you know the script is good.'[1]

Long before the film was even finished, Bowie's new self-confidence became obvious when he flew to London just for a day on 20 February 1978 to announce his forthcoming world tour. A press conference was held at the Dorchester Hotel primarily as a photo call; the conference lasted 15 minutes. Asked why he was touring again after such recent success with *Heroes*, Bowie said with what appeared to be a sheepish smile, 'I need the money.' It was a good quote, and quite probably planned with care – right down to the smile – but it was untrue. Bowie now had regular income from performance royalties and record sales.

His announcement included details of his first British tour in five years, but by the time the stories appeared in the evening newspapers he was already on his way back to Berlin to finish *Just A Gigolo* before another brief holiday in Kenya, this time to show his son lions, elephants, giraffes and antelope living wild. No one was allowed to photograph them. Their relationship was the most private part of his life, with Bowie arranging for Joe (as he now called him) to attend the Scottish public school Gordonstoun, and timing his working year so they were always together during school holidays, eventually seeing him through university with a doctorate in philosophy.

On the set of *Just A Gigolo*, Bowie even disclaimed being a rock musician, telling Michael Watts of *Melody Maker*: 'I've decided that I'm a generalist now. That just about covers all grounds. It encompasses anything I wish to do, really. I find, for instance, I really want to paint seriously now and not toy with it, and I am painting very seriously now, every available moment. I'd like to be known as a painter one day when I get up enough courage to show them, but at the moment I want to be known as a generalist, rather than as a singer or composer or actor.'

Bowie concluded that he would 'live and die an artist', which was what he had been saying for ten years but still rang true, as he prepared to begin rehearsals for the world tour in Dallas on 16 March, readily travelling everywhere now by plane. (This was another odd coincidence. As Angie's influence faded, he conquered his fear of air travel, readily using aircraft when he toured with Iggy Pop and now accepting it as a better way to make use of his time.)

When Bowie said he needed the money, he avoided saying that this tour would make him more than most musicians earn in a lifetime. He was arranging it himself through his own company; local promoters in every city would handle the detail, but the lion's share of the profits would go to Bowie with everyone but him employed on a salaried basis – and still only 5 per cent going to MainMan. Under the terms of his contracts with MainMan and RCA, Bowie was required to provide RCA with three more albums – so he did; no more and no less, with the first being a live album recorded on the tour, *Stage* (1978). This was recorded as a double-LP, with Bowie arguing it should therefore count as two LPs – and RCA maintaining it was one recording, made in one place at one time. The dispute delayed its release, but Bowie eventually conceded the point and gave them *Lodger* (1979), before recording his last album under the contract, *Scary Monsters (And Super Creeps)* (1980), taking care as he did so to make sure his RCA career ended on a high note with two hit singles. This was all rock 'n' roll politics – and there was no mention of that when Bowie announced the new tour.

*    *    *    *    *

Natasha Korniloff had not heard from Bowie in six years, when suddenly she received a call saying he wanted new tour outfits, and asking if she would fly to Berlin where he was still filming. Coco met her off the plane, drove her to the film set, and when Bowie finished for the day drove them to the hotel where they had booked her a room. 'We had about an hour to discuss what he wanted,' she said.[2] 'We both did drawings on the back of envelopes…. David wanted trousers that were big, Hawaiian-style shirts and jackets similar to a double-breasted one he had seen in a magazine … and velour track suits, which was something quite new at the time. Everyone wears track suits now, but David was trying something different, corduroy suits, a dark green and a brown with big shoulders.'

She saw him again when he flew to London for the day on 20 February, deciding how many copies he wanted of each design with less than a month before he was due in Dallas. 'His initial idea had been that I would prepare this large wardrobe and that he would wear one or two different combinations for each concert.' Instead, Bowie preferred a snakeskin jacket with loose-fitting white drill breeches which Korniloff based on a Jacobean design – and by the time the tour arrived in London, this had been taken up by Bowie's fans.

Bowie again chose a simple set, a plain black backcloth with suspended lighting, but varied spotlights to alter the atmosphere for different songs with a change of colours, and he increased his accompaniment from five musicians to seven, still retaining Carlos Alomar, George Murray and Dennis Davis as his rhythm section, but augmenting them with Adrian Bellew, lead guitar, who Bowie saw playing with Frank Zappa; Roger Powell, synthesizers, recruited from Todd Rundgren's Utopia on Eno's recommendation; Sean Mayes, keyboards, after their appearance on *Top Of The Pops*, and Simon House, electric violin, who had been playing with Hawkwind and was astonished to receive a phone call from Bowie. They were at school together 15 years earlier, and had not seen or spoken to each other since.

The tour opened at the San Diego Sports Arena on 29 March. and from there moved on, with minimal touring crew to save costs, to Phoenix, Fresno, Los Angeles and numerous major cities through April, including two nights at the Spectrum Arena in Philadelphia, where Bowie had established a strong local following, making this the place to record the *Stage* double-LP. This time, there were no rows between the musicians over extra fees – or, if there were, no one heard of it, for Bowie was now leading his touring company from the front, mixing with the musicians after each show, sometimes going off to dinner or to check out local clubs, play bowls or listen to new groups.

Visconti mixed the tapes for *Stage*, and, after the aforementioned short delay, RCA released it in the first week of September, while the world tour was still in progress, having left America months before. *Stage* is interesting to listen to now for only one reason; the songs sound almost identical to the original studio recordings. This shows how well Bowie could work with his musicians but misses the point of a live album – there is no life. There was no explanation for this from Bowie, but it may have been that he was intentionally denying RCA anything really new as part of his long-running grudge against MainMan; this was another situation where the bootlegs were better than the authorized LP.

The North American leg of the tour resumed at the Toronto Maple Leaf Gardens (1 May), and concluded with three concerts at Madison Square Garden, New York (7th to 9th). The 31 shows in this first North American leg must have grossed at least $3m, for Bowie rarely appeared before audiences of less than 20,000, and by the time he reached New York every show was sold out (although he had been less successful in the south). Andy Warhol complained in his diary that 'only two tickets came for the Bowie concert and everyone wanted to go'[3] – and when he wanted to lunch with Bowie the following day, Bowie said he was too busy and, instead, spent much of the day and night with Brian Eno and Bianca Jagger.

From New York, the tour moved to Europe, starting with Germany and Switzerland (Hamburg, Zurich, Essen, Cologne, Munich, Bremen); then Austria (Vienna); France (Paris, Lyons, Marseilles); and then flying north to Scandinavia as May ended (Copenhagen, Stockholm, Gothenburg, Oslo), then south to Holland for three concerts in Rotterdam, and two more in Brussels. The British leg began with concerts at Newcastle City Hall (14–16 June), followed by Glasgow and Stafford, and the first stage of the tour concluded with three nights at London's Earls Court Arena (29 June to 1 July), where the acoustics had been dramatically improved since Bowie's first appearance there five years earlier.

This was a triumphal return home, but another nightmare for RCA. Bowie refused to engage in any other form of record promotion or to give any interviews; the tour was enough, in his view – and neither RCA nor his own musicians were told where he was staying as the tour travelled circuitously from Newcastle to London. Bowie avoided all the usual hotels, preferring instead to book into rented apartments – which saved him money, avoided all the usual pressures that accompany such tours and gave him privacy. No one knew whether or not Bianca Jagger was travelling with him.

His mother was allocated the Royal Box at the final Earls Court concert, where the audience included Bianca Jagger, Bob Geldof, Brian May and Roger Taylor of Queen, Iggy Pop, Dustin Hoffman, Ian Dury and David Hemmings, who was filming the occasion. Afterwards Bowie disappeared again, probably to Switzerland with his son, although he was also spotted over the next four months in Berlin with Iggy Pop (mid-August), shopping in London (late August) and filming a photo session for *Vogue* in Paris (September), and was also known to have spent part of September in Montreux working on the next LP, *Lodger*. Bowie was keeping a low profile, having so far grossed around $5–6m purely from his first 66 concerts, quite apart from the advance he would have received for the *Stage* LP ($200,000) and the money that kept flowing through from his record sales and performance royalties. As he relaxed that early autumn, there was probably another $8m or $10m tucked away in his Swiss bank accounts – enough to bolster his confidence as he prepared to engage in a further round of business poker with MainMan and RCA. None of the details were disclosed, but it was an open secret that Bowie was banking cash just in case he found himself engaged in a legal conflict with RCA.

On 8 October, after prolonged speculation in the trade press, Bowie made a formal announcement to 'clear the air and set the record straight': 'At present and for the foreseeable future I am under contract to RCA Records and at no time have I engaged in any negotiations to alter that status. My relationship with RCA has been a long and rewarding one and any rumours that I am signing with another label are completely false and erroneous.'

This did not clear the air at all. After this, it was generally understood that Bowie was observing his contract to the letter, producing LPs as required and respecting every clause – thereby leaving himself free to leave RCA when the moment came without any risk of litigation. How they discovered it, no one would ever know – but the press gradually established that David Bowie would be free of all contractual obligations to RCA, MainMan and his publishers by 31 December 1982. And then he would be free.

Meanwhile, there were still four years to go. Bowie ended his year with six concerts in Australia, beginning on 11 November in Adelaide, then Perth and then Melbourne Cricket Ground, where with every ticket sold long in advance, a crowd of over 20,000 sat in the pouring rain to hear his show. On stage Bowie and the musicians were terrified of touching the microphones or sound equipment for fear of electric shocks. The show moved on to Brisbane (21 November) and two performances at Sydney Show Ground, with rumours in the local press that Bowie was paid in gold bars to avoid Customs duties and local taxation. Without confirming or denying this, Bowie quietly moved on to Japan where he rented an apartment in Kyoto for a Christmas holiday with his son, and performed in Osaka and Tokyo. They stayed in Japan over the New Year, before returning home to Switzerland in early 1979 for the start of the skiing season.

With *Lodger* now in its final stages of mixing, *Peter And The Wolf* and *Stage* both in the shops, and *Just A Gigolo* ready for release, Bowie engaged in another exhaustive publicity burst similar to his campaign promoting *Heroes* a year before. He travelled from Switzerland to London, on to New York, back to London, and then returned to New York once more; he repeated the journeys *again* before returning to Australia, finally returning to London and New York a third time – within the space of a mere two months: all this, just to promote his current product with TV and radio interviews and the briefest of press conferences. His press conference at the Café Royal to launch *Just A Gigolo* lasted only 15 minutes, essentially no more than a photocall with Sydne Rome. Only very rarely now did Bowie ever give an interview of any depth. He was maintaining his momentum as a world star, without doing anything that would inhibit his freedom to act when his management, recording and publishing contracts expired. It was a shrewd campaign, and not a hint of its purpose came through in the press.

When he did speak to journalists, his comments were those of a man withdrawing himself from the everyday battles of life, as well he might with a fortune now banked in Switzerland. 'I think, without being pompous, that my way of working is as important as Method,' he told a journalist in Japan, adding, 'Style is only a superficial juxtaposition of things as they are, arranged against each other to offset their individual qualities and meanings' – a remark that would have baffled most of the fans who bought his records – while in a London interview with the Welsh TV interviewer Mavis Nicholson, Bowie said, 'Thematically I've always dealt with isolation in everything I've written, I think. So it's something that triggers me off. It always interests me in a new project.... I have often put myself in circumstances and positions where I am isolated, just so that I can write about them.'

In moments like these the deep, puzzled, searching, intellectual nature of the man comes through. Bowie was very capable of deflecting anyone who thought they might be penetrating his reserve, but once in a while, a question would provoke an answer that revealed the deeper Bowie – as when Nicky Horne asked him on Capital Radio[4] about the influence of Lindsay Kemp: 'Oh God, an extraordinary amount .... I borrow and steal everything that fascinates me. I'm a sort of jackdaw, or is it a magpie? I can never remember. Lindsay introduced me to things like Cocteau and The Theatre of The Absurd ... and the whole idea of restructuring and going against what people generally expect; sometimes for the shock value – and sometimes as an educational force. He just gave

me the idea that you could experiment with the arts and do things
and take risks that you wouldn't do in real life.'

And, in a tribute to Eno's influence, Bowie said that until they
worked together he had driven himself, but now realized that 'you
could do all the experimentation in creating music and not actually
have to put your body through the same kind of risks'.

Bowie only gave one British interview of any length that year,
and again it was with Jean Rook of the *Daily Express* whom
Bowie beguiled so skilfully three years before. A suite was hired
at The Dorchester to ensure the interview was conducted in an
ambience of luxuriant calm. Experienced though Jean Rook was,
Bowie ran rings around her, not letting one single question
penetrate his reserve.

'How does he do it?' she asked in her article,[5] noting that Bowie
looked younger than ever, perhaps 17 years old, with his hair now
pale brown and cut short, back and sides, 'the unmade-up face'
'guileless and spotless'. He looked 'like a public schoolboy. Or
like Edward before he met Mrs Simpson.' The word 'guileless'
revealed that she had not got through to him at all.

'I hated the pop lifestyle but it's hard to kick the habits of a
lifetime,' said Bowie. 'I'm learning to be happy. To go to bed at
night instead of 5 a.m. and get up in the morning instead of
halfway through the day. I'm painting pictures nobody wants to
buy, but I love it. I've grown my hair back to mouse. I'm even
practising walking down the street .... For years I daren't walk out
of my front door. I was paranoid about it, terrified ... now I look at
other people. I even go into shops and, if somebody talks to me, I
chat back. Now, every day, I get up more nerve and try to be more
normal and less insulated against real people.'

And of his son, he said: 'I want him to be a real person. Thank
God he doesn't associate me with the awesome thing he sees on
stage. He thinks of that as the way Daddy makes his money.... To
him, I'm Dad – the man in the next bedroom who has breakfast
with him every morning. For me, that's being real people.'

It was a good interview, reflecting the latest image Bowie was
presenting of himself. Jean Rook could see Bowie was 'a modern
rock poet.... A probable genius. The nearest thing to Christopher
Isherwood, whom Bowie idolizes.' However, the interview told
the reader nothing about his real life as a hard-nosed businessman
protecting his growing fortune and a multi-millionaire tax exile

totally secretive about his investments, with homes in Switzerland, Berlin and Mustique.

Bowie maintained a home on Mustique for nearly 20 years until he sold it early in 1995. The house – Britannia Bay House – was built and decorated to Bowie's specifications, Balinesian-style; Mick Jagger also had a home there, built Japanese-style. For many years, Bowie and Jagger stayed on Mustique at Christmas and Easter, with Jagger hosting a champagne party on New Year's Eve. Bowie sold his home for £2m.

The bland new image displayed to Jean Rook was carefully crafted. Bowie was moving back into the mainstream again after his three Berlin albums, which he now called his 'triptych' – 'because I like the word. I've been longing to find an excuse to use it.' However, he gave *Lodger* only limited promotion, despite producing videos for *Boys Keep Swinging*, *D.J.* and *Repetition*. When given a two-hour slot on the BBC radio programme *Star Special*[6] to coincide with the release of the LP, Bowie said caustically of *Boys Keep Swinging*, 'that song really does have a problem' – and did not mention the other two at all. Bowie was marking time. *Lodger* was another album with minority appeal, a good example neither of his collaboration with Eno nor of Bowie's best work in the rock mainstream. According to Zanetta, an internal memorandum was distributed within RCA saying 'It would be fair to call *Lodger* Bowie's *Sgt Pepper*, a concept album that portrays the Lodger as a homeless wanderer, stunned and victimized by modern life's pressures and technology.... It is absolutely necessary that you listen to *Lodger* until you hear it. The music *is* there.'

If this was what Bowie told RCA, I suspect he was having them on – the album lacks coherence and bears all the hallmarks of having been put together without enough thought. Listening to it, I have the impression that much of the material was left over from his previous sessions for *Low* and *Heroes*, with one or two later tracks added, using the musicians on his 1978 tour. Although Bowie may refer to *Lodger* as part of his 'Berlin triptych', he actually vacated his Berlin apartment shortly after finishing *Just A Gigolo* (although the lease did not run out until three years later).

More interesting than the album itself is the use Bowie made of film to record the three promotional videos. This was a relatively new departure (though he had made a video for *Heroes* – on a low budget, with Bowie walking through a curtain of light to sing, without stage props or backcloths – and film survived from his earlier tours that could be recycled in video form). Each of the three new videos is a minor work of art. Video was still a new tool for rock musicians, for there were few outlets for it. At the time The Beatles made what is now generally seen as the first pop video, their own visual interpretation of *Strawberry Fields* and *Penny Lane* (1967), they used cinema film. The expense was justified because their records sold all over the world, so copies were distributed for promotion on a global basis. This was not repeated until Queen produced *Bohemian Rhapsody* (late 1975), hiring the Australian director Bruce Gowers themselves and making the video at the extraordinarily low cost of £5,000. Although *Bohemian Rhapsody* earned vast royalties, record companies were still reluctant to invest in videos before the arrival of MTV in August 1981.

As so often in his career, Bowie saw this coming and bought his own Sony equipment to make black and white films in the mid-70s, starting with the *Diamond Dogs* tour. Several of those films have still not been seen, and remain within his collection in Switzerland, while his three videos for *Lodger* predate MTV by two years. He made them with David Mallet, who was directing Kenny Everett's TV series when Bowie appeared on the programme in April 1979 and who had worked on the innovative US TV shows *Shindig* and *Hullabaloo*.

On *Boys Keep Swinging*, Mallet filmed Bowie singing jerkily, almost epileptically, against a backcloth with harsh, angular designs, dressed in a semi-formal black suit with shirt and striped tie. These catatonic movements caught the eye, making one concentrate on the lyrics: 'When you're a boy/you can wear a uniform'; and 'They'll never clone you when you're a boy/you can buy a home of your own,/learn to drive and everything'. This was Bowie using camera to make the political point that women seldom have the same rights as men ... and two of his three backing singers removed their wigs and make-up, while the third walked on a stick as if on the set of the film *The Prime Of Miss Jean Brodie*, winking as the video ended. All three were David Bowie in drag.

For the *Look Back In Anger* video, filmed in a garret, Bowie and Mallet based their storyline on Oscar Wilde's novel *The Picture Of Dorian Gray*, with Bowie caressing a portrait of himself as an angel while his skin bubbled and he metamorphosed into a monster. Music and visuals complemented each other against a literary storyline, instead of the music being treated as little more than a backing track. In the equally innovative *D.J.* video, Bowie satirizes another branch of the music business, dressing in a flamboyant pink suit to mimic the disc jockey who allows the nature of his job to unbalance his brain: 'I am a dee-jay/I am what I play'; and, in a repeated refrain, he says 'I've got believers/ believing in me'.

Bowie was again pointing the way forward. Videos were to become an increasingly important part of his work, with Bowie choosing the directors, developing the storylines, producing the films himself and then licensing them out through his own companies to promote his music. By the time MTV started, Bowie had six videos in the can – and thereafter made new ones to accompany each important piece of music.

The virtue of video from an artist's point of view is that it enables him to promote his music in any part of the world without having to engage in the kind of travelling schedule Bowie and MainMan employed to sell *Ziggy Stardust, Aladdin Sane* and *Diamond Dogs*. Bowie could make more effective use of his time, market his videos – and then vanish. Which was what he did in 1979, leaving New York in June, retreating to Switzerland, holidaying again in Kenya, making two brief visits to London and then Australia, before returning to New York in December to spend Christmas there with his son.

On 16 December 1979, Bowie went to see the Broadway production of *The Elephant Man*, later visiting the club Hurrahs, where he was introduced to the play's director Jack Hofsiss, unaware that Hofsiss was looking for someone to replace the Tony Award-winning lead, Philip Anglim. They discussed the character-ization, with Hofsiss telling Bowie, 'The important thing about this play is that the elephant man must be played as a character ... the actor must not use his deformity to capture the audience's sympathy.' Just after Christmas, they met again in a restaurant and Hofsiss mentioned that Anglim was leaving, and expressed the view that the character was similar in some ways to Bowie's role in *The Man Who Fell To Earth*. 'They're both isolated from society,' said Hofsiss, offering the role to Bowie and explaining that the play was being taken on a tour of American cities and might then return to Broadway.

Bowie thought about the offer carefully. The timing could not have been better. His contracts with RCA and MainMan now had three years to run, and he was required to deliver one final album and knew this would have to be stronger commercially; he would not be needed for *The Elephant Man* until July 1980 – and that left him time to record the LP, make videos to promote it, and then devote the rest of his year to *The Elephant Man*. Financially, there was little in it, since top Broadway incomes are far below those of the music industry, but promotionally it gave him the chance to prove his capacity as an artist while waiting for his contracts to expire.

*     *     *     *     *

After appearing on the TV shows *Saturday Night Live* and *Dick Clark's Salute To The Seventies*, Bowie returned home to Switzerland for a skiing holiday (characteristically, Bowie had taken lessons in both skiing and swimming since settling in Switzerland to make himself good at both). When his son returned to school, Bowie returned to New York in early 1980, where he now had an attic apartment in Greenwich Village, and began recording his new album at the Record Plant Studios with Tony Visconti. Once again, they recorded the backing tracks first with Bowie's usual rhythm section (Alomar, Murray and Davis), with guest lead guitar overdubs from Robert Fripp, Chuck Hammer and Pete Townshend, plus Andy Clark on synthesizers and Roy Bittan, piano. The musicians could see Bowie was more concentrated. Instead of composing the lyrics on the spur of the moment, he crafted them in advance, marrying what he wanted to say with the shape of each song. Bowie had the ability to produce hit singles on demand – but there always had to be another incentive. The title track was *Scary Monsters (And Super Creeps)*, but the two songs that stood out from the rest were *Ashes To Ashes* and *Fashion*, which both combined a contemporary, hard-driven rhythm with directly personal lyrics, designed to appeal to an audience that had been following Bowie's career since *Space Oddity*, growing with his music.

*Ashes To Ashes* – aided by a brilliant Mallet video showing Bowie in Pierrot costume, dressed as both a spaceman and a deep-sea diver and walking along a shoreline with a woman who could have been his mother – took up the early theme of the spaceman lost in space: 'Ashes to Ashes funk to funky/We know Major

Tom's a junky' sang Bowie, linking his original success with his career since, so that his lyric became a parable, describing his battle against drugs and his desire to stay clean, despite 'little green wheels' that still kept chasing him. Bowie made no secret of the fact that he occasionally returned to drugs, but this was largely tongue-in-cheek, like his observation 'I ain't got no money I ain't got no hair' when he certainly had plenty of both. Its underlying message was simple: Bowie had not lost touch with his audience and was still reaching out for those intangible, elusive objectives that grip every artist: 'I've never done good things/I've never done bad things/I've never done anything out of the blue'.

*Fashion* was written to a disco beat, with Mallet's video filmed in a small club, a dance studio and out in the New York street, using models, dancers and actors of many races to convey an impressionistic feeling of light, movement and colour. But even in this song (frequently used at fashion shows) Bowie had a wry twist in the lyric: 'People from good homes/are talking this year'.

While he was making the album, Bowie received another approach from Hofsiss, who said *The Elephant Man* would play Denver and Chicago in July and August and then, all being well, open in New York. They discussed money, and Hofsiss agreed Bowie would be paid top Broadway wages for a production of this kind – 10 per cent of the box office gross (although 10 per cent of Bowie's money would go to MainMan).

'How much time do I have to make up my mind?' asked Bowie.

'Twenty-four hours,' said Hofsiss.

Bowie grinned. He knew he would be accepting the role the following day; but it was still good to have time to think about it.

This left him with three clear months before opening in Denver. Bowie promoted a new single, reviving the Bertolt Brecht/Kurt Weill number *Alabama Song* coupled with an acoustic guitar version of *Space Oddity* – two recordings that were more satisfying than remunerative (the single reached No. 23 in the British charts) – and then flew off to Japan to make a television commercial promoting a new rice wine drink, *Crystal Jun Rock*, for which he wrote the music. When asked why, Bowie replied: 'No one has ever asked me to do this before ... and the money is very useful.' It was wholly in character for him to spend one part of his time promoting a song that he loved without thought of money – and another making money without thought of the product. Bowie then holidayed in Switzerland with his son, visited

Iggy Pop in Berlin – joining Iggy on stage during a concert at the Nollendorf Metropol, playing piano – before returning to London to add some finishing touches to the new album, including the guitar track from Pete Townshend, and to research the character of John Merrick, the grossly deformed cripple upon whom *The Elephant Man* is based.

Merrick, rescued from life as a circus freak by the Victorian surgeon Frederick Treves and installed in a suite of rooms at the London Hospital, suffered from neurofibromatosis. This was a condition affecting both the skeletal frame and muscles, giving him a very large, misshapen head with folds of skin hanging loosely over his chest and back, and a very large tongue; he was unable to run because he had no hips. After Merrick's death in 1890, moulds of his body were made and preserved in a museum at the Hospital, together with his skeleton, clothes, walking stick and a model of a cathedral that Merrick made. Bowie studied all these carefully; he did not intend to reproduce Merrick bodily, but was anxious to understand what he had to interpret for, besides these deformities, Treves always insisted Merrick was a highly intelligent man, with a romantic streak in his character.

Once he had returned to the United States, Bowie also observed how Anglim played the role. Anglim relied more upon facial make-up and bodily padding, whereas Bowie drew on his knowledge of mime and theatre, wearing a cloth around the hips and under the crotch similar to the garment that he had worn during his Japanese tour in 1973. This reduced him bodily to an almost naked frame that he could then, with his naturally lithe physique, twist out of its normal shape to convey deformity. Bowie accompanied these physical movements with a distorted pattern of speech, having listened to tape recordings of victims of cerebral palsy. This unusual use of technique may have been intensely personal, for Bowie knew a high intelligence lay beneath his brother Terry's mental abnormality just as a lively, enquiring mind lay hidden within John Merrick's deformed frame. Once again, Bowie was using his artistry to make a point, knowing this can be more effective than words.

The play opened at the Denver Center of The Performing Arts on 29 July 1980. Every ticket was sold for that week, making this the most successful venture in the Center's 38-year history. *Variety* reported:

Drawing on an early mime background and the resourceful staging of his rock shows, Bowie displays the ability to project a complex character. Playing a man too ugly to draw a freak audience, and too human to survive within a distorted body, Bowie shows a mastery of movement and of vocal projection.

Bowie takes the stage with authority.... Vocally, he is both quick and sensitive. In scene after scene he builds poignantly, crying for the chance to become civilized, though he knows he will always be a freak; pleading for a home, though he knows his presence disturbs; and questioning the rules of society, though his well-being depends on their acceptance. Judging from his sensitive projection of this part, Bowie has the chance to achieve legit stardom.[7]

The takings for the week were $186,466 ($18,646.60 for Bowie, $1,864.66 from that for MainMan). With eight shows a week, he was earning approximately $2,000 per show – but the value of these appearances was beyond measurement, for he was being hailed as a highly skilled artiste of wide accomplishments, and not just as a rock musician.

After its week in Denver, *The Elephant Man* moved to The Blackstone Theater in Chicago for three weeks and there, with Bowie able to settle into a daily routine, he co-operated with RCA in a promotional campaign designed to make the most of this opportunity. Journalists were flown in from Europe and other parts of North America, to see him in *The Elephant Man*, with interviews to simultaneously promote *Scary Monsters (And Super Creeps)* and the single taken from it, *Ashes To Ashes*.

For once, some writers were allowed to see him for an hour at a time. Angus MacKinnon from the *New Musical Express*, flown in by RCA, was allowed three separate interviews – and it was he who came closest to Bowie's present state of mind. Confronting Bowie with three lines in *Ashes To Ashes*: 'I've never done good things/I've never done bad things/I've never done anything out of the blue', he asked whether this reflected the way Bowie felt about his own career. After a long pause, drawing on a cigarette, Bowie admitted 'a continuing, returning feeling of inadequacy over what I've done.... I have an awful lot of reservations about what I've done ... I don't feel much of it has any importance at all,' adding that he was always aware of 'this long chain with a ball of middle-classness at the end of it which keeps holding me back.... I keep

trying to find the Duschamps* in me, which is harder and harder
to find.... class consciousness is a very great wall of contention
with me, always getting in my way.'

By the time *The Elephant Man* opened at The Booth Theater on
Broadway on 23 September, media interest was intense. *Ashes To
Ashes* and *Scary Monsters* brought Bowie a hit single and hit
album just as he was entering the New York crucible. Two whole
days were set aside for TV, radio and newspaper interviews, with
each journalist this time given just 15 minutes for exclusive quotes
– an arrangement that suited Bowie well, for it left him in total
control. The opening night became a planned media event,
attended by celebrities in all branches of the arts, including
Bowie's Swiss neighbour Oona Chaplin, widow of Charlie
Chaplin, who flew in especially for the occasion at his invitation,
Aaron Copland, Steve Reich, Brian Eno, Andy Warhol, Christopher Isherwood, David Hockney and Diana Vreeland.

Whatever Bowie's state of nerves (and he is often ill before
appearing in front of a live audience), his performance stunned
even the New York theatre critics, with John Corry of the *New
York Times* describing it as 'splendid', *Theater* magazine saying
Bowie possessed 'the exquisite stillness that the best actors have',
*Village Voice* confirming that Bowie 'commands the stage' and
the *New York Post* headlining its review 'BOWIE BLAZING ON
BROADWAY'. *Back Stage* magazine affirmed that Bowie
'acquitted himself magnificently', the *New York Daily News*
applauded his 'restrained, tortured eloquence', and the London
newspapers reported that his appearance in *The Elephant Man* was
'one of the events of New York's theatrical season' (*The Times*).
By any criteria, this was a triumph – and the producers confirmed
that every ticket for each performance in the three-month run had
been sold.

Every night, fans gathered at The Booth Theater hoping to meet
Bowie or collect his autograph, and he would cheerfully stop to
talk to them, relaxed about his own personal security. He often
walked from his Chelsea apartment to the theatre: 'The most you
get is, "Hi, Dave. How's it going?" It's very neighbourly. They
don't get as excited at meeting you as they do in London, which is

---

* This is Bowie being typically oblique. Marcel Duchamp (1877–1968) was the younger
of the three Duchamp brothers who were associated with the Cubist period of art. Marcel
was the most rebellious, renouncing his middle-class background as he went on to
embrace advanced art forms. Their name is often spelt Duschamps.

still a bit star conscious. Here, you see Al Pacino walking around or Joel Grey jogging. It's quite easy to do that, it's great.'[8]

That freedom vanished with the murder of John Lennon on 8 December. The fact that they knew each other, worked together and became friends heightened Bowie's anxiety. He was walking the streets every day, appearing on stage each night in a small, intimate theatre with an audience of only 735 people for each performance, nearly all of them strangers and any one of them a possible killer; it could have been him. Checking with security the following day, Bowie discovered there were 27 different ways of approaching The Booth Theater, and within the auditorium four entrances with access to the stage. Thereafter, a bodyguard sat by each entrance, checking people as they came in – and Bowie declined Hofsiss's invitation to continue in the role after its initially scheduled three-month run. The play ended on 3 January 1981, with the other members of the cast holding a party for him and presenting him with the play's backcloth as a personal souvenir.

\* \* \* \* \*

Bowie's career continued to operate on several levels. During the run of *The Elephant Man*, he appeared on the main TV talk shows in the United States and by satellite link to Australia and Europe, his videos continued to be shown world-wide and his press coverage was constant. The simultaneous success of his stage play and his music brought him many offers.

A studio was hired for one day so that Bowie could recreate one of his 1978 concerts for a sequence in the German film *Christiane F*, a story about a teenage heroin addict whose only focus in life is her love for David Bowie. This gave him free use of a ready-made set the following day to make the *Fashion* video with David Mallet. *Christiane F* was a major film in Germany, with Bowie's performance reproduced on cinema film, in video form and on a soundtrack LP that he delivered to RCA – but for him it was still just one day's work. Bowie made even more money, without even having to do a day's work, when K-Tel, the company that packages 'greatest hits' albums and sells them via television, offered to market the LP *The Very Best Of David Bowie*. This was agreed by RCA. K-Tel chose the tracks and oversaw the packaging – all Bowie had to do was bank the proceeds when the

LP became one of his most successful, reputedly selling over 1m copies, and reaching No. 3 in the British LP charts.

Money had long ceased to be a problem for Bowie by the time the stage run ended and, with all rock's leading stars now increasingly anxious about their personal safety, he slipped quietly out of New York to return home to Switzerland, having usually managed to arrange his diary so that he could go skiing every February. He and his son have both become accomplished in the sport, with Joe winning many medals. Tony Visconti, who had a skiing holiday with Bowie in 1979 (when he was also a witness in Bowie's divorce case), says Bowie taught him the basics within two days, making him walk up and down a hill with his legs crossed and toes pointing inwards, and then sending him off down a 1,000-metre slope. 'He's an excellent teacher – very, very patient ... [but] Joey passed us about eight times going down the most dangerous slopes like a streak of lightning, leaving David and I tottering down like old men.'[9]

Bowie spent most of 1981 in Switzerland, visiting London briefly at the end of February to receive awards as The Best Male Singer and for The Year's Best Video after the annual *Record Mirror* readers' poll, and returning to London again in August, in total secrecy, to rehearse and film a BBC TV production of Bertolt Brecht's play *Baal*, but spending most of his time in his studio developing his interests in screen-printing, woodcuts, and so on.

Bowie had long been familiar with the works of Brecht and Kurt Weill, but even after his acclaim in *The Elephant Man* he was reluctant to take on a part like this. The producer Louis Marks and director Alan Clarke flew out to Switzerland to discuss the project with him (as always, Bowie booked a suite for the meeting at a hotel in Montreux rather than invite them to his home). 'He was very nervous about it,' says Marks. Bowie asked to see tapes of Clarke's previous productions before making a decision. 'We discussed all aspects of it – not simply the play itself, but how it would work for him, coming into a totally new medium, something he hasn't really worked in before, the whole working structure of the production.' Bowie flew to London to start work on the production, for 'the basic BBC fee.... He worked for the same kind of money any actor working at the BBC would be paid. In other words, he did it because he wanted to do it ...' (The fee was about £1,000.)

Quite apart from it being Brecht, the part was perfect casting;

Bowie played the role of Baal, an amoral troubadour who seduces his patron's wife, goes through life abusing women and working in sleazy bars, losing all sense of personal values, until eventually he murders his only true friend, escapes police custody and dies. The film was shot at the BBC Television Centre, with Bowie coming in each day then vanishing, just as he had on the set of *The Man Who Fell To Earth*. No one was allowed to know where he was staying, not even the producer and director. A bodyguard accompanied Bowie wherever he went and if the producer wished to contact Bowie he had to phone RCA, who would then phone Coco Schwab, who would, in turn, relay the message. Says Marks, 'There was this wonderful contrast between the artificial way one had to deal with him because of the security and then the total informality and friendliness and relaxed atmosphere of the actual work.'

Although he knew there would be little money to be made from a recording of a production of this nature, Bowie called in Visconti to produce his versions of the songs *Baal's Hymn, Remembering Marie, Ballad Of The Adventurers, The Drowned Girl* and *The Dirty Song*, packaging them beautifully as an EP with a gatefold sleeve illustrated with photographs from the production, portraits of Brecht and himself and a woodcut by Frans Masreel, with a lengthy description of the production by John Willett, who adapted the play for television with Clarke. Little more than 20,000 copies of this EP were sold by RCA, but making money was not the point of the exercise. 'He wanted to record this as a souvenir,' says Visconti. 'David said it wasn't going to be any big deal and probably wouldn't sell, but he felt it should be recorded for posterity ... and we recorded it with one violin, one viola, one trumpet and one accordion, so that it sounded like a German pit orchestra.'

The press were not told Bowie was in London making the film. The set was closed to all visitors – and he was back in Switzerland before an announcement was made by the BBC, with Marks saying: 'Baal is someone who lives his life to the full, experiencing everything. He's rather like a rock star of today.... Bowie, of course, was ... a natural for the part. For one thing, he certainly knows his Brecht. He's very well read and is particularly interested in pre-First World War German drama and art. Working with him, it was apparent that he had an instinctive understanding of the character. Baal is very close to his own nature, one might say.'[10]

Still marking time, Bowie spent the next six months in Switzerland, apart from one short trip to New York to discuss a film project with Mick Jagger and to see The Rolling Stones' latest stage show. That autumn of 1981 he had another No.1 hit single with *Under Pressure*, a song recorded with Queen at their studio in Montreux. They co-wrote and co-produced the song, sharing the royalties, with Bowie and Freddie Mercury singing the lyric – but he did not leave Switzerland to promote it. In the age of video, promotional trips were no longer as necessary as they used to be – and he had no wish to talk to the press.

## 23

# The Fifty-Million-Dollar Man

As 1982 began and he passed his 35th birthday, Bowie still had a year to go before he could finally break free from Defries and negotiate a new recording contract. Like all major musicians with global status, Bowie knew his future contracts would be balanced more in his favour, giving him almost total control of music and packaging, allowing him to regain the rights to his work within five years, and leaving the record companies as little more than hired distributors, required to pay in advance for the privilege of marketing his work. The industry changed in the first 20 years of his career – musicians now called the shots. But Bowie still had another 12 months before being able to prove the point.

Meanwhile, with the worldwide success of *Under Pressure* underlining his strength in the marketplace, Bowie continued to live quietly on his Swiss mountainside, skiing in January and February, before returning to Britain at the end of the month just as *Baal* was being shown on BBC Television, and RCA were releasing the *Baal* EP. For anyone looking for clues to the direction his career might be taking, it was all here in the *Baal* EP – but Bowie was still giving no interviews, making no explanations, for he knew that a word said out of place might prejudice his contractual situation.

At the beginning of March, strict security was again enforced when Bowie began work on his third film, *The Hunger*. 'I don't know why David's making a film like this,' Pitt commented to me. It was a sci-fi horror movie in which Bowie appeared as a seventeenth-century aristocrat, John Blaylock, who has not aged in 300 years and now finds himself, still only 30 years old, living in modern-day New York with a gorgeous vampire who has also been pickled by time, even though she was born 4,000 years before Christ. The couple spend their lives picking up victims in punk discos and disposing of them in their own private basement crematorium. In one scene, set in a doctor's waiting room, Bowie ages by over a hundred years, his skin wrinkling as he becomes suddenly raddled and haggard. The movie ends with Bowie climbing into his own coffin while the vampire discovers the joys of lesbianism.

A good manager might have advised Bowie not to make a horror film, despite the attractions of co-starring with Catherine Deneuve and Susan Sarandon. A manager would also have questioned the track record of director Tony Scott, who was making his first cinema film after making some highly rated TV commercials. The fact that his brother Ridley Scott had made *Alien* was not a strong enough recommendation. At this stage in his career, Bowie needed to be making vibrant movies with all-star casts and top directors – and it looks as if this was the best he could get.

The box office failure of *The Man Who Fell To Earth* (despite the acclaim) and *Just A Gigolo* should have rung the warning bells; nonetheless Bowie came back to London for filming with Tony Mascia and the ever-loyal Coco Schwab, keeping the real world at bay. No one knew where they were staying, but every morning at 6.30 a.m. Mascia would deliver Bowie and Schwab to wherever they needed to be for that day's scenes, with Bowie having to spend up to five hours in make-up before filming could begin. The main locations were a house in Mayfair; the gay disco Heaven, beneath the arches near Charing Cross Station, and the opulent country house Luton Hoo in Bedfordshire. Some scenes were also shot in the Yorkshire fishing port of Whitby, with its steep, narrow streets and air of mistiness. (Whitby had been chosen by Bram Stoker as the place where the long-dead Dracula escapes from his coffin.)

Scott and the screenwriter Michael Thomas found Bowie pleasant enough to work with, anxious to please and quietly spoken, with Thomas observing that Bowie was 'so bloody confident, as if he was the biggest star in the history of mankind. He feels he can't lose. He hasn't got any fears or doubts about himself.'[1] There was one scene where Bowie was required to play the cello. 'Most actors would have faked it,' says Thomas. 'Not David. He fucking learnt how to play the cello! He worked like a bastard until he could play a decent Bach cantata!' Bowie was giving the part all he had, anxious to make a name for himself in cinema, but the right roles were not being offered to him. Instead, having played a crazy, mixed-up alcoholic alien in one film, a confused gigolo in another, and a pathetic deformity in his only stage play, Bowie was in some danger of being always cast as a 'character actor' rather than in leads.

\* \* \* \* \*

During the run of *The Elephant Man*, Bowie was visited backstage by the Japanese film director Nagisa Oshima, whose work he knew well, being fascinated by Japanese films, theatre and music. Oshima's third film *Ai No Corrida* (or *In The Realm Of The Senses*) – a finely filmed monochrome study of the passion of a geisha girl and her mistress's servant, which develops into an obsession and leads to their mutilation and death – is still said to be, nearly 20 years later, the most sexually explicit film ever granted a certificate by the British Board of Film Censors. Oshima's visit was more than just a courtesy call. He now had a shooting script for his next film, *Merry Christmas Mr Lawrence*, written by Paul Mayersberg (who wrote the screenplay for *The Man Who Fell To Earth*). This latest project, set in a Japanese prison camp, was based upon a short story by Sir Laurens van der Post, himself a former Japanese prisoner of war. The story could be viewed from different perspectives, as a study of Japanese character as it expresses itself in wartime, or one of homosexuality. The key moment comes when Major Jack Celliers (Bowie) kisses the Japanese commandant on the lips to distract him from executing another, more senior British officer. Celliers pays for this 'crime' with his own life, buried up to his neck in sand beneath a blazing mid-day sun, and one is led to the conclusion that both Celliers and the commandant have been driven towards this climax by the repressed homosexuality in their lives.

Bowie's co-stars were the celebrated Scottish actor Tom Conti (as an intermediary who tries to save Celliers' life) and the former Japanese pop star Ryuichi Sakamoto (as the Samurai-style commandant). Even so, as with his previous films, Oshima was having great difficulty raising the $5m needed to begin production, and having promised to send him the script – which arrived within two or three days – Oshima warned Bowie that he could not say when he would be ready to start.

\* \* \* \* \*

While Bowie was in London making *The Hunger*, he flopped back
into his old habits, turning up late at night at clubs and discos with
Mascia and old buddies. Some days, when not required on the
film, he was spotted visiting theatres, dining out, and calling in at
the HMV, Virgin and Tower Records stores, checking out the
latest releases and stocking up with a broad selection of rhythm 'n'
blues records, including James Brown, Otis Redding, John Lee
Hooker, Sam and Dave, Sam Cooke and Etta James, which he was
planning to take home to Switzerland while he prepared himself
for his next album. Bowie also saw his mother regularly, which
inevitably became known to her sister Pat, who was still visiting
Terry once a month at Cane Hill. Terry had now been incarcerated
nearly 16 years, apart from one brief period when he married and
set up home with a fellow inmate (a tragic relationship that ended
in divorce). Pat phoned the *Sun* after Terry tried to commit suicide
on 2 June 1982, throwing himself from a second-storey window at
Cane Hill and breaking an arm and a leg. She told the paper that
Bowie repeatedly ignored the plight of his brother, accused him of
being 'callous and uncaring' and said it was 'time his fans knew
the other side of David Bowie – and time he faced up to his
responsibilities'.

This was not the first time Pat had chosen to sink her teeth in
Bowie's jugular, but this time her criticism really wounded him.
The fact that Terry had tried to commit suicide made her story
seem all too credible, so Bowie went down to Croydon to see
Terry in the Mayday General Hospital, where he was recovering
from his injuries, confined to bed with his arm and leg bandaged
and in plaster.

Bowie arrived with a selection of LPs, a radio and some
cigarettes, walked down the ward to his brother's bed, said 'Hi,
kid', sat down, and began to talk, remembering the old days, their
childhood, the experiences shared. According to Pat, Bowie
'promised Terry he would look after him for life, pay for
operations on his crippled arm and leg and set him up in a private
clinic…. He told him, "From now on, Terry, what's mine is
yours." Terry was happier than he had been for years. He finally
had something to look forward to and he was on cloud nine.'[2]

To Bowie's deep and understandable distress, his private
meeting with Terry was reported in the *Sun*, with their conversation reproduced and the story headlined 'I'M TERRIFIED OF
GOING MAD, SAYS BOWIE'. Full details of the visit were

included, together with comments on Bowie's family background and the insanity that runs through his mother's side of the family. In typical tabloid style the story began 'In a sad, old Victorian hospital in South London, two men met a few days ago with tears in their eyes ...' and went on to develop its second-hand account of his reunion with Terry, and alleged promises to provide him with accommodation in a private clinic.

Bowie was mortified, and his first instinct was to leave town as fast as he could to avoid the inevitable follow-up stories by other newspapers. At that moment, just as he was finishing *The Hunger* and planning to return to Switzerland with his cache of rhythm 'n' blues records, a phone call came from Oshima, nearly two years since their last conservation, saying he had now managed to raise the $5m from funding sources in London and New Zealand. 'We're going to start filming in Raratonga in three weeks' time. Do you still want to do it?' asked Oshima.

'Of course,' said Bowie. 'I'll be there.' He cancelled his plans to go home to Switzerland, and flew to the South Seas, basing himself in the Cook Islands, and travelling around the other islands, listening to rhythm 'n' blues, while he waited for the production crew to arrive. Oshima and his company of technicians and actors spent five weeks filming in Raratonga and then two weeks in New Zealand towards the end of 1982. Working to such a tight budget, Oshima rarely allowed himself more than two takes, often edited his movie mentally while filming with the cameramen, and after each day's work sent that day's rolls of film straight back to Japan for processing and post-production work.

\*     \*     \*     \*     \*

Bowie had a reason for refreshing himself with rhythm 'n' blues, the music that first brought him into rock in the early 60s with The King Bees and The Manish Boys. He was going back to basics, returning to the sounds and the rhythms that first attracted him – and as soon as he finished filming *Merry Christmas Mr Lawrence* Bowie returned to his loft in New York and booked four weeks' studio time at the Record Plant Studios in November and December.

Initially, he was planning to make his next album with Tony Visconti and asked Visconti to set this period aside for the recordings – but when Visconti phoned Coco Schwab to ask for his plane tickets, he learned that Bowie had now 'met someone else'. This was the producer and rhythm guitarist Nile Rodgers, whom Bowie happened to meet in a New York nightclub. Rodgers was riding a run of success that began with Chic, the disco band he formed with bass player Bernard Edwards and drummer Tony Thompson, whose three fine albums, *C'est Chic*, *Risqué* and *The Best Of Chic*, outsold every LP in the history of Atlantic Records. More to the point, Chic were still musicians-for-hire, willing to work with top artistes in other fields, including Diana Ross, Sheila B. Devotion, Sister Sledge and Debbie Harry.

Bowie knew Rodgers could give him something new, basically the sound of a new rhythm section – and by combining that with another discovery of his own, the largely unknown Texan blues guitarist Stevie Ray Vaughan, whom he heard at the 1982 Montreux Jazz Festival, Bowie had all the ingredients for a fusion of rock, rhythm 'n' blues and disco that sounded new, and yet was firmly rooted. One cannot fault Bowie at moments like this. His instincts rarely let him down – but, there was, of course, the added incentive that his contracts with RCA and MainMan had nearly run their course.

By recording the *Let's Dance* album, and particularly the stunning title track, Bowie was able to pick and choose before deciding which record company to sign with. He asked the staff at his New York office, Isolar, to provide business profiles of the six main record companies, detailing their commercial strengths and weaknesses, their key personnel and their willingness to invest in promotion, gradually whittling them down before signing a contract with EMI America, who were willing to meet his main financial demand – an advance payment that was widely reported to be £10m in cash (then $17m). For this, EMI America received distribution rights to *Let's Dance* with Bowie being also contracted to deliver two more LPs within a five-year period.

Having signed the contract with EMI America in January 1983 Bowie set out to make himself extremely rich within the course of just one year. My estimate is that he made at least $50m in 1983 – and in all probability had it paid to him in Switzerland in such a way (i.e. via intermediate holding companies) that he became liable only to minimal levels of Swiss taxation. This can be done. I have discussed the way it is done with a Swiss banker and a Swiss lawyer, which leads me to the conclusion that, in all probability, Bowie banked his $50m – and quite cheerfully paid the minuscule taxes levied annually under Swiss law upon the *share capital* of holding companies. I cannot believe Bowie moved to Switzerland for any other reason, having in the meantime established his own management, record production, film production and song publishing companies, each of which would have had a nominal share capital. With there being no tax payable on net profits under Swiss law, I would be astonished if Bowie paid more than $10,000 in taxes; and thereafter that $50m was his to invest, no doubt wisely.

Bowie's 1983 money-making began with the advance payment of $17m. Once he had been given the money and signed the contract, Bowie travelled to Australia where he produced videos with David Mallet for the two strongest tracks on the album, the title number *Let's Dance* and *China Girl*, a song Bowie wrote six or seven years earlier with Iggy Pop. Both videos were innovatory. He juxtaposed a small-town bar, the Australian desert landscape, scenes with Aborigines and children, together with Sydney's skyline, as the backdrop to *Let's Dance*, underlining unexpectedly its compelling disco rhythm with the simplest of storylines: 'Put on your red shoes and dance the blues/to the song they're playing on the radio' and turned all this into a vivid video that was all it was meant to be: a promotional tool that would guarantee time on all the world's top TV rock shows – with a fee for Bowie whenever it was broadcast.

*China Girl* was a totally different concept: the world's first erotic rock video, taking the beach scene from the film *From Here To Eternity*, with Bowie assuming the Burt Lancaster role and a delicately beautiful Chinese girlfriend, Jee Ling, Deborah Kerr's. They were lovers in the sand, totally naked, with the tidal surf rolling up over their toes. If anyone still believed Bowie was bisexual, he was clearly disabusing them now – and the video was duly banned by some TV stations.

With his videos ready for world-wide distribution, and both the *Let's Dance* LP and the double-A-side single *Let's Dance/China Girl* timed for release by EMI America upon the same day around the globe, Bowie immediately threw himself into his heaviest round of press promotion since *Ziggy Stardust*. He flew from country to country, with his London promotion beginning on 16 March. He hosted a press reception at Claridges the following day, announcing his first world tour in five years, while also carefully projecting his new image as the wholly respectable, established World Star, immaculately suited in beige, with fashionable wide lapels to his jacket and the kind of glowing tan that only comes from either rich living or constant exposure to a sun-ray lamp.

Once 'the product' had been given its push (and both the *Let's Dance* single and the LP sold well, with the single quickly selling over 1m copies and the LP grossing 5m sales), Bowie flew straight home to Switzerland with Coco Schwab and his son to begin planning the world tour. Mark Ravitz, who worked with Jules Fisher on the *Diamond Dogs* tour, was flown over from New York and agreed to prepare a set for the new tour, which Bowie decided to call his 'Serious Moonlight Tour' (from *Let's Dance*, in which two lovers look into each other's eyes 'under the moonlight/this serious moonlight').

In New York, Isolar staff began planning Bowie's schedule, liaising with local promoters in all main cities as they drew up a seven-month schedule that would take him to 59 cities, presenting second concerts where demand was high and performing in all 90 concerts in 15 countries, opening in Brussels.

As with all his tours since breaking with Defries, Bowie kept costs to a minimum, allowing himself only one luxury – and that arguably an economy, given the scale of the tour. Bowie hired a customized Boeing 707 to take the company around the globe, complete with accommodation for his musicians and a separate apartment for his own use with comfortable settees rather than aircraft seating, a spacious private bedroom, space for his travelling library, all the latest films on video – and a personal chef. Expensive though this must have been, it minimized travelling time and delays at airports, enabled them to move from city to city giving concerts night after night – and left Bowie with few days when the tour was not earning money.

The sets devised by Ravitz were simply constructed, relying upon columns of light and movable backcloths rather than rigid stage furniture, and just as on the album Bowie concentrated on being the singer, fronting the band, presenting his songs and playing no instruments, while Carlos Alomar led the musicians.

Alomar was dropped from the *Let's Dance* recording sessions to make way for Stevie Ray Vaughan and Rodgers's chosen rhythm section, and initially Bowie hoped to take Vaughan on tour – but that plan fell through when Vaughan's management refused to let him work for only $300 a night. As always, Bowie was keeping his musicians on a tight financial rein. They were each paid $1,000 *per week*, with a daily cash allowance to cover out-of-pocket expenses and unspecified 'tour bonuses' midway through the itinerary and again at the end. Once again, it was a tight musical unit – essentially a six-member band with two backing vocalists. Besides Alomar on lead guitar, the band was largely new to Bowie. The Chic drummer Tony Thompson worked with him on the *Let's Dance* sessions and came in to replace Dennis Davis, who had joined Stevie Wonder's backing band since the last Bowie tour. Bass player Carmine Rojas and the backing singers, brothers Frank and George Simms, also stayed on with Bowie after *Let's Dance*, augmented by Lenny Pickett (saxophones) and Dave Lebolt (synthetic piano).

Apart from Alomar, who wore a Nehru-style jacket with no fold-back lapels, they all dressed casually, looking just like Bowie wanted – 'a 50s Hong Kong bar band' – and giving extra contrast to his neatly tailored, grey and green pastel-coloured suits, as he stood out front, at the apron of the stage, looking bronzed and fit, reaching out to their audiences with his repertoire of songs, a solo artist presenting his work just as he said he might one day when we ran through his future career 14 years before.

It would be hard to assess Bowie's total daily running costs, for there were sets to be carried, costumes replaced, a light show maintained, etc., but with his musicians and backing singers costing no more than $10,000 a day, and the size of the touring company kept to a minimum, he quite possibly kept his daily costs down to $50,000, including the rented Boeing and some hotel accommodation. Even if the costs came to double that, to $100,000 a day, which I doubt, Bowie was still making 'Serious Money' as one can tell from the box office receipts reported in the trade magazine *Billboard*.

For a single concert in Los Angeles on 30 May – the 'US Festival' organised by Steve Wozniak, one of the founders of Apple Computers – Bowie received a flat fee of $1,500,000. This was widely reported at the time as the highest one-night concert fee ever paid to any performer, but it was not far out of line with the other money Bowie was making that year. His three concerts in Chicago grossed $716,000, in Dallas he grossed $235,000; in Toronto, $2.3m; in Vancouver, $1.3m, and in Edmonton, $1.2m. Only occasional figures like these were reported during the seven-month tour – but even in Sweden Bowie played to 60,000 people a night, and at Milton Keynes, north of London, his audiences at three concerts totalled 175,000. All told, his touring show was seen by 2.5m people – and by the time he had taken his percentage of the box office receipts, a large slice of the income from the catering concessions and also from the merchandising, I would be very surprised if he earned less than ten dollars a head, i.e. another $25m, after all expenses had been paid. One has to remember that rock tours had now become huge commercial operations, attracting maybe 60–70,000 people a night. Every ticket is sold weeks in advance, and the punters arrive with money in their pockets, determined to take home their personal souvenirs – the concert programmes, posters, commemorative books, LPs, scarves, T-shirts, sweat-shirts, tie-pins, badges, etc., etc. Solo stars such as Bowie take the lion's share of the receipts, with their travelling tour accountants actually gathering in the cash on the night before the show leaves the arena. It is more than likely that $25m is an underestimate – and that is never the end of the story, for after the tour there was a 'Book of the Tour', an hour-long TV film made for screening in the United States by the Home Box Office and later released as a video. Another documentary film, *Ricochet*, was also issued in video form.

Even then – whether it was $25m, $35m or $40m – this was only part of Bowie's income from promoting his *Let's Dance* LP. All the albums that he recorded with RCA were rereleased, as well, for the concert tour act only included three new songs – and with those he had already covered his advances and was now in profit. Bowie actively encouraged this, supplying RCA with his tour schedule far in advance, agreeing their plans for yet another 'Greatest Hits' LP, and so ensuring that in every city local record shops were mounting David Bowie promotions, with the disc jockeys on the local radio and TV stations also caught up in the enthusiasm of 'the big tour', playing his music over and over again, with more and more royalties filtering back to Switzerland.

David Bowie was now becoming very, very rich. With his $17m advance from EMI America, the advances that he would have received for his song publishing rights, an estimated $25m from his tour, royalties flowing through from all his past work, he probably earned $60–70m during this one year. At a conservative estimate his net earnings came to $50m.

*     *     *     *     *

The London music papers, who had done so much to create the

Bowie myth, were dismayed by his new pre-eminence. They did not understand the finances, and made no attempt to explain them, but could tell that a huge rock 'n' roll marketing operation was rolling successfully around the world – and it starred their Ziggy, the original anti-hero who predated punk. The young left-wing radical writers who came into rock journalism in the late 70s, galvanized by punk and its anti-Establishment, anti-money message, found all this hard to take. For several years, they had written about punk to the exclusion of nearly everything else that was happening in world music – and punk had proved a disaster to the music industry, driving down record sales generally. None of the British punk stars broke through in the world market. There wasn't enough money in the British market to keep the punk movement going. And now here was David Bowie, looking as svelte as Frank Sinatra, presenting a smooth and confident stage show, never appearing anywhere without a suit and tie, and quite clearly walking off with the loot, while all their punk heroes were falling like flies.

In *Sounds*, Bowie was dismissed as 'the thinking man's Frankie Vaughan ... musical fish and chips'. In the *New Musical Express*, which had slavishly chronicled punk, Bowie was compared to the one-time singing bus conductor Matt Monro, with its readers told that 'the new, very visible Bowie says much to us about the rewards of mediocrity', while *Melody Maker*, whose staff had done more to mould the Bowie myth than anyone, now proclaimed that his work could 'be safely filed away under family entertainment' – although they did have the grace to add that 'all the family is buying'.

Whatever such critics might say, Bowie was reaching out above their heads to a global audience that was willing to buy the whole Bowie package. Shrewd use of publicity, employing local agencies to back up his own travelling PR team, ensured that every concert in his seven-month tour became an event. In Los Angeles, 32,000 tickets were sold in 90 minutes, while in London the promoter Harvey Goldsmith found himself oversubscribed eight times over, a far higher demand than for The Rolling Stones. But this was only part of the story, for the promotion was handled in such a way that those who did not have tickets would envy those who had, being left with the feeling they had missed something potentially important in their lives.

At strategically important venues, where the media were

powerful, Bowie hosted backstage parties after his concerts – with guests ranging from British and European royalty (Princess Michael of Kent and Princess Caroline of Monaco) to the true aristocracy of the media age, the Jaggers, Bill Wyman, Prince, Bryan Ferry, Susan Sarandon, Ron Wood, Yoko and Sean Lennon, Sissy Spacek, Raquel Welch, Tina Turner, Elton John or the Chaplin family. In the United States, Bowie was front-covered by *Time* magazine and hailed by *Playboy* as its Man of the Year; in Britain, he won two more Ivor Novello Awards for his song-writing, while continuing throughout to keep the world's press at arm's length, with no one outside the tour party allowed aboard his aircraft and a total news black-out on all but his public appearances. Every member of the tour party was forbidden to speak to the press, and Chet Felippo, who was contracted to write an authorized 15,000-word account of the tour (to accompany authorized photos in a 'book-of-the-tour'), had to give a written undertaking that he would not say or write another word to anyone. Bowie now had total control.

The tour ended with a final concert in Hong Kong on 8 December 1983, and as the show drew to a close an emotional Bowie stepped forward, waiting for a moment to speak. 'The last time I saw John Lennon was here in Hong Kong,' he told them, reminding the audience that it was exactly three years to the night since Lennon's murder. 'We went to the Hong Kong market and there was a stall, and I did something that's not usually in my character. I saw a Beatle jacket on that stall and asked him to put it on so that I could take a photograph. I've still got the photograph. The jacket doesn't fit properly. It looks like John had outgrown it …' and with that, he started to sing the most-loved of all Lennon's songs, *Imagine*, fighting back tears. A few moments later, Bowie was gone.

\*     \*     \*     \*     \*

By the end of 1983, Bowie had no real need ever to work again – other than to deliver two more albums to EMI America. Having already stashed away a fortune before the year began, he could now live comfortably on his investment income, continuing royalties from his past albums, and the performance royalties every time his music was played on radio and television, anywhere in the world – but he clearly felt the artist's need to progress.

Eighteen months after the release of *Let's Dance*, Bowie issued his second LP for EMI America, *Tonight*, duetting on the title track with Tina Turner, and promoting the strongest number, *Blue Jean*, with a 22-minute film which he produced himself, *Jazzin' For Blue Jean*, directed by Julien Temple, who also made the films *Absolute Beginners* and *The Great Rock 'n' Roll Swindle*. It was a classic in its field, a neatly crafted study of rock 'n' roll fame. Bowie, in what could be described as typically schizophrenic mode, appears as a fan in the audience who loses his girl to The Star – playing both parts. Despite its brevity, the film was released on video with its final segment, Bowie performing *Blue Jean*, used to promote the song on television. The LP and single were as poorly reviewed in Britain as his tour the year before, but this made no difference to the record-buying public. *Tonight* went to No. 1 in the British LP charts and No. 6 in the United States, with the *Blue Jean* single a hit in both territories and throughout Europe.

Bowie himself was rarely seen in public, his private life a mystery – and nothing would be heard from him for months on end, other than when he released a video to promote a new song, made a film or wrote the theme music for another movie. From this period comes *Loving The Alien*, one of his better songs, with a strong melody line and a strange lyric inspired by the mediaeval wars between the Saracens and Crusaders – but he mostly remained at home in Switzerland, painting more than writing, working in his studio, moving on from lino cuts, woodcuts and litho prints to portraits in oils. When he did leave Switzerland, to make the films *Absolute Beginners* and *Labyrinth*, or to produce a video, it was always in conditions of utmost secrecy, for after Lennon's murder, stars of Bowie's celebrity became increasingly fearful for their personal safety, surrounding themselves with bodyguards – and Bowie had more reason to fear than most, having maintained such a high profile, and being aware of the risk that his son might be kidnapped.

Bowie was barely seen for 18 months. There were even rumours that he might have retired, and he chose to stay in Switzerland rather than attend the funeral when Terry committed suicide, throwing himself in front of a train. Then Bowie was back, like a genie from a lamp, returning for the Live Aid Concert at Wembley Stadium on 13 July 1985. As always, he took far more care than anyone else to prepare for his performance, spending two weeks in constant rehearsal and choosing his wardrobe with a sense of occasion. While other musicians flopped around in jeans and T-shirts that looked in need of a wash, Bowie suddenly stepped from behind a curtain, smartly dressed in a light grey suit, collar and tie, and not a hair out of place, to almost steal the show with an 18-minute performance that included *Rebel Rebel* and *Modern Love*, choosing *Heroes* as his finale with its neatly symbolic message: 'We can be heroes/just for a day'. It was as stunning a performance as any he had given, and yet coldly calculated with nothing left to chance. Unlike many of the other rock stars who performed that day, Bowie's act was timed to the second, a professional to his fingertips – leaving the stage with his message ringing in the ears of a billion viewers around the globe. His presence was felt throughout the day, for he and Jagger recorded a video version of *Dancing In The Street* by Martha and The Vandellas, which was used as a space-filler whenever the stage was being rearranged for another group, and duly went to No.1 when released as a single, with Jagger and Bowie donating all proceeds to Live Aid.

Bowie was setting a standard for himself, sensing the historical importance of this occasion when others were being far too casual – and in the years that followed every subsequent Bowie artefact was launched with this same meticulous attention to detail. As in the worlds of film and theatre, whatever he did was finely crafted.

Once the show was over, Bowie vanished again. There were to be no more live appearances in 1985 and 1986 – but with *Absolute Beginners* and *Labyrinth* one could see Bowie was consciously broadening, fusing his work in different media into one achievement, writing music, performing title songs but also bringing his other skills into play. *Absolute Beginners* received a surprisingly mixed press, praised by the national papers but sharply criticized in the music papers. I suspect *Absolute Beginners* will one day be seen as a classic. Based on the novel by Colin MacInnes, the film is set in the Soho and Notting Hill of 1958, when rock 'n' roll was just beginning to take root, superceding the greyness of the post-war years, with a racial mix starting to gel and the whole world opening up for the young and ambitious. Director Julien Temple amplifies these themes with a startling use of primary colours and dance routines, set against the bright lights and darkened doorways of Soho's streets. This gives the story extra dimension, quickening the pace, enlivening its characters to capture a sense of the

moment, and of the future awaiting the young, now they have
money, music and a feeling of hope – and it's then that the mood
subtly changes with Bowie's entrance. Initially observing its
central character from a balcony, Bowie steps forward as if
walking centre stage, a tall, imposing, classless, American-suited
man, with a not-quite-right mid-Atlantic accent. This is Vendice
Partners, the advertising man who spots the newly developing
teenage market as his chance to make money, and quickly acts.
'You have integrity, just the thing my agency stands for,' Partners
tells the young photographer who has been trying to capture these
moments – and from this point because of his sense of stillness, his
ability to hold the screen with a minimum of movement, the film is
Bowie's. But you do not like him, for you know that the spivs are
moving into the market, squeezing the young, removing their
innocence.

In *Labyrinth* Bowie played Jareth, The King of the Goblins, co-
starring with a young child lost in a world of fantasy and a cast of
gargoyle-like goblins. These were the latest creation of Jim
Henson of Muppets fame, who conceived a new family of
characters for his first full-length cinema movie, a $25m produc-
tion directed by Henson with a script by Terry Jones of *Monty
Python*. Once again, Bowie was ridiculed by the rock music
weeklies, but when asked why he was making films like this
Bowie had an answer. 'What I do now is pure entertainment.' he
said[3] – and it was. I suspect that this – like *Absolute Beginners* – is
going to be another of those David Bowie 'products' that will be
seen as timeless in 20 or 30 years' time.

In April 1987, four years after his last concert tour, Bowie and
Peter Frampton undertook a two-man world tour – to hold press
conferences announcing they would be back later in the year to
present Bowie's 'Glass Spider Tour', with Frampton playing lead
guitar. This was a novelty, a world tour to promote a tour, but one
must remember that by my calculation Bowie earned at least $25m
last time around – and by publicizing the show in advance he was
making sure promoters could bank the ticket money, and pay him
his share, before the tour began. The tour's title was taken from a
song on Bowie's third LP for EMI America, *Never Let Me Down*,
which was a disappointment. The title track was an obvious single,
which Bowie promoted with another video, and reached No. 34 in
the UK singles chart. In *Day-in, Day-out* (which as a single
reached No. 17 in the UK) Bowie came up with a strong song for

performing on stage with a dance routine, but overall he seemed to be trying to satisfy himself with experimental sounds rather than pleasing the mainstream audience. Already, one could hear him moving on to the music and lyrical construction of his next project, Tin Machine.

The stage presentation of the 'Glass Spider' show was more adventurous than any of Bowie's concerts since *Diamond Dogs*. The set was dominated by a vast glass spider, maybe 30 or 40 feet tall, its legs columns of changing light and its body a glass shell that turned from green to red to pink to purple as the show unfolded, with Bowie making his entrance from it, suspended on a chair as if being lowered from a helicopter. The posters, programmes and subsequent video all emphasized that this production was 'Conceived by David Bowie' and he held the stage throughout, presenting over 20 songs, accompanying himself occasionally on guitar, but mostly working only with a microphone, and nearly always down at the front apron, reaching out to the audience, happy, smiling and bonding with them more openly and freely than in any show since *Ziggy Stardust*.

Besides Frampton, there were five other musicians, led by Carlos Alomar (guitar) and strongly featuring Erdal Kizilcay (keyboards, congas, violins and trumpet), who has become one of Bowie's closest friends in recent years. The other musicians were Richard Cottle (synthesizer and saxophone), Alan Childs (drums and percussion) and Carmine Rojas (bass). For this tour, Bowie also employed five dancers – Melissa Hurley, Constance Marie, Viktor Manoel, Stephen Nichols and Craig Allen Rothwell. Bowie choreographed their routines with Toni Basil, incorporating costume changes and creating a sense of movement that zipped the show along.

This was a stage show designed for large auditoriums seating up to 60,000 people. Much of its subtlety was lost in these vast arenas, with the audience too far from the stage to be able to see what was going on. In the *Independent*, Marek Kohn described Bowie as having 'the visage of the rock idol with the polish of the Vegas crooner', saying of the concert as a whole, 'The star was there; what was in alarmingly short supply was taste .... Bowie has built a career on making hollowness inspirational so it's surprising that such a past master should have lost the knack of structuring a spectacle.'[4] And yet, the show looked good on the subsequent video, filmed in Australia and directed by David

Mallet. All the routines and costume changes could be seen for what they were, devices to keep the audience's attention. Initially released as a double-video set, *Glass Spider* was later reissued as a single, 100-minute video, capturing Bowie in full flight, making good use of his props and dancers, reinterpreting songs like *Fame, Fashion* and *Loving The Alien* and updating numbers by earlier heroes, Iggy Pop's *I Want To Be Your Dog* and The Velvet Underground's *White Light, White Heat*, which has been part of his repertoire since the late 60s. In years to come, I believe this video will rank with *Absolute Beginners* and *Labyrinth* to show how Bowie was trying to fuse his ideas in the 80s.

Part of the charm of the *Glass Spider* video is the way it captures another, unexpected side of Bowie – happy, relaxed and clearly falling in love with the American ballet dancer Melissa Hurley, having claimed for years he would never fall in love again after his disastrous marriage and the end of his affair with Hermione Farthingale. In the show, Melissa is plucked from the audience, using one of the old tricks of music hall where a key member of a troupe was often sitting in the stalls in disguise, waiting to make an unexpected entrance. Excitedly she steps up on stage, changes costume, puts on a dress and starts to dance with Bowie, a fan meeting her idol – and as they dance, in this routine and in others, one can sense a genuine tenderness between them, although Bowie was to say later that their affair did not begin until after the tour ended.

When choosing musicians and dancers for the tour, Bowie says he was fascinated by her 'black Irish look ... lovely dark hair and a wholesome peach complexion'.[5] They saw each other throughout the tour, dancing together each night, and he says that 'as it petered out I kept asking myself, "Are we going to see each other again?" We fell in love after the tour was over, while having a holiday in Australia. I realized then that I did not want us to go our separate ways.'*

Dismissing any suggestion that he might be too old for her (he was now 40, she 23), Bowie said: 'I know many couples far closer in age who have absolutely nothing in common.... Love has

---

* It's the sense of tenderness that surprises. During another part of the tour – in Dallas on 9 October 1987 – Bowie was arrested and accused of rape. A woman named Wanda Lee Nicholls claimed Bowie assaulted her in his hotel room, crawling over her in 'a Dracula-like fashion'. Bowie admitted having spent the night with her, but denied any assault – and the case was eventually dismissed.

nothing to do with age. I've had more than my fair share of girls in the past but I don't need that any more. We actually enjoy each other's company. She fulfils something within me that I don't have. She has a very bright, solid, totally buoyant attitude towards how wonderful life is that I find irrepressible and most irresistible. I try not to be apart from her for more than four weeks, which means I have to spend a lot of time in Los Angeles.... I know I said in the past that I'd never get married again because it was such a painful experience the first time. But we are engaged and generally engaged people get married.'

Periodically, they would be photographed together – sometimes going to the theatre or ballet, but more often at airports, travelling between Bowie's homes in Switzerland, New York, Los Angeles, Mustique and Australia – and in 1989 and 1990 there were frequent reports that they were about to marry, either in New York or on Mustique, where Jagger was said to be standing by as Bowie's best man.

Eventually, after three years together, they parted as silently as their affair started, with Bowie deciding marriage would not work out. Melissa never discussed their relationship, and Bowie did not mention it ending until three years later,[6] when he described her as 'such a wonderful, lovely, vibrant girl' and said, 'I guess it became one of those older men, younger girl situations where I had the joy of taking her around the world and showing her things. But it became obvious to me that it just wasn't going to work out as a relationship – and for that she would thank me one of these days. So I broke off the engagement.'

24

# With riches, love and the minotaur
# – is this just fame or is it art?

And so, in 1987, at the age of 40, Bowie became what he had set out to be, the self-christened 'generalist', the polymath of rock 'n' roll. As was said of Pinocchio, he could dance and he could sing, he could do most anything – which made Bowie awkward to categorize.

This does not bother him; Bowie has long been part of rock's global aristocracy, which has become so phenomenally wealthy that it is able to live by its own terms and customs, choosing which media to work through, never needing to explain, and admitting no outsiders. Contrary to newspaper opinion, its wealth comes not from record sales or concert tours – although these may earn them many millions – but through the constant broadcasting of their music by radio and TV stations in nearly every part of the planet. Every time songs are played, a fee is paid to the composer – and the most popular are played thousands of times each day around the world. Details are never published because the collection agencies do not disclose how much their members earn, and the fees are usually channelled through offshore tax havens, but it is an open secret within the music business that some individual songs earn millions of pounds every year – and will continue to do so for as long as they remain in copyright, i.e. until 70 years after the writers' death under the new copyright provisions agreed by the European Union. What makes Bowie's career so intriguing is that he has now spent 20 years of his life using the freedom wealth has given him to push himself in many other directions, taking chances, experimenting, trying his hand in different fields, never feeling the need to conform or to apologize to anyone, yet managing to convince his audience that this is Art for Art's Sake. Bowie has done precisely what he said he would 25 years ago in Ken Pitt's apartment.

Writers, artists, film stars or musicians rarely take risks on the

Bowie scale, preferring to make their reputation in one field and then ploughing that furrow assiduously. Bowie, however, seems driven by something he cannot control – which he described in the brochure for his first retrospective exhibition of paintings, drawings and sculpture at the Cork Street Gallery, London, in April 1995 as 'a bloody-minded determination to create something that WAS NOT there before'. Frequently, this coincides with other dramatic events in his life – and then critics say he is reacting against fame, fleeing Los Angeles, seeking refuge in Berlin, discovering something new in Japan or Africa, changing characters like a chameleon, or sloughing skins – but it must be something deeper, perhaps an ability to see life through abnormal perspectives. More literally, a man born with a gift.

That has always been his appeal. It was why a musician of the calibre of Boy George says that *The Man Who Sold The World* first turned him on to music, and a whole generation still clings to Bowie's songs, listening to the lyrics or watching his films, searching for hidden meanings. One has the sense of an artist unfolding before one's eyes, finding more and more within himself, realizing one can only explore one's own resources by first mastering technique. Bowie told me many years ago that there was no logical progression in his early music, and I think that is still true of his work as a whole; this is the career of a man finding the means to explore within, and as with so many true artists his early output stands *pari passu* with his most recent.

Kenneth Pitt, one of the few to have known both Bowie's parents well, often told me that Mr and Mrs Jones realized during his childhood that they had produced an unusually gifted son 'and bore the consequences bravely'. Those gifts are almost certainly in his genes, something Bowie was born with, and there is little doubt that when he talks about 'the madness, real fucking madness' in his family he is describing traits frequently observable in those blessed, or cursed, with genius. They are literally borderline cases – or as Dylan Thomas described it in the essay mentioned in the Introduction, their borderlines are 'more difficult than the majority of people, comparatively safe within the barriers of their own common-sensibility, can realize'.[1]

Bowie has several strange characteristics. He looks odd with that spindly frame, despite thickening out a bit in recent years, and those disconcerting eyes, one blue, one brown. Stranger still is his temperament, his volatility, the ease with which he bursts into tears – or turns to sudden coldness. His mind works rapidly. He still reads three or four books at a time, switching from one to another, and who else but Bowie would walk up to a microphone in a recording studio and start to sing, without a word being written in advance? Who else would record five albums at a time, or complete 300 major canvases, mostly in acrylic oils, without stopping to test his public's reaction? Who else would feign such indifference to the whims of the marketplace? Is it all an act? I think not. Bowie is a generalist, all right – but one who can turn his hand to rock whenever it suits him without being totally driven like Eric Clapton or Keith Richard, who live and breathe their music. Bowie can produce great rock music whenever he wants to, which he seldom does. For him, there is always more than one purpose in life.

Realizing that creative achievement is not enough and that true stars have to be commercial, Bowie also has that gift of being able to pluck the hit album from the hat without lowering his sights, and yet, being also anxious not to be pigeonholed like so many musicians before and since, changes character, creating new personalities for himself, shedding the Ziggy, Diamond Dog or Aladdin Sane imagery like worn skins, re-emerging whenever he wants as the re-born chansonnier on the darkened stage, the eternal Thin White Duke.

But it has all been a means to an end, and as soon as the need arises, whether breaking free from Defries or laying out the ground for a new recording contract, Bowie can always find the sound for the moment, whether with *Fame* or *Golden Years*, with the brilliant video for *Ashes To Ashes* or the totally commercial *Let's Dance*, playing the game with an immaculate sense of timing, before going back to the drawing board, and again taking risks, whether with films such as *Labyrinth* or *Absolute Beginners*, with his painting and sculpture (which lay hidden in his studio in Switzerland, accumulating for 20 years before being suddenly shown in 1995), or experiments in music like the two Tin Machine albums, the gentler *Black Tie, White Noise* LP, his *Buddha of Suburbia* concerto (which is what it will surely be seen as in years to come), or the more recent sessions with Brian Eno, continuing a collaboration that has also lasted two decades, bringing him back together with Mike Garson, Reeves Gabrels and Erdal Kizilcay to record the albums *Outside* (1995) and *Inside* (1996).

Interspersed between them all are the forays into other fields, from *Baal* to *The Elephant Man* and tiny roles in arthouse movies, whether playing Pontius Pilate in Martin Scorsese's *The Last Temptation Of Christ*, his strange, ethereal manifestation in David Lynch's cinema adaptation of *Twin Peaks, Fire Walk With Me*, or the films Bowie has partly financed himself through his own company Isolar, *The Linguini Incident* or the still-unseen *Mesmer*, in which Bowie was executive producer, working to a Dennis Potter script and starring with Alan Rickman.

At heart, Bowie has never been a rock 'n' roller, but this was the convenient medium when he was searching for ways to express himself. Bowie could have been a poet, a novelist, a playwright, an actor or a painter. All the necessary attitudes lie within him, though sometimes he is short on technique. When Bowie strays outside his own expertise, as in writing the long essay that was part of the packaging for *The Buddha Of Suburbia*, his writing is wooden and imprecise. But because he sometimes uses five words where two would be more effective, or employs long words when shorter would have more impact, it is wrong to describe him as 'pseudo-intellectual' or 'suffering from literary pretensions', which are the kind of phrases usually used in the British music press. Within his own field as a lyric writer, Bowie is spare and precise, never wasting a word or note.

\*    \*    \*    \*    \*

At the time we first met, Bowie's intellectual interests – in art, literature and music – were much as they are today. As he says himself, they have barely changed since he was 12 years old. Since then, he has travelled, studied, learned and listened, reading insatiably and using every opportunity to visit the world's churches, museums and art galleries, and yet the shape of the man remains the same.

That there's also a somewhat manic quality within Bowie, I do not doubt. For much of his adult life, Bowie has been driven by sexual compulsions, but that's not an unusual corollary to artistic genius. And one always had the feeling that within the driven man, there's been a bruised romantic looking for love. It's the same story with drugs. They were available, too – much too available. Bowie tried everything, as an obsessive would, but it was cocaine that did the damage. Couriers maintained his supplies, knowing him a willing buyer, and he would be snorting day and night, eating hardly any food, living on cigarettes and coffee, but maintaining his workpace and sexual momentum, going six or seven days without sleep – but never missing a performance. However far he fell, some part of his character was holding on to reality – when others were not.

'My life turned into a nightmare,' he says of the 70s,[2] admitting his brain was probably damaged, that he now has 'enormous memory lapses' and that part of his brain fell through his nose. 'Cocaine is a devious companion,' he adds. 'It crushes you totally. If you really want to break with friends and relatives, don't hesitate – cocaine is the way.... I told everyone, and lied to myself, that I was not dependent because I was only using it occasionally, but, of course, those occasions got closer and closer, so I stopped doing drugs and turned to alcohol. That was an absurd situation. I said to myself, "I've stopped the dope – and now I'm an alcoholic." Drinking is the most depressing habit there ever was because you go from the heavens to the pits.' Now he does not drink at all. His past life has been put behind him. Only the art remains.

It is a miracle Bowie survived. So many did not, killed by the pace and tension, the drugs and excess, the need to keep going and the general craziness that has surrounded rock 'n' roll since Bowie first picked up a saxophone and told his teachers, 'I want to be a saxophonist in a modern jazz quartet.' An appalling catalogue of unnecessary death surrounds the history of rock 'n' roll, like some hideous shroud – and David Bowie has lived through it all, pushing his body to its limits, defying the odds, and survived. That in itself is astonishing, and I suspect it's because, whatever he does, however crazy his life has been, there is an iron will within the man – a determination to keep control on some levels, while letting go on others.

Whenever it is necessary, Bowie is ruthless – in dispensing with Pitt, Defries and Lippman; in protecting his wealth from the British and American tax authorities, who seem to delight in stripping artists to the bone; in firing musicians and producers, and in divorcing a wife – and one cannot look at any aspect of his career without thinking of money and his attitude to it. As I said earlier, he once told me he intended to make enough money by the time he was 30 to be free to spend the rest of his life however he wished. This was a genuine determination, and I sensed a steely will. And this was what he did, but instead of resting on his laurels, and living on the small fortune and steady income that he had established for himself by 1977, Bowie went on to make a huge fortune.

*     *     *     *     *

From the way the financial structure of his career has been organized, I would suspect Bowie was able to treat the fortune that he earned in 1983 as capital – investing it safely and allowing it to steadily increase in value, probably doubling every five or six years through the normal capital growth of the 80s. If this was what he did (and I would be amazed if he did not) there would have been no need for him to touch the capital. All those other continuing royalties, augmented by fees for appearing in films and licensing out videos, would have been more than enough to fund his lifestyle. If I am correct in my analysis, that conservative estimate of $50m for 1983 would have doubled to $100m by 1988/9 and to $200m by the mid-90s – but that was only the beginning of Bowie's accumulation of capital.

His 1987 'Glass Spider Tour' may not have had the same excitement as his 1983 tour, without the multi-million-selling LP to accompany it, and it may have been more expensively staged, with a larger travelling company – but by then ticket prices had increased rapidly, and through his merchandising, pulling power at the box office and total control of costs, I would be surprised if Bowie took less than $30–40m back to Switzerland – and again, that may have doubled by now.

And then there was his biggest moneyspinner of all, the recycling of all his past work – and promoting this on a global basis in 1990 with his 'Sound and Vision Tour'. Once again, Bowie came up with a marketing operation no one else had thought of – though it has been widely copied since. In 1986, all the rights in his Mercury and RCA albums – i.e. nearly all the songs recorded prior to 1983, apart from those for Decca, Pye and Deram – reverted jointly to Bowie and MainMan under the terms of their settlement. These were then digitally remastered in Switzerland, thereby creating a new 'sound' copyright* – and extending their copyright life. In the meantime, the music industry

---

* In the music business, there are two copyrights in every song – one exists in the song itself while the other is in the sound recording of that song. Thus by re-recording their early songs, musicians are now establishing a new 'sound' copyright.

switched over to compact disc – and in agreement with Defries, with MainMan also based in Switzerland, Bowie recycled the whole of this Mercury/RCA catalogue, not only on compact disc but also as vinyl LPs in their original packaging (but with 'bonus tracks') and on audio cassette. In Britain, this licensing operation was handled through EMI Records – presumably with another multi-million-dollar payment upfront – and in the United States through Rykodisc. *Hunky Dory*, *Ziggy Stardust*, *Diamond Dogs*, *The Man Who Sold The World* and *Aladdin Sane* began selling all over again, in all formats – aided by this 1990 tour, which saw Bowie performing 110 concerts in 15 countries. To give this promotion additional thrust, Bowie announced that this would be the last time he would ever perform his past work in public – and repeated his 1987 ploy of travelling around the world first to promote it, thus guaranteeing that most of the tickets were sold and a major part of his money banked before he even had to leave home. Never one to miss an opportunity, Bowie also repackaged his best songs for yet another compilation LP, once again calling this *Changesbowie*, but subtitling it *Sound And Vision*. There was nothing wrong with his commercial judgement; this LP went straight to No. 1 in the LP charts, and stayed in the charts for six months. This overall concept earned Bowie a Grammy Award for 'Best Packaging' of any musical product in 1990. He would have split the record royalties with MainMan – but the tour money and merchandising spin-offs were all his, and he probably earned another $40–50m to tuck away in his Swiss haven.

If my analyses are correct – and they are based on the scale of the tour, concerts played and probable per capita income – David Bowie was worth in total, counting the 1983 and 1987 tours and capital growth since, at least $300–350m by the end of 1990 – and it has been growing ever since. If anyone doubts my arithmetic, I would point out that Lennon's estate was officially computed at $400m on his death in 1980 – and Lennon never made solo tours to compare with David Bowie's, had to share his Beatle recording income with three other Beatles and with Brian Epstein, and shared only 50 per cent of his Beatle songwriting income with Paul McCartney (the other 50 per cent went to Northern Songs Ltd). Lennon's solo career was also relatively brief – at a time when record prices, artistes' royalties and concert tickets were all much lower than in Bowie's key earning period. By taking control of his finances as soon as he could and then basing himself in

Switzerland, Bowie prepared himself to make great wealth in the 80s. And he did it. My estimates veer on the side of caution.

There were other reasons for Bowie's determined money-making. Not for the first time, he was closing the book on one phase of his life and beginning another – or so he thought, for it can never be quite as simple as that for someone with such a high-earning profile. Surprisingly, a degree of naïvety seems to have entered his planning. He appears to have thought he could suddenly – by mere expression of will – cease to be David Bowie, Solo Star, and become part of something else, Tin Machine.

Bowie tried hard to persuade his fans and the music papers that he was no longer a solo performer. Anyone hoping to gain access to Bowie by expressing interest in Tin Machine found himself face to face with all four members of the group – Reeves Gabrels, Hunt Sales, Tony Sales and Bowie – with the maestro barely saying a word, and the others contradicting each other, not knowing how to play the game – but still Bowie persisted with the notion that he was a musician reborn, his identity lost within the new group, relying on the old basics of lead guitar, drums, bass and vocals. The name was no misnomer, for the music was a cross between early Hendrix and high-volume, crashing heavy metal – but without that powerful tenderness that made Hendrix a man apart.

It was not Bowie's first journey down this road. Back in the early 70s, when given a free hand by RCA and Defries to work with other musicians, his then friend Lou Reed veered off into heavy metal with *Rock 'n' Roll Animal* (1974), before completely losing himself in the double-LP *Metal Machine Music* (1975). This is where I suspect Tin Machine found their inspiration. It was not a good place to start. The sound was hard and tinny, with little melody or subtlety, and a rhythm more mechanical than musical – and this was the route Bowie now chose to take.

Throughout his career, Bowie has tended to continue working with the same rhythm section for several years, finding a new sound with a change of lead guitarist – and what he did with Tin Machine (for I have no doubt he was the motivating force) was to graft lead guitarist Gabrels on to Iggy Pop's rhythm section and then front the band himself, writing most of the music and nearly all the lyrics, and functioning as lead singer. This made his attempts to project himself as one of the boys look silly.

The experiment had its roots in Iggy Pop's 1977 tour when Bowie joined the band anonymously on keyboards, travelling across Europe and the United States, playing alongside Hunt Sales (drums) and his brother Tony Sales (bass). They may have known each other before that, for the Sales brothers toured and recorded with Todd Rundgren in the early 70s as members of his group Runt. Their father was the American comedian Soapy Sales, so their roots in the entertainment business ran deep. After the Iggy Pop tour, they returned to Berlin with Bowie to record Iggy's next album and were thus familiar with each other's tastes and skills.

Ten years later, when Bowie was engaged upon his 'Glass Spider Tour', he was handed a demotape featuring Gabrels on lead guitar. Almost immediately he phoned Gabrels, suggesting they might record together, resulting in an eight-minute reinterpretation of Bowie's *Look Back In Anger*, which he and Gabrels performed at the Dominion Theatre, London, in April 1988 in a fund-raising concert for the Institute of Contemporary Arts. The relative intimacy of the 3,000-seat venue clearly made Bowie nostalgic for his early days when he could see and 'feel' his audience, and when he happened to meet Tony Sales again, Bowie suggested the four of them might like to get together in Montreux and see how they got on in a recording studio.

Through 1988 and 1989, between holidays in Indonesia, Italy and Australia with Melissa Hurley and filming his small part in *The Last Temptation Of Christ*, Bowie worked hard at Tin Machine, recording 35 songs together in Montreux, rehearsing for two months in Australia and meeting up again in Montserrat for another burst of rehearsals. The group was launched at the first International Music Awards ceremony in New York on 31 May 1989.

When EMI received the tapes for Bowie's next LP, they were more than mildly surprised to find that it was titled *Tin Machine*, without his name on the cover. Largely on the strength of his connection with the project, this went to No. 3 in the LP charts in June 1989 – reportedly selling strongly in mainland Europe, too – and was credited with more than 1m sales world-wide. Two singles taken from the LP, *under the god/sacrifice yourself* and *Tin Machine/Maggie's Farm*, also achieved respectable sales.

Still determined to promote the group the traditional way, playing small gigs to begin with and then slowly working their way up, Tin Machine did the briefest of tours that year – three shows in America, five in Britain and four on mainland Europe. Every time, they insisted on playing to venues with a capacity of rarely more than 2,000. When Tin Machine were booked into a venue in Amsterdam that could accommodate 900 people, relay screens had to be erected outside to pacify a crowd of 25,000 who wanted to see Bowie. In Britain, fans travelled from all over the country, willing to queue for up to four days to see Bowie at small venues he had chosen, such as the Town and Country Club in North London. Had Bowie responded to this enthusiasm by booking himself into larger arenas, seating around 10,000 people, Tin Machine would have been taken seriously. Instead, they were seen as a joke – a toy-thing for a self-indulgent millionaire – and abused by fans and critics alike.

Musically, they had something going for them. Their stage act included new-sounding heavy metal interpretations of Bob Dylan's *Maggie's Farm*, John Lennon's *Working Class Hero* and The Moody Blues' classic *Go Now*. Their first LP featured several good new Bowie songs with strong lyrics – especially *crack city*, *baby can dance* and *under the god* – but these were overwhelmed by the crashing, clattering, tinny sound of a heavy metal band going catatonic with no one person in control. One day, I suspect, Bowie will rerecord some of the songs on this LP and give them their proper due.

Immediately after launching Tin Machine with this brief tour, Bowie went straight back out on the road, presenting his 'Sound and Vision Tour'. This was Bowie back on the big stages again, playing to arenas and stadiums holding up to 60,000 people – which emphasized even more that strange perversity in his personality, the non-star one day and the world star the next. He performed 110 concerts in 15 countries and earned many more millions, and then went straight back to Tin Machine to record another album. *Tin Machine II* had all the flaws of the first – imaginative lyrics and strong tunes, notably *You Belong In Rock 'n' Roll*, *Baby Universal* and *A Big Hurt*, but drowned by a sound more noise than music.

When Bowie took the tapes to EMI Records, they refused to release the album – in my view, understandably – and so the LP was licensed to the London label, instead, with Tin Machine still persisting in the second phase of their plan, a much more lengthy tour of better (but not large) venues through Britain, mainland Europe and the United States, through the summer and autumn of 1991 and the spring of 1992. By new band standards, the tour was a success – but when I saw them at the Royal Court in Liverpool, there was no disguising their discomfort. The audience were calling out for Bowie's music all through the show – but what they got was this intensely metallic sound performed in a confined space, bouncing off the walls, with some fine, soaring, jazzy saxophone from Bowie; a solidly reliable rhythm section and a few brilliant guitar-breaks from Gabrels – and a ringing noise in the ears afterwards, like tinnitus.

From a packaging point of view, Bowie could not be faulted. Both Tin Machine LPs were marketed skilfully, with superior artwork, clever use of photographs, the lyrics printed in full – and imaginatively sold in various CD, mini-CD, vinyl and audio cassette forms – but all the clever salesmanship could not disguise the fact that Bowie had made a mistake, regressing rather than moving forward.

For many musicians, an error of this magnitude could be catastrophic. And perhaps it was for Reeves Gabrels and the Sales brothers, but not for Bowie who was now so firmly ensconced financially that he could take a year off whenever he felt like it, or dabble with something new – and I have more than a sneaking suspicion that his audience actually expect him to share his mistakes with them. In any case, his life was changing, too. Late in 1990, Bowie told Melissa Hurley their engagement was off – and some weeks later, to be precise on 14 October, Bowie found himself at a private dinner party in New York. He had just finished the 'Sound and Vision Tour', and was about to make the film *The Linguini Incident* with Rosanna Arquette. Sitting next to him at dinner was the stunningly beautiful model Iman. Bowie had frequently been drawn to black women in the past, but these were usually backing singers, dancers or receptionists – and Iman was in a different league; a tall, graceful and highly sophisticated international model, with a flawless complexion, used to wearing the latest designs in haute couture and working with a personal hair stylist and make-up artist. Bowie fell head over heels in love – and behaved like a perfect gentleman. From all that I have read and heard, I have not the slightest doubt this really was what the French call a *coup de foudre*.

Iman, then 34, was born in Somalia. Her family name is Abdulmajid, her father being a diplomat and former ambassador and her mother a gynaecologist. She married first at 16, as an act of rebellion against her parents, but later moved to Kenya to study economics and political science at Nairobi University. While walking down a street in Nairobi she was spotted by the photographer Philip Beard, who asked her to pose for him. At first, she refused – but changed her mind when told the fee would be £4,000. This led to her becoming a model, moving to New York and being chosen to star in the Tia Maria advertising campaign, with her face featured on TV commercials and in the glossiest magazines in the world. Iman's second marriage, to the millionaire American basketball star and former Olympic gold medallist Spencer Heywood, also ended in divorce, and by the time of this dinner party she was living alone with their 12-year-old daughter Zulekha. As a top model, wearing her age with ease and reputedly earning more than $700,000 a year, Iman was already part of the international jet set, with a flat in New York and her own house in Laurel Canyon, Los Angeles, complete with swimming pool and Mercedes convertible. She was seen at the more fashionable parties on both coasts and pursued by many suitors, among them Warren Beatty.

Bowie admits falling in love at first sight. 'I make no bones about it, I was naming our children on the very night we met,' he says.[3] 'I knew she was for me. It was absolutely immediate. I just fell under her spell. I'd never been out with a model before so I was surprised to meet one who was wonderful and not the usual sort of bubblehead.' Bowie insists that he wooed her in 'a gentlemanly fashion' with 'lots of being led to doorways and polite kisses on the cheek. Flowers and chocolates, the whole thing. It was precious from the first night, and I just didn't want anything to spoil it.'

After finishing *The Linguini Incident* – an oddly inconsequential film in which Bowie plays an immigrant nightclub barman who has a strange affair with a female escapologist – at the close of 1990, Bowie and Iman flew to Switzerland and spent their first Christmas together in a romantic setting, a new home overlooking Lake Geneva, surrounded by snow-topped mountains. He says they barely discussed marriage, but spent six weeks the following summer cruising along the Côte d'Azur and holidaying in Florence, viewing Renaissance paintings and touring churches – and in October flew to Paris, the city of lovers. There, Bowie proposed, travelling down the Seine by boat, dining by candle-light, with a pianist playing. He had planned it carefully, and when the pianist began to play *April In Paris*, Bowie started to sing of *October In Paris*, and then dropped to one knee as the song ended, offering her a rose plucked from a table display, and asking, 'Will you marry me?' It would have been a huge embarrassment had she said 'No' but Iman immediately said 'Yes' – and was apparently so stunned by the suddenness of his romantic gesture that she almost fell off her chair and into the river. 'I knew I had to sing to express how I felt in the best way I can,' says Bowie.[4] 'Luckily, it worked. Everything was perfect … it was not something we had discussed at any length and she was not expecting it. She was shocked, but she didn't hesitate for a second.'

Just as the proposal was private, so was the wedding – with Bowie returning home to Switzerland after the Freddie Mercury Memorial Concert and quietly slipping down to Lausanne Town Hall for a civil marriage ceremony on 24 April 1992. Even that was kept secret, with not a word appearing in the press until the Swiss Sunday newspaper *Sonntagsblick* broke the story on 3 May, reporting that the couple arrived at the Town Hall with two friends as witnesses, with Bowie wearing a black silk suit and grey silk tie with a white rose in his lapel, and Iman, hidden behind dark glasses, dressed in a plain white trouser suit with a black top and a choker of pearls, carrying a bouquet of white flowers.

Just over a month later, largely catching the press unawares, the couple were married again, in a religious ceremony at the St James Episcopal Church in Florence by the Rev. Mario Marziale, with Bowie's son Joe as best man. This time it was a sumptuous occasion in a Renaissance setting, with them both wearing designer clothes and Iman attended by her personal hair stylist and a make-up artist, who had both flown in from New York. A local newspaper broke the news that morning, but it was too late for the overseas press to make it to Florence – although time enough for a crowd of over a thousand people to gather in the street outside the church, watching their families and closest friends arrive. For several days, a wedding party of 68 had been gathering at the Villa Massa, a luxury hotel in the Tuscany hills ten miles outside Florence, with Bowie and his son among the last to arrive, flying in from Mustique where Joe celebrated his 21st birthday. It was very much a family affair, with Iman's parents, her brothers and other near relatives, besides Bowie's mother, his cousin Kristina and those closest of friends that he had known since childhood, George Underwood and Geoffrey MacCormack. From the world of show business, there were only Yoko Ono, Bono of U2, Brian Eno and his wife Anthea, and Eric Idle.

As they arrived at the church, a small orchestra of Italian musicians played classical music – and later a suite that Bowie had written for the occasion. In the evening, there was a formal dinner at the Villa Massa with the couple flying out via Rome the following day for a month's honeymoon in the Far East.

If this formal wedding was meant to be a symbolic occasion, something more than than an expression of love between a man and a woman, it certainly achieved their intention – for the whole world could see that Bowie had once again changed planes, now merging the disciplines of fashion with those of music, art and theatre. He wore a formal black suit with tails, a white shirt with winged collars and a white bow tie, but designed by Thierry Mugler so that the lines were sleekly cut away, creating the impression of formality, but without its ordinariness – and Herve Leger created for Iman a flowing, oyster-coloured gown to underline her beauty, with Teddy Antolin arranging her hair and Jose Luis applying her make-up. This was a marriage between a Christian and a Muslim in an Episcopal church, with them both avowing their personal faith.

'I'm not a religious person,' said Bowie.[5] 'I'm a spiritual person. God plays a very important part in my life – I look to Him a lot and He is the cornerstone of my existence – even more as I get older. But it is a one-to-one relationship with God. I believe man develops a relationship with his own God.' Iman added: 'Getting married did not convert me from a Muslim into a Christian. I am not a religious person – but I do come from a religious family and the most important thing to me is that I have their blessing. What matters to them is that we are happy and have faith in each other and in God.'

Now David Bowie seemed to have it all – astonishing riches, the love of one of the world's most beautiful women, a 'real marriage, sanctified by God',[6] homes in different parts of the world so that he could plan his life on a global basis, the strength and warmth of a bonded family, the trusting intimacy of lifelong friendships that have survived even the music business, and the spiritual contentment of his one-to-one relationship with God. But, when all is said and done, can this ever be enough for an artist?

\*   \*   \*   \*   \*

Throughout his career, Bowie's music has been marked by

coldness, a sense of detachment or isolation, the musician describing what he sees rather than how he feels. But now, since his marriage, even that is changing. In 1993, Bowie released his first solo album in six years, *Black Tie, White Noise* – and then six months later another album, *The Buddha Of Suburbia*, based on theme music he had written for the BBC TV serial drama written by Hanif Kureishi. He even found himself with a hit single, *Jump They Say* – taken from the first LP – and being the master salesman that he is, used this as an opportunity to release a two-volume *Singles Collection*, featuring no fewer than 37 of his hit singles, and also *Bowie: The Video Collection*, a compilation of his music videos. With each new creation, he never misses the chance to recycle his past work.

*Black Tie, White Noise* saw Bowie expressing his own emotions, instead of writing about urban desolation or a future without hope – and that in itself was a welcome departure. He teamed up again with Nile Rodgers for the first time since *Let's Dance*, but chose to explore with him rather than repeat their first success. In *Jump They Say*, he even managed to express his distress at his brother's suicide. This provoked another venomous letter to the tabloid press from his Aunt Pat. Her angry handwriting always explained more than she realized, and this time she wrote: 'I only wish he could have shed his tears and showed his feelings towards him when he was still alive. He did disown him, right from the beginning of Terry's illness…. Now he is using his tragic death to put his record in the charts and I find that not only macabre but pathetic.' Referring to the song's video, she went on: 'The picture of David with his face scarred so much upset me terribly. There is a real resemblance. David looks just like Terry did when he became schizophrenic and started to lose weight …'

Her inchoate anger made one perceive how far he had come; how much he had left behind in his triumph of will over background. The LP itself, with its tender wedding music, its fusion with rock in Morrissey's *I Know It's Gonna Happen Someday* and in Cream's *I Feel Free*, and his freer-than-ever use of jazz saxophone and trumpet, saw the real man at last beginning to emerge from behind his many masks. Significantly, he felt able to work again with the dying Mick Ronson on *I Feel Free*, a song that was a constant part of their stage act twenty years before, and willing to bare his emotions in *Miracle Goodnight*; 'I love you in the morning/I love you in my dreams/I love the sound of making love/The feeling of your skin'.

Bowie and Brian Eno spent the early months of 1994 in Montreux, recording enough material with Reeves, Gabrels, Garson and Kizilcay for five albums, with the first, *Outside*, released 18 months later in September 1995, and the second, *Inside*, without a release date or its time of writing.

Meanwhile, Bowie dibbled and dabbled here and there, using his freedom to the full. Happily married and more relaxed than he had ever been, Bowie joined the editorial board of the magazine *Modern Painters*, regularly attending their quarterly board meetings, dining afterwards at The Gay Hussar and no longer reluctant to discuss or exhibit the artworks that have been a constant part of his life since he left Los Angeles in 1976 and settled in Switzerland and Berlin. These first surfaced when he helped Brian Eno stage the exhibition *Little Pieces From Big Stars* at the Flowers East Gallery in London Fields, East London, between 29 September and 9 October 1994. The exhibition was arranged to raise funds for the charity War Child, which was established in 1993 to help children who had become victims of war in any part of the world. Already it had funded a mobile bakery in Bosnia, supplied insulin to children in Sarajevo, Maglaj and Mostar, and established links between children in Bosnia and Britain. Now with this exhibition, War Child was hoping to start raising money to finance a therapy centre for children in Sarajevo whose lives had been shattered by the conflict between the Croatians and Serbs.

Many leading musicians responded to Eno's request to donate paintings, photographs, drawings and works of sculpture, among them Paul and Linda McCartney, Charlie Watts, Pete Townshend, Bono, Jerry Dammers, Bryan Ferry, Boy George, Adam Ant, Iggy Pop, Dave Stewart, Kate Bush, Neil Tennant, Billy Bragg, Hugh Cornwall, Robert Fripp, Bob Geldof, Michael Hutchence, Julian Lennon, The Levellers, George Michael, Michael Nyman and Nigel Kennedy, but one only had to walk through the door to realize that Bowie's contribution stood head and shoulders above them all. It was an extraordinary experience to walk through the exhibition rooms and suddenly come across his mounted series of 17 mixed media prints, *We Saw A Minotaur*, each designed to be preserved in a handmade red velvet-style box, produced on handmade paper, and numbered and signed by Bowie in an edition of 14.

Once again, Bowie was ridiculed in the music papers and accused of pretentiousness, but one only had to see the collection in this setting to realize he was now an accomplished artist, largely self-taught, perhaps, but no less an artist for that. *We Saw A Minotaur* was designed as a series of prints describing how a playwright Joni Ve Sadd (an anagram of Bowie's real name David Jones) set out to create a futuristic stage play in the year 2003, devising his imagery on a Macintosh Quadra 650 computer, printing each sheet on Arches paper, and hand-colouring his frontispiece. Typically, the content of Bowie's work was totally ignored by the music trade press and the critics from the national newspapers but one could see from the frontis, the two decorative pages and the fourteen sheets of imagery that Bowic had once again devised something new and challenging, with one of his characters being Ira Beno (another anagram, this time for Brian Eno) and the work as a whole revolving around his concept of The Minotaur, a mighty masturbating beast who, like so many of Bowie's creations from the Diamond Dog through to the cover of the second Tin Machine album, was overwhelmed by the size of his own penis.

The critics may have ignored him once again, but when the two boxed sets were put up for auction in aid of War Child at the Royal College of Art on 4 October they fetched among the highest prices in the whole exhibition, with one raising £5,000 and the other £5,100, while Bowie's signed and hand-coloured portrait of The Minotaur was bought for £5,600. This was the first indication that Bowie's work as an artist was now being taken seriously. A few weeks later, between 17 November and 3 December 1994, Bowie's Minotaur images were included in the *Minotaur Myths And Legends* exhibition at the Berkeley Square Gallery, London, alongside the works of internationally renowned artists Michael Ayrton and Elizabeth Frink, with a Bowie-designed exhibition poster.

In April 1995, Bowie staged his first fully retrospective exhibition, *New Afro/Pagan And Work 1975–1995* at the Cork Street Gallery, London, and this, too, was convincing proof that he had used those 20 years of quiet seclusion to become a highly proficient artist with a mastery of several techniques. I particularly liked his 1976 portrait in acrylic oils of Iggy Pop, his more recent

1994 charcoal portraits of Mike Garson, Reeves Gabrels, Erdal
Kizilcay and the drummer Sterling Campbell, completed during
their recording sessions in Switzerland, and a large canvas in
primary colours, *Dry Heads*, showing a black man and a white
woman sharing a shower. Bowie began this impressive work in
Johannesburg in February 1995 while accompanying his wife on a
photo-shoot for *Vogue* magazine, posing with the South African
President Nelson Mandela.

*     *     *     *

And so the point was made – Bowie had become an accomplished
artist besides being a musician, actor, composer, writer, mime
artist, film producer, company director and business executive; not
just a jack of many trades, but a man capable of producing lasting
work in all of them. Next comes the cinema study of *Mesmer*,
already in the can and awaiting distribution when legal disputes
are settled; the movie based on the life of Andy Warhol, which
Bowie began filming with Gary Oldman and Dennis Hopper in
June 1995; the release of *Outside* and *Inside* and the other albums
recorded in Montreux, and the videos made to promote them, and
his current world tour, establishing, if there still remains any
doubt, that rock is truly an art form, and more than that, high art.

Now, approaching his 50th birthday but still looking barely a
day over 35, what may we expect of Bowie after these ventures?
Another rock album? Further excursions into ambient music,
modern jazz, Tin Machine or even, God help us, a return to punk?
Occasional exhibitions of his portraits in acrylic oils, charcoal
drawings or works of sculpture? Concert tours, films, novels or
more learned essays in worthy journals?

The answers are even broader than the questions. As I was
finishing this manuscript, Bowie was winding up his 1996
European tour with a July 21 concert in the town sqaure at
Bellinzona, Switzerland, close to the borders with Italy. He was
then planning a short holiday before further concerts in New York,
Boston and the main Canadian cities at the end of August.

By the time of Bellinzona, Bowie had taken to heart the many
criticisms that he was concentrating too much on his new music
and not giving audiences the chance to hear the songs that first
attracted them to him. His stage act had broadened out to include
*Scary Monsters*, *Heroes*, *Alladin Sane*, *Under Pressure*, *All The*

*Young Dudes* and *The Man Who Sold The World*, as well as his more recent material, and – just like the early Seventies – Bowie was again including Lou Reed's *White Light, White Heat*, always one of his favourite songs. The implication was clear: he was becoming commercialy-motivated again, giving the fans what they want, and preparing to make 1997, his Fiftieth Birthday Year, another big earner.

As always, the plans were being made on a scale that would faze most of David Bowie's contempories. There were art exhibitions being planned in Italy and New York (opening January 1997); a new album being recorded with Brian Eno in the autumn of 1996, and four more songs to be recorded with The Pet Shop Boys; promotion for a new orchestral recording by Philip Glass, who has now produced a symphony based on *Heroes* to follow the *Low* symphony ... and more and more music flowing through, a boxed CD set of Bowie's work for the BBC; music recorded specially for Kodak for a worldwide campaign promoting a new camera; another CD to coincide with the release of the Warhol film *Basquat*, on the Island label, and the latest David Bowie single, *Telling Lies* which is due to be released by RCA as a 12" vinyl single in the autumn of 1996.

At the same time, Bowie was also planning to mark his Fiftieth Birthday Year with a tour of Australia, Hong Kong, Singapore and Japan early in 1997, followed by tours of Britain and Europe (from March onwards), and then a major tour of the United States and Canada, all the while promoting the CDs, films, videos, books, tour merchandise and even the David Bowie calendars that carry his imprint.

Bowie has left every option open, knowing as well as anyone that the music business now runs in three- or five-year cycles with groups like U2, Pink Floyd or The Rolling Stones, or solo stars like Elton John, Eric Clapton, Rod Stewart, Phil Collins or Bowie pacing themselves, never competing for the same audience at the same time, planning their tours so that a new circus never rolls into town before the fans have had time to save up for the tickets, albums and merchandise.

'Do you think rock 'n' roll is going to last?' asked the Father of The Man, and, of course, it has – though everything has changed but the music. Nothing is left to chance any more. Millions of pounds spin upon the turn of a three-minute single, and a global tour may generate £200–300m in revenue.

# Notes

## INTRODUCTION

Almost wholly based on my five-hour conversation with Bowie on 19 November 1969 when he mapped out his future career, explaining that he saw himself more as a writer and artist than a musician, expected to be a millionaire by the time he was 30, and to devote his life to other interests in the arts. Even then he was talking of going to the United States, spending time in Berlin, pursuing intellectual interests, and opting for self-imposed exile.

## CHAPTER 1

Based on interviews with Bowie between 1967 and 1969, two conversations with his father, and my many conversations with Ken Pitt that began on 11 July 1966 and continued through to the mid-80s. Supplemented by my own interviews with other artists, and quotes from other sources:
1. *David Bowie ... In Other Words*, p. 8
2. *Arena*, Spring 1993
3. *Rolling Stone*, 12 February 1976
4. *Rave*, January 1970

## CHAPTER 2

Also based on the 1967–9 Bowie interviews, conversations with his father, my own research at Somerset House, continuing conversations with Pitt, and my contemporary interviews with Peter Frampton, Dick James, Les Conn, etc., supplemented by:
1. *Alias David Bowie*, p. 45
2. *David Bowie: A Chronology*, p. 21, and *The Pitt Report*, p. 21
3. *Alias David Bowie*, p. 107

## CHAPTER 3

Drawn largely from my own recollections of the period, continuing conversations with Pitt and Tony Secunda and other managers, notably Brian Epstein, Tony Calder, Peter Walsh, Larry Parnes, Gordon Mills, Larry Page and Andrew Loog Oldham, and with Ralph Horton, whom I met several times after Secunda hired him as road manager for The Moody Blues. The only time I saw Bowie perform live during this period was when he was with The Manish Boys. It was not impressive. Also:

1. *The Pitt Report*, p. 41

## CHAPTER 4

Based on my continuing conversations with Pitt, particularly on 9 May 1967 at 35 Curzon Street when he told me of his meeting with Andy Warhol, and on my first lengthy interview with Bowie on 5 September 1967. Background information based on my interviews with Marc Bolan, Rick Wakeman, Peter Frampton, Steve Took, Mickey Finn and the continuing guidance of Tony Secunda. Also:

1. *The Pitt Report*, p. 56
2. *The Velvet Underground Story*, p. 11
3. *The Velvet Underground* by Michael Leigh, published by Macfadden Books with a cover showing high-heeled lace-up boots, a whip and a mask, suggesting sado-masochism.
4. The Velvet Underground and Nico released their first LP in the US on the Verve label in March 1967 and in the UK on the Verve label in October 1967.
5. Oscar later changed his name to Paul Nicholas, starring in the film *Tommy*, many West End shows including *Cats* and several TV series. His Christian name really is Oscar. His father is the leading show business lawyer Oscar Beuselinck. Stigwood went on to manage Cream, launch The Bee Gees and produce the film *Saturday Night Fever*.

## CHAPTER 5

Drawn from my interviews with Kenneth Pitt, supplemented by contemporary press reports and background information from Tony Secunda. And:

1. Interview with Kurt Loder, *Rolling Stone*, MTV, 1990

2. *New Musical Express*, 2 September 1978
3. MTV interview, 1990
4. *Alias David Bowie*, pp. 171–5. Their account differs from the one Bowie told me. My understanding is that Terry began receiving full-time treatment in 1966.
5. *Alias David Bowie*, p. 173
6. *The Pitt Report*, p. 76
7. *Alias David Bowie*, pp. 174–5
8. Nothing came of *Orpheus*. The script was sent to the Lord Chamberlain under the old censorship rules and he objected to a scene in which a naked Orpheus kisses another naked man. So the project was dropped.
9. *David Bowie: A Chronology*, p. 39
10. *David Bowie: The Starzone Interviews*, p. 90
11. *In Other Words ... David Bowie*, p. 16

## CHAPTER 6

Based largely on my interviews with Bowie in February and May 1970, my conversations with Pitt after Bowie left him, and with Bolan and Secunda. And also:

1. *Twentieth Century Boy*, pp. 77–8
2. *David Bowie: The Starzone Interviews*, p. 21
3. *The Pitt Report*, p. 86
4. In later interviews, Bowie claimed to have made his film debut in *The Virgin Soldiers* – but he failed the audition and ended up with only six days' work as an extra, for which he was paid £40. His scenes ended up on the cutting room floor.
5. *In Other Words ... David Bowie*, p. 16
6. Reports in the *Independent* (August 1991), supplemented by later stories in the *Guardian* and the *Observer*.
7. *The Pitt Report*, p. 99
8. *In Other Words ... David Bowie*, p. 19

## CHAPTER 7

Based largely on my interviews with David Bowie on 17 November 1969 and 5 February 1970. On the second occasion we spoke for two hours at 39 Manchester Street, and then caught a taxi down to the BBC studios in Lower Regent Street where he introduced me to Mick Ronson and Tony Visconti. Material gathered on these two dates is also used throughout Chapters 8 and

9, supplemented by continuing conversations with Pitt and Secunda, two meetings with Angie Barnett, and later press reports.
1. *The Pitt Report*, p. 119
2. *The Pitt Report*, p. 120
3. *Free Spirit*, pp. 30–1
4. *Backstage Passes*, pp. 9–10
5. *The Pitt Report*, p. 139
6. *David Bowie: The Starzone Interviews*, p. 21

CHAPTER 8

1. *Alias David Bowie*, p. 208
2. *Backstage Passes*, pp. 24–5
3. *Backstage Passes*, p. 11
4. *Free Spirit*, pp. 37–8. My account also includes detail from *Backstage Passes*, supplementing the information Bowie gave me himself on 17 November 1969 and 5 February 1970. Naturally, he did not give me the sexual detail – and I doubt if this would have become known had they not married and divorced.
5. This quotation repeats Bowie's words to me and also paraphrases Angie's third person account in *Backstage Passes*, p. 14. Her comment on his disclosure was, 'He had reason to worry, I think, as events were to demonstrate.'
6. *The Pitt Report*, p. 151
7. *The Pitt Report*, p. 154
8. This last detail and the Angie quote comes from *Backstage Passes*, p. 39. Pitt told me the rest of the story.
9. *Backstage Passes*, pp. 40–1. Pitt told me all this at the time I wrote *The David Bowie Story*, but I decided not to include the material. Peggy phoned him constantly with complaints about Angie and their frequent confrontations, and on two occasions this happened when I was visiting Pitt. Peggy thought they were treating her like a child.

CHAPTER 9

1. *David Bowie: The Starzone Interviews*, p. 23
2. *Observer*, 7 December 1969
3. *The Pitt Report*, p. 183
4. *Backstage Passes*, p. 46. This error is one of many. The Ivor Novello Awards were announced at the end of March after

Bowie and Pitt parted company. Bowie duly appeared at the
Awards Ceremony at The Talk of the Town.
5. *Backstage Passes*, p. 48
6. *Jeremy*, January 1970
7. *Backstage Passes*, p. 96

## CHAPTER 10

Based largely on my interviews with Tony Visconti, Mick Ronson
and Bowie; my long interview with Bowie on 5 February 1970
and then several casual meetings at GEM, where Tony Defries
then had an office. GEM also had an interest in the careers of Gary
Glitter, The New Seekers and the record producer Mike Leander,
and I was a frequent visitor to their offices during this period when
I was also still in constant contact with Ken Pitt and Tony
Secunda. Material also drawn from meetings with Angie, Tony
Defries, and telephone conversations with Defries's family.
1. This key statement is based on Bowie's description to me, *The
   Pitt Report*, conversations with Pitt and Angie's two books.
2. *Backstage Passes*, p. 56
3. *Free Spirit*, p. 47
4. *Backstage Passes*, p. 72
5. *Backstage Passes*, p. 86
6. *The Pitt Report*, p. 212
7. *The Pitt Report*, p. 215
8. *Backstage Passes*, p. 88
9. *The Pitt Report*, p. 218

## CHAPTER 11

The impressions of Defries's character and personality are based
on my own meetings with him. We met at GEM and spoke
occasionally on the phone, and I frequently compared notes with
Pitt, who seemed to know everything that was going on within
Bowie's 'family'. Bowie himself gave me all the background info
on Haddon Hall and Arnold Corns.
1. *Bowie*, Hopkins, p. 61. This is clearly a quote from another
   source, but Hopkins takes quotes from many sources without
   identifying them.
2. *Backstage Passes*, p. 100
3. *In Other Words ... David Bowie*, p. 35
4. *Alias David Bowie*, p. 288

5. *Stardust*, p. 116
6. *Stardust*, pp. 117–19
7. *In Other Words ... David Bowie*, p. 35
8. *Backstage Passes*, p. 109
9. *In Other Words ... David Bowie*, p. 42

## CHAPTER 12

Largely based on my own interviews with David Bowie in February 1971 and on 23 April 1971 at the Chrysalis offices with Angie, and again in October 1971 when he returned from New York and gave me an enthusiastic account of his visit, meeting Warhol and Lou Reed, and watching Elvis perform. We discussed his songwriting at length during this period. Pitt continued to have a constant flow of information about Bowie's affairs, and it was my view that they still might get back together again.
1. *Backstage Passes*, p. 110
2. *Bowie: An Illustrated Record*, p. 24
3. *Bowie: An illustrated Record*, p.24
4. *The Bowie Companion*, pp. 51–9
5. *Alias David Bowie*, pp. 305–6

## CHAPTER 13

Also based on the interviews with Bowie mentioned above, supplemented by discussions with Pitt, who also knew what was happening down at Haddon Hall, partly because Mrs Peggy Jones kept phoning him. Some information also comes from *Stardust*, although Zanetta is much better in his reportage on later events within MainMan.
1. *Stardust*, p. 128
2. John Mendelsohn compares Bowie to Lauren Bacall in *Rolling Stone*. Bowie sniffed dismissively when I asked him what he thought of the comparison.
3. *Stardust*, p. 129
4. *Alias David Bowie*, pp. 317–18
5. *Stardust*, pp. 130–2
6. *The Pitt Report*, p. 219
7. *The Life And Death Of Andy Warhol* by Victor Bockris, p. 262
8. *Backstage Passes*, p. 115
9. *The Life And Death Of Andy Warhol*, p. 61
10. *Backstage Passes*, p. 119

CHAPTER 14

Based on my interview with Bowie at the Royal Ballroom, Tottenham High Road, on 19 January 1972 when he was rehearsing The Spiders from Mars. We ran through the songs on the *Hunky Dory* LP, discussed the material written for Ziggy Stardust, and the problems of fusing rock with theatricality. I also had conversations with Defries and Pitt and interviewed Ronson, Bolder and Woodmansey, but it was already apparent that they were no more than hired hands.
 1. *Backstage Passes*, p. 58
 2. *Backstage Passes*, p. 107
 3. *Backstage Passes*, p. 108
 4. *Rolling Stone*, 28 February 1974

CHAPTER 15

Also based on my January 1972 interview with Bowie, supplemented by discussions with Defries, Pitt and Secunda. The nature of the managerial gamble fascinated me. During this period I was also in frequent contact with staff at MainMan.
 1. *Alias David Bowie*, pp. 356–9
 2. *Rolling Stone*, 9 November 1972
 3. *Stardust*, p. 187
 4. *Alias David Bowie*, p. 379
 5. *Stardust*, p. 184
 6. *Backstage Passes*, pp. 137–9

CHAPTER 16

It was Ken Pitt who told me The Spiders had found God, and he knew MainMan's finances were becoming dodgy. At the time I did not believe him, but it all turned out to be true. This chapter is largely based on information from Pitt and Secunda, with descriptive material based on Pennebaker's film and contemporary reportage. I also discussed all this with Marc Bolan, who was suitably scathing.
 1. *Stardust*, p. 204
 2. *Bowie*, Hopkins, p. 98
 3. *Backstage Passes*, p. 143
 4. *New Musical Express*, 9 June 1973

5. *Backstage Passes*, pp. 140–4
6. *The Pitt Report*, p. 222
7. *Backstage Passes*, p. 148

## CHAPTER 17

Inside material on the MainMan empire comes from Zanetta – no one else talked! *Stardust* is very good on this period. Pitt and Secunda continued to advise me on the significance of the many Defries managerial decisions that were largely misunderstood by the music press.

1. *In Other Words ... David Bowie*, p. 62
2. *Backstage Passes*, p. 152
3. *Stardust*, p. 216
4. *Stardust*, p. 216
5. *Backstage Passes*, p. 173
6. *Bowie: An Illustrated Record*, p. 64
7. *Rolling Stone*, 28 February 1974

## CHAPTER 18

Surprisingly, this and the next chapter are largely based on Kenneth Pitt. Even though they parted with some bad feelings and Pitt had initiated High Court proceedings to recover monies invested in Bowie's career, Bowie nevertheless turned to him both for advice and as a shoulder to lean on when his relationship with Defries fell apart. Between mid-December 1974 and the end of February 1975, Bowie repeatedly phoned Pitt from New York, often talking for several hours – and because I knew them both and had broken no confidences, Pitt kept me fully informed. Zanetta saw the dispute with Defries from within MainMan and recounts their side of it in *Stardust*. The music papers knew Bowie and Defries were communicating through lawyers, but no more than that.

1. *Stardust*, p. 229
2. *Stardust*, p. 230
3. *Stardust*, pp. 231–2
4. *Stardust*, p. 235
5. *Stardust*, pp. 235–6
6. *Stardust*, p. 243
7. *Alias David Bowie*, pp. 472–4

8. *Bowie*, Hopkins, pp. 134–6
9. *Loving John: The Untold Story* by May Pang and Henry Edwards, pp. 190–1

## CHAPTER 19

At the time, it seemed more likely than ever that Bowie and Pitt would start working together again. Pitt told me on 14 March 1975 that Bowie now seemed to be broke and was convinced he had been conned into believing he was a 50:50 shareholder in MainMan when he possessed no equity at all – although he had managed to block RCA's payments to MainMan with a New York court injunction. Angie was now back in London, fighting off creditors – and the situation was so grim that even Bowie's £50 a month allowance to his mother had been cancelled. 'I am afraid the Mafia might get to David before he sorts himself out,' Pitt told me, for that was another secret of the times. The Mafia had by then cornered key sectors of the American music industry. Information also comes from Zanetta, Secunda, the BBC TV documentary *Cracked Actor* and contemporary reports.

1. *Stardust*, p. 287
2. *Stardust*, p. 295
3. *Stardust*, p. 305
4. *David Bowie: The Starzone Interviews*, pp. 118–20
5. *Stardust*, p. 310
6. *Loving John*, pp. 282–4
7. *The Lennon Tapes: John Lennon and Yoko Ono in Conversation with Andy Peebles* (BBC, 1981). This discussion was recorded two days before Lennon's murder and was his first interview in five years.
8. *John Lennon*, Ray Coleman, p. 440
9. *Stardust*, p. 312
10. *David Bowie Profile*, Charlesworth, p. 52
11. *David Bowie: The Starzone Interviews*, pp. 44–50
12. *Bowie*, Hopkins, p. 145. As usual, Hopkins does not identify his sources.
13. *Stardust*, p. 320
14. *Backstage Passes*, pp. 228–9
15. *Arena*, Spring 1993
16. *Backstage Passes*, pp. 244–5

## CHAPTER 20

Largely reconstructed from contemporary press reports. Bowie's flight from Los Angeles to avoid the tax authorities was well concealed at the time, and he managed to keep his Swiss residency secret for nearly three years, pretending to be living wholly in Berlin. The Gillmans managed to trace some information through US court records. For me, it was fascinating to see Bowie travelling along those routes we had discussed six years earlier and finding inspiration just where he thought he would.
1. *David Bowie Profile*, Charlesworth, p. 51
2. *New Musical Express*, 13 September 1980

## CHAPTER 21

Also largely reconstructed from contemporary press reports and my own interpretation of his work during this period.
1. *Backstage Passes*, p. 244
2. *Free Spirit*, p. 148
3. From the radio interviews gathered for *In Other Words ... David Bowie*.
4. This would have been Roy Martin.
5. *New Musical Express*, 12 November 1977
6. *Free Spirit*, p. 148
7. *In Other Words ... David Bowie*, p. 88

## CHAPTER 22

Largely reconstructed from US reportage, augmented by Pitt and Secunda and my own interpretations of the ways Bowie's music was developing.
1. *New Musical Express*, 13 September 1980
2. *David Bowie: The Starzone Interviews*, p. 89
3. *The Andy Warhol Diaries*, p. 132
4. 13 February 1979
5. *Daily Express*, 14 February 1979
6. *Star Special*, 20 May 1979
7. *Variety*, 6 August 1980
8. *The Times*, 29 November 1980. John Lennon used to make the same observation.
9. *David Bowie: The Starzone Interviews*, p. 26
10. BBC Press Release, 7 September 1981

CHAPTER 23

Based on my own researches into the finances of the music industry, studying Bowie's films, contemporary press reportage when he signed his $17m contract with EMI America, critics' reactions to his work in the 80s, and continuing advice from Tony Secunda.

1. *Bowie*, Hopkins, p. 239
2. *Sun*, 11 May 1992
3. *Telegraph Sunday Magazine*, 22 June 1986
4. *The Independent*, July 1987
5. *Sunday Mirror Magazine*, 25 February 1990
6. *Arena*, Spring 1993

CHAPTER 24

For this last chapter I have endeavoured to put Bowie's work in a broad perspective, listening to his music over and over again (although not all those bootlegs!), watching him perform with Tin Machine, revisiting his films and videos, reading his own writing, and studying that small part of his work as an artist, painter and sculptor Bowie has been willing to reveal through his *Minotaur Myths And Legends, War Child* and *New Afro/Pagan* art exhibitions.

1. *Genius And Madness Akin In The World Of Art*, 1933, published in *Dylan Thomas: Early Prose Writings*, J. M. Dent & Sons Ltd., 1971
2. *Globe Hebdo*, Paris, April 1993. Extracts from this interview were published in the *Daily Telegraph*, 15 April 1993.
3. *News Of The World*, 6 June 1993
4. *Hello*, 13 June 1992
5. *Hello*, 13 June 1992
6. *Sun*, 31 March 1993

# Bibliography

Most of the books relating to David Bowie's career are picture books rather than biographies and they tend to be repetitive, so I have given an indication of those that are essential reading:

Anon. *Bowie Lives and Times: Bootleg Records Illustrated*, Babylon Books, Manchester, England, 1979. A useful guide to the bootleg field.

Bockris, Victor, and Malanga, Gerard. *Up-tight: The Velvet Underground Story*, Omnibus Press, London and New York, 1983. Predates Bowie's involvement with Lou Reed but explains Reed's intellectual appeal to Bowie.

Bowie, Angie (edited by Don Short). *Free Spirit*, Mushroom Books, London, 1981. Some useful detail but little insight.

—— (with Patrick Carr). *Backstage Passes: Life On The Wild Side With David Bowie*, Putnam, New York, and Orion, London, 1993. Basically *Free Spirit* recycled, with more attention to the sordid side of their marriage but still little insight.

Cann, Kevin. *David Bowie: A Chronology*, Simon & Schuster, New York, and Vermilion, London, 1983. Packed with useful information but not always correct.

Carr, Roy, and Murray, Charles Shaar. *Bowie: An Illustrated Record*, Avon Books, New York, and Eel Pie, London, 1981. A well-researched analysis of Bowie's music.

Charlesworth, Chris. *David Bowie Profile*, Proteus Books, New York and London, 1981. Brief but balanced cameo.

Claire, Vivian. *David Bowie: The King Of Glitter Rock*, Flash Books, New York and London, 1977. Dreadful.

Currie, David (edited by). *David Bowie: The Starzone Interviews*, Omnibus Press, New York and London, 1985. Good-quality fan-magazine background interviews with Bowie associates. Recommended.

De La Parra, Pimm Jal. *David Bowie: The Concert Tapes*, Amsterdam, 1985. Superb, loving research into Bowie's work, concentrating on the 400-odd known pirate recordings. Find it if you can.

Douglas, David. *Presenting David Bowie*, Pinnacle Books, London, 1975. Superficial with little to commend it.

Edwards, Henry, and Zanetta, Tony. *Stardust: The Life And Times Of David Bowie*, Michael Joseph, London, 1986. This is the best of the later books, taking up the story where my first book finished. Zanetta moved from Warhol's Factory to become President of MainMan and observes the 1972–4 period well – and it's essential reading because no one else had accesss to Bowie at the time. Has little to say beyond 1974. Highly recommended.

Fletcher, David Jeffrey (edited by Rose Winters). *David Robert Jones Bowie: The Discography Of A Generalist 1962–79*, Ferguson, Chicago, 1979. Highly regarded – but almost impossible to find.

Gillman, Peter and Leni. *Alias David Bowie*, Hodder & Stoughton, London, 1986. Tangentially well researched, but the authors admit they do not know the music business – and this is painfully clear. Often inaccurate.

Hoggard, Stuart. *David Bowie: The Illustrated Discography*, revised and updated by Chris Charlesworth. Omnibus Press, New York and London, 1982. Valuable study.

Hopkins, Jerry. *Bowie*, Macmillan, New York, 1985. A few good moments, but without Zanetta's insight or Angie's angst.

Hunter, Ian. *Diary Of A Rock 'n' Roll Star*, original paperback, Panther, 1974. Written by the Mott The Hoople singer. One of the few authentic accounts of rock on the road. Highly recommended.

Jarman, Marshall. *David Bowie's World 7" Discography 1964–81*. Privately published glossy discography. Essential for Bowie collectors.

Juby, Kerry. *David Bowie*, Midas Books, London, 1982. Limited.

—— *In Other Words ... David Bowie*, Omnibus Press, New York and London, 1986. Based on his original radio interviews. Good, strong original material. Highly recommended.

Kamin, Philip, and Goodard, Peter. *David Bowie: Out Of The Cool*, Virgin, London, 1983. Every bit as bad as the title.

Kelleher, Ed. *David Bowie – A Biography In Words And Pictures*, Sire Books, New York, 1977.

Lynch, Kate. *David Bowie: A Rock And Roll Odyssey*, Proteus Books, New York, 1984. Misses the point.

Matthew-Walker, Robert. *David Bowie: Theatre Of Music*, Kensal, 1985. I have been unable to find this book, despite advertising for it extensively.

Miles, Barry. *David Bowie's Black Book*, Omnibus Press, New York and London, 1980. Very good illustrations.

—— *Bowie In His Own Words*, Omnibus Press, 1980. A useful compilation, largely taken from press cuttings.

O'Regan, Denis, and Felippo, Chet. *David Bowie's Serious Moonlight* Doubleday, New York, 1984. An account of Bowie's 1983 Serious

Moonlight Tour with some splendid performance photos. A coffee table book.

Pitt, Kenneth. *Bowie: The Pitt Report*, Design Music, 1983. A fascinating account of Bowie's early career, expanding on the material Pitt gave me for *The David Bowie Story*. Thoroughly recommended.

Rogan, Johnny. *Starmakers And Svengalis*, Queen Anne Press, 1988. The first book to study rock managers. Includes a chapter on Pitt. Recommended, although the true villains escape lightly.

Thompson, Dave. *David Bowie: Moonage Daydream*, Plexus, London, 1987. Thorough analysis. Recommended.

Thomson, Elizabeth, and Gutman, David. *The Bowie Companion*, Macmillan, London, 1993. Useful compilation of essays, with some innovative material, but the overall tone is prissy and pretentious.

Tremlett, George. *The David Bowie Story*, Futura, London, 1974. My first rock book and the first to be written on Bowie.

Various. *The Melody Maker Book Of Bowie*. Not so much a book as a magazine-style account of his early career with contributions from staff writers Allan Jones, Michael Watts, Chris Brazier and *MM* editor Ray Coleman. Highly recommended.

Various. *Rock's Nova Bowie*. Undated. Interesting compilation of essays by Michael Gross, David Douglas, Eric Van Lustbader and Mick Rock.

Various. *David Bowie – A Portrait*, Wise Publications, 1974.

# Appendix: Timeframe

This appendix puts the events of David Bowie's life in sequence. When *The David Bowie Story* was published, so many readers wrote to me commenting on the chronology that I made them part of each subsequent book, compiling the chronologies before writing the first chapter, thereby establishing boundaries for each book as a whole. Most other rock writers have since adopted a similar device. It is not an easy one. The difficulties lie in gathering and cross-checking the material. One cannot rely upon any one source for fear of inaccuracy, and so one has to cross-check with trade papers, music magazines, radio, television, books, record companies and, best of all, by being there.

*1933*

November 21          On his 21st birthday Haywood Stenton Jones inherits £3,000.

December 19          Claiming to be 23, Jones marries Hilda Louise Sullivan. He uses his inheritance to launch her career as a singer.

*1934*          His venture fails. Jones opens a drinking club The Boop A Doop.

*1935*          The club fails. Jones becomes a porter at the Russell Hotel, later joining the staff of Dr Barnardo's Homes.

*1937*

November 5          Birth of Terry Burns, illegitimate son of Peggy Burns by Jack Rosenberg.

*1938*

January          Birth of Annette, illegitimate daughter of Haywood Jones and a Birmingham nurse. The child is adopted by Jones and his wife.

1943
August     29        Birth of Myra Ann, second illegitimate child of Peggy
                     Burns, following her affair with a married man.

1946                 Jones returns from the War to find his wife living with
                     another man. He meets Peggy in a restaurant in Tun-
                     bridge Wells.

1947
January    8         David Robert Jones – i.e. DAVID BOWIE – born at 40
                     Stansfield Road, Brixton, London.
June       26        Hilda Jones granted decree nisi.
August     11        Decree nisi made absolute.
September  12        Haywood Jones marries Peggy Burns. Terry and Annette
                     live with them intermittently.

1951
November   12        Bowie's first day at Stockwell Infants School.

1955
autumn               Terry joins the Royal Air Force. Myra Ann marries an
                     Egyptian.

1957
early                The family move to 4 Plaistow Grove, Bromley. Bowie
                     attends Burnt Ash Primary School, joins church choir
                     and Wolf Cubs. His friendship begins with George
                     Underwood and Geoffrey MacCormack.

1958
September            Bowie starts at Bromley Technical High School.
November             Terry returns home after three years in the RAF.
                     Introduces Bowie to jazz, Soho, the Beat poets and Jack
                     Kerouac.

1960                 Bowie takes saxophone lessons with the jazz musician
                     Ronnie Ross.
                     In their third year at High School, Bowie and Underwood
                     fall under the influence of art teacher Owen Frampton
                     whose son Peter also becomes a musician.

1961
spring               Bowie and Underwood fight over a girl. Bowie's left eye
                     is permanently injured. He has several operations and is
                     off school for eight months.

1962
July                 Bowie and Underwood form their first group The Kon-
                     Rads, with Bowie calling himself Dave Jay. Later they
                     call themselves The Hooker Brothers.

| 1963 | | Bowie and Underwood trawl the rhythm 'n' blues clubs, especially The Crawdaddy and Eel Pie Island. |
|---|---|---|
| July | | Bowie leaves school with O-levels in Art and Woodwork. Begins work in an advertising agency, with a Saturday job at Vic Furlong's record shop in Bromley. |
| August | 30 | The Kon-Rads audition for Decca Records. They are turned down. |
| | | Bowie and Underwood form The King Bees with Dave Howard (bass), Roger Black (lead guitar) and Bobby Allen (drums). |
| *1964* | | |
| April | | Bowie seeks finance from the washing machine tycoon John Bloom. Introduced to Les Conn who also manages Marc Bolan. Conn books The King Bees for Bloom's wedding anniversary party, finds them dates and a recording contract. |
| June | 5 | Davie Jones and The King Bees release *Liza Jane/Louie Louie Go Home* (Vocalion). |
| June | 6 | Bowie seen fleetingly on *Juke Box Jury* (BBC TV) when the record is played. |
| September | | The King Bees release *You're Holding Me Down/I've Gotta*. Bowie leaves to join The Manish Boys. |
| October | | The Manish Boys appear occasionally at The Marquee. Bowie meets Dana Gillespie. |
| November | 2 | Bowie's first publicity stunt. Claims to have founded The International League for the Preservation of Animal Filament on behalf of people with long hair. |
| November | 12 | The stunt leads to an interview on *Tonight* (BBC TV) with Cliff Michelmore. Jimmy Page and Screaming Lord Sutch also took part in the stunt. |
| December | | The Manish Boys booked to tour with Gene Pitney, Gerry and The Pacemakers, The Kinks and Marianne Faithfull. |
| *1965* | | |
| March | 3 | Another stunt. The national press report that Bowie is refusing to have his hair cut before appearing on TV. |
| March | 5 | The Manish Boys release *I Pity The Fool/Take My Tip* (Parlophone). The B-side was Bowie's first recorded song. Jimmy Page played lead guitar. |
| March | 8 | Despite the long hair stunt, The Manish Boys appear on *Gadzooks! It's All Happening* (BBC TV). |
| April/May | | The Manish Boys break up, with Bowie joining The Lower Third. |
| August | | Ralph Horton becomes their manager. Books them for concerts with The Moody Blues and The Who. Other members of the group were Dennis 'Teacup' Taylor (lead guitar), Graham Rivens (bass) and Phil Lancaster (drums). |

| August | 20 | Bowie releases *You've Got A Habit Of Leaving/Baby Loves That Way* as 'Davy Jones' (Parlophone), writing both songs. |
| August | 21 | Begins Sunday afternoon gigs at The Marquee. |
| September | 14 | Signs publishing contract with Sparta Music. He receives £10 each time one of his songs is recorded and 50 per cent of all subsequent royalties. |
| September | 15 | Horton contacts Kenneth Pitt, who suggests Davy Jones needs to change his name: he becomes DAVID BOWIE. |
| December | 31 | First overseas appearances, supporting Arthur Brown at the Golf Drouet Club, Paris. |

*1966*

| January | 14 | David Bowie with The Lower Third release *Can't Help Thinking About Me/And I Say To Myself* (Pye). Produced by Tony Hatch. |
| January | 29 | The Lower Third break up after a row over money. Bowie advertises for new musicians. |
| February | 7 | Begins rehearsals with new group The Buzz – Derek Fearnley (bass), Derek Boyes (organ) and John Hutchinson (guitar). First gigs in Leicester (10th) and The Marquee (11th). |
| February | 12 | *Can't Help Thinking About Me* creeps into the *Melody Maker* chart at No.45, rises to No.37 (9 February) and No.34 (26th), and then disappears. |
| February | 26 | Collapses on stage in Chelmsford. |
| March | 4 | Debuts on *Ready, Steady, Go!* TV show, dressed in a white suit. Also on the show that week were The Small Faces and The Yardbirds. |
| April | 1 | David Bowie's first solo single *Do Anything You Say/Good Morning Girl* (Pye). Produced by Hatch. Issued in US by Warner Brothers. |
| April | 3–5 | Visits Scotland promoting the single. Appears at Green's Playhouse, Glasgow, with Johnny Kidd and The Pirates. |
| April | 17 | Meets Kenneth Pitt for the first time at The Marquee where he appears on Sunday afternoons in *The Bowie Showboat*. |
| August | 19 | David Bowie's second solo single *I Dig Everything/I'm Losing You* (Pye). Produced by Tony Hatch. |
| September | | Leaves Pye. Pitt arranges for him to sign a recording contract with Denny Cordell's new label Deram. Cat Stevens and Denny Laine also sign to Deram. Cordell's assistant is Tony Visconti. |
| November | 8 | Pitt goes to New York to discuss a record deal. Meets Andy Warhol and Lou Reed. Brings back The Velvet Underground and The Fugs LPs. |
| November | 13 | Pitt offered $30,000 advance for Bowie's songwriting contract. Later returns to London to find that Bowie and Horton have agreed a £500 deal with Essex Music in his absence. |
| November | 25 | With Pitt still out of the country, Bowie sacks his backing |

group. Their final appearance was in Shrewsbury (2 December).

**December 2**  David Bowie's third solo single *Rubber Band/The London Boys* (Deram). Produced by Mike Vernon.

*1967*

**January 18**  Bowie asks Horton to release him from his management contract.

**January 30**  Oscar releases *Over The Wall We Go* (Reaction), written by Bowie. His first song recorded by another artist. Oscar now better known as the TV and stage star Paul Nicholas.

**April 14**  David Bowie's fourth solo single *The Laughing Gnome/The Gospel According To Tony Day* (Deram). Produced by Mike Vernon.

**April 25**  Bowie signs five-year management contract with Kenneth Pitt.

**June 1**  Bowie's first LP *David Bowie* released by Deram, making him the first British artist to record an album without first having a hit single.

**June 11**  Leaves home and moves into a room at Kenneth Pitt's apartment at 39 Manchester Street, London.

**July 7**  Ronnie Hilton releases his version of *The Laughing Gnome* (HMV).

**July 14**  David Bowie's fifth solo single *Love You Till Tuesday/Did You Ever Have A Dream?* (Deram). Produced by Mike Vernon.

**September 13**  Spends three days making 14-minute film *The Image* (Border Films).

**September 15**  Slender Plenty release their version of Bowie's *Silver Tree Top School For Boys* (Polydor).

**October 28**  Joins the actors' trade union Equity.

**November 10**  Appears on Dutch TV show *Fan Club* to promote release there of *Love You Till Tuesday*.

Begins attending Lindsay Kemp mime classes at The Dance Centre, Covent Garden. Kemp asks him to write music for *Pierrot In Turquoise*.

**December 1**  The Beatstalkers, then managed by Pitt, release *Silver Tree Top School For Boys* (CBS).

**December 18**  Appears live on *Top Gear* (BBC Radio).

**December 24**  Appears live again on *Top Gear*.

**December 28**  First mime appearance as Cloud in *Pierrot In Turquoise* at the Oxford New Theatre. Kemp plays Pierrot and Jack Birkett, Harlequin.

*1968*

**January 3–5**  Travels with Kemp, Birkett and costume designer Natasha Korniloff to present *Pierrot In Turquoise* at the Rose Hill Theatre, Cumberland.

**January 30**  Wearing powdered wig and eighteenth-century costume, appears in BBC TV play *The Pistol Shot* with Hermione Farthingale, dancing a minuet.

| February | 26–7 | Goes to Hamburg to record three songs for TV programme *4–3–2–1 Musik für junge Leute* (ZDF). |
| March | 5–16 | Appears in *Pierrot In Turquoise* at the Mercury Theatre, Notting Hill Gate. |
| March | 22 | Billy Fury's version of Bowie's song *Silly Boy Blue* released by Parlophone. |
| March | 26–30 | *Pierrot In Turquoise* presented at The Little Theatre, Palmers Green. |
| April | 22 | Leaves Deram complaining they have failed to promote his records. The Beatles' company Apple turn him down. |
| May | 26 | Another appearance on *Top Gear*, listed as David Bowie and The Tony Visconti Orchestra. They perform five songs with Steve Took of Tyrannosaurus Rex on backing vocals. |
| June | 3 | Presents a 12-minute mime act at the Royal Festival Hall, supporting Tyrannosaurus Rex, Roy Harper and Stefan Grossman. |
| | | With so little money coming in, Bowie takes a part-time job operating a photocopying machine at Legastat, a printing and stationery shop in Carey Street. |
| June | | Auditions twice for the London stage musical *Hair* and also for the films *Triple Echo* and *Sunday Bloody Sunday*; all unsuccessful. |
| June | 21 | The Beatstalkers release Bowie's *Everything Is You* (CBS). He sang backing vocals. |
| July | | Auditions for a lead role in the film *The Virgin Soldiers*; ends up with a tiny role. |
| August | | Bowie and Hermione Farthingale move to 22 Clareville Grove, South Kensington, and form the multi-media trio with guitarist Tony Hill, who is soon replaced by John Hutchinson. They call the trio Turquoise. |
| September | 14 | Turquoise make their debut at The Round House and soon change their name to Feathers. |
| September | 19 | Goes to Hamburg for another appearance on *4–3–2–1 Musik für junge Leute* (ZDF). |
| October/November | | Films his part in *The Virgin Soldiers*, but most of it ends up on the cutting room floor. |
| November | 17 | Feathers appear at Hampstead Country Club. |
| December | 6 | Feathers appear at The Arts Laboratory, Drury Lane, London. |
| December | 7 | Feathers appear at Sussex University. |

*1969*

| January | 11 | The Beatstalkers release their third Bowie song *When I'm Five* (CBS). |
| | | Feathers appear at The Round House where they are seen by Angie Barnett and Calvin Mark Lee. |
| January | 22 | Bowie films a TV commercial for Lyons Maid's new ice cream LUV, which was being marketed as 'the pop ice cream'. The commercial was filmed on a London bus. |

| | | |
|---|---|---|
| January–<br>– February | 26<br>8 | Makes the film *Love You Till Tuesday*, which was originally intended for German TV. Pitt financed the film and Bowie wrote a new song specially for it – *Space Oddity*. Hermione Farthingale left him while the film was being made. |
| February | 11 | Now just a duo, Bowie and Hutchinson appear as Feathers at Sussex University. |
| February | 15 | Supports Tyrannosaurus Rex during short tour, visiting Birmingham, Croydon, Manchester, Bristol, Liverpool and Brighton. |
| April | 9 | Calvin Mark Lee invites Bowie to dinner with Angie Barnett and takes them to King Crimson's reception at The Speakeasy. They become lovers. |
| April | 14 | Bowie moves to 24 Foxgrove Road, Beckenham, becoming Mary Finnegan's lover. Angie Barnett later moves in. They form Beckenham Arts Laboratory. |
| April | 22 | Concert at Wigmore Hall with Tim Hollier. |
| May/June | | Calvin Mark Lee, who works for Mercury Records in London, introduces Bowie to the parent company in Chicago. |
| June | 14 | *Colour Me Pop* (BBC-2) with The Strawbs. |
| June | 20 | Bowie signs Mercury Records contract. Receives £1,250 advance plus £20 a week when working in recording studio. Records *Space Oddity*. |
| July | 5 | *Space Oddity* played when The Rolling Stones stage their free concert in Hyde Park. Bowie records an Italian version *Ragazza Solo, Ragazza Solo* (Philips). |
| July | 11 | David Bowie's sixth single *Space Oddity/Wild Eyed Boy From Freecloud* (Philips – Philips had taken over Mercury since he signed the contract). |
| July | 15 | Hounslow Arts Laboratory with Dave Cousins of The Strawbs. |
| July | 16 | Begins recording LP with Tony Visconti as producer. With some breaks, they work through until mid-October. |
| July | 20 | The US Apollo 11 space craft lands on the moon with *Space Oddity* played constantly on TV and radio to accompany the live coverage. |
| July | 24 | Malta for the International Song Festival and then Monsummano, Pistoia, Italy, for the Premio Internazionale Del Disco where he wins the Best Produced Record award for *When I Live My Dream*. |
| August | 3 | Returns for appearance at Beckenham Arts Laboratory and hears that his father is ill. |
| August | 5 | Haywood Stenton Jones dies of pneumonia. Bowie hears the news while recording with Visconti at Trident Studios. |
| August | 11 | His father's funeral. |
| August | 16 | Plays at and helps to organize Beckenham Free Festival, which prompts his song *Memory Of A Free Festival*. |
| August | 25 | Holland for appearance on TV show *Doebidoe*. |
| September/November | | Belatedly, *Space Oddity* becomes his first hit record, entering the Top 10 charts in all the British music papers. |

| October | 8 | Tours with Humble Pie and Love Sculpture for 18 days, presenting an acoustic set which is jeered by audiences who boo and whistle. Bowie shaken by the experience. |
|---|---|---|
| October | 9 | First appearance on TV show *Top Of The Pops* (BBC). |
| October | 28 | Berlin to appear on German TV show *4-3-2-1 Musik für junge Leute* (ZDF). |
| November | 2-4 | Switzerland to appear on TV show *Hits-a-Gogo*. |
| November | 4 | David Bowie's second LP, also titled *David Bowie*, released by Mercury. This was later reissued with the title *Man Of Words, Man Of Music*. |
| November | 7 | Begins nine-day Scottish tour. |
| November | 20 | Presents *An Evening With David Bowie* at Purcell Room, London – and is angry when he hears most newspapers had not been invited. |
| November | 21 | Appears at Devizes Poperama; Bowie made many one-night stands that autumn, but this one was for the new young promoter Mel Bush who went on to become a top promoter. Bush presented Bowie's seven-week British tour in 1973.<br><br>Bowie awarded an Ivor Novello Award for *Space Oddity* by the Songwriters' Guild. |
| November | 30 | Save Rave Charity Concert at the Palladium with Dusty Springfield, The Equals, The Mojos and Tiny Tim. Attended by Princess Margaret. |
| December | 5 | Dublin to appear on TV show *Like Now* (RTE).<br><br>Readers of *Music Now* vote David Bowie the Year's Best Newcomer.<br><br>Angie Barnett returns to her family in Cyprus after a row with Bowie; he proposes marriage to her by letter and by phone. |

| *1970* | | |
|---|---|---|
| January | | Scotland to appear on *Cairngorms Ski Night* (Grampian TV) with Lindsay Kemp and to film a programme for Scottish TV. |
| February | 5 | Mick Ronson performs with Bowie for the first time at the BBC Paris Cinema, Lower Regent Street. They form Hype with Tony Visconti (bass) and John Cambridge (drums). |
| February | 14 | Voted Brightest Hope for 1970 by readers of *Disc And Music Echo* in their annual poll. |
| February | 22 | Hype debut at The Round House, supporting Country Joe McDonald and The Fish. |
| March | | Bowie invited to write a musical adaptation of Sir Walter Scott's *The Fair Maid Of Perth*.<br><br>Pitt arranges for Bowie to make a TV commercial for Wall's Sausages. Bowie angrily rejects it. |
| March | 6 | David Bowie releases his seventh single *The Prettiest Star/Conversation Piece* (Mercury). Marc Bolan plays lead guitar on the A-side. |
| March | 12 | MENCAP Charity Show at the Royal Albert Hall. |

|            |    | Afterwards, Bowie tells Pitt that he and Angie Barnett are to marry. |
|------------|----|---|
| March      | 20 | Bowie marries Angela Barnett at Bromley – and finds his mother waiting on the registry office doorstep. She has invited the local press. |
| March      | 25 | Records two *Sounds Of The Seventies* shows with The Hype (BBC Radio). |
| March      | 30 | John Cambridge leaves The Hype after their gig at the Star Hotel, Croydon – and is replaced by Woody Woodmansey. |
| March      | 31 | Bowie tells Pitt he wants to manage himself. |
| April/May  |    | Records his third LP *The Man Who Sold The World*, again with Visconti as his producer. Tells Olav Wyper at Philips that he is unhappy with Pitt. Given the names of three lawyers, including Tony Defries. |
| May        | 7  | Visits Pitt with Defries. They fail to agree a settlement, so Bowie bides his time waiting for his contract with Pitt to expire. Defries later becomes his new manager. |
| May        | 10 | Bowie receives his Ivor Novello Award during a ceremony at The Talk of the Town which is broadcast to the US by satellite. The Rolling Stones and John Lennon appear on the same show. |
| June       | 8  | David Bowie releases eighth single *Memory Of A Free Festival, Parts I and II* (Philips). |
| August     |    | Plays alto sax on *Oh Baby/Universal Love* as member of Dib Cochran and The Earwigs (Bell). Both were Eddie Cochran songs. Marc Bolan, Mickey Finn, Rick Wakeman and Tony Visconti also played on this single. |
| October    |    | Marc Bolan shortens his group's name to T. Rex and has first hit with *Ride A White Swan*. He targets the teenage market and goes on to sell 37m records in three years. |
| October    | 23 | Bowie signs a £5,000 publishing agreement with Chrysalis. He agrees to deliver at least a hundred songs over the next five years. |

*1971*

|            |    |   |
|------------|----|---|
| January    | 17 | David Bowie's ninth single *Holy Holy Holy/Black Country Rock* (Mercury). A-side produced by Blue Mink, B-side by Visconti. Appears on TV to promote the single wearing a Mr Fish frock. |
| January    | 27 | Visits US to promote *The Man Who Sold The World* LP, touring radio stations wearing frocks. His feminine appearance provokes an angry response. |
| February   |    | Forms group Arnold Corns with dressmaker Freddi Burretti, whom he renames Rudi Valentino. Mick Ronson, Trevor Bolder and Woodmansey join in. |
| April      |    | *The Man Who Sold The World* LP released in the UK with a front cover portrait showing Bowie wearing a dress and looking more feminine than ever. |
| April      | 24 | In an interview with the *Daily Mirror*, Bowie insists: 'My sexual life is normal'. |

| April | 30 | Peter Noone releases *Oh You Pretty Things*, with Bowie playing piano. They record three other songs with producer Mickie Most. |
|---|---|---|
| May | 7 | Arnold Corns release *Hang On To Yourself/Moonage Daydream* (B&C), written and produced by Bowie, who also sang the vocals – although he did not admit this at the time for contractual reasons. |
| May | 28 | The Bowies' son Duncan Zowie Haywood Jones born at Bromley Hospital, prompting Bowie to write *Kooks*. |
| June | 5 | Appears *In Concert* with John Peel (BBC Radio), performing *Hunky Dory* with Ronson, Bolder and Woodmansey plus Underwood and Dana Gillespie. |
| June | 20 | Memorable acoustic set at Glastonbury Fayre. Bowie goes on stage after a wet night, just as dawn is breaking, with the sun shining directly upon him. |
| July/September | | Begins recording songs for the LPs *Hunky Dory* and *Ziggy Stardust*. Defries in New York negotiating a record deal with RCA. |
| July | 28 | Performance at Hampstead Country Club with *Pork* actors in the audience. Bowie later sees many performances of the Andy Warhol play, and members of the cast subsequently join Defries in promoting Bowie's career. |
| August | 1 | Bowie signs recording agreement with GEM, the company jointly owned by Defries and music business accountant Laurence Myers, and also a management contract with Defries. |
| September | | The Bowies, Ronson and Defries go to New York to sign the RCA contract (9th). RCA pay $37,500 for each of three LPs. Meets Lou Reed and Iggy Pop, visits Andy Warhol and sees Elvis Presley at Madison Square Gardens. |
| September/November | | With the *Hunky Dory* LP finished, Bowie continues recording *Ziggy Stardust* and other songs. |
| October | 15 | Peter Noone releases *Walnut Whirl/Right On Mother* (RAK). Bowie plays piano on the B-side. |
| November | | Holidays in Cyprus, staying with Angie's parents. On the way home, their plane hits an electrical storm. Bowie reluctant to travel by plane thereafter. |
| December | 17 | Signs an agreement whereby his Mercury LPs are assigned to RCA with copyright passing to GEM. David Bowie's fourth LP *Hunky Dory* released by RCA. |

*1972*

| January | 7 | David Bowie's tenth single *Changes/Andy Warhol* released by RCA. |
|---|---|---|
| January | 22 | *Melody Maker* front-pages the interview in which Bowie says: 'I'm gay and always have been, even when I was David Jones.' This is headlined 'OH! YOU PRETTY THING'. When his mother phones, Bowie says: 'Don't believe a word of it, Mum' – but he goes along with the image the story gives him and the story makes his name. |

| February | 3 | Begins seven-month British concert tour, with his clothes designed by Freddi Burretti and his Ziggy Stardust stage personality evolving as the tour progresses. |
| | | Iggy Pop arrives in London. Travels with Bowie and they also record together. |
| February | 11 | Terry Burns marries Olga, a fellow patient at the Cane Hill mental institution, moving into a bedsitter near Bowie's home in Beckenham, Haddon Hall. |
| April | 25 | Bowie's contract with Pitt expires. |
| April | 28 | David Bowie's eleventh single *Starman/Suffragette City* released by RCA. |
| June | 9 | David Bowie's fifth LP *The Rise And Fall Of Ziggy Stardust And The Spiders From Mars* released by RCA. This proves to be his break-through LP with 8,000 British sales in its first week. |
| June | 30 | Defries establishes MainMan after buying an off-the-shelf company and changing its name. Bowie believes he holds a half-share. Defries opens an office in Gunter Grove, Fulham, and then a New York office, largely staffed by actors from the cast of *Pork*. |
| July | 8 | Bowie appears with Lou Reed in Save the Whale concert at the Festival Hall, London, staged by Friends of the Earth. *Melody Maker* headlines its review 'A STAR IS BORN' and in *The Times* he is acclaimed as 'T.S. Eliot with a rock 'n' roll beat'. |
| July | 14–16 | RCA fly US journalists into London to see Bowie perform at the Friars Hall, Aylesbury – and he startles them all by appearing in luminous green with bright orange hair and performing his Ziggy Stardust routine. |
| July | 16 | Defries stages a happening at The Dorchester Hotel – Bowie dresses outrageously, kisses everyone in sight (including Lou Reed and Iggy Pop), while the US press are ushered in for individual 15-minute interviews – and then he goes home to his £8-a-week flat. |
| July | | *Glastonbury Fayre* LP released, to pay off the debts of last June's festival. Bowie contributes the song *Superman*. Other songs from Marc Bolan, Pete Townshend and The Grateful Dead. |
| July | 28 | Mott The Hoople release *All The Young Dudes* (CBS), written and produced by Bowie. |
| July/August | | Bowie and Ronson co-produce Lou Reed's LP *Transformer*, with Bowie temporarily living at Grosvenor House to save travelling time. |
| August | 19–20 | Presents his Ziggy Stardust stage show at the Rainbow Theatre, London, with posters by Underwood, choreography by Lindsay Kemp and costumes by Natasha Korniloff. Roxy Music open the show, which is then taken to Bournemouth, Bristol, Manchester, Sunderland, Sheffield and Liverpool. |
| September | 1 | David Bowie's 12th single *John I'm Only Dancing/Hang* |

| | | |
|---|---|---|
| | | *On To Yourself* released by RCA. |
| September | 8 | Mott The Hoople LP *All The Young Dudes* released by CBS. Produced by Bowie. |
| September | 10 | Leaves to begin his first US tour, which opens in Cleveland (22nd), criss-crossing North America in a hired Greyhound bus. In Britain, his success prompts RCA to rerelease *Hunky Dory* and *The Man Who Sold The World*. |
| September | 28 | Sell-out concert at Carnegie Hall brings rave reviews in New York press. Lillian Roxon's review in *The New York Daily News* headlined 'A STAR IS BORN'. |
| November | | Lou Reed releases *Walk On The Wild Side/Perfect Day* (RCA). Both tracks produced by Bowie. This becomes Reed's most successful single in both Britain and the US. |
| November | | Bowie remixes the *Raw Power* LP for Iggy Pop. |
| November | 24 | David Bowie's 13th single *The Jean Genie/Ziggy Stardust* released by RCA. |
| December | 2 | Bowie's US tour ends with two sell-out concerts in Philadelphia. |
| December | 8 | Lou Reed's LP *Transformer* released by RCA. Produced by Bowie and Ronson. Backing vocals by Bowie, who writes the track *Wagon Wheel*. |
| December | 23–4 | Bowie presents two Christmas shows at the Rainbow Theatre. The audience asked to bring toys for Dr Barnardo's. |

*1973*

| | | |
|---|---|---|
| January | | After concerts in Glasgow, Edinburgh, Preston and Newcastle, Bowie returns to the studios to finish his next LP *Aladdin Sane*. |
| January | 17 | Appears on the *Russell Harty Plus* show (LWT) singing a new song *Drive-In Saturday*. |
| January | 25 | Leaves Southampton on the *Queen Elizabeth 2* to begin a 100-day world tour in the US. |
| February | 14 | The US leg of the tour opens at Radio City Music Hall, New York. Mike Garson joins Bowie on piano. Salvador Dali attends the concert. |
| April | 6 | David Bowie's 14th single *Drive-In Saturday/Round And Round* released by RCA. |
| April | 8–20 | Begins the Japanese leg of the tour with eight concerts, including one at Hiroshima. |
| April | 13 | David Bowie's sixth LP *Aladdin Sane* released by RCA with British advance orders totalling 100,000. |
| April | 21 | Leaves Japan by boat for Vladivostock. Catches Trans-Siberian Express to Moscow and Orient Express to Paris. Stays over in Moscow to see the annual May Day Parade. |
| May | 4 | Arrives back at Charing Cross Station, London. Several hundred fans are waiting. |
| May | 10 | The Bowies visit Pitt for the first time in three years, with tickets for the Earls Court concert. |
| May | 12 | Begins seven-week British tour at Earls Court, wearing |

|  |  |  |
|---|---|---|
|  |  | new costumes by Japanese designer Kansai. Visits 37 cities in 45 days, with 150,000 people attending his concerts. |
| June | 1 | Iggy Pop's LP *Raw Power* released by RCA, after being remixed by Bowie. |
| June | 22 | David Bowie's 15th single *Life On Mars?/The Man Who Sold The World* released by RCA. |
| July | 2–3 | Final shows at Hammersmith Odeon filmed by D.A. Pennebaker, who also directed Bob Dylan movie *Don't Look Back* and *Monterey Pop*. Bowie shocks the audience by announcing retirement – although it was only Ziggy who was being laid to rest, not Bowie. |
| July | 4 | Bowie hosts his 'retirement party' at the Café Royal in Regent Street, London. |
| July | 9 | Leaves for Paris to begin recording at the live-in studio Château d'Herouville, where Marc Bolan and Elton John have also recorded. |
|  |  | By the end of July, Bowie has five LPs in the Top 40, with three in the Top 15. |
| August/September |  | Bowie holidays in Rome, working on a stage musical adaptation of George Orwell's *1984* for which he writes twenty songs, without establishing that the rights to *1984* are available. |
| September | 8 | Decca rereleases *The Laughing Gnome* (1967) which now becomes a hit, selling 250,000 copies. |
| September | 29 | Sweeps the board in the *Melody Maker* readers' poll. Voted Top British Male Singer, Top Producer and Top Composer. *The Jean Genie* and *Drive-In Saturday* voted top singles. |
| October | 12 | David Bowie's 16th single *Sorrow/Amsterdam* released by RCA. |
| October | 18–20 | Films 90-minute *Midnight Special* (NBC TV) with The Troggs and Marianne Faithfull. Calls it *The 1980 Floor Show*, a punning title as he is unable to secure the rights to *1984*. |
| October | 19 | David Bowie's seventh LP *Pin-Ups* released by RCA with advance orders totalling 150,000. |
| October |  | Moves to a flat in Maida Vale for three months and then to Oakley Street, Chelsea, renting a house from actress Diana Rigg. |
| December | 11 | RCA host luncheon to mark his success in having five LPs in the charts at the same time for 19 weeks. In Britain alone Bowie sold 1,056,400 LPs and 1,024,068 singles during the year. |
| *1974* |  |  |
| January/February |  | Spends two months recording at Olympic Studios, Barnes, adapting much of his *1984* material for his next LP *Diamond Dogs*. |
| January | 12 | Lulu releases *The Man Who Sold The World/Watch That Man* (Polydor), written by Bowie and jointly arranged |

|  |  | and produced by Bowie and Ronson. Bowie on backing vocals and saxophone. |
|---|---|---|
| January | 26 | Mick Ronson releases his first solo single *Love Me Tender* (RCA). |
| February | 15 | David Bowie's 17th single *Rebel Rebel/Queen Bitch* released by RCA. |
| March | 1 | Mick Ronson's first LP *Slaughter On 10th Avenue* released by RCA. Bowie wrote *Growing Up And I'm Fine* and co-wrote *Music Is Lethal* and *Hey Ma Get Pa*. |
| March | 15 | Steeleye Span release *Now We Are Six* (Chrysalis) with Bowie playing saxophone on one track. |
| March | 22 | Dana Gillespie releases LP *Weren't Born A Man* (RCA), co-produced by Bowie. Includes his songs *Andy Warhol* and *Backed A Loser*. |
| April | 11 | David Bowie's 18th single *Rock 'n' Roll Suicide/Quicksand* released by RCA. |
| April | 11 | Bowie leaves London for New York, living almost openly with black singer Ava Cherry. They stay initially at the Sherry Netherlands Hotel. Ava introduces him to soul music. Corinne (a.k.a. Coco) Schwab becomes Bowie's Personal Assistant. |
| April | 24 | David Bowie's eighth LP *Diamond Dogs* released by RCA. |
| May |  | Begins rehearsing with a new touring band that includes Mike Garson (piano), Herbie Flowers (bass), Tony Newman (drums), Carlos Alomar and Earl Slick (guitars). |
| June | 14 | David Bowie's 19th single *Diamond Dogs/Holy Holy* released by RCA. |
| June | 14 | *Diamond Dogs* concert tour opens in Montreal, fusing dance, mime and music with stage sets by Jules Fisher, choreography by Toni Basil and Michael Kamen as Musical Director. |
| July | 14–15 | Tower Theatre, Philadelphia, concerts recorded for live LP. Musicians threaten strike when demanding more money. |
| July | 20 | First leg of tour ends at Madison Square Gardens, New York. Defries cancels London dates because of tour costs. |
| July | 21 | Bowie distressed on learning that he has never owned 50 per cent of MainMan. |
| August | 11–18 | Returns to Philadelphia to record next LP at Sigma Sound Studios, mainly with black musicians. |
| September | 2 | *Diamond Dogs* tour resumes at Los Angeles Amphitheatre. Show filmed for BBC TV documentary *Cracked Actor*. Bowie begins to slim down the stage show, concentrating more on soul music. |
| September | 12 | Bowie revives Eddie Floyd classic *Knock On Wood* for his 20th single, coupled with *Panic In Detroit* (RCA). |
| October | 29 | The Philadelphia-recorded double-LP *David Live* released by RCA. His ninth LP. |

| December | 1 | What began as the *Diamond Dogs* tour ends in Atlanta. Police raid the after-tour party at the Hyatt Regency Hotel. |
| December | 3 | Bowie returns to New York. Mixes his next LP *Young Americans* at Record Plant Studios where he co-writes and records *Fame* with John Lennon and Carlos Alomar. They also record The Beatles song *Across The Universe*. Bowie tells Lennon he has lost confidence in MainMan and Defries. Lennon urges him to take control of his career. |
| December | | Bowie and Ava Cherry move to 21st Street, New York. Bowie divides time between there and Los Angeles, still seeing Lennon. |
| December | 29 | Bowie telegrams Defries that his services are no longer required and that legal action will be taken to terminate their contract. |
| *1975* | | |
| January | 26 | *Cracked Actor* TV documentary shown on BBC-2. |
| February | 21 | David Bowie releases his 21st single *Fame*, co-written with Lennon and Alomar/*Suffragette City* (RCA). His first US No.1. |
| March | 1 | Bowie upset when Aretha Franklin receives Grammy Award and says on TV: 'I'm so happy I could even kiss David Bowie.' |
| March | 7 | David Bowie's tenth LP *Young Americans* released by RCA. |
| March | 10 | Defries issues restraining order in New York halting distribution of *Young Americans* LP. Bowie settles dispute by allowing MainMan 50 per cent of all future royalties from his existing RCA and Mercury LPs, 25 per cent of publishing royalties and 16.66 per cent from records completed before his MainMan contract expires 30 September 1982. |
| | | Bowie also asks his lawyers to settle dispute with Pitt by payment of £15,000. |
| March/June | | While this settlement is still being negotiated, Bowie moves in with new manager Michael Lippman in Los Angeles and then into house there with Angie. Learns that Iggy Pop is in hospital and visits him, urging him to resume his career. |
| June | | Travels down to New Mexico to begin filming *The Man Who Fell To Earth*. Joined there by Angie. Clear to their friends that the marriage is under increasing strain. |
| September/December | | Returns to Los Angeles and begins recording at Cherokee Studios with the musicians who worked on the *Young Americans* LP. |
| September | 26 | RCA release three-track single *Space Oddity/Changes/Velvet Goldmine*, one of several issued without Bowie's encouragement. |
| November | 17 | David Bowie's 22nd single *Golden Years/Can You Hear Me* released by RCA. |

| November | 23 | Appears on *The Cher Show* on US TV singing *Fame*, *Young Americans* and a medley with Cher. |
| November | 25 | Announces on satellite link-up with *Russell Harty Plus* (LWT) that he will be returning to Britain in the New Year during next world tour. |
| December/January | | Stays at Keith Richard's house in Jamaica while rehearsing for tour. Dismisses Michael Lippman, claiming that he has taken 15 per cent and not 10 per cent commission. Bowie also accuses him of withholding $475,000. |

*1976*

| January | 23 | David Bowie's 11th LP *Station To Station* released by RCA. |
| February | 2 | Begins first world tour since 1973 in Vancouver. Backdrop taken from Salvador Dali/Luis Buñuel film *Un Chien Andalou* (1922). Dressed in white in a white spotlight, Bowie earns sobriquet The Thin White Duke (which is the title of a bootleg LP). Visits 45 North American cities. Bowie admits he is now earning 'obscene amounts of money'. Travels with only two assistants and a press officer, who are paid wages, and says: 'My office is a suitcase which stays in my room.' |
| February | 11 | Meets David Hockney and Christopher Isherwood after Los Angeles concert. |
| February | 13 | Contents of Bowie's home in Stone Canyon Drive removed for shipping to Switzerland where Angie has found them a house. |
| February | 28 | Bowie tells *Melody Maker*: 'Over the last year I've become a businessman. I used to think an artist had to separate himself from business matters but now I realize you have more artistic freedom if you keep an eye on business.' |
| March | 18 | *The Man Who Fell To Earth* premiered in London. |
| March | 21 | Bowie and Iggy Pop arrested with two friends in Rochester, New York. Charged with possessing marijuana. |
| March | 25 | Bowie and Pop granted bail. The case was dropped a year later. |
| March | 26 | The North American leg of *Station To Station* tour ends with Madison Square Gardens concert. |
| April | 7–30 | The European leg begins with concerts in Germany and France; takes two days off to visit new home in Switzerland, before appearances in Sweden and Denmark. |
| April | 26 | Tells a Swedish journalist: 'I believe Britain could benefit from a Fascist leader. After all, Fascism is really nationalism.' Comments widely criticized in Britain. |
| April | 30 | David Bowie's 23rd single *TVC 15/We Are The Dead* released by RCA. |
| May | 2 | Returns to London for first time since April 1974, having established he is not liable to British taxation. Angie |

|  |  | arranges for them to become formally resident in Switzerland. |
|---|---|---|
| May | 3–8 | Appears six nights running at Wembley Empire Pool, London. |
| May | 13–18 | European leg ends with concerts in Rotterdam and Paris. Bowie settles in Switzerland. |
| May | 20 | Bowie's first compilation LP *CHANGESONEBOWIE* released by RCA. |
| June/December | | Begins recording at Château d'Herouville with Iggy Pop for LP *The Idiot*. Moves to Berlin with his musicians in September, and leases a flat in Schöneberg where he stays on-and-off for the next two-and-a-half years. |
| July | 9 | David Bowie's 24th single *Suffragette City/Stay* released by RCA. |
| September | | Having finished Iggy Pop LP *The Idiot*, Bowie begins work on his own album *Low*, working with Brian Eno and influenced by German group Kraftwerk. |

*1977*

| January | 14 | David Bowie's 12th LP *Low* released by RCA, whose executives are none too happy with it. The LP is followed by *Heroes* and *Lodger*, to form what Bowie calls his 'Berlin triptych'. |
|---|---|---|
| February | 11 | David Bowie's 25th single *Sound And Vision/A New Career In A New Town* (RCA). |
| March | 1 | Iggy Pop's British tour opens in Aylesbury with Bowie playing keyboards. Group includes Hunt Sales (drums) and Tony Sales (bass) with whom Bowie formed Tin Machine twelve years later. |
| March | | Angie tells the *Daily Express* they are broke and says: 'David's been robbed blind'. |
| March | 10 | Bowie, Iggy Pop and the Sales brothers leave for US Bowie travels by plane for first time in over five years. They perform in 15 US cities over the next 34 days. |
| April | | The tour finishes. Bowie and Iggy return to Berlin to record next Iggy LP *Lust For Life* and Bowie LP *Heroes*. |
| June | 17 | David Bowie's 26th single *Be My Wife/Speed Of Light* released by RCA. |
| July | | Bowie joins Bianca Jagger in Paris and then holidays with her in Spain. |
| September | 9 | Bowie visits Britain to guest on Marc Bolan's Granada TV show *Marc*, singing *Heroes*. The only time they were ever filmed working together. |
| September | 9 | Iggy Pop LP *Lust For Life* released by RCA. Bowie co-wrote seven songs and performs throughout with Hunt and Tony Sales. |
| September | 11 | Films duet with Bing Crosby, performing *Little Drummer Boy* for a Christmas TV special. Crosby dies a month later. The record is a hit when released by RCA five years later. |
| September | 16 | Marc Bolan killed when his car hits a tree on Barnes |

| | | |
|---|---|---|
| | | Common. Car driven by his girlfriend Gloria Jones. |
| September | 20 | Bowie flies in from Switzerland to attend Bolan's funeral at Golders Green, London. |
| September | 27 | David Bowie's 27th single *Heroes/V2 Schneider* released by RCA. |
| September | 28 | Bolan's TV show with Bowie screened. |
| September | 29 | Bowie says he is establishing a trust fund for Rolan, the son of Marc Bolan and Gloria Jones. |
| September | 30 | Iggy Pop releases single *Success/The Passenger* (RCA), partially written by Bowie who plays keyboards and produced the record. |
| October | 14 | David Bowie's 13th LP *Heroes* released by RCA. |
| October | 19–21 | Bowie returns to London to promote *Heroes*. Appears live on *Top Of The Pops* (BBC-1), meets press – and leaves for Kenya to holiday with his son. |
| December | | Attends New York wedding of his bodyguard Tony Mascia, and records narration of Prokofiev's *Peter And The Wolf* with Eugene Ormandy and The Philadelphia Symphony Orchestra. |
| December | | After dispute with Angie, leaves Switzerland for Berlin with their son. He is due to begin filming *Just A Gigolo* in Berlin with Sydne Rome and filmed guest appearance by Marlene Dietrich, directed by David Hemmings. |
| December | 23 | Angie flies to New York and stays with a boyfriend over the Christmas holiday period. |

*1978*

| | | |
|---|---|---|
| January | 2 | Angie returns to Switzerland, finds house empty and phones the London *Sunday Mirror* to say she is penniless. They send a photographer and journalist to interview her. She attempts suicide with an overdose of pills and a kitchen knife. Tells the *Sunday Mirror* she and Bowie have not slept together in five years. |
| January | 6 | David Bowie's 28th single *Beauty And The Beast/Sense Of Doubt* released by RCA. |
| January | 9 | Bowie issues press statement in Berlin: 'My wife was not aware that my son was with me. A few days before Christmas she decided she would leave Switzerland and spend the holidays with friends elsewhere. From that day to her arrival back on 2 January she didn't phone me or the boy to say where she was.' |
| February | | Bowie leaves Berlin for another holiday in Kenya. |
| March | 16 | Begins rehearsals in Dallas for next world tour, visiting 65 cities and not performing to less than 18,000 people at any venue. Natasha Korniloff designs him a new stage wardrobe. |
| March | 29 | The world tour opens in San Diego. |
| April | 7 | Iggy Pop releases the single *I Got A Right/Sixteen* (RCA), co-produced with Bowie. |
| April | 28–9 | Both performances in Philadelphia recorded live for the *Stage* double-LP. |

| | | |
|---|---|---|
| May | 7–9 | The North American leg of the tour ends with three concerts at Madison Square Garden. |
| May | 12 | Bowie's 14th LP *Peter And The Wolf*, recorded with the Philadelphia Symphony Orchestra, released by RCA. |
| May | 12 | Iggy Pop's live album *TV Eye* released by RCA. Recorded on his tour with Bowie, featuring four tracks written with Bowie and four with the Sales brothers. |
| May | 14 | European leg of the tour opens in Hamburg with further concerts in Germany, Austria, Switzerland, France, Denmark, Sweden, Norway, Holland and Belgium. |
| June | 14 | British leg opens with three concerts at Newcastle City Hall, followed by four nights at Glasgow Apollo, Stafford Bingley Hall and three nights at Earls Court. All three London concerts filmed by David Hemmings. |
| June | 29 | With the end of the first stage of the tour, Bowie goes to Vienna, working on a film based on the life of Egon Schiele (which is later aborted). Holidays in Switzerland for three weeks before beginning work with Eno on their next LP *Lodger*. |
| September | 25 | David Bowie 15th LP, the live double-LP *Stage*, released by RCA. |
| November | 11 | Bowie resumes his world tour with a concert in Adelaide, the first of seven in Australia. |
| November | 16 | Bowie misses the world premiere of his film *Just A Gigolo* in Berlin. |
| November | 17 | David Bowie's 29th single *Breaking Glass/Art Decade/Ziggy Stardust* released by RCA. All three tracks are from *Stage*. |
| December | 6 | His world tour ends in Japan, with three concerts in Osaka and two in Tokyo. |

*1979*

| | | |
|---|---|---|
| February | | Visits London to promote *Just A Gigolo*, with appearances on TV and radio. |
| February | 14 | Attends premiere of *Just A Gigolo* at Prince Charles Cinema, London. A soundtrack LP released with Bowie contributing *The Rebels: David Bowie's Revolutionary Song*, co-written with Jack Fishman. |
| April | 27 | David Bowie's 30th single *Boys Keep Swinging/Fantastic Voyage* released by RCA. Both tracks are from his new LP *Lodger*. |
| May | 25 | Bowie's 16th LP *Lodger* released by RCA. Six tracks jointly written with Brian Eno. |
| June | 29 | David Bowie's 31st single *D.J./Repetition* released by RCA. Both from *Lodger*. |
| June/December | | Bowie travels between London, New York, Los Angeles and Switzerland, giving some radio interviews but generally keeping low profile. In November, he holidays again in Kenya. |
| December | 7 | David Bowie's 32nd single *John I'm Only Dancing (1975)/John I'm Only Dancing (1972)* released by RCA. |

Returns to London for New Year's Eve TV show with Kenny Everett, performing acoustic version of *Space Oddity*; then leaves for New York to appear on *Saturday Night Live* and *The Dick Clark Show*. Returns to Switzerland.

*1980*

| | | |
|---|---|---|
| February/April | | Works on new LP *Scary Monsters (And Super Creeps)* in New York. |
| February | 8 | His divorce from Angie becomes final under Swiss law. Bowie retains custody of his son and pays her $750,000 over ten years. |
| February | 15 | David Bowie's 33rd single *Alabama Song/Space Oddity* released by RCA. Bowie recorded the A-side in Montreux. The B-side was an acoustic version of his first hit. |
| March | | Goes to Japan to make two TV commercials for Crystal Jun Rock, a sake drink. Wrote the music. Released in Japan as *Crystal Japan/Alabama Song* (RCA). |
| April | 27 | Returns to Berlin and joins Iggy Pop on stage at the Metropol, playing keyboards. Meanwhile in Chicago, Kenneth Pitt was a guest at first David Bowie Convention. |
| May/June | | Completes *Scary Monsters* LP and goes to London to research life of John Merrick, The Elephant Man, whose remains are kept at the London Hospital. |
| July | | The Cuddly Toys release *Madman*, written by Bowie and Bolan when Bowie appeared on *Marc* in September 1977 (Fresh Purr Records). |
| July | 29 | Makes his stage acting debut in *The Elephant Man* at the Denver Center for the Performing Arts. |
| August | 1 | David Bowie's 34th single *Ashes To Ashes/Move On* released by RCA. This gives him his second British No.1 hit. |
| August | 5 | *The Elephant Man* begins a three-week season at The Blackstone Theater, Chicago. |
| September | | Promotes *Scary Monsters* LP and *The Elephant Man* with appearances on *Good Morning America* (ABC) and *The Tonight Show* (NBC). |
| September | 12 | Bowie's 17th LP *Scary Monsters (And Super Creeps)* released by RCA. His last LP for RCA under his MainMan contract. Bowie refused to record another LP until his RCA and MainMan contracts ran out. |
| September | 13 | Bowie tells *New Musical Express*: 'The reason why I haven't given any interviews in recent years is simply because I have become, I think, very private.' |
| September | 23 | *The Elephant Man* opens at The Booth Theater on Broadway. Andy Warhol and David Hockney attend the opening night. |
| October | 24 | David Bowie's 35th single *Fashion/Scream Like A Boy* released by RCA. |
| October | 24 | Angie Bowie's memoirs *Free Spirit* published in London |

|  |  |
|---|---|
| | by Mushroom Books. |
| October | Bowie films the sequence in New York for the German film *Christiane F*, describing the downfall of a teenage girl addicted to drugs who focuses only on David Bowie. |
| December 5 | *The Best Of Bowie* LP released by K-Tel. Includes 16 of his songs. Sold only by TV advertising, this becomes an unexpected British hit, reaching No.2 in the charts. |
| December 8 | John Lennon shot dead in New York, causing Bowie to increase his personal security at the Booth Theater. |
| December | Bowie spends Christmas in New York with his mother and son; their first Christmas together in seven years. |
| *1981* | |
| January 2 | David Bowie's 36th single *Scary Monsters (And Super Creeps)/Because You're Young* released by RCA. |
| January 3 | *The Elephant Man* ends its Broadway run with Bowie reluctant to continue after Lennon's death. Returns home to Switzerland, living in seclusion and painting while his RCA and MainMan contracts run out. |
| March 20 | David Bowie's 37th single *Up The Hill Backwards/ Crystal Japan* released by RCA. |
| May | *Christiane F* soundtrack LP released in Germany. *Christiane F* reportedly the most successful film in the history of German cinema. 25,000 copies of the LP imported to Britain. |
| July | Bowie and Queen write and record *Under Pressure* at Queen's studio in Montreux. He also writes and records vocal track for film *Cat People* with the music written by Giorgio Moroder who won an Oscar for the film music for *Midnight Express*. |
| August | Insisting on secrecy, Bowie films Bertolt Brecht's play *Baal* for BBC TV in London for the standard BBC actors' fee. |
| August/February | Continues to base himself in Switzerland, with brief visits to London and New York, refusing all media requests while RCA continue to repackage his work. |
| November 2 | Bowie and Queen release *Under Pressure* (EMI). An immediate No. 1 hit in Britain. |
| November 19 | David Bowie's 38th single *Wild Is The Wind/Golden Years* released (RCA). |
| November 19 | RCA release their second compilation LP *CHANGES-TWOBOWIE*, which he does not promote. |
| December 17 | The *Christiane F* film released in Britain. |
| *1982* | |
| January 30 | Bowie voted No. 1 Male Singer in the annual *New Musical Express* readers' poll. |
| February 26 | The *Baal* EP released by RCA in a gatefold sleeve illustrated with photos from the TV play. Five songs – *The Baal Hymn, Remember Marie, Ballad Of The Adventurers, The Drowned Girl* and *The Dirty Song*. |
| March 1 | Begins filming *The Hunger* in London and Whitby with |

Susan Sarandon and Catherine Deneuve.

| | | |
|---|---|---|
| March | 2 | *Baal* broadcast (BBC-2). |
| March | 11 | *Cat People (Putting Out The Fire)* released by MCA for contractual reasons. Bowie featured only on the title track. |
| June | 2 | Terry Burns tries to commit suicide, throwing himself out of a window at Cane Hill. Bowie's Aunt Pat tells the story to the *Evening News*. |
| July | | Bowie visits Terry at Cane Hill for the first time in nearly ten years, prompting headline 'I'M TERRIFIED OF GOING MAD, SAYS BOWIE'. This causes him intense distress as he leaves London. |
| August/November | | Bowie holidays in the South Pacific before beginning to film *Merry Christmas Mr Lawrence* in the Cook Islands, New Zealand and Tokyo. He co-stars with Tom Conti. |
| November | 4 | RCA reissue ten of Bowie's best-known singles in a picture disc format. |
| November | 18 | RCA release *Peace On Earth/Little Drummer Boy/Fantastic Voyage*, featuring songs Bowie recorded on TV five years earlier with Bing Crosby. Reaches No.3 in the British charts over Christmas, with no promotion by Bowie. |
| November/December | | Bowie records for four weeks at the Record Plant Studios in New York and then holidays over Christmas at Acapulco where Eric Idle finds him sunbathing on a beach and invites him to appear in the film *Yellowbeard* with Spike Milligan and Marty Feldman. |

*1983*

| | | |
|---|---|---|
| January | 27 | With his RCA and MainMan contracts expired, Bowie signs a distribution contract with EMI America for an advance of $17m. Bowie has to deliver three LPs in five years. And because he is contractually free, all the money goes to him.<br>Completes the LP *Let's Dance* with Stevie Ray Vaughan on lead guitar. Produced by Nile Rodgers of Chic. |
| February | | Films videos in Australia for *Let's Dance* and *China Girl* with director David Mallet. Latter track originally written and recorded with Iggy Pop in 1977.<br>In Australia, Bowie tells *Rolling Stone*: 'The biggest mistake I ever made was telling that *Melody Maker* writer that I was bisexual. Christ, I was so young then! I was experimenting.'<br>Bowie buys a ranch in Australia. Already has houses in Mustique and Switzerland and also apartments in New York and Los Angeles – but he tells *Rolling Stone* that he retreats to Mombasa, Tokyo and Berlin for privacy. |
| March | 16 | London press conference at Claridges to announce first world tour in five years with 90 concerts in 15 countries over next five months. The shows will be seen by 2.5m people. |

| March | 18 | David Bowie releases his 39th single *Let's Dance/Cat People (Putting Out The Fire)* (EMI America). A No.1 hit in the US, Britain and throughout Europe. |
| March | 23–5 | Bowie exhibits lino cuts at a New Expressionist Exhibition in Berlin. |
| April | 11 | The *Let's Dance* LP released world-wide by EMI America, giving EMI their most successful LP since The Beatles' *Sgt Pepper*. No.1 in Britain, No.5 in the US and a hit throughout Europe, Far East and Australasia. Reported that EMI have recouped their $17m advance. |
| May | | David Bowie's 40th single *China Girl/Shake It* (EMI America). |
| May | 18 | His 'Serious Moonlight World Tour' opens in Brussels after rehearsals in Dallas, moving on to Frankfurt, Munich, Lyon, Frejus and Nantes. |
| May | 20 | Bowie flies to San Bernardino, California, for just one concert for which he is paid the then record $1.5m fee. Resumes tour in London. |
| June | 2–4 | British leg opens with three Wembley concerts and two in Birmingham. Promoter Harvey Goldsmith says he could have sold eight times as many tickets. Moves on to Paris, Gothenburg, Bad Segeburg, Sochum and Edinburgh. |
| June | | His former company RCA reissue twenty of Bowie's singles with new picture sleeves, each in an edition of 25,000 copies. |
| June | 30 | 'Serious Moonlight' Charity Show at Hammersmith Odeon to raise funds for the multi-racial Brixton Neighbourhood Community Association, who are active in the area where Bowie was born. |
| July | 1–3 | Three open-air concerts at Milton Keynes Bowl each attract audiences of 60,000. |
| July | 12 | The tour moves on to North America, opening in Montreal and then criss-crossing the US with Bowie travelling in a private Boeing 707 with his own office, bedroom, lounge and video room. |
| September | | David Bowie's 41st single *Modern Love/Modern Love (live version)* released by EMI America. RCA release *White Light, White Heat/Cracked Actor*. |
| November | | More than 11 years after the event, the D.A. Pennebaker film of the last Ziggy concert at Hammersmith Odeon is released with the title *Ziggy Stardust: The Motion Picture*. Soundtrack album released by RCA. |
| November | 24 | The tour crosses the Pacific, opens in New Zealand followed by Australia, Japan and Thailand. |
| December | 8 | The tour ends in Hong Kong with Bowie reminding his audience after the final show that John Lennon was murdered just three years ago – and then singing Lennon's quintessential *Imagine*. |

Having secured his personal fortune through the EMI America deal, the success of the *Let's Dance* LP, the singles, publishing income therefrom and his most successful tour yet, Bowie returns home to Switzerland with neither income tax nor corporation tax to pay on his year's earnings. David Bowie is now a very rich man.

*1984*

| | | |
|---|---|---|
| February | 21 | Voted Best British Male Artist at the annual Brits Awards ceremony in London. |
| April | 19 | Receives two Ivor Novello Awards for *Let's Dance* as Hit of the Year and also Best Rock Song. |
| May/July | | After nearly six months at home in Switzerland, Bowie begins making the 16-minute film *Jazzin' For Blue Jean*, hiring film director Julien Temple. |
| September | | David Bowie's 42nd single *Blue Jean/Dancing With The Big Boys* released by EMI America. |
| September | | Bowie's 19th LP *Tonight* released by EMI America. |
| December | | David Bowie's 43rd single *Tonight*, a duet with Tina Turner/*Tumble and Twirl* released by EMI America. |
| December | 27 | Terry Burns tries to commit suicide by lying down across railway track near Coulsdon South station. Changes his mind at the last moment, but is injured. |

*1985*

| | | |
|---|---|---|
| January | 16 | Terry Burns commits suicide, again lying down across the track near Coulsdon South station. This time, an express train is approaching and he is killed. |
| January | 25 | Funeral for Terry Burns at Elmers End cemetery. Bowie sends flowers, but remains in Switzerland – deeply distressed, not knowing how his family or the press would interpret his presence, or his absence. |
| January | | Bowie records *This Is Not America* with The Pat Metheny Band for the film *The Falcon And The Snowman*. |
| May | | David Bowie's 44th single *Loving The Alien/Don't Look Down* released by EMI America. |
| July | 15 | Two years after his last British concerts, Bowie presents a stunning 18-minute stage act at the Live Aid Concert in Wembley Stadium – and also makes a video with Mick Jagger of *Dancing In The Street*, which is shown on TV throughout the day. The video becomes one of the highlights of Live Aid. |
| August | | Bowie and Jagger release *Dancing In The Street* (EMI), promoting it with the video. This stays at No. 1 for a month. All profits for Live Aid. |
| | | Bowie films *Absolute Beginners* and *Labyrinth*, starring in both and also writing and recording songs for both movies. |

*1986*

| | |
|---|---|
| March | David Bowie's 45th single *Absolute Beginners/Absolute Beginners* released by Virgin who financed the film. |

| April | | *Absolute Beginners* panned by film critics, but Bowie's title song a No. 1 hit single. |
| June | | David Bowie's 46th single *Underground* released by EMI, coupled with an instrumental version. Both are from *Labyrinth*. |
| November | | Bowie soundtrack song from the film *When The Wind Blows* also released by Virgin who financed this movie, too. Instrumental version on the B-side. His 47th single. |

*1987*

| March | | David Bowie releases his 48th single *Day In Day Out/ Julie* (EMI America). The A-side is from his new LP *Never Let Me Down*. |
| April | 15 | In an interview with French magazine *Globe Hebdo* Bowie admits his life 'turned into a nightmare' when he was on cocaine. |
| April | | Bowie's 20th LP *Never Let Me Down* released by EMI America. |
| May | | Bowie begins his 'Glass Spider' World Tour in Rotterdam with schoolfriend Peter Frampton on lead guitar. Bowie's lover Melissa Hurley is a dancer in the stage show. |
| June | | The 'Glass Spider' show tours Britain with Big Country, Alison Moyet and Terence Trent D'Arby as support acts. |
| June | | David Bowie's 49th single *Time Will Crawl/Girls* released by EMI. |
| August | | David Bowie's 50th single *Never Let Me Down/87 and Cry* released by EMI America. |
| October | 9 | During the 'Glass Spider' US tour, a woman in Dallas accuses Bowie of sexual assault in a hotel after a concert. She says he behaved 'like Dracula'. Bowie admits spending the night with her. The case is dismissed. |

*1988*

| April | | Bowie appears with guitarist Reeves Gabrels at the Institute of Contemporary Arts, London, presenting an eight-minute version of his song *Look Back In Anger*. |
| | | Bowie and Gabrels contact Hunt and Tony Sales. In Switzerland, they record their first LP *Tin Machine* with Kevin Armstrong on rhythm guitar. Produced by Tim Palmer. |
| August | | Bowie leaves the Tin Machine sessions to film role of Pontius Pilate in Martin Scorsese's movie *The Last Temptation Of Christ*. |
| November | | Virgin release an extended version of Bowie's *Absolute Beginners* on compact disc. |

*1989*

| April | | All Bowie's previous LPs re-released through US distributors Rykodisc on compact disc. |

| | | |
|---|---|---|
| May | | After rehearsals in Montserrat, his new group release the first *Tin Machine* LP which reaches No. 3 in the British LP charts and No. 28 in the US. Includes their version of Lennon's *Working Class Hero*. Their LP is reviled by the music press – but still sells over 1m copies. |
| May | 31 | Tin Machine's first live appearance at the International Music Awards in New York. |
| June | 10 | Reported that Bowie is to marry Melissa Hurley at Christmas in Switzerland. |
| June | 14 | Tin Machine's concert debut at Wake Ballroom in New York. |
| | | Announced that Bowie is to be the Musical Director for Kylie Minogue's first film *The Delinquents*; he quietly withdraws. |
| June | 29 | Tin Machine's European debut at La Cigale, Paris, followed by four British concerts. |
| July | 15 | Bowie opens the £1m Brixton Community Centre. This was partially funded by his Hammersmith concert in 1983. Bowie reported to have contributed £150,000 to the Centre. |
| | | The *Daily Mail* reports that Bowie is to make *Mandrake The Magician* film with director Julian Temple. |
| | | Bowie holidays in Indonesia and then spends ten weeks in Australia rehearsing and recording with Tin Machine. |
| August | | Tin Machine single *Tin Machine/Maggie's Farm* released by EMI with extra tracks *I Can't Read* or *Bus Stop* in some territories and formats. |
| October | | Tin Machine release *Prisoner Of Love/Baby Can't Dance*, the latter being a live version. |
| | | Reported that Bowie was thumped and kicked by Axl Rose of Guns 'n' Roses after chatting up one of the band's wives. |
| October/February | | Still based in Australia, Tin Machine continue rehearsals and then move to New York for next recording sessions. |
| | | Bowie agrees to support Yoko Ono's $100m Greening The World Campaign, sponsoring environmental projects and sending students to other countries in memory of John Lennon. |
| *1990* | | |
| January | | Bowie launches retrospective collection of all his work, *Sound And Vision*. Marketed as LPs, CDs and cassettes by Rykodisc. Includes 18 previous LPs, all repackaged with extra tracks to appeal to Bowie collectors. The CD set is boxed with each set including a letter of certification personally signed by Bowie. |
| January | 23 | Bowie hosts Rainbow Theatre, London, press conference to announce six-month world tour with 110 concerts in 15 countries, promoting *Sound And Vision* set. Widely reported that he will receive a minimum of £20m for the tour. |

| February | 21 | *Sound And Vision* receives a Grammy Award for the Best Repackaging Concept. |
| February | 25 | Bowie tells the *Sunday Mirror* that he and Bob Dylan are better known for music than record sales. Says his total LP sales are only 30m. |
| March | 4 | 'Sound and Vision' World Tour opens in Quebec. Bowie also promotes *Changesbowie* double-LP saying this contains what he considers to be his best work. Includes remixed *Fame*. |
| May | 6 | Angie Bowie tells the *Sunday Mirror* that Bowie once tried to strangle her. Claims she found Bowie in bed with Mick Jagger. They both deny her story. Angie says: 'He used me for what he wanted then discarded me like a piece of rubbish … he got rid of me when he thought I was no more use to him.' |
| August | 4–5 | 'Sound and Vision' World Tour returns to Britain for two concerts at Milton Keynes Bowl. |
| August | 27 | Stevie Ray Vaughan, whose solo career began after working with Bowie on *Let's Dance*, killed in helicopter crash after appearing in concert with Eric Clapton. Clapton's agent, bodyguard and tour manager killed together with the pilot. |
| September | | Bowie performs to audience of 100,000 in Buenos Aires. First British artist to visit Argentina since the Falklands War. |
| October | | Shortly after ending his two-year romance with Melissa Hurley, Bowie meets international model Iman, who was previously married to baseball star and former Olympic gold medallist Spencer Heywood. |
| November/December | | Bowie films *The Linguini Incident* with Rosanna Arquette and then returns to Switzerland with Iman. They stay there next six months. |

*1991*

| August | 25 | Reported that Bowie is being sued for £3m damages by a man who claims his ears were injured during a Tin Machine concert at the New York Coliseum the previous year. |
| August | 27 | *Tin Machine II*, their second LP, launched at Los Angeles reception attended by Little Richard. |
| September | | *Tin Machine II* released in Britain by London Records after EMI express little faith in Bowie's project. |
| October | | Bowie proposes to Iman during candle-lit dinner on a riverboat travelling down the Seine, singing *October in Paris*. She agrees to marry him and then returns to Los Angeles to film a video with Michael Jackson and a new film, *Star Trek 6*. |
| October | | Meanwhile, Bowie begins Tin Machine world tour in Europe with eight concerts in Britain, the last two being in Brixton where Bowie was born. |
| November | 11 | Bowie injured at last concert in Brixton when a fan |

throws a Marlboro cigarette packet which hits his eye. After bandaging his eye, Bowie continues with concert.

*1992*

March 19
Bowie and Iman reported to be house-hunting in Ireland after Bowie spends time there recording with U2. Said to have made an offer for Homewood Castle near Kiltegan, Wicklow – an area where Mick Jagger and Eric Clapton already have homes.

April 20
Bowie recites Lord's Prayer at Wembley Stadium tribute to Freddie Mercury. Performs duet with Annie Lennox singing *Under Pressure*, the song he recorded with Mercury and Queen. Joined on stage by Mick Ronson and Ian Hunter when singing *All The Young Dudes*. Show seen by one billion TV viewers in 73 countries.

April 24
Bowie marries Iman at civil ceremony in Lausanne, Switzerland.

May
Bowie holidays in Mustique with son Joe. Celebrates Joe's 21st birthday there on 28 May, then flies to Florence.

June 6
David Bowie and Iman's church wedding at St James Episcopal Church, Florence. Guests include Yoko Ono, Bono of U2, Eric Idle, Brian Eno and his wife, Jerry Hall and Bianca Jagger. Eno said afterwards: 'You couldn't tell what was sincere and what was theatre. It was very touching.' Other guests included Bowie's mother, George Underwood, Geoffrey MacCormack, and Iman's parents and immediate family from Somalia.

July/August
Bowie and Iman honeymoon in France.

November
Iman appeals to US Senators and incoming President Clinton to intervene in Somalia. Tells a Washington press conference that US may have to act as midwife to restore stability. Returns to Somalia with BBC TV camera team to make programme strengthening her appeal.

December 31
Reported that Bowie has been paid £50,000 for 10-minute guest appearance in TV series *Full Stretch*, playing tired, irritable rock star who spends most of his time asleep.

*1993*

January
Angie Bowie's second book *Backstage Passes: Life On The Wild Side With David Bowie* published in Britain by Orion.

March
American composer Philip Glass releases *Low Symphony* LP (Point Music/Philips Classics) based on Bowie's LP *Low*. Glass describes *Low* as 'a fairly complex piece of music, masquerading as a simple piece'.

April 15
David Bowie releases his 21st LP *Black Tie, White*

|              |      | *Noise*, his first LP in five years, including a piece written for his marriage to Iman, *Wedding Jump*, and a song about Terry Burns's suicide, *Jump They Say*. |
|--------------|------|---|

*Noise*, his first LP in five years, including a piece written for his marriage to Iman, *Wedding Jump*, and a song about Terry Burns's suicide, *Jump They Say*.

In a *Sunday Times* interview, Bowie says cocaine nearly killed him: 'I blew my nose and half my brain fell out.'

April/June   *Jump They Say* (Arista) brings Bowie his first hit single since *Absolute Beginners*. The LP is successful in Europe – but not in the US where newly formed Savage Records collapses mid-way through the LP's launch.

April   29   Mick Ronson dies in London of liver cancer.

June   25–7   Bowie visits Glastonbury Festival, scene of one of his early triumphs – as a spectator, listening to The Velvet Underground, Donovan, The Kinks, Lenny Kravitz, Van Morrison and Robert Plant.

September   Records soundtrack for BBC TV serial adapting Hanif Kureishi's novel *The Buddha Of Suburbia*, and then expands upon this to create the album *The Buddha Of Suburbia*, which becomes his 22nd LP.

November   1   *The Buddha Of Suburbia* LP released (Arista).

November   3   The four-part BBC TV series *The Buddha Of Suburbia* commences. Controversy in press over sex scenes.

December   1   Bowie comperes the Concert of Hope at Wembley Arena, starring Mick Hucknell, George Michael and k.d. lang, as part of World Aids Day. Show attended by the Princess of Wales.

December   10   *Black Tie, White Noise* TV documentary shown on BBC-1 followed by repeat of *The Man Who Fell To Earth* with *Absolute Beginners* on Channel 4.

*1994*

January/May   Bowie in Switzerland, recording with Brian Eno for the first time in 15 years, laying down enough material for five albums. Accompanied by lead guitarist Reeves Gabrels from Tin Machine; pianist Mike Garson and rhythm guitarist Carlos Alomar, who have worked with Bowie on-and-off since 1974, Erdal Kizilcay on bass and synthesizers, and drummer Sterling Campbell.

March/April   Joins the editorial board of the London Fine Arts quarterly *Modern Painters*.

May   29   Interviews the artist Balthus (i.e. Comte Balthazar Klossowski de Rola) at the Balthus family home in Switzerland.

June   Posthumous release of Mick Ronson's third LP *Heaven And Hull*. Bowie guested on Ronson's version of Bob Dylan's *Like A Rolling Stone*.

September 29 – October 9   Collaborates with Brian Eno in staging *War Child: Little Pieces From Big Stars* exhibition at the Flowers East Gallery, London Fields, East London. Exhibitors include Paul and Linda McCartney, Bono, Pete Townshend and Charlie Watts.

October   4   Auction of War Child exhibits at the Royal College of

Art raises £70,000, with Bowie's works commanding some of the highest prices.

Bowie's 12,000 word interview with Balthus appears in the autumn issue of *Modern Painters*.

Bowie buys the painting *Croatian And Muslim* by Peter Howson for £18,000 after its rejection by the Imperial War Museum.

MTV cancels Bowie's appearance on their *Unplugged* series when he refuses to perform his old hits, saying he only wants to play his newly written work. Eric Clapton, Nirvana, Phil Collins, Bob Dylan and Rod Stewart had all previously appeared featuring their back catalogues.

| | |
|---|---|
| November 17<br>– December 3 | Bowie's prints included in the *Minotaur Myths And Legends* exhibition at the Berkeley Square Gallery alongside other works by Michael Ayrton, Picasso, Elizabeth Frink, Igor Mitoraj and Francis Bacon. |
| November 24 | Bowie and Iman attend a special showing of the *Minotaur Myths And Legends* exhibition. |
| December/January | Bowie and Iman spend Christmas and the New Year at their home on Mustique, Britannia Bay House, for the last time before putting the house up for sale. |

*1995*

| | | |
|---|---|---|
| January | | Asked to contribute 'something' to the 100th issue of *Q Magazine*, Bowie surprises them all by sending in a short story *The Diary Of Nathan Adler*, with three of his own signed computer-drawn illustrations, and a bizarre 1,500-word conversation recorded with Brian Eno over the Internet, in which he reveals that he has 'the same goose bumps as 1976' over their recent recordings. |
| February | | Bowie accompanies Iman to Johannesburg for her *Vogue* photo-shoot with Nelson Mandela, and completes a series of paintings for his upcoming exhibition. |
| March | | Bowie sells his Mustique home to the publisher Felix Dennis for £2m, and says he will be spending more time in future in Tuscany where he is currently building a new home. |
| April | 18 | Bowie's first solo art exhibition *New Afro/Pagan And Work 1975–1995* opens at the Cork Street Gallery, featuring his paintings, charcoal drawings and sculpture, and two wallpaper designs produced for him by Laura Ashley. |
| June | | Bowie begins filming the Julian Schnabel movie, based on the life of Andy Warhol, with Gary Oldman and Dennis Hopper.<br><br>An article describing the African art he had seen in Johannesburg in February appears in the summer issue of *Modern Painters*. |
| July | | Bowie designs the poster for the annual Jazz Festival in Montreux, which he usually attends every year. |
| September | 14 | Begins his first world tour in five years at Hartford, |

|                       |                                                                                                                                                                                                                              |
|-----------------------|------------------------------------------------------------------------------------------------------------------------------------------------------------------------------------------------------------------------------|
|                       | Connecticut, calling it The Outside Tour and supported on his US dates by the pioneers of 'industrial music' Nine Inch Nails.                                                                                                 |
| September 25          | The first of his new albums recorded with Brian Eno, *Outside*, released world-wide by BMG (other than in the US, where it was issued by Virgin America). A single was also released, *The Heart's Filthy Lesson*.            |
| October 3             | Reported that Bowie and Iman have bought a five-bedroomed town house in Chelsea, London, for £1.2m and are spending £300,000 on its renovation.                                                                               |
| November/December     | Bowie begins the British leg of The Outside Tour with three concerts at the Wembley Arena (14, 15 and 17 November), followed by Birmingham, Belfast, Dublin, Exeter, Cardiff, Aberdeen, Glasgow, Sheffield and Manchester, with Morrissey as the support act. |